First Intermediate Period

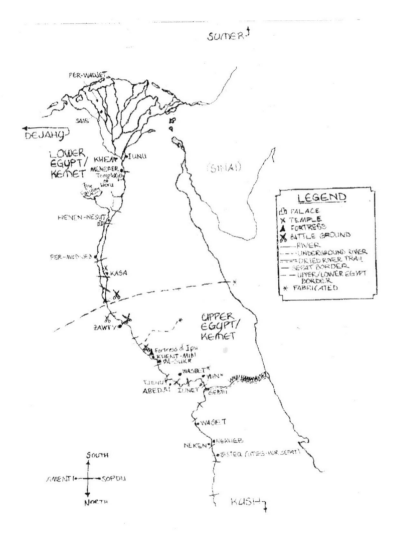

The King of Egypt

This book is whole-heartedly dedicated to Alexia Lewis who believed in it first, most and always.

From the first day I mentioned to Alexia (as a joke) that I was going to turn a college English paper into a novel, she responded with enthusiasm and began announcing to everyone we knew (and didn't know) that I was going to write a book. To make her stop, I quickly broke it to her, stating, I was just joking about the whole 'writing a book thing.' But, Alexia stood by her proclamation, said she thought it was a great idea, and insisted I would write a bestseller. I told her she didn't even know if I could write. I believe I even threw in a statement or two about her being a little off her rocker.

For a long time, I had a great desire to gag Alexia, and even better, concoct some memory loss serum. Yet, the truth be known, when I first declared my thought to her, deep down I truly wanted to write this novel.

As the years went by, with no start on the book, Alexia never lost faith. It was her undying belief that made me begin to believe I was going to write the novel—that, and the shame of not doing it since she had convinced everyone I would. Soon enough I found myself climbing on Alexia's bandwagon and making the same announcement, "I'm going to write a novel." With that statement, I now had to, and it was all Alexia's fault.

So, this is for you Alexia. Thank you for always believing in me. Thank you for never losing hope. Thank you for pushing me onto my path and for your unwavering support. I love you.

Also, to Nan, who boasted proudly of my novel, who never got to see its birth, and whose parting gift was once again, to be the one to get me what I wanted. Thank you, Nana. You've always been my blessing.

The King of Egypt

War would end if the dead could return.

—Stanley Baldwin

Every end is a new beginning...

ON THE PALACE halls when everyone laid lulled in sleep, a man sheathed in dark clothing slipped through the corridors. The long dark shadows helped to conceal him as he quickly moved to his destination. He stopped briefly to watch a guard sleep noisily at his post before he determined all was safe and disappeared into a passage. Igniting a lamp, the hooded intruder glided through the narrow walkway until he came to his exit. He paused; listened--behind the door all was silent. Slowly, he pushed the panel open and peered into the stillness of the room.

Across the chamber on a majestic bed, the General slept soundly as the cloaked, ghost-like figure slid across the floor. He halted beside the bed, peered down onto the Great General for a quiet moment before he carefully pulled back the sheer, covered the unsuspecting commander's mouth and startled him awake.

The General gasped.

"Do not stir, my Lord," whispered the invader. The dark stranger lowered his hood to reveal himself. "Quickly, to the council chamber. Do not draw attention along the way. There will be others alike waiting for you." He returned to the opened panel across the room. "Ask no questions," he said before the General could sail a sound through his parted lips. "All will be answered there." He pulled up his hood, slipped into the passage and made his way towards the other unsuspecting parties.

≈

IN THE PRIVY Chamber of Council, men gathered disturbed from

1

their sleep. Each arrived one-by-one, until there were seven. They grumbled curtly to each other, trying to determine if the other had an answer or at least knew something more. But, no one knew why they'd been summoned well into the night.

Two passageways led to the chamber: the main passage, which those who sat in council knew and the second, an escape—known only to the Pharaoh and the Vizier.

The chamber itself, although large, was not much bigger than the huge round table placed in the middle of the room. A low fire burned in the centre of the stone table as well as from the torches hanging from the walls. Chairs lined the table in a horseshoe and where they gaped apart at the far end, a high throne looked down upon everything from a raised level. The thick arms of the stone throne held a golden flail and crook at their tips, which represented power. And, it was here, in the privy Chamber of Council, where some of the most important decisions in Egypt were ordained.

The circular room amplified the growing voices of the men. But, the walls were thick and the chamber was tucked in the lowest, outermost part of the palace to ensure nothing within could be overheard.

The men grew more impatient as time slowly passed without any answers: one paced, one observed and another sank listlessly into his own thoughts while the rest questioned with bitter anticipation.

Long anxious moments passed well after the seventh man had joined and before three more officials entered the room—one of whom had woken them all.

Everyone fell still. They looked at the three men knowing their answers arrived.

The Vizier, who led the entering troop, was the first to speak. "Come, sit down," he ordered, gesturing towards the seats. He said nothing more as he advanced to the round table.

"Why have we been summoned at such an hour?" demanded the Governor of Upper Egypt. He was an older man, frail in body but not in mind. His grave was in sight, and he knew it; but until that moment came, the Governor would command with a power that compelled respect from the strongest of men.

The Vizier took a stand in front of his chair while the others moved in to sit down. He waited until everyone was settled before he replied, "There is much to discuss, for change must befall us all. But, before I speak of why you have been gathered here tonight, I must express the urgency of this meeting. The mighty goddess Sekhmet has risen up with vengeance, denouncing our Pharaoh and demanding we take arms against the kings and men, who at this very moment storm towards Egypt, threatening to conquer our beloved land." He looked at each of their faces: the Great General of the Armed Forces; the General's brother and First Officer; the Superior Commander of the Legions; Admiral of the Royal Vessels; Commander of the Ships; the two Governors of Upper and Lower Egypt; and, the two men who had plotted with him—the High Priest and the Chancellor of the High Courts.

Although a man of forty years, the Vizier held his stresses on his face. Lines cut into his skin by his deep set eyes that were hungry for control. He seemed to have aged since their last meeting. His expression was solemn, tired, concerned. But, there was a force in him that tinged of danger.

The Vizier's expression hardened. "You have all been chosen wisely and are expected to play an important role within the hours to come."

"Where is the Pharaoh?" demanded the General, drawing to the oddness of his absence.

Although the Vizier spoke to everyone, he looked steadily at the General, his voice stern. "I bid you all not to speak until the very end, as time is imperative. To hear me out shall answer all the questions you wish to know." He raised his arm to silence the gatherers and took to eyeing each man so they could see the importance of his intent. Then, he withdrew to a softer tone. "It has become of grave concern between us three..." He opened his arms to indicate the two officials who had entered the room with him and who were now seated at his sides. "We have spent many nights contemplating solutions for the crisis of which I now speak." He studied the expressions of the selected men. His words needed to be chosen carefully. All the faces in the room were high-ranking officials chosen because they too would see--or at least be convinced--this affair was of severe importance and great measures needed to be taken to eliminate their burden.

Yes, he had to persuade them—it was the only way. Egypt was crumbling. The King of Sumer, Puzar-Sin, was seen marching towards Egypt with his ravenous desire to rule the land. In a few days, he would breach the border and the Vizier knew their Pharaoh Wadjkare would do nothing. He wallowed in wine and was no longer capable of ruling the empire. But, the Vizier would not stand by and watch their fallen Pharaoh take Egypt with him. No, at all costs he would prevent it.

"Egypt is at stake!" he erupted. "Our Pharaoh, son of Egypt, is failing her!" He lowered his voice. "We anxiously sit by and wait for his command to restore our great nation to what she once was and what she can still be, but he does not command. You—" he pointed in the direction of the men, intensifying the moment. "Mighty men of soldiers born, deprived of your birth right, able yet unable to glorify your names and die in honour. Leashed here at Men-nefer while our enemies storm our borders and our King, mad with ale, boldly drinks a smile upon his face!" His hand slammed the table.

The soldiers stirred in their seats knowing the truth of what he said, enraged at the very mockery of their titles. They knew all too well the adversity befalling Egypt—her riches dwindled, her crown powerless and her enemies thrilled by the ease of conquer. Already the surrounding countries were moving in, warring with each other in order to take over her land while Egypt's army panged for their instructions to defend and regain order.

The Vizier drew out the moment of muted fury lending time to the soldiers who were engrossed in thought—their blood curdling in frustration and rage at the very picture he painted so clearly. He knew he had to anger the men with a passion of longing in order to make them agree and abide by the undertaking he was about to present.

"I see by the expressions upon your faces that your hearts join ours in this affair." He allowed his words to sink in; it was crucial they agree. He couldn't bear the consequences if they did not.

A nervous feeling crept within him. As the Vizier stood in front of the superior commanders of the Egyptian army, the room seemed to close in. The stone walls felt as if they squeezed against his body with great pressure. The words he had to push from his lips risked death.

But, he knew he had to speak. If they did not stand up against Puzar-Sin, all would be lost. Now was the time—the only time. Seven powerful men sat before him, waiting to know what he was about to propose. He believed in their hearts they longed for someone brave enough to lead them. Indeed he would. He had designed this opportunity, this night, when they could wait no longer. If all went well they could have an army at the borders before Puzar-Sin could step on their glorious land. Then, they could begin to regain order.

The Vizier took a deep breath, forced the words out of his mouth knowing the pressure of saying and doing nothing was much heavier than the pressure of the room.

Carefully, slowly, he continued, "I beg you, quiet your tongues and hear me through, if not in agreement, then out of respect because what I am about to propose places my neck and the necks of my two conspirators beneath the axe." He looked directly at the General. "This moment is of dangerous regard and I pray before you act, you consider our beloved Egypt—for her, I speak."

The Vizier inhaled deeply. He allowed the air to seep at length back out from his pursed lips. Sweat began to break out along his forehead. But, he thought of Egypt's demise; it restored his courage.

"It is apparent our Pharaoh yields this chaos to unconventional order. His mind, enslaved by liquor, no longer gifted to make the proper decisions or lead a force, slowly drowns. Why must we wait for him to drown himself? To wait means to sacrifice Egypt! And, if you are willing to give Egypt away to those desiring to take her, I demand you get up and go back to your beds, but forget not this day when Egypt is just a memory, you gave up the choice to save her!" The Vizier looked at each man sitting at the round table. No one moved.

"Then, here is the choice I give you."

Attention amplified.

"We can wait until our Pharaoh drinks himself to inevitable death—a slow suicide. Or," he whispered, "we can quickly make his grave."

No one moved. No one spoke. Everyone weighed his conscience against the scheme at hand.

The Vizier felt his body loosen, the pressure gone, the words now exposed and threatening his life with subversion. He felt drained but it was done.

He glimpsed their faces. "I, my friends, have struggled with this purpose for some time and I know, although my mind is fearful, my heart is strong."

He stood straight, stiffening his body, putting power back into his voice. "I stand for Egypt! All those with me rise to my side." The Vizier stood tall, his heart pounding. All it took was a single opposition to ruin his plans, which would undeniably destroy the Egyptian Empire.

He glanced around the table.

The first to stand were his two counterparts but no one else stirred. He eyed the men again. No one looked at him. They all had dropped their eyes or covered them, perhaps in shame of the thought.

The Vizier's chest grew tight. He could feel his conspirators eyeing him nervously—the men's response was taking much too long. What if no one agreed? He wasn't prepared to die.

The Vizier shoved the thought from his mind. He didn't move. He stood tall, strong, quietly praying they would consent. He studied each man, taking note of their demeanour.

Perhaps this is good, he thought. Perhaps this meant they were considering the unspeakable offer—they must be, or they would have dragged him off already.

For what seemed an eternity, no one else moved. Then, a chair screeched away from the table and the Great Chieftain, General of the Egyptian Army, carefully stood up. The rest followed one-by-one, slowly, yet deliberately until the last man remained seated. He struggled nervously with his decision as pressuring eyes urged him to join.

"This is anarchy," he muttered, looking around in a state of confusion at the developing coalition.

"This is imperative." The General spoke this time. His influence amongst the men was strong. He was the Pharaoh's first man and ranking officer of war. From the onset of the Pharaoh's reign, he had taken them to the battlefields and defended Egypt's power; he yearned to do it again.

Now, he felt it necessary to add to the conviction. His eyes burned with fury at the commander who sat in disbelief, unable to concede.

"The Pharaoh is the traitor!" the General declared. "For it is treasonous to stand idly by when Egypt's enemies ravage and plunder her. It is treasonous of the Pharaoh not to command defence! And, if we too sit here and do nothing while this Kingdom is annihilated, then what are we but his *accomplices?*" The General's voice rang through the air like horns that called out for war. His words held a strong regard in everyone's heart and he knew it.

The officers glared at their comrade.

The moment intensified.

The commander closed his eyes, considered the consequences, held his breath. "What's best for Egypt," he finally exhaled as he stood.

〰〰

THE GENERAL PACED back and forth in his room. Everyone had a role in the assassination; however, his was by far the most difficult. It was already decided by the council he would be elected to the throne—they would see to it. In this tragic time Egypt needed a warrior at its reign, not a boy, and indeed, the people would agree.

He paced while he waited for his signal as it helped to settle his nerves. Time was causing his burden to grow heavier. Forever had already come and gone.

"*Oh, what sin,*" he huffed.

More disturbing than what he faced right now was soon he would have a different weight to carry. His palms sweat at the very thought of it. Anxiety grew in his stomach as the moments passed with the eerie realization life would be different. He would be Pharaoh; ruler of Egypt; God of men. It seemed ideal but not this way.

The General exhaled with a long and drawn out breath. He stepped to his bed, kneeled before it. Clasping his hands together, he whispered to the walls, "When all is said and done, and to my deathbed I one day go, I fear my conscience will outweigh the feather of Maat. So heavy is it now, I just solemnly pray, fair goddess, you will consider Egypt before giving Ammut my heart to devour--"

A soft rap on the panel door ended his prayer. He went to the hidden passage. It was the moment he dreaded, yet, cherished.

The Great Chieftain closed his eyes, drew in a breath. "For Egypt," he whispered before he opened the panel and disappeared into its darkness.

※

THE BOY OPENED his eyes. His bedchamber was still dark. Outside the full moon glowed through his window. Although morning was still sometime away, he couldn't sleep. He peered around the moonlit chamber and already felt bored. It would be torturous to lie in bed and wait for the sun to end the night.

He looked at his toy sword leaning against the wall and thought to play his favourite game—stealing around the palace, going unnoticed by the guards, fighting imaginary enemies lurking in the corridors. Yes, that's what he would do. The morning would come quicker for it.

Throwing back the covers, the boy swung his legs off the bed, stood on the cold stone floor and shivered. His linen tunic draped loosely to his knees, which offered no protection against the cold night. He slid into his papyrus woven slippers and went to his wooden sword. Grasping its handle, he held the sword high in the air then dashed from the room.

※

THE CHANCELLOR AND the General scurried along the narrow corridor. They exited the secret passage, discreetly crossed the palace hall, and slipped into another passageway. For some time, the two men moved through the halls without speaking a word until the Chancellor broke the growing unpleasantness of their silence.

"The dawn has opened the day. We must hurry before the people wake and spy our acts." His pace quickened. The General pursued. "They have awoken the Pharaoh and have taken him to the Temple of the Gods of War. They feel it will aid your deed." He glanced back at the General. "He is expecting your discussion. Say nothing for your pity may be strengthened by the speech."

The two men came to the next exit. They left the safety of the passage, hurried down the palace hall, turned a corner.

A soft light pierced in from the windows as the sun began to rise outside. The General's skin burned, not from the rising sun but from the strike of reality. Everything around him seemed to intensify—he could hear the air moving past him, the Chancellor's breathing...

Footsteps.

The two men stopped abruptly.

A guard approached.

"Get back!" whispered the Chancellor, pulling the General behind a column. They pressed against the wall.

The guard rounded the corner, stopped. He peered down the hallway. "*Iiti?*"

"He has heard us. I should order him to continue," whispered the General, beginning to step out without thinking.

"No!" exclaimed the Chancellor, grabbing the General's arm and holding him back. His whisper was frenzied, "Stay still! We must not create suspicion!"

The guard took a step forward. He listened intently, searching for the slightest noise as he peered further down the hall. He couldn't see anyone. He stepped closer to get a better look. Waited.

"*Iiti?... Iiti em hotep?*"

Silence. There was no one in sight and he wasn't about to go and search. His bladder was full. He peered down the hall for a moment longer before concluding it was nothing. "Euphrates," he finally mumbled to satisfy himself as he turned and headed towards the lavatory.

The Chancellor peeked out from behind the column; decided it was safe, motioned to the General to follow. Time was not on their side. He knew the Pharaoh would already be waiting in the sacred temple. Outside the sky was growing bright. It was better to be masked in the solitude of darkness as people slept. The Chancellor glanced out a window at the fading darkness, quickened his pace. The deed would be done this night before the sun woke the earth.

The senior officers stopped in front of the last secret passage, looked around apprehensively, slipped into its darkness.

〰〰

THE YOUNG BOY swung his small sword in the air at the imaginary enemy towering above him. In his other hand he held a clay pot lamp, which illuminated the secret tunnel in front of him. His *enemy*

9

was crumbling; he had fought him long and hard and had worn him down. Now, for the final blow; the boy jabbed his blade forward and froze. He strained to listen.

Could it be? Footsteps—*real* footsteps hurrying along. No one had been in the passageways at this hour before—at least not since he had discovered them. His heart raced with excitement; his game suddenly turned real.

The boy stood motionless, listening to the sounds of sandal hitting sand calling to him. The footsteps headed deeper into the tunnel where he had not yet been brave enough to venture. He shuddered, tightened his grip on his toy sword, and stared down the passageway, which the darkness swallowed in the distance.

At last, a real mission! he thought.

♒

THE TUNNEL LED deep under ground, past the fortress' outer walls and into the Temple of Horu. The two men marched on, through the maze of passages beneath the earth's surface: some led nowhere, others to different chambers, but theirs had a distinct destination.

The Chancellor proceeded to lead, moving speedily through the passage, turning corners without hesitation as if the route was mapped out in his mind.

The General followed, dazed by the images which repeatedly played in his thoughts. Everything was drawing to a close; all was happening at a dizzying pace. His anxiety turned the air thick and sticky. He found himself taking longer breaths with each step that brought him closer to his altered future.

The General was a man of stature. Strong. Powerful. Well respected. Once friend of the Pharaoh.

What am I doing? he agonized. What sin am I about to commit? And, why, when I know it is a horrendous deed, am I still possessed to do it? The General clenched his fists. It is not for greed, he reminded himself. It is to save our blessed empire.

Sweat dripped from his brow. He swiped it away. He had fought in many battles yet even under the glint of a sharp blade swinging towards him, he never felt as uneasy as he did now. He had to remain strong but more so, he had to show only strength—especially if he was to become Pharaoh.

〜

THE BOY CHASED the sound to its whereabouts. When he caught up to the rhythmic beat of the falling steps, he stopped, peeked around the corner. Two officers were rushing down the hall.

Who were they? Why were they up so early stealing through the secret tunnels? He could tell by their attire they were men of rank.

The boy sparked with excitement. Something important was taking place and he would be witness to it.

The young boy blew out his light, placed the clay pot on the ground and pushed it to the side, out of the way. He removed his sandals so they wouldn't hear his movement, tucked them under the arm holding his sword and used his free hand to navigate his way through the darkness.

Remaining in the shadows, the boy followed the officers further down the forbidden tunnel. The pound of his heart quickened as he slid along the corridor in pursuit. The air thickened in his throat, drying out his mouth. He could even taste its staleness and smell the scent of dirt. Fear began to swell up inside him and yet, he persisted—curiosity motivated him; mystery beckoned him.

Onward the two officers went, deeper into the cryptic passage where the boy was not permitted to go. They rounded a corner and stopped.

〜

THE CHANCELLOR SPUN to face the General whose usual great, noble manner seemed to have fallen on their course to their chosen destiny. The General looked worn, tired, defeated even.

They stood in a moment of silence—uneasy silence—before the Chancellor broke their spell. "This is where we part," he murmured. He took a deep, overwhelmed breath but his expression imparted resolve.

Their eyes locked with understanding.

"For Egypt," the Chancellor broke in. He grasped the General's hand, then briskly turned and made his leave.

11

The General watched the Chancellor of the High Courts walk down the tunnel for a moment longer. Then, he opened his hand and studied the clay vial given to him by the Chancellor.

Fate held in such a small container, he thought. And, here it is in my hand. *Left in my hands.*

The General stole a deep breath before he pushed open the wall's disguised door and stepped into the room

♒

FROM WHERE HE stood, the boy could see the intensity of their expressions. He witnessed the Chancellor utter something to the General before he turned and made his way back along the passage.

The boy froze in fear. Something wasn't right—he had seen it on their faces. *The Chancellor of the High Courts. The General of the Armed Forces.* Something serious was about to happen; something he felt he should stay away from.

Frantically, he spun and scrambled back up the tunnel. There was a turn a short way back; he hoped to reach it and hoped the Chancellor returned the way they had first travelled.

The boy's chest tightened with fear causing him to pant for air. His movement felt heavy; his body numb with the dread of being caught. Although the darkness masked him, his fear slowed him down. He tripped over himself with anxious steps and crashed to his knees. The sandals fell, smacking the ground and echoing in the boy's mind. His chest grew tighter—incredibly tight. He began to panic, gasping uncontrollably.

Glancing over his shoulder, the boy judged to see if he'd been heard. He hadn't. The Chancellor continued his pace, completely unaware.

Move, the boy encouraged himself as he struggled to hold back his gasps. The light from the Chancellor's torch closed in. The boy desperately slid his hands across the floor in search of the sandals. With each passing moment, breathing became more difficult, his stomach more nauseous, and his heart raced at such a speed it began to hurt.

The light was growing closer; another step, closer. He had to find the slippers. He moved slightly, patting the cool dirt ground, glancing back to judge the time he had left before his presence was revealed. His heart sunk. It would only be a matter of moments.

The light edged in.

The boy leaned forward, patted—nothing! He shifted—patted—nothing! His eyes locked on the Chancellor, though he went on searching, groping the damp ground. *Nothing! Nothing!* Still, *nothing!*

Then the boy's fingers touched *something.* He recognized the feel of the papyrus woven slipper. He scooped it up aware there was still another missing. How far could it have fallen?

The light fell within steps of him and he knew if he didn't move he would be spotted. He was shaking but willed himself to get up; giving up his blind search of the missing sandal, hoping it would be overlooked. He snatched his wooden sword from the ground beside him. His palms drenched with sweat, caused him to fumble the one shoe he clung to as he crawled clumsily along the passage.

The light almost touched him, illuminating the tunnel behind him. He clambered to his feet, stumbled down the tunnel faster. He slid his hand along the wall in search of the opening hidden in the darkness.

Please, let me make it, he prayed.

The grit on the walls tickled his fingertips in a soothing manner. He allowed its sensation to calm him. Then, the feeling stopped. Instead of a wall, there was sudden emptiness. He dove down the adjacent passageway and pressed against the wall. There was no time to run; he had to remain still—and pray.

Around the corner the footsteps grew louder. The boy panted, tried to calm himself. He feared his heart could be heard pounding loudly throughout the tunnel. He pressed tighter against the wall as the Chancellor approached.

The torch shone bright; its glowing flame exposing him crouched just past the turn as the footsteps closed in with their pace at a steady beat. The boy could hardly bear the moment; his fear urged him to run but he dared not move. He tucked his head and closed his eyes, listening to the fall of each step, waiting for the missing sandal to be discovered. He held his breath, which felt as if it would suffocate him.

The Chancellor approached. He was behind the corner. A step—he was there; but he tramped by—past the turn, past the boy, past the slipper. His footsteps grew faint—gone—almost gone. The boy heaved in air, relieved. He was safe! *Unseen and safe!*

He sat up and held his head to stop it from spinning. He took a moment to gather himself, to regain his breath before he scurried to the corner to make sure all was clear.

The torchlight disappeared.

〰

STANDING IN THE hall of the great temple, the General felt his anxiety heighten. *The Temple of War*, he thought. How he longed for combat in order to revive Egypt.

For a lingering moment, he took in his surroundings, which gave him strength. High ceilings added to the grandeur of the room and colourful hieroglyphs covered the walls, telling tales of death and glory. The hallway was long and wide with massive columns, which led to a large chamber.

Torches burned on the walls, guiding the way, waving him forward. Now was his time. He turned to face the main chamber. Everything seemed painfully quiet.

"Forgive me in the name of Egypt," he whispered, before treading forward to the temple's great room where the Pharaoh awaited.

〰

SEVERAL MOMENTS PASSED before the boy's eyes were able to adjust to the darkness. He squinted, blinked them into focus as he peered down the hall in the direction of where the two officers had stopped. No one was there. His heart raced but he forced himself to continue. He moved down the tunnel and stopped at the spot where the men had departed. He pushed his weight against the hard stone wall until at last the wall gave way and opened to an opulent room.

The boy entered the great temple. Giant pillars loomed over him, their presence cautioning those who did not belong with their daunting magnitude. He read an inscription on the wall. His eyes widened in astonishment as he realized he stood in the Temple of War, the Great Temple of Horu. Shrill excitement pumped through his veins. The temple was a place where the highest warriors met for their ritual,

14

before marching out to battle—a place he longed to one day become a part of.

Remembering his mission, the boy looked at the General who made his way down the hall towards the Great Chamber of the Gods.

INSIDE THE GREAT Chamber, the Pharaoh watched the door, sipping his ale, already intoxicated. He was forced out of bed and rushed to this temple on the notion of urgency in spite of his protests.

War, they had mumbled. He didn't care—he wanted to, but didn't.

Wiping his mouth, he looked back at the doorway as the Great Chieftain, General of the Egyptian Army, finally entered the room. The Pharaoh glimpsed his royal officer up and down through bleary eyes.

So strong; so controlled, he thought. For many years they had battled side-by-side and were close friends. When had it all gone wrong?

The Pharaoh took another gulp of his drink. *War.* He was tired of it; tired of them pestering him to go to battle. Even the thought annoyed him.

"What is so important that you must have me up before *Ra* sails across the skies?" he demanded, a hint of hatred emanating from his voice. "And, why this temple?" His glare pierced for only a second before his face softened. "Is my bed not worthy enough for such matters of discussion?" He let out a drunken laugh and stumbled forward awkwardly.

THE GENERAL STUDIED his King—he looked so pathetic; red faced, frail. He was no ruler. His insubordinate behaviour disgraced Egypt. The Vizier was right—they had waited much too long.

THE BOY DARTED from one column to the next making his way towards the General who just stepped through the doorway into the Chamber of the Gods.

Someone from inside the chamber began to speak.

The boy froze. The voice—it was a familiar sound he had heard all his life. From behind the wall, in the main chamber, his father spoke.

The boy's heart pounded as intrigue replaced fear. He moved to hide behind a column in clear view of the room and looked into the face of the Great Chieftain, General of the Egyptian Army.

The young boy studied the General admiringly. He hoped to grow up and become as strong of a warrior as the Great General. He glanced at his father; he too was strong once. He could be again—perhaps tonight. Perhaps his father was here to command the Great General to go to war with him. Yes, it must be. Together they stood in the Temple of War; the Pharaoh and the General, the most powerful men in the country.

The boy smiled broadly, giddy with the thrill of witnessing their acts—longing for the day he would follow his father's crown and become Pharaoh of Egypt.

"You want to go to war?" spat the Pharaoh. "Well, not now, I already feel like death." He rubbed his head, took another swig from the decanter dangling from his fingers.

The boy studied his father. Why was he so weak? Only a short time ago the Pharaoh was mighty, glorious. What happened to the great King to make him this way?

Yes, go to war, he wanted to advise his father. He watched him stagger forward. He wanted to help him—help him to become strong again.

The Pharaoh shook his head. "I cannot discuss Egypt at this time—"

"You don't have to, my Lord." The General charged towards his King. He snapped open the lid of the vial. Before the Pharaoh knew what was happening, the General grabbed his jaw and forced open his mouth.

"For Egypt," he toasted, pouring the contents of the tiny clay container down the King's throat. He cupped the Pharaoh's mouth, held it shut so he couldn't spit or spew.

The boy's heart stopped momentarily. He watched with fright. Something horrifying was happening; something he knew he should stop, he *must* stop! *Father,* he wanted to call out but his fear held onto the word. Instead, he sunk against the column to the floor. The General was so strong. What could he do? What could he do but cry? He covered his face, peeked through his fingers, and watched his father struggle. His heart hurt. It ripped inside him with guilt and sorrow.

Tears flooded his cheeks. But, what could he do? He was only seven. He was too young and too afraid.

〜〜

THE KING COUGHED and choked in a desperate effort to disgorge the venom. He struggled feebly but it was impossible—the General was strong and he forced him down.

The Pharaoh felt his death trickling rapidly down his throat. His body weakened. He lay in the arms of the Great General who watched as all signs of life swiftly left his King.

Using his last bit of strength, King Wadjkare looked into his traitor's eyes. "Curses to you and yours!" he managed before his eyes rolled back taking his last breath with them.

The Pharaoh's body trembled then stiffened.

The son of Egypt was dead.

Egypt.
2153 B.C.E.

I

$\mathcal{A}$LLEGI SAT ON his horse, slumped over its neck with his hands tied at the wrists behind his back. The straps cut into his skin but he said nothing. His protests fell upon deaf ears. It was pointless. He would have to wait until its moment to discover what his captor intended. *Death? Torture?* No, it couldn't end this way. He needed to escape and warn his Pharaoh. But, the horseman kept Allegi's reigns tightly wound around his hand and Allegi at his mercy. There was no escaping, at least not now.

Allegi closed his eyes. Give me a chance, he prayed.

As if the gods heard his plea, for the first time in hours, their horses were halting. Allegi looked at the horseman and tried to gather a hint from his expression. His eyes were squinting, looking into the distance, looking around. He was calculating where they were.

Allegi followed his captor's gaze to the desert's end, which was signalled by the ripe tree line. They were many stretches from the trees, dry barren desert surrounded them, yet still it was a sight for hope. Allegi knew just beyond the lush greens was the river and upon it his ship. His crew would await his return for at least another few days before they would consider him dead and abandon their stay. Now, only to make it.

Suddenly, Allegi's attention was drawn to the horseman who swiftly turned towards him, dagger drawn. He lunged before Allegi could react. He sliced at his wrists, pushing Allegi from the horse.

"Off!" growled the horseman, ripping the water pouch from Allegi's neck before he fell, crashing to the earth.

Allegi rolled over, gripped himself in pain as he coughed and spit the sand from his mouth. He rubbed at his wrists where the straps had bound them together and glared up at his captor. "Your fight is fruitless against our Majesty!" Allegi spat.

The horseman tilted his head back and laughed. He poured what was left of Allegi's water over his face, gulping some of it down before he threw the empty pouch into the sand next to him. Then, he drew a parchment from his sack.

"To *your* Pharaoh," snarled the horseman, throwing the scroll down.

Allegi snatched up the letter before the wind had a chance to steal it away and tucked it into his skirt. He did not take his eyes off the looming figure above him.

"See to it that it reaches." The horseman ripped his canteen from around his own neck and roughly tossed it down. He reared up on his horse and turned, the reigns of Allegi's stallion still in his grip.

Allegi suddenly realized the horseman was setting him free but taking his steed.

He can't! thought Allegi. The thief! I will die! "Release my horse!" he shouted. "I command you! It's of royal property!"

The horseman forced a devilish cackle. "And, so it shall be returned." His voice cut the air like a knife and seemed to quake the earth with its deep, hollow tone. "Let your fraudulent Pharaoh know, he will not stop until he obtains what's rightfully his." The man's eyes narrowed. He leaned forward on his horse as he spoke in a low throated growl, "*Egypt* is his. He's declaring war." The horseman dug his heels into his horse and galloped away.

By the time the dust settled, the horseman was a small figure in the distance; Allegi was completely alone. He was heat stricken, parched, hungry, sore—never before did he feel so helpless. But, he was aware of what the desert could inflict if he didn't keep moving.

Allegi wiped his brow, willed himself to look up into the bright sky. Vultures already began circling over head. He knew they would follow him.

The river was far away, his mouth extremely dry. If he was to survive the journey, he needed water. Allegi reached for his water pouch despite having seen the horseman empty it. He grabbed the bag from the sand, desperately tried to squeeze water from the skin but nothing came out. He shook it vigorously, almost cried in frustration—a few tormenting drops dripped into his mouth only causing him to crave more.

He whipped the empty container aside, yelling with grief. The bag flew through the air, landed beside the horseman's pouch, which was almost completely covered by the rolling sand--the desert's vengeance. Starved of water, it sought to swallow everything that dared to cross its land.

Allegi eyed the horseman's water pouch. *Please, let there be some left*, he prayed as he unsteadily picked himself up, stumbled to the canteen and collapsed to his knees. He dug the pouch from the earth, lifted it up. He was stunned for a moment, frozen in disbelief—the pouch was *heavy.*

Allegi opened the lid and drank back half the contents leaving the rest to ration for his journey. Despite the weakness he felt in his body, he forced himself up. He peered towards the tree line, which seemed impossible to reach and glanced at the merciless sky.

The sun was hot and had been cooking the sand since morning, which burned the bottom of his bare feet as he stood. Overhead, the vultures waited for his collapse so they could feast; but, they would have to wait—he would not give up easily, he would not die this way. *He couldn't!* He had to reach his Pharaoh.

Allegi remembered the scroll. Taking the letter out from where he had tucked it into his skirt, he unrolled it. The words on the page were piercing, horrific, and they gave him new strength.

Time only benefited the enemy.

II

*T*IGRIS STOOD IN her dressing room while her chambermaids dressed her. Two of them held the rich linen in place as another stitched it on so her gown had a tight, contour fit. The final touches of her make-up were carefully being applied and she stood still as the bone carved stick drew the *msdmt* around her eyes extending out towards her temples.

Before her, the wig and jewellery makers patiently waited until the eye paint was complete and the artist stepped aside before they began showcasing their works of art.

Tigris paid them no mind. Instead, her eyes rested in the shadows, which beckoned her to escape deep within her thoughts.

Soon, she thought. Yes, today, all shall be answered.

The two craftsmen continued to hold up her choices despite her absent stare. The jeweller opened an elaborately hand-carved wooden box displaying an elegant gold necklace with the amulet *djed*—symbol of stability. He hung his head low, looked up under his brow and awaited her decision. But, without even glancing, Tigris shook her head to reject it.

The box was quickly passed to a servant in exchange for another container picked from one of the many piles organized on the jeweller's cart. As the jeweller prepared his next item, the wig maker seized his opportunity. He pulled a plaited wig from a reed container, which was perched on top of a wooden head. He bowed as he presented his handwork. Again, Tigris shook her head with disapproval sending the wig-maker back to his assistant for another style.

Both men continued taking turns, stepping forward, removing an item from its box, holding it up and watching for the slight movement of her head, which gestured rejection or acceptance.

Within the room, the tension seemed to swell with each refusal. Silent messages were passed amongst the servitors questioning the odd behaviour of their Majesty. But, no one spoke. They continued despite the fact her rejection became more of a habit than an answer and her eyes were looking past them towards the wall.

Her servants knew when she initiated a mood of fun the air was relatively relaxed and informal but when she did not, dutiful respect was to be carefully employed. This morning, it was the poor maidservant who stood holding a dish of fruits, bread and cheese, well aware she would not have a bite that gave clue to all that her mood was preoccupied by her thoughts, which were not to be interrupted. And, in spite of her endearing nature it became common knowledge, or rather a warning, what one poet once regarded, "...when she is, she *is*; when she is not, she *is not*."

So, everyone managed properly, uncomfortably but indeed in the manner a servant was supposed to, in the presence of the Pharaoh.

Tigris stared into the shadows, unable to focus on selecting her attire. She mulled over a more important matter as she waited for her messenger to bring news of a rumour brought to her attention almost a month ago. This information leaned mightily upon her crown and at the rate the situation was growing, something quickly needed to be done. But, the Pharaoh knew what needed to be done would be better organized once she understood what was happening. Thus, she was doomed to wait.

Tigris pressed her hands together and tried to manage her tension through her breathing. She had been informed her Royal Messenger would come today—his ship had been seen returning on the Nile.

Funny, she thought, how the knowledge of the messenger's arrival always arrives before the messenger himself.

Tigris glanced around the room. She felt to pace but too many people surrounded her--she couldn't let them see her worry. No, she was Pharaoh, she had to remain impervious and hold the mask of strength even though her nerves quietly tormented her.

Tigris discreetly clenched her fists, pretended to be calm.

What if the rumours proved real? No. They couldn't be. Why now? Why after she had secured peace in Egypt?

She glimpsed at the door again, wishing it would open. How much longer did she have to wait before she would discover the truth? Such torture in waiting.

To wait, Tigris seethed. She glanced at the water clock. Only three hours since the sun had risen from the earth—three hours, which had lingered by like a year. The day would be long—waiting would make it that way.

The Queen's thought was distracted by the jeweller. She turned her attention towards him. He held an item bearing a large gold necklace plate with intricate carvings and a beaded string of calcite linked around the bottom edge. Although, it wasn't beautiful, Tigris was drawn to it. She looked at him and nodded. His face lit up.

The two chambermaids, who were holding the gown in place, stepped aside to allow the jewel-maker room while the girl servant remained to finish the last stitches on the hem.

Smiling, the jeweller took a bow and moved forward to fasten the piece around the Queen's neck. "A wonderful choice, Majesty," he beamed. "I made it only two days ago after discovering a man selling the calcite in the village. He told me he had mined it from the river outside of Hatnub. I thought to add it to the necklace to soften its edge. There are earrings to match." He snapped his fingers.

The servant attending the cart was quick to find a smaller box and held it forward. The jeweller snatched the box from the servant, opened it and proudly held the earrings against his own ears to display their splendour.

Tigris gave a small nod.

"I know the calcite doesn't shine like many stones but their white tone looks lovely against your olive complexion."

Tigris closed her eyes, inhaled deeply. Did he not take note she craved the silence? Petty details of jewellery hardly interested her at this time. In fact, the entire adorning process seemed frivolously prolonged.

She opened her eyes and studied the jeweller. Perhaps he was proud, she thought as she looked at the two men before her, their carts almost picked through, their faces grim. She suddenly felt guilty, realizing the poor man was actually relieved. She had dragged this on, unaware she had allowed the dressing to help pass time while she waited.

Tigris smiled appreciatively before returning her stare back into the shadows, into their darkness where she could think. *Her heart skipped.*

Soon the wait would be over and then what? She knew the possibility of what would follow though she didn't want to consider it before it was certain. Tigris pushed the thought aside, drew a deep breath and closed her eyes for a moment. *What lies ahead, great Goddess Bastet? I embody you.*

The chambermaids made some final adjustments to her dress then took a large step backwards, lowering their heads to await approval. The jewel-maker straightened the necklace one last time then followed suit while the wig-maker still tried to seek acceptance for one of his wigs. He now held one with plaits joined together at the end to make a fringe. But, instead of giving her decision, the Pharaoh-Queen turned to face the full-length mirror.

The mirror was a polished copper with accents of gold. It leaned against the wall over ten feet high and four feet wide. There was little else in the room except for a vanity, a stool, a lounge chair and a few pots, chests and rugs placed as decoration.

The mirror reflected all of the servants, who quickly took to lowering their heads while fixing their eyes upon their Pharaoh. Tigris, however, did not pay mind to even her own reflection. Instead, she studied the necklace.

What is it about the ugly piece? she wondered as she unconsciously moved her hand up to touch her chest and rest her fingertips upon the calcite fringe of the necklace. She remained still, staring at the calcite, listening to the drops of water count the hour as they dripped into the clay pot, mocking her torture.

Soon, she prayed.

The door burst open, breaking her trance. The servants jumped but the only movement from the Queen was the shifting of her eyes to catch a glimpse in the reflection of the mirror.

Her anxiety heightened as her heart raced. He had returned—her Royal Messenger had returned. The wait was over.

Tigris spun to face him. She nodded towards the door, signalling the dismissal of the servants attending her. They bowed, stepped back and scurried out of the room almost in single file. The chambermaids led the line followed by the jeweller whose servant pushed the cart behind him. The wig-maker's cart followed the procession but the wig-maker himself hesitated. He pondered for a moment before detouring from the line. Walking over to the vanity, he slammed the wig with its wooden-head down on top of it. Abrasively, he arranged the braids before being the last to exit.

While the messenger struggled to regain his breath, Tigris said nothing. She forced her patience as she went to her vanity and sat down. Picking up a brush, she placidly moved it over her head, her own hair a straight and even cut. The two maidens, who stood fanning her with palm leaves, followed and continued their duty where she now sat.

The breeze was always welcomed during the daylight hours when the sun mercilessly beat down upon the earth. It was especially desired in this long, narrow room where the opened window seemed only to procure light. Yet, as much as it was her servants' obligation to keep all they heard and saw silent, Tigris knew trust need always be given with caution. With regard to the matter of which she was about to contend it was necessary rumours were not spread.

"Leave me," Tigris commanded.

The maidens immediately lowered their leaves, gave a short bow before hurrying out of the room.

Tigris breathed deeply to subdue her eagerness. Her bosom raised and fell under the tightly draped linen of her dress, which was the colour of a sun-kissed beach and flawlessly clung to her delicate curves.

She was tall, thin, with a fair olive complexion, and her teeth were like pearls. She was known as 'the noblest and loveliest woman of her time, braver than all the men, most beautiful of all the women, fair-skinned with red cheeks.' The Pharaoh possessed such stunning beauty it was once written she won wars because her beauty weakened men. Even greater than her outer beauty, Tigris had passion, a heart kind and giving and intelligence beyond measure. She was never careless with her kindness and so her people respected her, loved her, yet, feared her for her power was of frightening but gentle perfection.

Tigris eyed her messenger as he caught his breath. At twenty-one, he was her most dedicated servant and indeed, her truest friend. He looked as though life had been sucked out of him, yet he held an inner strength.

The Queen managed herself patiently, studying him in the mirror as she ran the brush through her onyx hair. The fate of the country lied in his knowledge—the next few words he would deliver—but she would not rush him.

〰〰

IN THE DOORWAY, Allegi stood hunched, his arms stretched out to the door frame in an effort to hold himself up. His legs slightly trembled, his skirt dirty and his knees scratched. For days he travelled without rest to bring her the news with little food or drink. The message pushed him onward. Now, it weighed down on him like stone upon a tomb worker's back.

Allegi looked into his Pharaoh's stare. "Lost... taken... everything..." he forced between his gasps, unable to stop panting. He had run at full speed from the barque station to the palace, through the grounds and into the inner building of the royal residences to reach her. His body was exhausted. He hadn't been able to sleep since his meeting in the desert over a week ago.

When Allegi finally regained control of his breaths, he raised his head but didn't meet her eyes. He was ashamed—ashamed of being left a fool by the enemy. "I was stripped of my horse, pouch, everything but a canteen of water." He almost wished not to tell her, but he was due to return days ago.

Tigris shifted her attention to the guard who stood outside her chamber with his back to the room pretending not to listen. "Fetch him some water," she commanded as she turned on her seat to face her messenger. Within a moment, the guard returned with a goblet.

Allegi presented a grateful nod, took the cup and chugged the water. He handed the empty goblet back to the guard who had returned to his post. Closing the door, he turned to face Tigris. "He says..." Allegi looked steadily at the Queen knowing the news he brought would spark fury. He stole a breath. Found his will. "He says he won't quit until he obtains what's rightfully his." Allegi stepped further into the room, hesitated. "He says..." He dropped his head. He dreaded this moment even though Tigris was sensible at times when most men would have lost their minds, able to keep composed when chaos was at its peak and always managed to remain calm. He thought of her peaceful nature, her desire to make everything fair, everyone happy. He remembered, when anger was heavy amongst the council, Tigris would take a breath and deliver logic that would ease tension. Still, Allegi could hardly bring himself to say the words. He didn't fear her--he dreaded the wretched feeling inside stirred by this horrific speech. The words alone held a sense of betrayal and he hated having them spill from his mouth even though it was his duty.

Lifting his head slightly, Allegi looked at his Pharaoh whose eyes implored him to speak. Slowly, reluctantly, the messenger whispered, *"Egypt is his."*

Tigris' cheeks burned. Rage flared through her. She clenched her teeth. "It's *my* land and *my* people. He will *never* have it!" She swung back to face the mirror, clutched the brush tightly, swept it through her hair with gentle, measured strokes.

Allegi allowed her anger to ease for a quiet moment before he added softly, "The people of Sopdu have turned against you. They feel a King is better for Egypt."

Her arm dropped, the brush dangled in her fingertips. *The east? That was half the land!* Tigris glared at her messenger through the mirror with blazing eyes but her voice was calm. "How much does he have?"

"Reportedly only as far south as Abedju, mostly on the eastern flank-- he hasn't crossed the Nile." Allegi moved towards her. "He has taken Upper Egypt but he aims for complete take-over." Lowering his head again, Allegi stretched out his arm and handed her the scroll. "He's declaring war."

After a long still moment, Tigris delicately placed the brush on the vanity, took the parchment, stood. "Do the people under Amenti know about this?"

"Only the farmers along the river bank."

"Where do they stand?"

"By you—he hasn't reached them, yet." Allegi glanced up, realizing what he had alluded to, but she didn't catch it or at least she didn't show it. Instead, her expression remained in bitter thought.

When at last she spoke, her words came slowly, from deep inside, instilled with power. "This is *my* Egypt! *Rightfully* mine and no one will take it from me!"

She turned towards Allegi. "We still out-number him," she stated. Although she looked at him, her stare was very distant—somewhere deep in thought, somewhere calculating. Her breathing slowed, her voice lowered and her teeth clenched as she announced, as if to herself, "If it's Egypt he wants... then to the *death* it is."

Gracefully, Tigris spun and left the room.

〰️

ALLEGI WAS STILL. He watched the secret panel swing close behind the Queen before he left her chamber to walk down the hall to his room.

Allegi's room was the closest to the Queen's apartments. Normally, it was reserved for children but since Tigris had none and Allegi was her closest friend, she had moved his quarters onto her floor.

His room was reasonably large with a large bed covered with pillows. Urns, pots and statues were added for decoration but other than a functional table and stool, the chamber was quite basic.

Allegi entered the bedchamber, removed his skirt. He went over to a basin partially filled with water, which sat on top of a table near the bottom of the bed. Picking up a cloth kept next to the bowl, he dipped it in the water. He dragged the wet cloth over his face and down his body, soaking in its pleasure before he placed the basin on the floor, sat on the stool and washed his feet. Later, he would go to bathe but for now this would do.

For some time he sat with his feet in the water, thinking about the future of Egypt. He didn't want to think about it but he couldn't prevent the thoughts from springing to mind.

"Egypt against Egypt," he mumbled, shaking his head, "...which one will win?" It almost seemed surreal.

Allegi stood, looked around the chamber, stepped over to his bed. Although it was still morning, he slid onto the cushion, pulled the net shut, which hung from the canopy and functioned to keep the bugs out while he slept. In that respect, the net promised a much more comforted sleep than even the feathered cushions.

He stretched out across the cool linen, pressed his eyes with his fingers. His body was exhausted yet his mind raced with tragic thoughts. He didn't want them. But, in the silence of his room, he couldn't help but ponder the fate of Egypt and more importantly his Pharaoh.

Tigris *must* win, he thought, but a woman on the throne? How long would her subjects remain loyal? His stomach churned with worry.

Even though she is adored, there are those who revel in traditional belief of Pharaoh being a king, and those who could easily be convinced, Allegi had heard the Vizier whisper.

A thought flashed before his mind. A horrible thought.

"Cursed!" Allegi spat out loud as he buried his face in his hands. If it were any other nation coming against her they would meet with defeat but Egypt and the rise of a male Pharaoh.... No, he couldn't think with such ill faith.

Allegi rolled over and tried to lie still, to not think—but, his mind was filled with doubt, forcing him to imagine horrible thoughts.

"I would sleep if curiosity would stop denying it from me," he groaned, rubbing his eyes, trying to rest, tossing and turning from the thoughts, which took control of him; thoughts of the war certain to consume the land.

War. He pushed the vision from his mind as he tossed with fury onto his back.

A crow landed on the windowsill. Allegi watched it poke at its feathers trying to find the unwelcome pest. Its head moved quickly although never losing sight of its surroundings. Allegi looked beyond the bird into the bright blue sky. The sky was clear as usual; however, as he continued to gaze into its emptiness, his stare turned the sky grey.

He blinked hard to clear his vision.

Allegi drew his focus back to the big black bird. The gnat must have been discovered because the crow was still. It cocked its head to one side so one eye peered out the window and the other back into the room.

Even a bird, considered to be free, was imprisoned by its fear, Allegi thought. He waved his arm and the bird immediately took flight.

"Egypt," he sighed, closing his eyes. "What will become of Egypt?" *Bloodshed.*

Allegi opened his eyes, blinked hard, tried to rid himself of the wretched thought that flooded his mind. But, it clung like dried blood to a wound. He jumped up from his bed, went to the jug of water on top of the table in his room. He poured some water into a cup, drank it back, and turned to face his bed. He stared at the bed as if it were guilty of poisoning his mind.

"Curiosity versus sleep—there's my true war," he mocked. Allegi walked back to the bed, dropped onto the cushions and lay on his back, arms outstretched across the soft linen feeling almost defeated. His body throbbed. His eyes ached. A heavy beat pounded behind them tightening his head with each thump. He couldn't rest—not now. Too much was about to happen.

More disturbing images of war and bloodshed flashed through his mind. Everyone was dead—*everyone.*

He pressed his temples. *Why think with such doom?* He felt guilty.

Rolling onto his stomach, he drew up onto his forearms, clutched a pillow and tried to picture the adversary who was attempting control of Egypt. He had heard the man was young and strong and to Allegi's knowledge, many did not see him as an enemy. He was told his face was gentle and his eyes kind—but, why war?

Another deathly image.

Allegi shook it away but it returned with a haunting chorus that chanted, *How does it end? How does it end?* The words were his but they questioned so loud it seemed as if they echoed off the walls of his room.

"How does it end?" Allegi whispered.

"With death," he answered himself as if to satisfy his mind. "Death," he repeated, dropping his weight back onto the pillow. We all die, he thought.

Allegi slowly climbed out of bed. He needed to leave his room, needed to escape the confinement of his thoughts

In the town of Henen-nesut, just beyond the palace walls, the day was lively as usual. Merchants lined the streets and the markets bustled with trade. Allegi slipped by people, listening intently on the conversations he passed, studying their expressions and movements. It seemed surreal that everyone was unaware of the change falling upon him; unaware of the tragedy, which would separate their families, their country and their Pharaoh.

As a group of people sitting on a terrace broke out into laughter, Allegi realized this could very well be the last moment of tranquillity Egypt would see for a long time.

Everything was about to change.

III

*C*IGRIS SAT IN her audience chamber contemplating the inevitable coming events. She clasped the scroll tightly in her hand. How did this arise so quickly without her knowledge? she wondered. And, with all the Great Overlords of the Northern *Sepats*—why did none send word until now? Were they all corrupt?

Slowly, she unrolled the scroll and began to read it for the countless time.

How many times had she read it since Allegi placed it in her hand? Too many, and still not enough. She was troubled by its words or perhaps she was still baffled by its surprise....

> *My sovereign sister, crowned Pharaoh of Egypt under the name of* <u>Nitiqreti</u>, *it is my duty as the true soul of Re to inform you of your illegitimate embrace of the royal flail and crook. With this regard, I announce to you* <u>my</u> *sovereignty with which I proclaim Egypt mine...*

She stopped to read the beginning over. The words infuriated her—the way her attacker chose them and even crafted them. And yet, there was something even more about the way in which they were written—an undertone. They disturbed her more than they should.

"What are you inferring?" Tigris whispered before she continued to read, the next part designed more in the manner she expected:

> *Respectfully, I wish to confer with you ere I declare war as I have only looked upon your statue erected here in Nekheb. Though war I understand I have declared already through my actions, I am certain your wish would only be the same in order to address he who has assailed you—for me you have not met. Therefore, I humbly beseech you to journey safely to the upper region beyond Abedju where we may openly converge. I promise you no harm until we meet on the fields of battle where all shall transpire as it must.*
>
> *A king is what Egypt always intended to have and at last I have come.*
>
> *Your brother and great enemy, Pharaoh, King of Egypt, enthroned as Usermaathor.*

A *King!* thought Tigris with disgust. A rebel wanting the crowns of Egypt and utilizing gender to support his cause. Where did he suddenly come from? She had been informed he was Egyptian and yet, held no office with her. Certainly a commoner could not have gained such power and formed such a force.

Tigris glanced down at the parchment skimming over his last few words.

Again, he returns to that suggestive undertone when closing, she thought. "Illegitimate embrace...Egypt always intended..." *What audacity!*

Tigris fanned herself with the scroll as she drifted off in thought. But, she couldn't keep her eyes away from the letter—the words called her in. She flattened the parchment's curling edges, turned her attention to his title. Her stomach tightened. Her blood burned with anger.

Enthroned. How dare he be so insolent as to give himself a throne name while I still sit upon it! And, with no coronation, she thought. Tigris reread the name, "*Usermaathor,*" she whispered. How deliberately you hide your birth name! Yes, you have my interest knave foe. I shall come!

IV

*T*IGRIS STOOD ALONE in her audience chamber. She fastened a thin cloak over her shoulders and moved towards the window to peer out over the courts. A soft breeze blew in from the river carrying the faint sent of lilies from the garden. Torches were beginning to be lit around the palace in order to help keep watch as night fell over the country.

Tigris had summoned a meeting of the Great Ten, a name she used to refer to the ten magnates of the High Council. Over the past week, several arrived from across the land and she knew her enemy would have watched and known.

All were received as guests in her palace, although a few already dwelled in residence in order to conduct their affairs and serve as political advisors. With the exception of those in palace office, Tigris had not yet convened with any of the officials. But, on this night, they would meet. Beyond discussing the issue of war she would most importantly study their eyes to determine who remained loyal. Indeed, the eyes revealed the secrets of the conscience.

Comprised of powerful men, the Great Ten included the Prime Minister, Ibimpetus, the Vizier—*tjat*; Amunken, the Governor of Lower Egypt who resided in Men-nefer; Anaten, Governor of Upper Egypt who resided in Waset; Siwadjet, Great Overlord of the Per-wadjet sepat; Ankhtify, General of the Royal Armed Forces, and Chephren, Admiral of the Royal Vessels who both led the military theocracy; Septoy, the High Priest of Men-nefer known as *Rekh-nesu*; Isetep, Chancellor of the High Courts; Mahorse the Royal Treasurer of God; and finally, the last member of the Great Ten, Allegi, Royal Scribe and Messenger of the court as well as Royal Confidant of the Pharaoh.

All ten men of the High Council would gather in the Great Chamber of Geb to discuss the critical steps they would have to take in order to keep Egypt in their clutches. The topic, of course, focused on Egypt's sudden upset: the rebel who came out of nowhere like a desert storm sweeping over the land—*her* land.

Tigris shook her head at the thought. She was still angry, still baffled at how this came about so unexpectedly. *How did no one know?*

It was a blow to her pride.

How did she not know until now! Her fist tightened, absorbing the anger brewing inside her. She wanted her assailant drawn from the sandpits in which he hid and terminated quickly. She would not be overthrown nor would she allow him to rule the north. No—Egypt would remain united under one crown. The one she possessed!

Narrowing her eyes with resentment, Tigris picked the dual red and white crown of united Egypt off of the chest by the window where she stood. She could feel the rage boiling inside of her from the thought of the unknown rebel. But, in spite of his strong beginning, she would see his end. She would bring him to his knees; have him admit Egypt was hers then watch him die.

Yes, Egypt was hers. She would not let him have it. Not as long as she lived.

"To the death..." the Queen whispered as she placed the united *pschent* crown of Egypt on her head.

Tigris climbed the three platform steps to the Great Throne of Geb and settled on her royal throne. Below, the councillors argued out of their seats. The Vizier's voice rang above the others, rage lashing from his tongue. Allegi was the only one who sat quietly listening, observing. He had proven to be extremely loyal and over a short period of their acquaintance, Tigris had taken him into her confidence—a privilege she did not trust with many or often. She had given Allegi the prestigious title of *Friend of the King*. And, even though the older men loathed his presence in the High Council, his title as *Friend of the King* forced them to silence their disapproval.

Tigris eyed Ibimpetus, her *Tjat*—Vizier. His deep set eyes were dark and foreboding. They could make a man quiver just by a glare. The lines that cut into the skin around them were pressed there by stress and anger. His brow clenched in a permanent scowl, making him look older than his years even though he was nearing seventy.

The Vizier had served under three Pharaohs including Tigris. He was an essential part of the government structure, the supreme architect for the Pharaoh and the foremost official of the nation. As much as the Queen hated to admit she needed anyone, she needed him.

Tigris watched the men. None of them seemed aware of the rebel she noted from their arguments and deep carved expressions of anger. That was good—their loyalty was still to the monarchy. She picked up the flail and crook from where they balanced in small cut holes on the tips of the chair arms and tapped their metals together to silence the men before she held them crossed against her chest, waiting for the councillors to be seated.

Each took his seat on one of the stools arranged in front of the Pharaoh's Seat of Estate. The seating arrangement curved like a bow so none of the men had his back to another, and so all were in frontal view to the throne. A small aisle divided the middle to allow servitors to pass.

Allegi sat at one end behind a small table equipped with his writing utensils and parchment; the Royal Treasurer sat at the opposite end in the same manner with his chest of most recent records by his side.

When, at last, they were all settled, Tigris began. "It has been brought to my attention, as I am sure you are all well aware, the calamity which is infecting our nation. It is most difficult for me to believe this has elevated to such purpose before ever passing by our knowledge." She looked at her cousin. "Governor Anaten, what have you to say?"

The vanquished region was under his jurisdiction and it was his responsibility as Governor of Upper Egypt to attend to this land and to keep the Vizier informed.

When Tigris' father left her the throne two years ago, the rebellious cities of Henen-nesut and Waset broke away from the centralized control of Men-nefer to stake their claim as the capital—*Ruling House of Egypt*. These petty warlords refused to be led by a woman and shunned Tigris' crowning. Within the first year of Tigris' reign she quickly regained control by placing her cousin Anaten on the seat of Waset and moving her estate from Men-nefer to Henen-nesut. To keep peace in the city of Men-nefer, which had long been the ruling state, Tigris made

37

frequent visits so the citizens would never feel their Pharaoh had abandoned them. And, in order to keep the Ruling House in Lower Egypt, Tigris moved the border dividing Upper and Lower Egypt further into the north but she left Amunken, Governor of Lower Egypt, to reign the south from the old capital.

Her cousin, Anaten, nonetheless, subdued the north. It was his duty to know if there were threats; his duty to know what went on in the northern *sepats*. How did he not know for so long?

The Governor of Upper Egypt stood up. His gown pleated around him, adding to his size. Fastened to one shoulder, a long piece of linen crossed over his mid-rift before draping to the ground—perhaps to flatten his potbelly.

Tigris eyed him. It was hard to believe they were even related. He was a very round man. His face, his stomach, even his arms seemed bursting with fat.

Self-consciously, Anaten folded his chubby arms over his stomach. "Your Majesty," he began slowly, "this knowledge has come as a shock to me as well. As always, I travel down the river every sixty suns to conduct my affairs with the *First of the Kings* in the northern *sepat*. During my last journey, upon reaching *Iunet*, I heard rumours that a... dare I say," he continued carefully, "a self-proclaimed King had taken over the eastern region of Upper Egypt. Naturally, I investigated further..." Anaten stopped and fidgeted his clammy hands as he slowly shook his head as if disappointed, "...and found these rumours to be true." He looked despairingly at the Queen. "Per'a, this rebel has gained the trust of many of our Egyptian people who follow him in aid of his cause. He has secured himself as far south as... as *Waset*—"

"The treasonous Wasets are always so hasty to take over Egypt!" grumbled Ankhtify.

Anaten acknowledged Ankhtify's words with a low-throated grunt. Everybody silently agreed.

"*Waset*?" pointed Ibimpetus. "Is that not your realm?"

Anaten shifted uncomfortably. "Yes, but... but, I've been away for some time and as Ankhtify mentioned, they are a hasty bunch." Anaten wiped his brow and looked at Tigris.

"Carry on," she said, sparing him of Ibimpetus' interrogation.

Anaten quickly sent a scowl to the Vizier before he continued.

"There's really nothing more to say—except, although in Iunet no one knows exactly who this enemy is, the one thing he did make certain was everybody knows he is Egyptian."

Tigris didn't move although inside she burned with despise. An attack of a foreign intruder was always much easier to swallow, but an Egyptian? It was his duty unto *Ra* to honour the Pharaoh as god! Where was his loyalty! she thought.

Anaten watched her, waiting for her to grant him his seat but Tigris remained in thought.

"Why were messages not dispatched immediately?" Ibimpetus questioned.

"Your Majesty," Anaten said, deliberately ignoring the Vizier, "I presume he has stationed men between Abedju and Tentere to obstruct messages from reaching you, hence, contriving your surprise." He looked at Ibimpetus with contempt. "Why I was permitted to pass down the river, I can only assume he was ready to make you aware." Anaten shifted his weight, making it apparent he was done.

Tigris watched him. His nervous twitches, his darting eyes—why could he not look directly at her? He was her cousin, her blood. They had played together as children and yet, she always felt wary of him. She remembered him teasing her, his pranks, his meanness when they were young. *He is a boy. That's how boy's are*, she was told.

Tigris nodded to allow Anaten sit; to his relief she had no questions. The Queen turned to Allegi. Although she heard his speech a week ago, the men should hear it too. "You met with him?" she probed.

"No," Allegi denied as he stood.

Confused, Tigris threw him a look to explain. Surely, when he arrived with the message he made it seem as though he had met with him— *Him!* Who was *he!* Tigris took a subtle deep breath. Why couldn't anyone identify this rebel!

"I travelled to Waset and inquired of his whereabouts. I was directed to Gebtu to search for a man by the name of Somiset who was expecting my arrival."

Allegi's words echoed in Tigris' mind—*expecting his arrival*. It burned her to know the enemy expected her while she knew nothing of his feat until *he* had decided to make it known. An unnamed Egyptian rising out of nowhere, seizing control of so much territory—so many people—and, yet, no one spoke of him until now. How was that possible?

She focused on Allegi who looked at her through honest eyes. Of all the men who sat before her, his were the most trustworthy.

"I was blindfolded, taken to a tent where I was instructed to bring correspondence to Somiset, in the uninhabited region near Abedju." Allegi saw Ibimpetus' lips begin to open. The Vizier would pound him with more questions than he had answers. Allegi continued preventing him the opportunity. "Before I was able to utter a word, I was dragged from the tent, tied and thrown upon my horse. Only when we reached within sight of the Nile was I released. I was then given the scroll with these departing words: 'He will not stop until he obtains what's rightfully his—*Egypt* is his.'" Allegi scanned the faces of the men. "He is declaring war.'"

Allegi noticed the smile that had spread across Ankhtify's mouth on the mere mention of the word *war* even though the General had quickly controlled it. Ankhtify was a warrior at heart and Egypt's peace was making him antsy for battle.

The messenger's last words roused the councillors from their seats to roar with rage. All but Allegi who had settled on his stool, Ankhtify who leaned back enjoying the idea of battle and Ibimpetus who sunk in heavy contemplation, were on their feet yelling, pointing, arguing.

Tigris' mind buzzed with her own thoughts. But, through the gripes and sneers she made out one voice.

"War," grumbled the Vizier in disdain.

Since the Pharaoh's coronation, aside from a few petty campaigns to administer order, Egypt had lived in peace. Now, they would face war with a woman at the helm.

Tigris ignored the men's scoffs, their doubts. She would prove them wrong. Show them she was a great Commander and Chief of Army like the best of Pharaohs before her. She only wished to see her enemy, know who took arms against her, look upon his face. Why did he choose to keep his identity hidden—the letter, not showing himself to Allegi.... *His Majesty!* she thought. What treason!

Tigris broke from her thoughts, looked at her councillors. She returned the flail and crook to their spots in the chair arms but kept her grip securely fixed around them.

"I will meet with him."

The men's voices immediately fell hushed. They looked at their Pharaoh, waited for her lead. This was her first war since her father's death, which she would have to command alone and prove her strength as Pharaoh. They would judge her, she knew. And, save for Allegi and Ankhtify their faces were filled with doubt.

Tigris cleared her throat. She peered directly into the eyes of each man as she spoke, slowly at first, gradually becoming more brisk as she delivered her orders. "Chephren, prepare the ships. I shall embark the day following Allegi's return.

'Tjat, I want the exact count of men in the regions up to Tjenu from the last population report. Enlist them in our army. I am sure it is safe to believe Abedju is the furthest he has reached towards the south." Tigris looked at the men to see if there was any disagreement. Indeed, "beyond Abedju" was mentioned enough times that it had to be in his safety. Tjenu was the next main city south of Abedju. Many warriors dwelled there. She needed to get to them first before her enemy corrupted their loyalty.

None of the councillors offered protest so Tigris proceeded. "Amunken, notify the northern regions to shield themselves against our enemy and find out from the Overlords if our borders have any reason to suspect intrusion. Be sure to include the Amenti." The west had not been mentioned and she did not want the old man to overlook it. "Test how far the borders keep allegiance towards Anaten's territory. Perhaps he truly is Egyptian and has not weakened our wall against our foreign enemies—that would distort his purpose if he were to succeed me." She paused for a moment to think. "Or, perhaps the borders now protect Egypt for him."

Tigris studied her cousin. Until she produced an heir, he was next in line for the throne. "Anaten, if it is possible to exchange letters between our *sepats* in the far north, attempt to discover how many of my officials are still devout. Find out their intentions by the Kingdom of Kush. They are more fickle than the Wasets."

Anaten nodded but his eyes still darted.

Tigris looked at Ankhtify. She held special favour for him adding to his nobility the honourary title of *Well-Beloved Friend*. He was a great warrior, loyal to the crown, ferocious in battle and a magnanimous chieftain who had earned the gold *Flies of Valour* in his younger years. He was her uncle and childhood teacher with whom she accredited her warlord attributes. With him, she trusted her life. For nearly twenty years, he had served under her father helping to bring the political and monarchical disorder of that time to an end. Now, he served faithfully under her.

Tigris allowed a smirk to crawl across her lips. His eyes beamed like a lion waiting for the lioness to complete her kill so he could go in and feast. "Ankhtify," she leered. "You may return that warrior smile to your face. It appears we have war on our hands."

Ankhtify gleamed as if fighting brought him to life. "He will regret the day he conjured up the idea to challenge your crown," he said in his rough and raspy voice.

Tigris returned a slight nod before becoming serious again. "Ready your men to depart from their families and prepare your necessary reserve.

"Mahorse, we will need to keep this army happy."

Mahorse nodded. His job was routine. He knew exactly what had to be done. In a time like this, he monitored Egypt's wealth and the expense of having a strong army.

Tigris looked at all the men hoping there was nothing she had forgotten. Until she was victorious, her every move would be judged.

V

ON THE AUDIENCE room of her bedchambers, Tigris stood on the skin of a zebra. The hairs beneath her bare feet felt good. Rugs overlapped each other all over the room. She loved their beautiful patterns and vibrant colours. Most were brought in from other countries, though some were Egyptian. Rugs heavily decorated the palace, as she constantly collected them but her favourites were the animal skins and of course, above all the tiger.

Tigris moved over to the seating area. Two long sitting cushions paralleled each other with many pillows scattered about them. One of the cushions was supported by a low bench with copper legs for the Queen, while the other rested on the floor. A short table sat in the middle. The Pharaoh's Royal Seat of Estate, a lesser version of her throne, was at the head of the seating arrangement for times when she'd meet with a councillor in the privy of her chambers.

Many nights, Allegi joined her in this room where they stayed awake talking the better part of the night.

Allegi now sat crossed legged on a single cushion, positioned close to the Seat of Estate. He pulled a small desk in front of him, placed his writing kit on the floor. He took out a piece of the papyrus, smoothed it out with a stone, preparing to scribe the Pharaoh's response to the enemy.

Tigris paced the room, thinking; remembering what the rebel wrote in his letter. *His Egypt. His Majesty.* Those words made her blood curdle. The rebel. The enemy. The Egyptian without a name. *The man she wanted dead!*

Tigris groaned heavily. Be brief, she warned herself. Do not let him know your rage—he may interpret it as weakness. She looked at Allegi who chewed on his brush to soften the hairs. "How long will it take you to arrive at his location?"

Allegi pulled the fibres from his mouth to answer, "About seven days."

"Then, scribe: I accept. Meet me—" she stopped, contemplated whether she should have him travel south into her territory or go into his. No, she decided. I must go into the north—show him I do not fear his threshold, that it's still mine.

She looked at Allegi. "Restart and scribe: I will meet you in the region beyond Abedju, by the eastern shore, two weeks from when you pass your message to my nobleman. Come aboard my ship. I will permit only two of your men for your safe feeling." She looked at Allegi with hardened eyes. "Sign it: *Your* Majesty and greatest enemy, King of Upper and Lower Egypt, Nitiqreti, Pharaoh of the Egyptian Empire."

She went to the window and peered out as Allegi read back the message. She was satisfied with it. There was no more to say for the time being.

Allegi rolled up the papyrus. He slid a copper ring, carved like a snake, over the scroll to prevent it from opening and packed up his equipment.

"Enough with matters of business." Tigris moved from the window, beaming at Allegi. "Are you tired?"

"No," he admitted, "I can't sleep."

"Then, play for me?" she asked.

With a slight smile, Allegi stood, went to the music chest, took out a small harp. Tigris kept her favourite instruments in her chamber, even though she played none. They were for Allegi to play during nights when they kept each other company but didn't feel to talk.

Tigris arranged herself comfortably on the low bench. A chambermaid immediately fetched her headrest. Tigris asked for some warm milk to be brought up then excused the chambermaid for the evening after it arrived.

"What would you like to hear?" Allegi asked, returning to the sitting area. He sat opposite Tigris amidst the pillows.

"Something soft."

Strumming the chords, Allegi sent a soft flow of music into the air. The beautiful notes drifted spiritedly from him, sweeping around the room with soothing melodies. The tune flowed through her, guiding her deep into her thoughts. She closed her eyes. How lucky she was to have Allegi as her friend, she thought. Allegi—her most trusted friend; her confidant. "Allegi, the great musician," she whispered. "I shall write it in my tomb."

VI

ᴇARLY THE NEXT morning, Allegi awoke in his own room. The sun was beginning to make its stand in the sky when he rode out of the stable gates, through the court towards the palace's wall of defence. He yelled to the gate guard who in turn yelled up to the tower guard. After checking if the entryway was safe, the guard opened the inner gate and ordered the outer gate to be drawn up.

Allegi galloped down the royal road towards the inner city of Henen-nesut where he would remain for a couple of days before setting out with the message.

The Queen requested he keep her enemy waiting. If their opposition was a respectable opponent, he would wait for her response before marching into combat—at least for a short while. Tigris hoped to hold him off for as long as she believed she could in order to lend time to her inquisitions.

Allegi was happy for the break. He was in no rush to return to the dead red lands or to rush the ugly fate of Egypt. He decided to spend his time in the city, away from the palace that was burdened with the coming war; away from the loneliness of his room that was haunted with questions of the future.

Allegi reached the busy streets of Henen-nesut, slowed Nefer to a walk. The scents of cooked meats and raw fish blended together in the thick air leading him into the market where wagons lined the main roadways, families spread out blankets displaying their trade for sale and beggars annoyed the shoppers with their pleas. Goats and pigs roamed the streets under the watchful eyes of their masters. People pushed their way through the crowds. Columns dwarfed the town's inhabitants but the buildings themselves were no more than three stories high, built in rows that left narrow streets. Palm trees grew on the outskirts of town but inside, the mud-brick houses dominated. Only the courtyards belonging to the Lords afforded a few trees for their gardens.

The city always bustled with people, settling down only well after nightfall. Several taverns and brothels stayed continually open and some combined together for an ideal spot. They provided music nightly, bringing life to the death of night.

Making his way out of the market and into the residential area, Allegi decided to tie Nefer in front of the guesthouse in which he would stay. The horse would be safe, as it was marked with the sign of royalty and death was the only punishment for theft or harm. He would spend the day at the market, strolling about the city, amusing himself by watching the town's people. Later, he would enter a *House of Pleasure* to enjoy its beguiling music, observe the drunken obscenities of its patrons, listen to their words—which always told more than they wanted to in their state—and watch the women pervade their seductive bodies. He preferred the city to amuse his time before journeying, especially now— the palace, quiet and passive, trapped him with his thoughts, which he was beginning to hate.

The sun finished making its slow crawl across the sky. Darkness sent the peddlers home, although a few determined and most likely homeless ones slept under torchlight in the main streets, hoping a drunken pedestrian would be stupid enough to spend his wage. The streets emptied quickly and fell hushed.

Allegi headed to his favourite nightspot, coined for its musical talent. He found his usual seat discreetly shadowed in the corner. As he sat down, one of the maidservants followed him across the room. She slapped a mug of ale down in front of him, smiled and winked when he paid her. She knew her customers and knew not to disturb him for the rest of the night as he only ever had one drink.

Allegi sipped his ale, observed the room. Although the singers and musicians entertained with upbeat songs, he found himself more entertained by the rowdy crowd. He looked across the room, caught the eye of a young courtesan who approached him. He quickly looked away.

Allegi never indulged in the indecencies of these women who gave themselves to men, drooping their bodies over them as they caressed their back and arms with flirtatious smiles curled across their lips, going from one man to the next, bound to no one and yet, open to all. He observed them but he never permitted himself the pleasure. He did not want to be like the men he viewed—many were known to become sick by their compulsion. Yes, the women were stunning but they were not wives.

The courtesan continued towards Allegi. He shook his head, moved his attention to a group of single women who frequented the spot looking for eligible men. They giggled and whispered, teasing the young men who came to flirt with them and not pay for a courtesan; they reminded Allegi of a pack of hyenas.

The courtesan was almost at his table. He looked away, but his dismissal did nothing to stop her. She sat down on a cushion close to Allegi and began to caress his arm. Allegi caught her hand, squeezed it. "Please," he said moving her hand away from him. "I'd prefer to be left alone."

"They say you always come in here and never touch a woman.

There's nothing to be afraid of; I will guide you through it." She gave a seductive smile as she attempted to touch him again.

Allegi stopped her. "I am not interested," he said sternly.

Insulted, the woman jumped up. "Then it is true, you must enjoy the company of men!" She stomped away.

It was not the first time Allegi heard the accusation. He allowed them to believe what they wanted. It soothed their bruised egos and granted him the solitude he desired. He had been with a woman. At one time, he thought he loved her. But, when he came into the Pharaoh's office, the love affair ended and he soon realized the feelings he had were not really love at all. That seemed so long ago even though it had only been a couple of years.

Allegi took another sip of his beer and turned his attention back to the musicians.

The next night, the young messenger returned to the same spot in the same dark corner, which no one else seemed to want to sit. He clutched his beer, slumped on the thick cushion and observed the room. Most of the patrons from the previous night were there again. Many royal nobles frequented the place though no one ever spoke of it in the outside world.

Allegi watched as one made his climb up the stairs behind the woman he had purchased for the next short while. Allegi knew the man was married, and his wife pregnant.

How terrible, he thought with disgust.

"If you don't come to pay then why bother to stay?" a voice groaned from the low table next to Allegi. Allegi looked over. There were four men sitting on a kilim around a game of Hounds and Jackals. They leered at him with dirty faces and rotten smiles. The harlot Allegi rejected the previous night was sprawled across the rug, leaning over the speaker's lap.

Allegi didn't answer. He turned away.

"He thinks he's too good. He's the Pharaoh's boy you know," said another man.

"Ya," laughed his friend, "but the Pharaoh must be poor in the bed if he finds his way here each night."

The table howled.

Allegi slammed down his mug, sprang from his seat, charged at the speaker. The man saw him coming. He pushed the whore from his lap, jumped to his feet. He was much bigger than Allegi, but Allegi didn't care. He grabbed the dagger from his waist side. His opponent did the same. Both lunged towards each other, almost colliding, pressing their daggers against each other's throat.

Allegi panted deeply, trying to tame his rage. His blade trembled with anger against the man's neck and he could feel the metal of his adversary's knife pressed to his skin.

Allegi stared the man directly in the eyes, spoke in a low voice. "Watch what you say about our Pharaoh or I will cut your tongue from your mouth and use it to hang you!" Allegi remained with his eyes locked on the man's. He didn't flinch.

The room fell quiet; everyone watched.

After a long, heavy moment, the man backed down. "You're only tough because you're protected by status," he sneered, pointing at the Gold Scorpion, which symbolized Allegi's title as *Friend of the King*. He looked Allegi up and down with cold eyes, spat at his feet.

Allegi didn't move.

The man turned back to his table. The onlookers resumed their conversations, disappointed they didn't get a fight.

Allegi kept his eyes on him until the man was once again seated on the floor. He slid his dagger back into its holder, went to turn.

Someone caught his eye.

Allegi turned to face the door. A girl stepped into the tavern. Allegi felt himself momentarily forget to breathe.

The girl was about his age. She wore a scarf draped over her head secured by a band around her forehead but her makeup was fashioned in the Egyptian way.

Uneasily, she entered the alehouse, looked around. She came alone and seemed unsure as she stepped further inside. The moment she was in the door, a man pounced on her, startling her by his sudden rambunctious presence. She slipped away from him, moving precariously against the wall.

Allegi went back to his seat. He fixed his eyes upon her from his reclusive spot. She was beautiful. Something about her was different from all the other women in the tavern. She seemed to be neither whore nor wooer. She didn't seem to belong.

Allegi picked up his mug, took a long gulp. He wanted to speak to her, but what could he say without seeming like all the other men who circled the bar swooping in on women? He didn't dare go to her. All he could manage to do was follow her with his eyes, hoping for an easy moment and the courage to seize it.

Allegi watched the girl make her way to the serving bar and buy some warm ale. She pinned her back against the wall. Nervously, she gazed around from under her brow as she took a small sip of her drink. When she almost looked at him, Allegi felt his stomach flutter.

Yes, he breathed, there was something about her. She seemed innocent, perhaps shy or even troubled—but definitely unlike the other women.

Go and speak with her, Allegi urged himself. But, he couldn't muster the courage to stand up.

The girl kept her eyes on the room even when she took a sip of her drink. Her eyes darted, glanced around. She spotted Allegi in the shadows. For a brief moment, their eyes locked. Allegi was almost certain he saw her hide a smile. But, before he was aware of what was happening, the girl set down her mug and headed for the door.

Within moments, she was gone.

A rush of disappointment flooded Allegi as he looked around the establishment at all the beautiful women. None had ever made his heart skip.

He sprang to his feet. This was it. If he didn't catch her he might lose his only chance.

A hand locked around his arm. Allegi looked down. The man from the other table noticed Allegi watching the girl. He had taken hold of Allegi's arm as he raced by and yanked him back. "Where you goin' in such a hurry?"

Allegi glared down at him.

"Don't go leavin' on our account. Stay and drink with us."

"Maybe next time." Allegi tried to move towards the door.

The man tightened his grip.

"Maybe next time you'll want to choose another place."

"Or, maybe if I slice your hand from your wrist you will no longer detain me." Allegi cocked his head as if to dare him.

The man let out a deep grunt before he let go.

"Goodnight," Allegi nodded.

The large man did not respond or if he did, Allegi was unaware. Without hesitation, he pushed through the crowd, bumping the patrons who were preoccupied with laughter and conversation to let him by. Eventually, he made it to the door but when he reached the alleyway, he found it empty. The only life outside the nightspot was the loud noises beckoning from within.

Allegi closed his eyes catching the breeze blowing up the narrow street upon his face. A crushing feeling lingered in his chest. How could such a fleeting moment cause so much grief? he wondered.

He walked to the guesthouse disappointed, yet, unsure of what he would have done had he caught up to the girl.

That night, as Allegi lay in bed, he found himself thinking about the girl instead of his recent disturbing thoughts—by comparison, it was a pleasant escape.

The next morning, Allegi rode out of the city before most of its inhabitants had stirred from their sleep and headed to the barque station. Set a short way in from the Nile, the royal ships were anchored in this water pit including the Vessel of the Royal Messenger. The small ship held thirty rowers and the master sailor. It housed two cabins— one for Allegi; the other for the Captain—and a stable.

When the Captain spotted him riding in, he immediately shouted orders to his men to take their places.

Allegi jumped off his horse. He led Nefer up the narrow wooden plank.

"Help yourself to some breakfast," the Captain called out, pointing towards a sack of bread loaves and jars of fresh water and ale. Dried fish hung underneath a cover to shade them from the sun.

"Thank you but I've eaten." Allegi stopped beside the stout tousled Captain who was busy grumbling to himself and gave him a pat on the back. "How does it go with you, Ramska?"

"Rough," replied the blithesome skipper with a grin. His smile grew as he added, "My head is still sore, my gut is still too big and my men are as always, poor rowers." He laughed in spite of himself before yelling at the men to commence rowing.

"Glad to hear nothing disturbs the usual then." Allegi smirked, "Though, might I suggest your cure?"

The Captain looked at him quizzically.

"Less ale for your head, your gut and your men!"

Ramska let out a bellow of a laugh.

The men rowed down the causeway, which led them out into the Nile. The river ride was always slower towards Upper Egypt as the men had to row against the current. The sun already hot, made the event even more torturous as the boat soon reeked of body sweat.

Allegi climbed onto the roof of the small cabin at the stern of the boat. A large piece of linen, tied off at poles hitched to each corner of the roof, created a canopy for shade. He sprawled himself out, catching the breeze from the moving vessel. Before long, the current rocked him to sleep.

About noon, Allegi awoke. His deep sleep much needed; he hadn't slept much over the past few days. He stood, stretched out his sore muscles and clambered down the ladder.

The men had stopped for lunch and were enjoying their break with food and conversation. Allegi passed them as he went to see about his horse. He poured buckets of water over Nefer's dark coat to help cool him off then returned to the cabin's roof where he ate in solitude.

Leaning back, Allegi stared down the river and bit into the fish. He thought of the girl from Sechemech tavern, her face painted perfectly in his memory. He imagined a different moment—catching her in the alley, talking to her, the girl liking him too. How quickly opportunity was lost; he would never be able to get it back. Why didn't he talk to her when he had the chance?

Allegi finished eating. He pulled out his writing kit and a blank piece of papyrus from his travel pouch.

In some ways, he believed his fate was sealed to a life of solitude. He would never leave the Pharaoh—to her, he owed his life. Although in many ways he was happy, he felt empty. He wanted to be in love.

The girl's image glowed in his mind. He closed his eyes as if in prayer. If the gods would only let them cross paths again, he would speak this time.

Allegi looked at the paper. He crushed some blue pigment with a stone, added a bit of water to turn it into ink. Dipping his brush in the ink, he wrote:

From a distance, I saw you close to me,
How I wish to speak your name,
But, the claws of fear had held me back,
Leaving me in pain.
My empty heart wants to love,
Though, what an evil game life plays,
To cast its spell of great desire,
Then steal one's strength away.

Allegi rubbed his eyes. He had only looked upon the girl and now she owned his thoughts. He felt so alone in the world—if not for Tigris he would have no one. Still, that was a friendship stipulated by protocol. She was a great friend, but she was also his Pharaoh. Although at one time Allegi revered her more, he soon realized it was a young and foolish infatuation. Since their friendship had grown closer, his affection matured into a love one would have for a sister and more so, a sister he felt the need to protect.

Allegi looked down into the river remembering the day they met—only two years ago, when he was nineteen:

〰〰

HIS MOTHER HAD caught a sickness crippling her to bed. While his father flooded his sorrows with ale, Allegi was made the parent of both. For a year and a half prior, he watched the demise of his parents until his mother slipped into the Underworld taking their spirits with her. That night, his father left the house never to return again save through a message: He was found dead on Khephritin hill.

A short while later, unable to bear the burden of life, Allegi made his way to the edge of a cliff. It was there Tigris found him as she was passing through Iunu.

"A careless place to stand," Tigris called to him.

"That depends upon one's intentions. For me, it is the perfect spot." He spun to see who spoke.

She was seated on her sedan with four men holding her up from its platform base. A line of well-dressed soldiers trailed behind, with some maidens among them. A large palm was held over her head to shade her from the sun in addition to being fanned. Her jewels were large and rich and the linen of her dress was fine and light.

Allegi immediately fell to his knees, bending his head to the earth. She had to be the Pharaoh, he remembered thinking. She was as exquisite as everyone had described.

"Why do you seek to end your life?"

Allegi hesitated before answering. "Because I have nothing to live for. Both my parents have left this world and I wish to join them."

A long moment lingered before she spoke again. "Stand and join my party. When we return to the Great Palace after our visit here, I will find purpose for your life."

Allegi obeyed. He stood but kept his head bent.

"Until you find your own purpose in life, you will remain under my rule. And, instead of to the valley, to me, your life you'll give." The Pharaoh looked to her chair bearers, motioned for them to continue.

Obediently, he followed her entourage. From that moment onward, Allegi had become the Pharaoh's subject.

The day they had arrived at the palace, Tigris called him to the *Great Throne of Geb* and asked, "What abilities do you possess other than flying?"

When she discovered he'd been studying hieroglyphs before his mother fell ill, she appointed him with the noble duty of scribe. He was re-schooled to learn the royal script. When his scribing was perfected, Tigris made him her personal scribe and messenger. Often she sent for his audience, which began their long talks.

Allegi long since realized why Tigris kept him close. Being without parents herself, and despite her position, or perhaps because of her position, she felt alone. Allegi reminded her she wasn't alone, that someone felt the same. More importantly, he offered what no other noble could—someone she could let her guard down with, if even a little.

〰〰

ALLEGI BROUGHT HIS thoughts back to the present. He peered down into the dark river, watched the synchronized oars dip into the water to pull the boat along. The bow of the vessel cut through the water smoothly. He continued to watch for a long while, hypnotized by the movement. His heart was heavy with emptiness and longing but his dedication bound him from his solemn wish to leave this world.

Inspired by the river, Allegi turned to the papyrus and wrote some more:

> *Beneath your murky currents,*
> *I hear you call my name,*
> *Cleanse me from my conscience,*
> *My spirit empty,*
> *Lets me go.*
> *Your undertow so strong,*
> *Whispers...*
> *So I come to you,*
> *Falling towards your depths,*
> *I collapse slowly.*
> *You hold up your mirror,*
> *And, I see the way you ridicule my frown—*
> *I am crying,*
> *Painful tears racing to you,*
> *Leading the way.*
> *My last memory is yours,*
> *Thus, you will not let me forget,*
> *So, you deliver me to my conscience,*
> *And, reflect upon your glistening surface,*
> *As I fall closer,*
> *My wisdom;*
> *   Closer*
> *My ignorance;*
> *   Closer*
> *My happiness;*
> *   Closer*
> *My sorrow;*
> *Until, at last, I am submerged,*
> *And, you rush over me,*
> *Cleansing me,*

Everything now so perfectly clear
From washing away the sins
That I hand clung to with a mortal price,
'Til finally, so surely I see my errors.
I smile.
My last labour bears only regret.

VII

℘ EVEN DAYS LATER the Vessel of the Royal Messenger reached the docking area closest to Abedju. They hugged the eastern shoreline searching for any clue of where Allegi was to find Somiset. The region, empty and lifeless, spanned some fifty odd miles before reaching Tentere.

Allegi and the Captain painstakingly peered through the bright Egyptian sun, searching for a flag, a sign—anything. There was no logic in the enemy withholding the exact location from his company unless of course, he himself did not know, which meant the enemy intended to march.

Allegi thought for a moment—that also meant the enemy had not yet passed Abedju. Certainly, he would not march further towards the south only to turn back just to receive the Pharaoh's response.

The Captain called out, "I think we've found your mark!" He was pointing towards a stake pitched into the sandy shore with the falcon god Horu perched on top of the copper rod.

Allegi raced to Ramska's side to look.

"A mark indeed," he said, smacking the sailor on the back.

The Captain and his men manoeuvred the boat as close to shore as possible. They anchored, drew the plank, planting it firmly into the ground beneath the crisp water.

Allegi departed on horseback. He eased Nefer towards the water. The river was cold and shocked the messenger's hot skin as he made his way into it. Nefer obediently moved towards the shore, rising out of the water, gaining speed.

"Go Nefer!" whispered Allegi, leaning close to the horse's ear. The water rushed off them as the last of Nefer's powerful body emerged from the river. Nefer moved faster, gaining more control, galloping from the river while his master urged him onward.

Allegi dug his heels into Nefer. They raced up the sandy beach towards the Horu rod. Allegi fixed his eyes on the pole, challenging himself to pull it from the ground as they sped by. He knew the Captain was watching—his attempt, a childish game, would prove embarrassing if he missed; yet, that added to the challenge.

Nefer brought them closer. Allegi bent low over the horse's back, reaching his hand out, aiming to lock his grip under the falcon. He steered Nefer arm's length from the pole, leaned further, grasped the falcon, pulled the rod successfully from the ground as they went soaring past. Behind him he could hear the faint cheer of the Captain.

Allegi continued racing all the way to the tree line, which followed the river before he slowed Nefer to a trot. He directed the horse through the dense strip of trees and eventually, they came out on the other side, leaving the river hidden behind. The land spread towards the mountains, gradually becoming drier as it left the river.

Allegi scanned over the open area for any sign of danger in its vastness. Everything was still, barren. He picked out the first cliff face, decided to wait for Somiset there.

Snapping the reins, Allegi sent Nefer into a steady speed up the modest incline towards the plateau. The land stretched further than its appearance, but before long they reached the cliff. Allegi drew Nefer to a stop, dismounted. He dug the Horu rod into the ground. The earth was hard and stony, which made the task difficult. He struggled with it until the rod held on its own, although it did so miserably. Allegi left the Horu rod leaning greatly to one side, thirty feet out from the cliff, then headed towards the shade leaving Nefer to roam freely—the horse would come by whistle.

The cliff was the perfect spot. Some twenty feet up, a ledge jutted out offering shade below. Allegi could see clearly down the slight hill in front of him and along the tree line in both directions. The mountains curled behind were steep, making them unsafe for entry or exit and thus, offering protection. From this point, his view gave him unobstructed visibility of whoever approached. Now, he could only wait.

The afternoon sun began to make its descent before the lone rider came out of the trees with great speed. He did not slow his pace until he left the tree line far enough behind.

Allegi watched as the rider slowed to a canter to subtly scope the land before rearing his horse and taking off again. He had picked out the copper staff glinting in the fading sunlight.

Allegi stood only when the rider was about him.

"I bring a message from Her Majesty, Pharaoh Nitiqreti, Tigris of Egypt," Allegi announced, trying to hold back the anger he felt upon seeing the man who had left him to the desert.

"Give it here," replied Somiset in his rough dialect. "I will take it to my King—"

"No, I will take it," Allegi cut in.

"Your presence is not welcomed."

Allegi gripped the scroll. "Why does your Lord find it essential to hide himself?"

"For his own purpose," Somiset answered, agitated.

"The Pharaoh wishes him to be described. I am a messenger and therefore, pose no threat—"

"Your Pharaoh will see him herself in due time," he snapped. He held out his hand.

Knowing the man would not give in, Allegi reluctantly handed him the scroll.

"Remain here. I will return tomorrow with my King's response."

After Somiset disappeared far in the distance, Allegi went to the Horu rod and removed it from the ground. He would return it at daybreak, but for now, he didn't need to draw attention to their meeting.

VIII

𝒯HE FIRES WERE just beginning to be lit as night arrived, smothering the light of day with a deepening azure. The temperature had cooled and would continue to do so considerably with the disappearing sun. The voices of men grew with the night—the ale seemed to reach their heads at the same speed darkness covered the land. Euphrates, however, had no desire to drink. He wanted to think about his quest, imagine how it would unfold—but, not tonight. Tonight he sat with a group of his closest men—the ones who were there from the beginning; the ones who were not just followers but also friends. He half listened to their stories and half listened to the voice within his own mind.

These men are all here for you, the voice told him. They are here because they believe in the cause with which you have brought them together to fight.

And, indeed they would all fight; unanimously marching towards bloodshed—their weapons raised, their hearts pounding and their passion urging them forward. *A King for Egypt!*

Euphrates knew he held a heavy weight of responsibility to these men, now rebels in the eyes of the unswayable Egypt. This endeavour was indeed perilous and, although some of them would only find but the afterlife in the end, they clung richly to the promise and fervently to its virtue.

What if virtue failed them? No, Euphrates decided, pushing the thought aside. He would not think that way. There was so much to lose, yet, so much to gain. Nonetheless he could not bring these men together and think of their despair, even if only for a moment.

Guilt struck him. He swore to himself never again to allow failure to cross his mind. He would lead them to victory. Every action, every thought, every movement and every spoken word that hence he did make would impress nothing but glorious success.

"What troubles your mind so much to place a furrow on your brow, my Lord?" asked Storithen, interrupting Euphrates' thoughts.

Euphrates looked at the lofty soldier. He exhaled deeply to allow whatever doubt remained to dissipate. "Nothing troubles me, my good man," he assured. "The furrow on my brow—which you speak so grimly of—is not of grief but rather of passion." Euphrates stood. "I bide my time with thoughts of the future and," he smiled, "you are all in it."

The men raised their cups to salute a cheer.

Euphrates continued boyishly, easing the air, which grew tenser with each passing day. He raised his arm and pointed. "You, Sir Storithen, I had made Lord of the Legendary Tales—fabled all by you, of course." Euphrates broke out into a chuckle as he sprang through the inner circle formed by the men around the low fire. Storithen could talk, tell a tale that would last for days; make a point twice as long as it needed to be. He stopped at where Storithen sat, looked at the large husky man of monstrous size, yet with a gentle face.

Euphrates knew doubt disheartened the men at times, especially when concern clouded his own face. Tonight, he decided, he would not confine himself to his regular deliberation. He was tired of preaching and tired of motivating them with promises he wasn't sure he could keep. For once, he thought he should provoke them with light-hearted fun and join them in their jests that so often accompanied the nightly fires and which he so often dismissed himself from.

Confused at first, the men quieted down to gather what Euphrates was doing but then playful smiles erased their puzzled looks. Storithen was the first to catch on. He stood tall as Euphrates drew his dagger to dub him. "With this title you shall continue to amuse all men with your stories naming me a hero of all heroes—"

The men snickered.

Euphrates turned, pointed his dagger at them. "Well, it is fable, is it not?" His expression implored them to agree. "Then I can be anything I want." He spun back. "Storithen, instead, make me a god to all men!"

Everyone laughed, their drinks endorsing the humour.

"I believe I'd make a better god, anyway." He struck a godly pose.

The men disapproved playfully.

"But, you are Son of Re, Euphrates," Storithen reminded him, raising his voice above the others. "Soon, the all of Egypt and the whole world will realize. You shall bring Maat back to Egypt in the palms of your hands and the people shall rejoice. You will make the laws for all eternity to the satisfaction of all people." He held his cup up high and brought the men into another round of cheer, this time with stomping and clashing of flasks.

Euphrates smiled. He patted Storithen on the shoulder. "Pray you are right."

For a moment, the air grew serious, quiet. Euphrates smiled, spun on his heels. "Who shall be the next nobleman to be given an excellent title?" he asked, cutting the austerity and bringing the spoof back to the group. He moved to the left of Storithen, nodded at Tuthiken's grinning face.

Tuthiken stood and bared a toothless smile. His face was cracked and weathered but his eyes were still bright.

"You, Tuthiken..." Euphrates paused to think. "You..." he stalled, trying to come up with the attribute to best describe the large man of muscular strength. Finally, it came: "You shall be Great Overlord of the Bale of Ale!"

Everyone laughed.

"Most befitting!" yelled one of the men clapping at the well chosen name.

Tuthiken loved to drink and had built an enormous tolerance for alcohol. Long after everyone else passed out, Tuthiken continued— never seeming to be numbed by its effects.

Euphrates tapped his blade on each of Tuthiken's shoulders as he announced, "With this title you shall be the superior guardian of drunken officials keeping a watchful eye over their limp bodies when the brew has stolen their noble stance."

The men groaned at the embarrassing thought.

Tuthiken bowed, grunted, lifted up a wooden barrel and poured the beer down his throat. His comrades rooted him on until he held the keg high above his head for a final applause.

The next man stood as Euphrates sidestepped towards him. "And you, good Menenthop, what title do you feel you bear justly?" he asked in a kingly voice.

Behind him, the men heckled out names. Euphrates laughed as he caught one of them. "Perfect! You shall be remembered as the Singing Duke of Lute."

Menenthop smiled. He carried his lute with him everywhere, seizing any opportunity he could to strum its strings and sing. He made his lyrics up at whim, annoying the men with taunting verses as he teasingly played. Menenthop contrived a song for just about anything and although he knew he wasn't very good, he enjoyed it nonetheless.

"Thank you kind Majesty. I shall wear my title well. In fact, I think I should sing a song about it!" He scooped up his instrument and began to pluck the strings.

Everyone cried out, begging him to stop. They grabbed small pebbles from the ground and tossed them in his direction.

The game continued around the circle, filling the night with laughter as they gave each other whimsical titles. Everyone was so engrossed they didn't hear the sentry until he stood in the middle of the ring, somewhat out of breath.

"My Lord! He's here!"

Euphrates' sober nature returned. He looked at the short thin man. "Somiset?" Euphrates questioned.

"Yes," replied Nefret. "I spotted him in the distance riding with the flag held high. He signalled his approach." The watchman beamed. "Soon my Lord your wish will be."

"Yes, my good man, very soon." Euphrates knew what Nefret referred to—their long and deliberate wait to strike war on Egypt's sovereignty. Until now, he had spent his time building his army, recruiting men far from the Pharaoh's region where he could safely organize some control and convince them of the truth.

Euphrates looked into the distance where Somiset would ride in with the Pharaoh's response. He was sure she would meet even though she held him off longer than expected. Another day, he would have began his campaign without the desired appointment. And, to think, his only purpose for the meeting was to go to war in honour.

Euphrates looked at the watchman who was still panting. "Return to your post and have Somiset bring the message to my tent."

IX

FIFTEEN DAYS AFTER Allegi left the palace he returned with the response. Later that night, he went into Henen-nesut in search of the girl at Sechemech Tavern. He was told by the bar maid she was there a few days earlier but to his disappointment she did not show that night.

♒

THE NEXT MORNING, by first light the royal ships were readied. Food was carried onto all the vessels but on the Pharaoh's ship, rugs, cushions, urns, statues and everything else to make her cabin as luxurious as possible were assembled. Trunks went down the roadway by the dozen with an entourage that seemed unreasonable for the short journey they would make. Cooks, cleaners, servitors, handmaids, dancers and entertainers prepared for the trip by order of the Vizier.

Ibimpetus intended to impress upon the enemy the magnificence of the Pharaoh in hopes to infect his mission with doubt. The Pharaoh's journey would not be discreet. Twenty vessels would row to the destination point reminding everyone they passed who their true Pharaoh God was and warning she was a force not to be reckoned with.

Jewelled golden statues placed at the front of each ship would glitter in the sun and reflect their prominence upon the surface of the river as their godly faces scorned disapproval of the enemy's quest. Flags would flap in the breeze to wave their approach and the drums would sound as the ships closed in on Abedju. Everything had to be perfect to demonstrate the supremacy of the almighty throne and the Vizier was fastidious to ensure it.

By early afternoon the ships would be ready to sail.

SHORTLY AFTER THE sun rose, Tigris awoke. The night had been difficult to sleep through with her anxiety of the coming affair. Opening her eyes, she lay for a moment staring blankly at the canopy before she threw back the sheet and sprang out of bed. Tigris darted from her bedchamber, across the adjacent audience chamber and out onto the terrace to peer down upon the courts below. She watched the men and women hustle about, getting everything ready, which made reality set in. Within the week she would meet the assailant who threatened her crown and who, in such a short time, altered her life. The idea of it weighed upon her and for a brief moment, Tigris felt doubt.

"Am I ready to bear the burden of war?" she whispered, covering her face with her hands and shaking her head.

Tigris turned away from the balcony. She began to pace. She knew the answer. She spent her whole life preparing for war and truthfully it was all she knew—though now she had to face it alone.

Tigris straightened. Yes, she decided, nothing to fear. Her steps quickened as her thoughts made the anxiety swell within her belly. The sensation almost hurt. She held her stomach.

"*My Egypt*," she whispered.

The Queen strode back to her bedchamber. She closed the door behind her, lowered the copper rod across it to keep it barred against the adjacent room, indicating to the chambermaids to leave her in privacy until she rang. She went over to the long mirror hanging on the wall and stopped in front of it. She momentarily studied her reflection before she grabbed the mirror's edge and pulled it forward. The mirror opened up to a dark narrow passage where just inside the doorway a torch hung on the wall waiting to be used. She lit the torch, stepped in.

Through the dark corridor, Tigris made her way to the staircase that wound downward until it was deep under ground. She raced down the uneven steps, pressing the wall for balance, holding the torch out in front. When she reached the landing at the bottom, she hesitated, staring at the door.

I should turn back, she thought. Sometimes it's best not to know. But, she couldn't will herself to turn around and despite her reasoning to do so she continued to stare at the door before her. At length, Tigris placed the torch in the holder on the wall and softly rapped on the door.

From inside, she could smell soft odours of frankincense, oils and inungent melding together and seeping out of the room, welcoming her with a scent that offered a feeling of comfort.

Tigris pushed the door open.

The room was dimly lit, casting an amber glow against the stone floor with long flickering shadows.

So many things in the room begged to be looked at. They were curiously extraordinary—both foreboding and welcoming to touch at the same time. But, the Queen knew not to disturb anything and even to poke around was considered a disturbance.

Tigris had been introduced to this hidden chamber as a child in Men-nefer long before she summoned the Vizier--her grand architect--to recreate it exactly when she moved her abode to the palace in Henen-nesut. Everything in the room was arranged as she remembered it as a child. Torches hung from the walls, dimly lighting the hidden chamber and casting long shadows across the stone walls and floors. Many chests, tables, statues and urns were scattered about the room, all bursting with contents. Scrolls and books were piled in and around everything with a low table holding a collection of *ostraca*, another table canisters, while another displayed stones spread out on a cloth. But, on a small high stand a lone book stood unequalled—it was the *Am Duat*—Book of the Dead. In front of a closed chest a long sceptre lay on the floor as if that was its intended spot. Everything within the room seemed out of place and yet, everything seemed to belong where it was. A particular part of the arrangement was more precious than anything else. To one side of the room rectangular rugs overlapped each other at the ends creating the shape of a hexagon. In the middle, a dark, shallow circular water hole was cut into the floor. Its depth was no more than a couple inches and the interior was tiled in a dark stone that made the water look black. Pillows were scattered all over the rug grouping but not a single corner fell near the hole. With the dancing flames around the room, the still water seemed to move. To Tigris, it looked like a black pond and since she was a child, it came to be known as such.

Often, stepping into this room brought back a rush of her first memory of the chamber. It was as if the door was the portal from hatred and anger to love and admiration. But, to get to the warm comforting feeling the room offered, Tigris had to succumb to the painful portage.

As Tigris closed the door and stood glaring at her reflection in yet another mirror, which hid the secret of the passage between the two rooms, the memory came bolting back to her:

I DON'T CARE, Tigris remembered chanting when her mother told her she wished not to continue their visits.

Tigris was convinced her mother was a child-hater and only gave birth to her because it was her duty in marriage. Queen Nefari—the woman Tigris had called mother—always feigned weak so she would only have to spend time with Tigris once a month. Any more than that she claimed was too much.

But, Tigris knew her mother was not a weak woman, which was quite apparent when they were alone. The queen resented Tigris for being born a girl and indeed she made Tigris pay for it. "You are nothing," she would tell her. "You are my curse. Do not fool yourself to believe you are loved. You are not worthy of it, cursed girl." Nefari's words were damaging, cutting Tigris like a knife.

The queen would also throw things at her—mostly things that wouldn't bruise her skin, but it was the fact she threw them at all that hurt Tigris the most.

"Do not believe your father loves you either. He is even more ashamed of your birth than me," Nefari would tell her often. But, Tigris refused to believe her. Unlike her mother, her father took interest in her.

Sometimes when Tigris visited with her mother, Nefari would ignore her altogether. This pained Tigris the most, more than her harrowing words, more than her spiteful lashes, the silences cut the deepest. The truth be known, Tigris yearned for her mother's love and acceptance. Hoped for it. Needed it. And, although she hated spending time with the queen because it was emotionally painful, she secretly hoped for the day her mother would change. Befriend her. Love her. Realize it was not so bad she was born a girl after all.

Tigris was mesmerized by her mother's beauty and wished to inherit its likeness. She would often stare into the queen's face believing her mother's beauty would transfer onto her. Tigris' handmaid Naat facetiously assured her the queen did enough habitual gazing in the mirror while pregnant that Tigris should not have to worry—a widespread belief in Egypt for making a developing child born beautiful.

While the staring drove Nefari crazy, it brought pleasure to Tigris. She was forced to sit quietly so in her bitterness, Tigris put effort into subtly making the queen uneasy with her perpetual gaze. It was how she received attention and although the attention was unpleasant, at least she got her mother to show she did exist. It became a struggle of will. Nefari would pretend she didn't notice but Tigris would continue until she finally broke her.

"Stop that! Why must you stare so?" the queen demanded looking up from a tapestry she was working on.

65

Tigris sat opposite the queen, studying her with contempt. Her mother hadn't acknowledged her presence and she was bored. "Would you prefer me to stare so?" Tigris twisted in her seat so she was upside down.

"You are not funny," Nefari balked.

Tigris smiled coyly. She loved doing that. *Winning*. That was what she considered it when she drove her mother to have to say something to her.

"Respect me! I am your mother!"

"Surprising. You don't behave so."

Nefari set her tapestry down. "Very well. If you wish not to come here anymore then consider yourself excused from the whole ordeal."

"Hmm, a rather tempting offer mother, I am surprised you've never suggested it before. Maybe because it is much easier said than done?" Tigris flipped back around in her chair. She provokingly waved her hand in a dismissing manner. "Away with the daughter is not so easy from where we sit. Besides, I come here with purpose," she shrugged.

"What? To drive me insane with your insistent staring?"

"Something like that."

"Well, I cannot take it any longer! For years I have put up with these visits, which have been more like a growing sore. There has to be a way to put an end to this before I burst!" Nefari huffed. She slouched back in her seat. She couldn't do much to Tigris anymore. Tigris was at the age where she fought back. Nefari would have loved to lock the child in the bedchamber until Naat came to retrieve her but she knew Tigris no longer feared her blows. The child couldn't be trusted. She would find the most precious thing Nefari owned and smash it in retaliation. The dutiful visits were becoming more and more taxing.

Nefari leaned forward and looked steadily at her daughter. "I will make you a deal. You, nor I, enjoy these visits. We carry on with them for the sole purpose of show. At most, we pretend for your father. I think it is time we cleverly do away with them." The queen stood up. She moved away. She sighed deeply, "I was just not meant to be a mother. I am sorry." Her tone was very matter of fact.

Tigris was shocked at the words spilling from her mother's mouth. How could she? Even though Tigris knew the truth; its sudden confirmation brought a lump into her throat. Self-pity swelled up inside her. Her mother was abandoning her and she felt a sudden pain creep through every part of her body. Desperately, Tigris didn't want to let go despite how much she thought she hated her. The queen was familiar—a visit she hated but needed; the mother she always prayed would one day come to her senses and open her arms to her—her *daughter!* Now, with apathetic words her mother was abandoning her.

"Why?" begged Tigris, still holding onto the lump within her throat. She didn't want to show her tears. She didn't want her mother to enjoy her grief because suddenly she believed the queen to be that wicked.

"The truth? How old are you now? Ten?"

"Eleven," Tigris said softly, the lump growing—her mother didn't even know her age.

"Old enough," Nefari shrugged. "The truth is I never wanted a child. I came to marry your father in an arrangement. It was perfect. I would see I'd never bear him a child and he could lay with other wives for the purpose." She stopped. Her stare peered off into a memory. "But then, the funniest thing—I fell in love. Me! Who ever would have thought the stubborn, self-absorbed, callous woman could fall in love?" Her trance broke. She looked at Tigris who sat frozen in her seat. "The heart *is* a powerful thing," she warned.

Nefari moved over to the window to gaze out. "You know, it's as if I've had five children already," she began, still gazing off into the distance. "I was the eldest of six with another on the way. It was a long and gruelling birth and I had sat many hours holding my mother's hand, watching this cursed fate of women cast excruciating pain before it took them both. My mother was not able to bear the last of my siblings, and thus, it condemned her to death and me to motherhood.

'I was angry with the gods for they had taken the one person who mattered most in my life and what's more, I hated the child who had conspired." The queen continued to glare out the window. "In those times, the poor had become wealthy; the rich poor, the robbers owned riches and servants plundered their masters. Although we were of nobility, my father could not afford a housemaid to look after the children. So, while other children played, I was forced to raise five miserable children. Dutifully, but not without despise, I raised my siblings hating every moment, vowing to never have a child of my own."

67

Silent moments passed before she resumed, "Indeed, I fell in love," she chuckled, her laugh cutting the air in a shrewd manner. Nefari's laugh ended as quickly as it began. She turned to study Tigris, looking her up and down with cold eyes. "And when I did, the thought of him having another wife left an unpalatable taste in my mouth. So, I did what I had to and everything else imaginable to make sure he was solely mine—I had you." Her voice changed to a vile tone: "A girl." The queen sized Tigris with contempt. "Of course, like all Kings he took lesser wives to have a son." Her eyes tightened even more. "I curse you for not being born a boy!" Nefari's face froze with the most dreadful expression. She held onto it for a brief moment before she smiled wryly, cocked her head and sent a piercing glare through Tigris. "My poor daughter, that is the wretched truth." She sighed, matter-of-factly, "Oh--but, what I have done for you to ensure our blood sits upon the throne—" Nefari hesitated, deciding if she should say. At length, she continued, "You should be grateful to me none of your half siblings survived to try to take your crown. Ah, sickness—it gets them when they're young."

Tigris felt her heart sink with sudden fear of the woman who stood before her. She couldn't believe her mother's horrifying honesty. Yet still, although a part of her hated her mother, Tigris suddenly found an unyielding desire to hang on to a mother she so desperately and secretly wanted.

A stabbing pain dug into her chest. "Why don't you love me! You are my mother! You must!" Tigris gasped, her tears, escaped down her cheeks.

The queen's smile disappeared; her head straightened. "I'm sorry. I just do not," she said, nonchalantly as she shrugged her shoulders. And then, as if it were nothing, she turned to face the window again.

Tigris couldn't speak. She was dumbfounded. She wiped her tears with the back of her hand. The last thing she wanted was to allow that wicked woman to make her cry. She pacified herself with thoughts of Nefari not being her real mother but instead the evil woman who killed her off to steal her place. Could a real mother be so cold?

Tigris soothed the lump in her throat while Nefari thought of a plan. After a long silence, the queen came from the window. She sat across from Tigris.

"I must admit," Nefari began, "you are right. Unfortunately, I cannot stop seeing you altogether. This show of mother-daughter bond is unremitting." Her eyes circled the room as she contemplated.

Tigris said nothing. She didn't move. She just stared.

The queen shifted her weight uneasily—she hated the way the child stared. And the crying.... Yet still, her daughter's tear-soaked eyes didn't make her want to mother her. In fact, it made her more irritated.

Nefari glanced away before she slapped her thighs with her hands and exclaimed, "I have an idea!" She leaned forward to add, "And, it is in your best interest to oblige." She threw a look of warning at Tigris before sitting up straight. "You will come as planned each month and I will receive you as always. However, when the door is shut I will escape through my passage only to return shortly before the close of our supposed engagement." The queen grinned, proud of her simplistic plan. "Oh, don't look so sad," she smirked, "I am not leaving you here for all that time alone. How would I possibly know you didn't wonder about giving suspicion to all those who knew you came?" Her tone was disgustingly jaunty. "Now, the question is—who do I trust to replace me?"

Tigris watched the queen with fear. She sat on the edge of her seat, her fingers tapping her mouth in thought. Why had she never taken leave through the passage before? All this time and this was the first she thought of it?

Nefari was looking up as though this helped her to think.

Why can't she love me? thought Tigris. Does she not see a bit of herself when she looks into my face? Does she not realize she could confide in me, that we could talk and laugh and I would be her closest friend? No, this can't be my mother. Who is she? Tigris jumped—

"I know the perfect person!" Nefari slapped her hand on her lap.

Tigris looked at her mother's smiling face and suddenly felt sick. I will not let her affect me, Tigris promised herself. *I don't care!* she chanted in her thoughts. *I don't care!* Whether it was all in her mind, the chant made Tigris feel a little better. She had closed a door on her feelings as she laid the first stones to the wall she built around her heart.

"She is quite old but I am sure you will be fond of her," Nefari was saying. She clasped her hands together. "I seek her myself quite regularly. You will be excited to know she charts the skies and upon painted papyrus and rocks, pictures speak to her of the future." The queen smiled proudly. Her eyes gleamed in the same manner as a mother who just gave her child a long dreamt about gift.

Tigris blinked hard, her expression blank.

"She practices *heka*," added the queen as if the word was forbidden.

A magician, thought Tigris, how common. Yet, clearly she did say *she*. Charting the skies was the job of a priest—but a priestess?

"She is very good," Nefari said. "But, you can find out on your own. I prefer to discuss the more important nature of this." Nefari slid back in her seat and folded her arms. "How do I ensure your silence?" She eyed Tigris for a moment. "I suppose I could order the magician to guard you with a spell," she chuckled wryly.

Her laugh made Tigris' skin crawl.

"Though, I would rather choose something more binding," Nefari's eyes darted as she entertained her thoughts.

Tigris watched as a mischievous smile gradually curled her mother's lips. Unfolding her arms, the queen looked sternly at Tigris. In a low, dangerous voice, she said, "If you breathe a word of our little arrangement to anyone I will see to it your dearest handmaid Naat is beaten and banished from you for good." It was the most potent strike Nefari could think of that would invoke obedience in the child.

Tigris felt a burning fury blaze up inside. She wanted to scream something horrible to her mother but she suppressed it. Instead, her eyes narrowed and in the same tone delivered by the queen she matched, "You are a wicked woman. Your heart may be even too hard for Ammut to gnaw."

The queen gasped, her hand launched to her chest. She was shocked at her own gesture. Embarrassed the child had struck her off guard, angered by her horrendous suggestion of fate, Nefari jumped up. "How dare you say such a thing!"

"How dare you do such things!" Tigris shouted back.

Nefari's hand belted across Tigris' face, knocking her over. The queen fumbled for words, "I... You... Agh!" she panted, hopelessly. Frustrated, she swung around, strutted to a pitcher of water on top of a table, which was always kept full. She emptied the liquid into the bowl the pitcher had sat in. Her arm shook, the water splashed everywhere but she didn't notice. She snatched a linen cloth from a small pile kept beside the bowl, dunked it into the water, wrung it out.

Tigris held her face where she could still feel the sting of her mother's hand. At first, she was so stunned she couldn't cry but now, as reality set in, it was all she could do to keep the tears from pouring down her face. They burned in her nose and behind her eyes but she held onto them. She would not cry.

Tigris slowly sat back up. She watched the queen's every movement.

Nefari finished wringing out another cloth. She spun, strode across the chamber towards the seating arrangement without even so much as a glance in her daughter's direction. However, as she approached, she tossed one of the wet cloths at Tigris before dropping onto her chair.

Tigris uneasily reached for the wet cloth that landed on her lap. She watched her mother who was slouched back in her seat, her eyes closed, the wet cloth draped over her forehead.

Strange, thought Tigris, the self-righteous, callous woman thought to give *me* a damp cloth.

〰

SOMETHING RUBBED UP against Tigris' leg pulling her back from her childhood memory.

"Heka," whispered Tigris as she bent down to scoop up the old cat. She stroked its soft fur before she set the cat back down on the floor.

Tigris stepped closer to the mirror, wiped it with her wrist so she could see her reflection more clearly.

The old priestess insisted mirrors close off the passages. She claimed their reflective surfaces kept the energy of the rooms in their own chamber so they wouldn't flow through the passage—even the energy of the priestess' chamber was not to be disturbed.

As Tigris stared at her reflection in the mirror, her vision blurred and she faded back into the memory:

〰

A MONTH AFTER her last visit with her mother, Tigris stepped up to the uninviting chamber of the queen's apartments with only the high door impeding the dreaded moment like a protective shield.

She stood behind her handmaid Naat who was moving to bang her fist against the thick wooden door. Queasiness grasped Tigris' stomach

71

as Naat's knock signalled their arrival.

There is nothing to fear, she forced herself to believe even though the door seemed to bear down on her with caution looming in its every grain.

What can the wicked woman really do? she questioned. She cannot put me in danger. I am to be Pharaoh. I glorify *her* name!

"Hold your chin up high," Naat coached her. "And remember, no matter what she says, it's her loss for not knowing such a wonderful daughter." That was Naat's famous line, which she always said when she walked Tigris down the hall to spend time with the queen.

Tigris looked up into Naat's gentle eyes. Naat winked as the door opened.

〜〜

INSIDE THE BEDCHAMBER Queen Nefari smiled in her seat. The thought of freedom from the torturous, pointless visits with the child was so pleasing. Everything had worked out better than originated. The old priestess refused to travel to the palace in the daylight—her eyes being sensitive to the bright desert sun—so, Nefari moved her to the palace. A perfect compromise.

The queen spent the past month having her architect construct a large apartment chamber under the earth within the palace grounds in which a hidden passage linked to her audience chamber.

The apartment was constructed to the magician's desires. There were no windows for sunlight and being so deep under ground, the air was always cool. A long passage led past the palace's outer walls to a hidden door that opened to the outside world, permitting Kafate the freedom to escape from the apartment's confines to venture into the city freely whenever she wanted.

Soon after construction was complete, the old woman and all her belongings were moved into the chamber.

Surely much better, Nefari thought as she stood and moved towards her bedroom door. What would she have done if she had to slip out instead of the child? Certainly, she couldn't be seen. Yes, all had worked out perfectly—she could stay in the comforts of her room and the child would deal with the confines of the dingy chamber.

Nefari adjusted her dress, grabbed the doorknob and let out a sigh of relief.

〰

NAAT LED TIGRIS into the room by the hand and stopped in the middle of the sitting area.

Tigris glanced around from her protective spot behind Naat. Nothing seemed different; there were no new faces. But then again, nothing would change until after Naat left.

There is nothing to fear, Tigris chanted nervously.

She looked towards the bedroom door as the queen appeared with a tight smile stretched across her face. The moment she glimpsed Tigris she opened her arms and gleamed in an exaggerated tone as she moved to embrace her, "My loving daughter!"

Normally, Tigris would return the embrace—not so much for the act but more for her secret need to steal her mother's affection, even if it was fake. But this time, Tigris stood rigid.

Nefari hugged her again. "I am so happy to see you! What would you like to do today? Your favourite? *Senet?*" Nefari stood up, smiled at Naat as if blameless for Tigris' strange behaviour. She stepped past the maiden to conceal a deep breath.

Tigris watched her mother. What's wrong with her? she thought. Why do people feel the need to give excessive performances when they are trying to hide something? The foulness of it made Tigris shudder.

Nefari turned back to Naat whose expression scowled with scorn towards the queen.

"That will be all," Nefari said firmly.

Tigris felt her stomach raise into her chest as the door closed behind Naat. She looked in every corner of the room expecting to see a monstrous person step out from the shadows. But, she saw no one. She turned to face her mother who stood watching the door until it made its final noise to indicate its close but the queen revealed nothing.

Nefari slowly walked across the room, her hands folded in front of her with that horrid grin upon her face. She stopped at a table, lifted a chalice to her lips. Every movement lingered as if she meant to draw out the moment of tension. Finally, she turned to face Tigris.

"Take her," she ordered in a low cracking voice.

Tigris looked from side to side. Her heart thumped faster. She looked at her mother, puzzled. Where? she begged with her eyes. But, the queen only offered a blank stare.

Confused and defenceless, Tigris looked around the room again. *What can the evil woman do? Although wicked, she won't let anything harm me,* she reminded herself—*she can't!*

Tigris tried to keep herself calm. *I don't care. There is nothing to fear,* she chanted in her mind.

♒

NEFARI STOOD CLASPING her goblet with both hands. She watched Tigris, empty of any emotion. *The girl looked frightened. It was her own fault. What did she possibly have to fear? Does she really believe I am foolish enough to have her harmed? After all, she is my only heir, even if born a girl.*

Nefari seethed with despise. *I shall let her suffer for the insult.*

The queen suddenly realized her chambermaid hadn't moved according to the previously arranged plan. She was frozen, watching. Nefari darted a harsh look in the chambermaid's direction, breaking the maid's stupor.

♒

THAT TIME, THE servant obeyed. She rushed over to Tigris, took hold of the child's wrist and pulled her towards the far wall. Her steps were fast, steady, striding across the room, dragging Tigris unwillingly behind her.

"Where are you taking me!" Tigris managed to cry. She looked at the queen. "Where are you taking me! I thought..."

A long mirror was swung forward like a door by the maiden. Another maid lit a lamp and passed it to her accomplice.

Tigris tried to pry her arm free. She looked at the maid who had passed on the lamp but the maiden kept her face turned away.

Before her, the dark tunnel seemed dangerous. Tigris gasped. *Oh gods, where did it lead?* Horrible images flooded her mind. She saw herself tied up in a dark room with snakes and scorpions. Her thoughts were wild with each grisly picture being replaced by another. She tried to blank them out. *There is nothing to fear,* she chanted.

Tigris twisted around to take one last desperate look at mother. But, the queen was standing across the room, her back turned. She gazed out of the window as if nothing was happening. Silhouetted by the sunlight, she appeared ghastly. The longer Tigris stared, the more her mother seemed to fade away into blackness, as if swallowed by the sun.

Tigris blinked hard, turned to the darkness before her. She stopped struggling, surrendered to whatever lay ahead.

They stepped into the passage. The mirror was shut behind them, closing them into the darkness where everything was dreadfully quiet. The light of the lamp glowed over the narrow walls of the passage, leading the way. Tigris obediently followed.

There is nothing to fear, she repeated.

Tigris focused her eyes as far down the tunnel as possible to see what awaited her. However, there was no end to be seen.

They walked further down the slanting floor before the chambermaid stopped. She looked towards the door they had entered, before letting go of the child's wrist. Gently, she stroked Tigris' arm, puckered her lips and placed her long slender finger over them. "Shh..." was all she said. She smiled softly, pointed her chin in the direction of the lower tunnel. Her smile grew slightly as she did.

Tigris watched, at first, confused. The maid was trying to tell her something but she couldn't speak. Tigris knew the queen had the tongues cut from her chambermaids' mouths to keep her secrets safe.

The chambermaid gave a soft smile and pointed down the tunnel. She took Tigris' hand delicately this time and walked forward.

At the end of the passage, the chambermaid pushed on the wall. A door opened forward to expose a dimly lit chamber with flickering shadows cluttered with books, scrolls, stones and magical tools.

The maid led the way into the room. She cleared her throat to signal their arrival.

Tigris was so captured by the mysterious room she completely forgot she was meeting someone with whom she would pass her time. She studied the magical tools, the odd devices she had never seen before and noticed even the burning wicks were placed precisely in the room so their light and shadows created a pattern.

Tigris watched the shadows dance. Something caught her attention. One of the dancing shadows became still, and yet, it was not still at all. It moved slowly across the floor. Tigris followed it, watched as it began to creep up the wall and slowly form the shape of a person. Tigris turned to look across the room. She saw the old priestess enter.

The woman was remarkably small—about Tigris' height. She hunched so far over she had to hold onto a staff to help her stand. A dark loose dress fell to the top of her feet, which were covered with an odd papyrus slipper that hid her toes. The long, wide sleeve of her dress covered the hand that dangled to her side. The other hand clasped the crooked staff and where the sleeve fell back revealing a part of her arm, a row of bangles concealed her flesh. Only her hand itself was visible, which was extremely pale, white and bony. A large ruby ring sparkled on her middle finger. A long, thin cape fastened around her neck dragged behind her.

Tigris watched the old woman shuffle further into the room. With all her loose apparel she almost seemed to float. How frightful she was to look at--a dark mass.

Tigris' heart began to thump hard. She moved closer to the maiden. I can't be left alone with her, Tigris dreaded. The old woman was eerie, scary, ugly, and Tigris had yet to see her face. But, the woman's hunch was so bad it forced her to look down at the ground. Her long grey hair streaked with black fell flat to the sides of her face, keeping it hidden. The only flesh that could be seen was the white bony hand gripping the staff.

Tigris felt the chambermaid letting go of her hand. She tried to grip tighter but the servant pulled away. A rush of fear sped through Tigris. She didn't want to stay alone with the old woman. She hugged the servant's waist but the matron unfastened her grip, stepped away.

Tigris looked towards the strange apparition—the eerie woman bent over and frail, yet, full of uncanny power.

The chambermaid took another step backwards, smiled softly with her kind eyes. She nodded her head as if to say everything was okay. Then, she turned, slipped back into the passage, pulled the door shut behind her.

Tigris looked at her own reflection in the mirror concealing the passage. Behind her was the reflection of the hunched woman, the dark mass, the eerie, ugly person who was nonetheless a magician! Oh gods, friend of the queen! She must be evil!

Tigris ran to the mirror. She grabbed its edge but as she reached out she heard a *click*—a latch! Tigris pulled at the side of the mirror, tears running down her face, fear flooding her body. In the mirror she could see the dark mass coming towards her. *There is nothing to fear*, Tigris repeated to herself.

〰

TIGRIS DRIFTED FROM her memory to the present. Her eyes refocused on her reflection standing in front of the mirror in her nightgown. The thought of first meeting Kafate made her smile— although at the time, she remembered how frightened she was. The old priestess had a terrifying look that deceived the true nature of her heart. Kafate had a good soul, which Tigris quickly grew to love.

Turning from the mirror, Tigris stepped further into the chamber. "Kafate?" she called in a loud whisper. "Kafate?"

A dark mass appeared in the doorway and the old woman shuffled into the main room.

"What is it child?" asked Kafate in her weak, accented voice as she slowly made her way towards Tigris. "It's very early in the morning."

"I know, but—"

"But, you can't just let things come to be." Kafate stopped close to Tigris, her bony hand clenched tightly on the staff as she used it to help her stretch up. The priestess strained to crank her neck in order to look Tigris in the eyes. "You want to *know.*" She let out a sigh as she relaxed. Then, she shuffled to a table.

Tigris went to the part of the room where the black pond was cut into the floor. She stepped around the glistening water and sat on a cushion, making sure nothing touched even the edge of the hole. Tigris watched the old woman fuss about.

Kafate came from a far away land to get away from the cold, harsh weather and settled in Egypt long ago. She was the oldest person Tigris knew and it seemed as though she had always been old. Wrinkles cut deep into her thin white skin, which was paler than anyone in Egypt and the lands beyond the southern border. Thick black liner traced the perimeter of her eyes and extended out towards her temples in the distinctive mark of the Egyptians, however, nothing else was worn in the Egyptian fashion. Her clothes were dark and loose and her jewellery was designed with strange carvings. Even more unusual than

77

her pale white skin were her eyes. One was blue and the other clouded over with blindness, which the priestess claimed was the eye that let her see all.

Kafate felt Tigris' stare. She looked at the Pharaoh, smiled—her teeth rotten and yellow. "I haven't been able to find my crystal in weeks. My mind is getting old."

"I could get you a new—"

"No. It's not the same. I need my crystal." She poked around some more before she gave up. "Agh. I'll look for it another day—if I remember," she laughed. The old woman clutched her staff and moved to join Tigris by the black pond. Her jewellery clinked as she walked.

Although the priestess held the Egyptian beliefs, her knowledge and religion were intertwined with many doctrines. She practiced magic unlike any Egyptian priest or priestess and she was able to foresee the future.

Kafate struggled painfully to lower herself onto a cushion across from Tigris. Tigris knew better than to help—the old woman despised it.

As Kafate settled in, a shallow deathly cough erupted from her chest.

"Are you okay?" Tigris jumped up to get some water.

"Sit down, dear. I've had this cough for over thirty years."

Tigris set the cup down next to the old woman then returned to her seat.

Kafate sipped the water. She studied Tigris carefully. "You leave today to meet *him?*" she asked in her thick accent.

Tigris nodded.

"And, you hate him."

"I don't even know him."

"But, you hate him nonetheless." Kafate leaned closer, squinting her eyes, studying Tigris some more.

"I hate what he is doing."

"But, you don't know what he's doing," Kafate said softly.

"He's disrupting my people, my land! I've been an amicable Pharaoh. I've fed those who were hungry, helped those who were sick. When the inundation was low, I lowered taxes. I've been fair and forgiving and I've kept peace in Egypt. Yet still, he rises against me just because I am a *woman!* Yes, I despise him!"

Kafate looked long and hard at Tigris. Except for the crackling of the torches around the room, all was silent. At length, the priestess opened a leather satchel, pulled out some stones. "Perhaps his purpose is distorted by something else," she said as she threw the stones into the pond then closed her good eye to stare at them with her blind eye. After a long moment, Kafate took a deep breath. "Horu," she whispered. She opened her eyes and looked at Tigris.

"Horu?" questioned Tigris.

"That's all I see." Kafate reached in the water, collected the stones.

Tigris was disappointed. "Horu," she repeated feeling deprived of a proper vision.

Kafate smiled. "Don't fret so much, dear. The future will soon become the present that will reveal all the secrets of the past." She fixed her skirt, stretched out on the long cushion and closed her eyes. "Go get ready. You will depart soon."

Tigris stood. She knew better than to ask for more. When the priestess was done, she was done; there was no use in pleading for more. Kafate would only say, "That is all you are meant to know."

Tigris went to the old woman, kissed her on the forehead, headed towards the mirror. Before Tigris got to the passage, Kafate was already asleep.

X

$\mathcal{T}$IGRIS WAS DRESSED in her thinnest linen to help make the hot journey bearable. A large jewelled collar was fastened around her neck and gold cuffs were slid onto her wrists and upper arms by the jeweller. The wig-maker straightened a short braided wig on her head, which would aid in protecting her from the sun.

"You look ravishing," announced the wig-maker as he stepped back.

Tigris smiled. "You are biased, Pendua."

The jeweller stepped up beside him. "I'm sorry Per'a, but I would have to agree with Pendua, you do look exquisite."

Tigris laughed. "And you, Kaper, are just as biased. It's your work you gawk at." Tigris walked over to the large mirror and studied herself. "Though I must admit, your crafts are beautiful." She laughed again as she turned.

Kaper shook his head. "You're much too modest. Even without accessories, your beauty will make the enemy crumble to his knees."

Tigris smiled, headed to the door.

The handmaids closed their trunk of linen dresses and sashes and carried it out behind Tigris to load on the ship.

In the outer walled enclosure the Vizier's apartments joined the massive state building where he was better able to run the administrative headquarters of the nation. His residence encompassed three stories with a private garden and rooftop terrace. Fully staffed, it was equipped with everything needed in a home, except a wife.

Two storerooms, a cellar, lavatory, bathing room, study and cookhouse, in addition to his bedrooms, study, dining suite, grand foyer and audience chamber made up his lavish apartment where he spent much of his time. Every room burst with scrolls, trunks, stelae, model structures and documented information he had gathered and kept for many years. Although it appeared cluttered, the clutter was very organized.

Ibimpetus never desired marriage. His life was studying Egypt's needs and he preferred to do so in solitude. He lived alone, save for his house servants, which he insisted were to be kept to a minimum.

Tigris went into the building and found the Vizier in his study reading over some documents. He looked up from his work as she entered unannounced.

"You are not coming?" Tigris asked.

"I am not needed. It's better for me to keep watch here." He studied her for a moment. "You need only to discover his requests—if there are any—and to lay eyes upon his mystery. Do not—"

"I am not worried. I know what to do," Tigris cut in. They looked at each other in silence. Their relationship was always so strained. Tigris studied him. She knew he despised her sitting on the throne but, as her father's only surviving child, he accepted it. "Do you agree with his plight?" she asked not taking her eyes from his.

The Vizier tensed his eyebrows.

Rephrasing her question, she asked again, "Do you agree with a King for Egypt?"

Ibimpetus looked away. He carefully picked an amulet off of the table next to him, put its string over his neck, and tucked it into his gown.

Tigris was unable to see what symbol the amulet bared.

Ibimpetus turned. He looked hard at her. "I believe in your father. He made Egypt great and entrusted it to you. I will serve you for Egypt as the royal bloodline that should descend."

Tigris burned inside. She clearly heard what the Vizier had said. "But, you will not serve Egypt for me?" she asked, pointedly.

Instead of answering, he changed the subject. "This rebel's quest is of no benefit to me. However, you must marry and produce a son." He looked back at his work and began to read its text. He was letting her know he was done.

Tigris ignored his gesture. "Marry?" she balked. "Let me know when *he* has arrived."

"You have had many suitors."

"I don't want just a suitor."

"Which is precisely why, it should have been arranged long before your father's death. You are a Pharaoh. Stop looking for a charming dream," he snapped.

Tigris remained glaring at him. She shook her head ever so slightly, somewhat in disbelief that he would be so blatant, and yet, she was somewhat not surprised.

The Vizier returned to his work. He moved some parchments around with jerky movements and dropped a stone text in front of him so it slammed down on the table. The conversation was over.

Breathing deeply, Tigris suppressed her feelings as she watched him before she gave in. "We shall speak when I return."

She spun, stormed from the room.

〜〜〜

THE VIZIER WATCHED her leave. He pulled the amulet out of his gown and rubbed it between his fingers. "For Egypt," he whispered before he turned back to the stones in front of him.

XI

$\mathcal{T}$OMORROW THEY WOULD reach the shores of Abedju when the sun loomed high in the sky. Despite the entertainment arranged for the Pharaoh's enjoyment, Tigris could not help but think of the meeting she would soon come to face. She tried to focus on the music and singers who belted their tunes up into the clear night sky. But, even the belly dancers who moved their bodies seductively around the contortionists weren't enough to distract her from her strife.

While everybody laughed and drank with the festivities of the night, Tigris remained listless. She barely touched her meal nor did she sip her wine.

"Are you nervous?" Allegi asked as he sat on the small chair next to the Pharaoh's royal seat.

Tigris eyed him, worried he may have seen it in her eyes. The last thing she wanted was for anyone to see her troubled, lest they regard her as weak—the thought made her shudder. As Pharaoh she needed to be composed, strong, assured—at all times—regardless of what took place.

She forced the muscles on her brow to relax, made her eyes look bright. "Of course not," she laughed. She looked back at the contortionist and applauded in sync with the audience. "I am excited!"

Tigris stood. She stepped down from her chair and walked away from Allegi over to Chephren, Admiral of the Royal Fleet.

The Admiral was surrounded by women who doted on him, feeding him fruits from a large plate and fanning him with palm leaves. He was somewhat drunk and giddy from the nightly entertainment or more so from the attention he received from the maidens. But, as soon as he spotted the Pharaoh approaching, he jumped to his feet and tried to collect his composure. The maidens took to bowing their heads to the deck floor.

"Divine Majesty." Chephren gave a slight bow, which Tigris returned.

"A dance?" she asked, holding out her hand.

Smiling, Chephren stepped out from the maidens clustered around his feet. He led her to the open area in front of the royal chair where

Allegi still sat, watching.

Tigris focused on the music, trying to let it sweep her away from her worries. She put great effort into pretending she was having an enjoyable time and that nothing bothered her thoughts. She beamed with joy while inside she quivered from the thought of losing her kingdom to a man. Nonetheless, Tigris wore the mask of contentment well; she wouldn't let her people see her worry. She was their ruler; she had to remain strong.

Yes, thought Tigris, to show anything but ease towards the situation is weak and I will never show weakness.

Tigris felt Allegi's eyes on her. She glanced over Chephren's shoulder; he was studying her. Allegi knew her better than anyone. His stare made her uncomfortable. Tigris smiled nonetheless.

I am Pharaoh. I am strong, she told herself. *I have nothing to fear.*

The Admiral spun her around. Tigris forced a joyful laugh. Though even as she laughed into the carefree night Tigris felt imprisoned by the one thought that made her spirits sink—

Tomorrow.

The red and white *Pshent* crown of United Egypt was placed onto Tigris' head. Adorned in her finest dress and wig with jewelled accessories, she was draped from head to toe in gold. She looked like a golden statue with her beauty pouring its radiance into the room.

Throughout the large cabin, rugs were spread across the floor, frankincense let off a subtle sweet aroma and beautiful plants and trees added luxury, providing a majestic background for the meeting. Tigris sat on the high Royal Seat of Estate, waiting. The chair was moved into the ship's cabin for privacy soon after the chambermaids finished helping her dress. Only two guards, Allegi, Chephren and three servitors, two of whom would fan the Pharaoh and the other who would stay bowing on the floor unless called upon, would remain present.

The Royal Messenger and the Admiral of the Royal Vessels would represent under their duties of councillors and were outfitted in their High Council regalia. Over their long white tunics they wore a wide gold stoned neckpiece that spread out to the shoulders with thick cuffs around their wrists. Both men had outlined their eyes with the only differences in their attire being the plaited wigs they chose to wear and their sashes. Chephren wore a blue sash tied at his waist whereas Allegi wore a black sash with a Gold Scorpion pinned at the bottom depicting his honourable title of *Friend of the King.*

To the right of Tigris sat Allegi and to her left sat Chephren. Statues of the gods Montu and Wadjet looked over the Pharaoh's shoulders bearing their powerful messages. Montu, a God of War--depicted as a falcon headed man with a sun disk and two plumes--protected the King in battle while Wadjet, the Cobra Goddess, Patroness of Lower Egypt, was ready to strike at the nation's enemies. Their messages were clear.

Tigris clutched the royal flail and crook still in the chair arms. She tried to breathe slowly. Four royal guards travelled out onto the land and it was reported they were seen riding back towards the Nile with the rebel and two of his men. The guard outside the cabin door would soon announce their arrival, which would be her cue to cross the flail and crook over her chest and lower her head until the enemy bowed.

The moment lingered almost painfully. Tigris peered out the high cabin window, gazed into the sky. Its clear blue colour was so peaceful compared to the atmosphere of the ship's cabin that she lost herself in the tranquility of the empty sky for a moment.

Very soon, she thought, *he* will be revealed.

Allegi looked at the Queen. She could see him watching her through the corner of her eyes—analyzing her.

"We already know we are set for war. What more can he say?" he comforted.

"I am not worried. I am infuriated by his nerve."

The door opened and a guard peeked in. "They are boarding the ship, great Majesty."

Tigris nodded. She lifted the flail and crook, crossed them against her chest, lowered her head, grateful to escape Allegi's probing stare. She forced herself to breathe calmly as the moments crept by while she waited for the door to open again. Everyone fell still sending the room into an unnerving silence save for Chephren's heavy breaths, which seemed to count the steps that brought the enemy to the door.

Huff. Huff. Huff.

Tigris' stomach tightened with each exhale the Admiral pushed from his lungs, knowing at any moment the door would open to reveal the self-proclaimed King—enemy of her empire.

Tigris closed her eyes.

The door finally opened.

Three men stepped into the room and despite her unbearable curiosity, Tigris did not look up.

〰〰

EUPHRATES STOOD BETWEEN Tuthiken and Somiset—two of the largest men in his army.

"Your associates may wait outside the door," Chephren snapped.

"Perhaps you should lead by example," retorted Tuthiken, shooting a hardened glower at both Chephren and Allegi perched beside the Queen.

Chephren scowled. "The other option is for me to have you removed."

Tuthiken went to speak but Euphrates stopped him with a nod in the direction of the door. Reluctantly, he obeyed. Somiset followed, leaving Euphrates to contend with the Pharaoh alone. The door closed behind them.

Euphrates stood tall. He was clad in a white knee length pleated skirt with a wide blue, gold and red sash slung from his left shoulder across his body. A thick gold plate collar was fastened around his neck with matching large gold cuffs adorning his wrists. His rich garments gave him a kingly air, but even more disturbing, he boldly wore the white *Hedjet* crown of Upper Egypt.

"Remove that crown and bow to your Pharaoh," ordered Chephren.

"She is *not* my Pharaoh and I have earned the right to wear this crown, for she no longer possesses Upper Egypt." Euphrates gestured towards Tigris who still kept her head bent and her eyes closed silently willing herself to remain calm, composed. "Tell *her* to remove her crowns and bow to the one true God of Men."

Chephren's face burned red. He motioned to the guards.

The two men charged at Euphrates. They reached out to take hold of him but he was too fast. Euphrates moved. He grabbed a guard, pitched him across the room. The guard crashed against some pots, smashing them into pieces. Already Euphrates had the other man on his knees with his arm twisted behind his back in pain.

85

The first guard jumped back onto his feet. He drew his dagger as he went to lunge at the unfaltering figure standing ahead of him.

≈

TIGRIS COULDN'T CONTAIN herself any longer. She opened her eyes, looked up under her brow to see what was happening. She saw the guard clambering to his feet, dagger pointed forward ready to pounce.

"Leave him," she said as she slowly raised her head.

The guard hesitated before putting away his knife.

Euphrates watched the guard until the man backed down. Then, he released the attacker still in his grip.

The large man stood. He turned to face Euphrates, his expression raging with embarrassment. With great speed the guard drew his knife and brought it to Euphrates' neck. Tension grew thick between the two men but Euphrates didn't flinch. Instead, his eyes seemed to dare the guard to try.

"I said, leave him," Tigris demanded.

Spewing hatred from his eyes, the guard slid the side of his blade along Euphrates' throat before he moved to join his partner near the door.

Tigris and Euphrates faced each other for the first time.

Their eyes locked.

Tigris could feel her stomach begin to spin; her heart beat high in her chest. She began to breathe deeply. The longer she stared at him the faster her heart hammered, not from fear but from a feeling she wouldn't admit.

The Queen scanned her enemy up and down; he was handsome—young, muscular and with a face that seemed chiselled by the hand of god—nothing like what she imagined.

He is the enemy, she forced herself to remember.

Yet, in spite of who he was, she couldn't help but enjoy staring into his dark eyes—they seemed so friendly, so sincere. Everything inside her body tingled at the sight of him.

Euphrates finally spoke, breaking the trance-like gaze they both had been caught in. "The infamous Nitiqreti."

"The rebel without a name," Tigris matched.

He didn't move his eyes from hers—she wished he would.

"Then permit me to introduce myself."

Tigris responded with a small nod.

"I am crowned under the name of Usermaathor—"

"As you've so boldly stated in your letter," Tigris cut in. "Do you realize the consequence of such contemptuous words not to mention a heathen crowning?"

Euphrates gave a slight smile as he raised his eyebrow and cocked his head. "Do you?"

"I am neither heathen nor self-proclaimed. I am a descendant of the gods!"

Their eyes locked again. Tigris' narrowed with a sinister scowl but Euphrates' eyes were almost smiling.

The enemy, she reminded herself again as she held her stare. But, her heart wouldn't stop beating. Something about him captured her. Perhaps it was his beauty; perhaps it was his eyes—*those eyes*. Dangerous, thought Tigris. Still, she dared not look away and give him the upper hand.

If you stare your enemy in the eyes and do not falter, you will no doubt tear down some of his confidence, she remembered her father saying. *Confidence is the only thing that makes warriors out of men. Thus, yours must be all the greater.* She had heard it many times from her father when he had taught her the secrets of having a warrior spirit. He had wanted to drive it into her mind, show her the way of exhibiting the air of a king. In fact, Tigris had witnessed it all her life. Soon, she came to notice that every leader—every man in power, held this confidence and those higher than the next always seemed to have more of it.

No, she decided, she would not look away, no matter how fast her heart dared to pound.

Euphrates stepped closer. "I have longed for this day almost my whole life though I had hoped it was your predecessor whom I would face." He took another step. "Still, at all costs, I will take back what's rightfully mine." Euphrates kept his eyes on Tigris; they had hardened with their sincerity. "Egypt is mine," he declared in a low voice.

Tigris froze for a moment. The way he spoke those words sent a chill through the muggy room. The friendliness in his eyes was gone. Something else replaced it; something she couldn't discern.

His words made her angry.

"Egypt does not belong to you," she finally returned in a powerful tone, fury blazing inside of her at the man who came to try to take away all that she cherished.

"I beg to differ, my Lady. It does not belong to you." Euphrates moved closer. He stood at the base of the platform her royal chair was raised on, looking up at her.

Tigris felt her stomach spin again. He angered her and yet he made her belly feel giddy and desirous. What was it with him? Those eyes, that face, his body—they all made her weak.

He is the enemy. *The enemy!* she repeated in her mind as she tried to stay focused.

Euphrates presented a short bow before standing tall. "My name, from birth," he said slowly, "is Euphrates."

Chephren choked.

Tigris looked at the Admiral. His face turned white—ghastly white. Something had set him off. He knew something—she suddenly realized—he had to. What did he know?

Tigris whipped her head back to look at Euphrates who was now curiously eyeing the Admiral. Again, she turned to Chephren. He couldn't even look Euphrates in the face. Certainly, he was hiding something!

"What do you know?" Tigris demanded.

Chephren turned to her, his expression filled with shock but he didn't speak.

"I asked, what do you know!"

"Allow me to divulge his secret."

Slowly, Tigris turned her head to face Euphrates. She didn't like this. Knowledge was power, which she clearly didn't have at this moment. She was at a disadvantage. Indeed, this wasn't good.

"My father was Wadjkare, Pharaoh of Egypt."

Tigris' eyes widened. *Wadjkare?* she thought. She looked at Chephren whose head was now lowered. No, this couldn't be good! Wadjkare, the Pharaoh preceding her father—

Euphrates continued, speaking slowly, "He was murdered for the throne and crowns of Egypt by *your father.*"

"No!" Tigris gasped. "Impossible!"

Euphrates knelt down on one knee. "Not impossible, Per'a. I witnessed it with these very eyes."

Tigris shook her head. "You accuse the wrong man!"

"And, you excuse him without knowledge!"

"I *know* of my father's honour!"

"Do you?"

He was looking at her that way again. His head cocked, his eyebrow raised, except this time there was no smile.

Tigris turned to Chephren. His eyes were darting. "Say it isn't so!"

Chephren glanced towards her, still unable to look her in the eyes.

"Say it!"

Very slowly, very softly, Chephren responded, "We all decided."

Tigris gasped.

Now what? Now what am I to do? she thought. What am I to go to war to defend? *Deceit? Conspiracy? Anarchy?* No, this can't be!

Tigris could barely breathe her chest felt so tight.

"Right your family wrong. Step down from the throne and return it to its rightful heir." Euphrates stretched out his arm towards Tigris, still on bended knee.

Chephren looked at Euphrates, finding the will to meet his eyes. Rage burned inside him. "If your father was left to rule there would be no Egypt for you to reign! He was a drunkard!"

"Nonetheless, the crowns of Egypt should have been passed to me!"

"You were too young! Egypt needed a warrior! The country was in dissolute!"

"If you had integrity, you would have awarded a regent to rule in my name until I was of age!"

Chephren didn't respond; Euphrates had him.

A state of disbelief engulfed Tigris with such heaviness she couldn't move. He was right. A regent to rule in Euphrates' name until he was old enough to take control would have been honourable. But instead, off with the Pharaoh and away with the boy.... No, no, it wasn't right. It can't be, she thought.

Still, Tigris watched Chephren—she couldn't bring herself to face Euphrates.

"Step down from the throne," Euphrates said again in a deep, piercing voice. "Or, we go to war!"

Chephren turned to Tigris, looked earnestly at her. "We would have never been able to save Egypt with a regent. We needed a commanding Pharaoh. Egypt was too weak at the time and your father knew it was the only way." His voice was strained, almost begging, "Defend what your father built, Nitiqreti. *Honour* your father."

"Crown or war?" Euphrates demanded. He stretched out his arm again, opened his fingertips towards Tigris.

Slowly, Tigris turned her head to meet Euphrates. She looked him up and down as she willed herself to take control and do what she thought was right.

"Alright," she finally responded as she uncrossed the flail and crook from her chest and rose to her feet.

The room fell deathly silent. Allegi and Chephren looked at her in dismay. Even the servant who bowed couldn't help but look up.

Tigris stared at Euphrates with eyes just as sincere. She took hold of both the flail and crook in her left hand and stretched her right arm out towards him.

"Crown," she said with a slight smile.

Allegi gasped.

A small voice escaped Chephren's throat, "No!" he whispered, shocked she would so easily part with the crown.

Euphrates returned her smile as he stood. He stepped towards Tigris, moved to take her hand. But, before he had the chance, Tigris pulled away. She lifted her hand above his outstretched palm and uncurled her fingers.

"Your crown," she said in a low voice, gesturing towards his head.

Euphrates felt his cheeks burn. His arm dropped; his voice growled, "*Never!*"

Silence fell over the room more deathly than the one before. Tigris and Euphrates stared at each other through blazing eyes. Neither backed down.

Chephren still held onto disbelief towards the figure standing before him. Allegi gaped in shock.

After a long, uncomfortable moment, Euphrates broke the silence. In a soft voice, he avowed, "So, it is war."

"So, it is," Tigris replied.

No one moved.

Tigris felt her body tremble internally. Euphrates stood before her, only an arm's reach away. They were both locked in that stare—that weakening stare. She felt trapped.

Those eyes, thought Tigris. Her stomach fluttered and her heart pounded as if moments ago there was no contention.

Stop this! she yelled to herself. *This is shameful! I cannot feel this way for the enemy!*

Yet, she felt lost in his eyes, overwhelmed by emotions. He even made her temperature rise, more so than the scorching sun.

For quite some time, they remained entranced before Euphrates turned and strode out.

He was gone.

Tigris was relieved and at the same time disappointed he was no longer in her presence. She wasn't sure how much longer she could have held that stare—her eyes deceiving her thoughts.

Why? was all she could think. Tigris took a deep breath, tried to soothe her emotions, and closed her eyes.

"Per'a?" Chephren said softly. "You must understand it was the only way."

Tigris whipped around to face him. A rush of anger flooded her body. Why didn't they tell her! "I don't want to hear it," she hissed.

"Your father had no choice—"

"I wish not to discuss it now, Chephren." She pressed her hand to her temple. Her head hurt.

"But, you must understand how important—"

"Get out," she commanded.

"But—"

"Out!" Tigris threw the flail and crook down onto the deck floor, interrupting the awkwardness with a powerful *clang!*

Chephren jumped.

"All of you—*out!*"

Chephren stomped from the cabin.

Everyone else followed and as each man exited, the uneasiness seemed to leave with him. She didn't want them there watching her. She was so confused. So utterly confused! Her chest hurt; it was tight and heavy and her head pounded with torment.

Allegi stopped at the door. He looked back at Tigris.

"Please," she said softly.

Gently, he shut the door behind him.

XII

$\mathcal{T}$HE ADMIRAL STORMED out of the cabin. He waited until Allegi was out of sight before he called the two guards aside.

"Take three soldiers and track him. I want to know where he hides and where he goes." He looked both men up and down with scrutinizing eyes. "I hope this time you'll have the strength to hold up to him if need be." Chephren could see the anger and humiliation blaze up in both men. Their stature, clearly larger than Euphrates', should have been superior and yet, two of them could not manage to fight against him.

Cheti turned his anger towards the desert. Already Euphrates and his counterparts were faint dots on the horizon. On camel they would never catch up and even if they went on horseback, the rebels had too much of a head start.

Chephren read his concern. "Take Montu. He is a superb tracker." The Admiral was pleased to see this concern on Cheti's face. His determination would not permit failure and with their earlier conflict with Euphrates, it was now a personal affair for the two guards—they could be trusted. "If you succeed, I will promote you to Commander of Troops," Chephren added to help ensure that Cheti sought only success.

Commander of Troops was a high rank aboard the ships, responsible for leading land-based duties, it ranked only under the Ship's Captain and the Captain's Mate. Chephren could see the desire glow in Cheti's eyes. He sized both men. "Remove your noble garb, you'll do better if you blend in," he added.

Both guards, Cheti and Iritu, nodded.

"Now, hurry and get off my ship. I must get to Henen-nesut immediately." Chephren spun. He went in search of his ship's captain as the two guards marched off to prepare their leave.

Moments later, Chephren found the captain lazing against the wall of the ship, hiding from the sun.

"Get up," Chephren barked, kicking the man's foot.

Haremhab jumped to his feet.

"As soon as Cheti has departed the ship with his troop, row at full force. We do not stop until dinner."

"But, Admiral, it's still morning." The tall, thin man looked at his superior, concerned for the men.

"We do not stop until dinner," Chephren repeated.

"But, sir, the men can't possibly row that long."

Chephren glared at his captain. He needed to get to Henen-nesut quickly and he didn't care about the men. Still, Haremhab was right. They would achieve more distance faster if the men were rested with content bellies.

"Then let them take breaks two-by-two but we do not stop until dinner. Am I clear?"

Haremhab nodded.

"Good. Now, send word that a vessel is to remain behind," the Admiral added before he stormed off leaving the ship's captain to contend with preparing their journey.

Chephren headed to the bow of the ship. His blood felt as if it were boiling inside him and his stomach was full of knots. He needed a moment to let everything settle in.

How could this be? he thought. Euphrates was supposed to be dead! They all had agreed it was the only decision.

Chephren wiped the sweat from his brow; his internal temperature even hotter than the sun beating down on him. The reality of the situation was far too daunting and too much for him to take. He couldn't believe it.

Twenty years ago they predicted this outcome if they let the child live. Certainly, Euphrates would avenge his father's death—he had witnessed it for gods' sake!

"Great Set!" Chephren whispered angrily. This was exactly what they wanted to prevent. And, now, the visage of vengeance showed its ugly face. How could Tigris' father be so stupid as to permit him to live?

"Weak!" Chephren spat out loud as if answering his own question.

He approached the bow, peered over the wall up the Nile as far as the eye could see. It would be at least seven days before they would reach the Great Palace, maybe even longer depending upon the wind— luckily, the men were rowing with the current and that was good.

Chephren gripped the wall of the vessel. At least seven days, he thought. Seven days of anxious torture! He slammed his palm against the top of the wall with seething frustration. He needed to inform the Vizier of the horrible, unexpected circumstance, and, he knew Tigris would look to confront him too—he just needed to warn him first!

Chephren began to pace. He breathed heavily, his chest tight with anxiety, still in shock. He glanced at the desert.

Where was Euphrates raised? he wondered. And, with what money? The King must have been paying someone to keep the boy. *The stupid, stupid man! Look what you've done!*

Again he wiped his brow. He needed to relax; his breathing was becoming short.

Chephren went to the bow and looked up the Nile again. They hadn't started rowing yet.

What was taking so long? He needed to get to the Vizier!

XIII

ℰUPHRATES RACED INTO the desert. He tried to race from his thoughts—the memories of the Queen, of first setting his gaze upon her, of her beauty, her voice, her eyes, everything! They all played like a vicious cycle in his mind.

Why did he not come against her father? To have been ready then, when the murderous sinner had lived! Life could be cruel.

The horse carried him up through the Wadi Hammamat towards their camp, which was hidden away in the dry cavernous mountain.

Tuthiken and Somiset stayed behind and Euphrates was glad for it. He didn't want to speak—he wanted to remain alone in his thoughts and the emptiness of the deserted land before him.

The rebels' camp was stationed not too far from the caravan trade route so those who watched them come and go would mistake them for merchants. Their path was hidden behind broken rocks and large boulders, which looked like every other part of the trade route; except, only they knew that shortly after the large bend, near the top of the climb, to veer from the path and head further down the mountain side. For those who didn't know the way, many misleading turns could end their journey.

Carefully, Euphrates and his two men rode through the unmarked trail. At several points, the path was so narrow they had to get off their horses and lead them through the rock, one behind the other. They pressed on, until within only a few hours after departing the Pharaoh's ship, they reached the base camp.

The men, waiting their return at the camp, saw them coming and rushed to greet them.

Euphrates watched the large group gathering together, anticipating his speech but he was in no mood to speak. He wanted to seclude himself, contemplate in solitude but he had to address the men--say something.

As he neared the group, he could see their anxious faces almost begging to hear him speak. With some effort, Euphrates willed himself to muster up the excitement he was expected to have. He jumped from his horse as he rode into the crowd, drew his sword, raised it high above his head and exclaimed, "To war we go!"

The men resounded in a cheer. They raised their weapons, thrusting them high into the air. Their rejoicing echoed through the mountains, letting all who listened carefully know where they hid. But, on this day of celebration, Euphrates would allow it, even though he knew it would continue late into the night. They had prepared for this day for much too long; he wouldn't stifle their spirits.

As the men set out to continue celebrating with a feast, Euphrates slipped into his tent. He would say more to them later, but for now he wanted to escape the noise and devise a plan.

ᨆ

CHETI, IRITU AND Montu along with Arman and Seti rode into a town at the base of the Wadi Hammamat. Montu was certain the rebel was stationed in the caverns off the trade route. Now, he was left to discover where. Nonetheless, Montu was confident he would find a sign. There were always signs left unintentionally and he would certainly find it. He was an excellent tracker—the best—and he believed what made him great was he always paid attention to his instinct.

The five men lowered themselves from their camels. Tonight they would rest in the town and make their inquiries—someone would speak and reveal something; someone always did.

〰

NIGHT HAD LONG since settled itself across the land. Outside everything finally calmed down. Most of the men were sleeping, the others not far behind.

Euphrates slumped in his chair, fidgeting with his dagger. He stuck the tip of the blade into the chair arm then flipped it onto the handle— back and forth again. The high and low pitched sounds fell into a rhythm that brought a sense of calm with it. A deep gouge formed in the chair arm where the blade repeatedly fell. *Thump. Tap. Thump.*

The tent door drew open.

Without looking, Euphrates whipped his dagger, the blade landing in the ground by the foot of the intruder.

The intruder stopped short; the knife barely missed his toes.

Euphrates looked up.

Tuthiken eyed him questioningly. He had a barrel of ale slung over his right shoulder.

"Pardon, my Lord. I've come to see if you need a drink?"

Euphrates gave a slight smile. Of course, he thought, the Great Overlord of the Bale of Ale.

"I didn't think it right for the men to drink it all without you, so I've saved you some." Tuthiken rested the bale down on the ground.

"A good man," Euphrates said as he stood. He walked over to Tuthiken, pulled his knife from the dirt.

"I'm sorry to have intruded." He went to leave.

Euphrates placed a hand on Tuthiken's shoulder. "There is no one more befitting for me to have my last drink with before we go to battle than the Great Overlord."

Tuthiken grinned at Euphrates, his face red, his eyes glassy. He was drinking with the men, but unlike them he was straight on his feet.

Euphrates moved to grab two goblets from the top of a trunk. "After tonight," he said, handing them to Tuthiken, "I will need you to keep a closer watch on the beer. We need our men strong and alert for battle."

Tuthiken finished pouring. He handed a cup to Euphrates. "No need to worry. This is the last of it until we reach the next town. I've already dumped three barrels over the hillside."

Euphrates laughed. "I knew there was no title more suiting for you."

Tuthiken raised his cup. "To war and to winning it," he toasted.

"Yes, to victory."

They chugged back the brew.

After Tuthiken left, Euphrates put out the lights, save one, and lay on his bed on the floor. He closed his eyes.

Her face. He couldn't get away from it—it hung in his mind, enticing his desires.

If only things were different, he thought. But instead, it was war—the one thing, and indeed the only thing, he spent his life preparing for.

Daylight approached soon after Euphrates had fallen asleep. He jumped out of bed, raced from the tent. The sun pierced across the sky towards him—three hours of morning.

Men were sprawled around the campsite, still sleeping off the effects of last night.

"Up and pack!" Euphrates shouted.

Some of the men stirred grumpily. Nefret was the first man to Euphrates' side. "My Lord," said the small sentry, "we can't leave. There is word a troop is on route to join our forces. Should we not wait?"

"We must be on the move," Euphrates stated, knowing more men were needed. They were still too small compared to the royal army. "They can meet us in Wasebet."

"But, how will they know?"

Euphrates stopped, looked at Nefret. "Take a man and remain here. I am stopping at the foot of the hills to meet up with the others who wait on my call before heading onward to Wasebet. We should reach

Wasebet in about two weeks. We will wait out the week for you to rejoin us."

"I will stay with Storithen."

Euphrates nodded with admiration for the small man whose courage was twice his size. "Do you know of the spring between here and Yun?"

"I know these lands well, we will be fine."

"If for some reason you are detained and don't make it to Wasebet before we leave, I intend to march on the Fortress of Ipu. Find us there." Euphrates gave Nefret a pat on the shoulder. He spun, yelled again at the men to ready themselves to depart.

XIV

ℴNLY NINETEEN SHIPS returned to Henen-nesut. The Pharaoh's was the first to reach the shore.

Tigris' servants prepared her palanquin and carried her up the long walk towards the palace gates. Everyone except eight royal guards who remained in front and beside her for protection, stayed behind in a long trailing line. The palanquin was closed off by a roof, a front and rear wall and curtains hanging on both sides, which could be drawn to allow in a breeze.

Inside the golden compartment Tigris sat upright. She could hardly sit still. She was anxious to confront the Vizier. She was sure he was a part of the conspiracy and still he kept it from her. *Everyone* had kept it from her.

Tigris twisted her hands together eagerly. She pulled back the curtain to see how much further they had to go. She wanted to order the chair bearers to run but she knew it wasn't fair. The road had quite an incline to protect it from enemy attacks and it was also quite long. She forced her patience, deciding to wait it out knowing the distance only seemed longer than it really was.

Dusk was just beginning to pull darkness across the sky. Around the palace the attendants began lighting the rooms. Soon Tigris and her entourage approached the gates. The musky smell of the Nile blew up the roadway, following them to the palace. They halted as the drums sounded to signal the Pharaoh's arrival.

One of the outer guards stepped forward, eyed each of the royal soldiers and the chair bearers before he pulled back the drape to peer in at Tigris. "Welcome, Per'a," he said with a bow. He allowed the drape to fall shut again, immediately called up to the tower to send rights to open the grand palace gates. Everyone who approached would be checked before being permitted to enter.

In the cookhouse, the staff hastily prepared dinner the moment they received word the Pharaoh's ships had returned. Though, Tigris was in no mood to eat. Instead of going to the small dining quarters in the royal residences to dine with Allegi, the Admiral and a few other nobles who would have a late dinner, she decided to forgo it altogether and attend to business.

As soon as they were moving again, Tigris rapped on the wall of the small compartment behind her head. The attendant, who followed alongside her palanquin, waiting to be needed, looked in.

"Have them take me to the Vizier's quarters," she ordered.

The servant nodded.

They moved through the palace grounds towards the far end of the outer building where Ibimpetus' apartment was located. Before long, the chair was lowered and a step placed on the ground. While the chair bearers held the palanquin steady, the attendant pulled back the curtain to help the Pharaoh out.

The royal soldiers had left the Pharaoh at the gate to take their horses to the stables.

Tigris stepped onto the box and looked about. There was no one around. At this hour, most of the palace workers had retired for the night and only the watchmen would make their rounds.

Stepping off the painted wooden box, Tigris moved away from the palanquin. The chair bearers jaunted off, the attendant followed.

Tigris stood alone in the court outside the Vizier's residence where everything was quiet and still. She took a quick breath before she marched forward through the front door into Ibimpetus' grand foyer. Large columns, marble floors and painted walls welcomed guests as they entered but Tigris focused on the stairway ahead of her.

A servant came forward. The look on his face seemed surprised. Whether he was shocked to see an intruder or to see it was the Pharaoh who entered, Tigris didn't know, nor did she care. She glanced at him with a small nod as she continued through the foyer towards the staircase. Tigris was sure the Vizier would be in his study where he spent much of his time.

The servant reached the steps first, stopped at the bottom, looked at her—his surprise still clinging to his expression. "Great Per'a, might I announce your arrival to my master?"

Tigris kept her pace. "There is no need. I will do it myself."

The servant glanced up the staircase. His surprise changed to worry. He backed up the steps, tried to keep himself from turning around altogether to race up the stairs ahead of her. But, Tigris was already at the staircase and keeping up.

The servant looked at her again. "But, Per'a, I should announce the arrival of any—"

"What you *should* do is bow in the presence of your Pharaoh," Tigris cut in, sharply.

The servant's eyes widened. It was customary upon seeing the Pharaoh for all to bow down. Only rank determined how long and low the bow was to be held. As a servant, he was expected to bow to the floor until either the Pharaoh passed or permitted him to continue.

"My regrets," whispered the servant. He immediately fell to the steps in a bow. The Queen strode past him. All he could do was look up the stairs ahead of her.

Tigris reached the top of the steps, rounded the corner, headed down the hall towards the study. The hall was dimly lit with a row of columns lining its length. Dark artwork hung on the walls between columns where there were no doors and chests occupied the floor beneath them.

Tigris quickened her pace until she came to the door at the end of the corridor. She gathered herself momentarily before she reached out, grabbed the handle, and pushed the door open.

Inside the chamber, quietly speaking to the Vizier, Chephren spun. Surprise covered his face just as it had the servant.

Tigris bitterly sized him as she entered. "News travels quickly with you, Admiral," she quipped. "Perhaps you'd be better suited as a messenger."

The Admiral lowered his eyes in shame. Tigris didn't remove her glare from him as she approached the two men.

Nonetheless, she was taken off guard. *How did he reach before me?* she wondered. *The moment the bridge was lowered from the ship I was carried off with only the royal guards ahead—the royal guards—no, he wouldn't!*

Tigris' eyes narrowed with their anger piercing the Royal Admiral, High Councillor, with contempt.

I would have him replaced, she thought. But, now they were set for war and she knew she couldn't replace the Admiral of the Royal Vessels in a time like this.

Tigris stopped beside the two councillors. "Your presence is not needed," she said to Chephren.

He looked at Ibimpetus who nodded his approval. The gesture angered Tigris even more knowing her command was not enough to govern obedience in the man—but, she bit her tongue, still eyeing him coldly as he turned away.

Chephren left the room and closed the door behind him. The moment the door was shut, Tigris shifted her glare towards the Vizier.

Ibimpetus turned, went to a high table and slid onto a stool.

"Why was I not informed?" Tigris demanded.

He picked up a brush, dipped it in ink, and proceeded to write something, ignoring her stare. Only after he allowed a quiet moment to linger did he finally respond without looking up. "It was before your time and it was not for you to know."

Tigris tried to control her fury. "It was not for me to know how my blood became of royal lineage?"

"This matter *never* should have concerned you." The Vizier looked up. His voice was angry. Tigris could sense the news came as a shock to him as well.

"But now," Tigris said, lowering her voice, "it's *all* of my concern." She looked steadily at the Vizier without blinking. He was bent over his paper with his head turned towards her, his expression hardened in the lines of his face. Only after he blinked did she move to a table where parchments were sprawled across it. She glanced over them—but she was too unnerved to read.

Ibimpetus was quick to spring from his stool and follow. He rolled the parchments up.

Tigris eyed him, resentfully. "I am Per'a. *Everything* regarding Egypt is privy to me."

The Vizier continued collecting the parchments. "This," he said holding up one of the scrolls, "is *not* regarding Egypt." He finished collecting the papers, carried them to a trunk, dumped them in and slammed the lid. He turned to face her.

For a long moment they glared at one another before Tigris broke the silence. "Tell me, how do I go to war against justice?" she asked, her words almost a whisper.

Ibimpetus' face tightened. He shook his head in disbelief. "This is precisely why women cannot rule a *king*dom—they lead with their emotions and they have too much pity!"

Tigris' cheeks flushed with rage. "My gender has nothing to do with it!"

The Vizier's glare turned colder. He lowered his voice so it resonated deep inside his throat as he spoke through gritted teeth, "Then you go to war as any *noble man* would—you go to war to protect what your father built!"

"You would have me go to war to protect you! For it would be your head first on the chopping block if he were to regain his claim to the throne!"

Ibimpetus stepped forward. "Are you really willing to step down from the throne? Do you have no *honour?*"

He moved back over to the high table; he pushed things around on top of it. "Let me tell you about justice," he began calmly. He set down a stelae and looked steadily at Tigris. "*Justice* was the day his shameful father was put to rest. *Justice* was the election of your father to the throne because he restored Egypt and thereby pleased the gods." His glare turned colder. "The crown rested upon his head. You are his descendant. But, only those whose heads are strong enough to hold the crown *are fit to wear it!*" His eyes narrowed. "Therein lies the question—*is yours?*" The words pierced out of his mouth.

Tigris was confused, overwhelmed by emotions. Justice, she thought.

She looked at the Vizier—the most powerful man in the country, whom she no doubt needed to have on her side. He was right. She couldn't just step down from the throne because the rebel's cause seemed just. Many Pharaoh's before his father were overthrown for less noble causes.

Yes, she had to protect the Egypt her father had resurrected and honour his claim and lineage; she knew it was the only thing to do.

Tigris took a long breath. "Send word to all the sepats that they are to pledge their allegiance. Those who do not, seize them." Her head nodded, ever so slightly, as if in agreement to a thought that entered her mind. "Egypt is *mine* and at all costs I will fight to keep her in my rule."

Tigris entered her bed chamber. She went over to a box on top of her writing table, opened the lid and lifted out a scroll. She carried it to her chair in the adjacent room and slumped down. Slowly, she unrolled the parchment and studied the words on the page, written by her new enemy:

> *...it is my duty as the true soul of Re to inform you of your illegitimate embrace of the royal flail and crook. With this regard, I announce to you my sovereignty with which I proclaim Egypt mine...*

Tigris took a deep breath. Euphrates' message was now so clear. She scanned down to his closing:

> *....A king is what Egypt always intended to have and at last I have come.*
> *Your brother and great enemy, Pharaoh and King of Egypt, enthroned as Usermaathor.*

Tigris leaned back in her seat. "Usermaathor," she whispered as she loosened her grip on the scroll, allowing it to roll itself back up.

"Usermaathor," she repeated over and over until it hit her. *Usermaathor—hor* as in the old royal titles. The Pharaoh's of Egypt had been enthroned under the sun god Re for over four hundred years and yet he used *hor*.

She opened the scroll.

"...it is my duty as the true soul of Re..." she read, realizing he did not deny Re. Tigris read his throne name again. "Usermaathor," she said as she studied the name in order to interpret it.

Many Pharaoh's had used the prefix *User*, which meant "to bring" and Maat was the Goddess of Justice. She looked at the last part of the name. "*Hor—*" she whispered as her eyes widened.

She jumped from her chair, raced to the bedchamber.

Horu! The god who avenged his father Oser's death by slaying Set.

Yes, his name—To bring justice to Horu—*Usermaathor!*

She pulled open the mirror, hurried into the dark passage not stopping to light the torch.

Her memory raced back to when she was a child visiting with Kafate instead of her mother:

≈

"TELL ME OF my future," she had begged the priestess.

"Go and play child while I finish preparing lunch."

"Send an attendant to the cookhouse."

Kafate stopped, looked at Tigris. "Do you see an attendant here?" she asked, pretending to be annoyed.

"Well, you should have one."

"Well, I don't want one. They're a nuisance and I have hands—two as a matter of fact." She used them to shoo Tigris away.

Tigris stopped in the doorway and pouted. "The queen said you could see the future but you always deny seeing mine," she complained, refusing to refer to Nefari as her mother.

"I see only what the future wants me to see," Kafate responded.

Tigris stood outside the small kitchen looking in at the old woman with a long face.

For awhile, Kafate tried to ignore her but she finally gave in. "Oh, alright, I will see what I can see."

Tigris' face lit up. She took Kafate by the hand and led her to the black pond. Sitting down, Tigris eagerly waited.

Kafate took her time to arrange herself on the cushions before she opened her leather satchel and dumped out the stones with the tiny symbols etched into them. Each stone bared its own symbol and was shaped differently from the next.

The priestess scooped them up, shook them in her bony hands, whispered:

Through cloud and darkness let me see
May the future's truths come to me.

She threw the stones into the black pond. They sunk to the bottom, landing in a way that spoke only to the priestess. The torches on the walls sparkled on top of the water, but under its shallow surface the white stones seemed to glow.

The priestess leaned forward, closed her good eye and peered at the stones with her blind eye.

Tigris watched the priestess' face, enraptured.

Kafate's stare slowly changed. The priestess leaned in closer with her eyebrows tightening her forehead. She blinked, opened her eyes and looked at Tigris.

Tigris waited for her to say something but instead the old woman collected the stones and stood up.

"I see nothing."

Tigris' face fell with disappointment. "You're lying," she accused.

Kafate set the leather pouch on one of the tables and smiled gently at Tigris. "You're still young. There is so much time for the future to change."

"Isn't it fated?"

The priestess laughed. "No dear, then there would be no point in living. Our choices play a strong role in it."

Kafate returned to the kitchen to finish making their lunch.

Tigris followed and stood at the door. "It was bad, wasn't it?" she asked softly.

Kafate stopped puttering around. She looked earnestly at Tigris for a long moment. "I won't lie to you. There is to be war," she stated with a comforting smile on her lips.

Tigris threw her arms up in the air. "There's always to be war when you are a Pharaoh." She smiled, not concerned. Her father spent most of his time campaigning and warring; she constantly pestered him to let her join—war was what she knew. In fact, most of her schooling was learning how to use weapons and to have the heart of a warrior. Indeed, she would be ready for it.

Tigris spun, went off to play.

"Unlike any you know," Kafate whispered after her.

≈

REACHING THE BOTTOM of the stairs, Tigris banged on the door twice before she threw it open.

Kafate was standing by a table stirring something in a small pot. She looked up at Tigris.

"Horu," Tigris said as she headed towards Kafate.

"Actually, it's hello," Kafate smiled, facetiously.

The Queen kissed the old woman on the forehead. "You are dear to me but at times you drive me crazy. You knew of this Horu. Why didn't you warn me who he was?" Tigris went to the black pond. She sprawled out on the cushions, stared up at the ceiling.

"I do not know all that you proclaim me to know," the priestess answered as she continued to mix her concoction. "I tell you only what the future permits me to." Kafate stopped to add some powder to her mixture, measuring it out carefully. "I only discovered myself who your pursuer was in a dream after you sailed to meet him. The tides were already set."

Tigris looked at the old woman. "I have to go to war," she said, softly.

"You have to follow your heart."

"Then, I must honour my father. He entrusted Egypt to me, his daughter—a woman. I cannot forsake him and I will not give up Egypt."

Kafate finished mixing her potion and poured it into a container. After closing it with a lid, she set the container down and moved to join Tigris.

As Kafate slowly managed to sit, Tigris turned on her side to face her. "Do you remember the first reading you gave me when I was a child in Men-nefer?"

The old woman grimaced in pain as she allowed her weight to drop the short way to the cushions. After the pain subsided, she set her staff down beside her and used the cushions to help prop herself up.

"You saw this war but you saw something else. Please tell me Kafate." Tigris studied the old woman who had replaced her mother.

106

It was the only great thing the queen had ever done for Tigris and the wretched woman had never known it.

Kafate shook her head, softly.

"I need to know what else you saw," Tigris begged. "Why did your face frown when you looked at the stones?"

Kafate remained in quiet contemplation before she let out a heavy sigh. "I saw a war with unnecessary suffering that you're not supposed to fight—"

"Not supposed to fight because he was to have Egypt but the choices of the Council changed his fate."

Kafate shook her head. "I cannot tell you any more. There are choices meant for you and you alone to make, which I do not have the answers to."

Tigris closed her eyes and rolled onto her back. "Dearest Kafate, please, why won't you tell me all?" she pouted, not expecting an answer.

But, the old woman responded with tenderness, "I wish I could child. But, you create your own fate by the choices you make and some choices cannot be guided, otherwise, it wouldn't be *your* destiny." Kafate pulled a blanket over her shoulders. "Only when you've opened yourself to the possibilities of change can guidance be given." She looked at Tigris, her eyes piercing with graveness. "Unless you've travelled so far down a road you've sealed the passages to alter it."

Kafate tapped her long fingernails against the stone floor. Heka entered the room and went to its master to be petted. As Kafate stroked the back of the cat, the bangles on her arm clanged back and forth in a soft rhythm.

XV

NEFRET AND STORITHEN waited six days before five lone travellers found them on the trade route.

"We're looking for the Pharaoh Usermaathor. We've come to join his forces," the leader said as he scanned the area. "Have you heard of him or seen him on your travels?"

Something about them Storithen didn't trust. "No—"

"You travel only as five?" Nefret cut in.

"For the time being. The rest wait on our response."

"We haven't seen this Pharaoh," Storithen assured, curtly, giving Nefret a look to keep quiet. "There is but one Pharaoh in Egypt and her palace is far from these lands."

The leader turned his attention back to Storithen. "You're right. There is but only one Pharaoh in Egypt, however, *his* name is Euphrates and we were told to say these words: 'Under the great Horu may Egypt be returned.'"

Nefret looked at Storithen who pretended not to notice. "We'll take you to him," he stated, ignoring Storithen's expression that clearly didn't want to welcome the men.

"I'm Nefret. This is Storithen," he introduced.

The leader turned to the men behind him and pointed. "Seti, Arman, Iritu, Cheti and I'm Montu."

XVI

*L*ETTERS WERE DISPATCHED to all the provinces stating the Pharaoh's proclamation of war and bidding the Overlords, high priests and noble dignitaries pledge their allegiance to the Pharaoh. The Vizier sent these letters during Tigris' absence and by the time she returned the highest-ranking men in the country had already arrived at the palace to kneel down below the Great Throne of Geb to honour their Pharaoh.

More than ever before, Tigris felt it was important to personify herself as a King in order to command the respect she deserved, and to remind everyone she was Pharaoh. She dressed in masculine attire with the *pschent* crown of United Egypt on her head. Today, she even wore the false beard—a hard braided piece of hair held on by the ears, which hung below the chin—often worn by previous Pharaohs to represent their power.

The Queen peered down upon her loyalists. Each man, prestigiously clad in his noble garb, paid his respects and declared his loyalty.

"May the crowns of Egypt be secured upon your head."

"A long and prosperous life, great Nitiqreti."

"May your name be spoken for all time as the true soul of Re."

After each wish, Tigris nodded her approval, permitting the speaker to make his leave. She sat high upon her majestic throne and watched as each man stepped forward, one-by-one, day after day. Of them, all the members of the Great Ten returned to bow down and proclaim their allegiance.

Tigris watched as Anaten approached the throne, knelt before her, tipped his head as he spoke. A wry smile curled his lips.

"Death to those unfit to wear the crown."

"Cousin!" exclaimed Tigris, repulsed at his chosen speech. "How indecent for you to seal your pledge with such treachery."

"I only wish destruction to the enemies of the throne," he replied, looking up at her.

Tigris sized him. "You pledge your loyalty with death and destruction without even honouring me as Pharaoh."

Anaten showed no remorse in his expression although he pushed sincerity into his response, "Of course, I honour you, cousin."

"Then mend your words."

Giving a small nod, Anaten said, "May the rebel find death for rising against you, Per'a."

Tigris was annoyed. "Must you tie death to your words of respect?"

Anaten looked at her blankly for a moment before he responded, "In such times, do you find it so dishonourable for me to wish death to the enemies of Egypt?"

"Your words disturb me."

"Then I apologize for my frankness," he said, smugly.

Tigris couldn't be bothered to argue. He was a stubborn man and she was in no mood to harp on the same point. She had spent most of her days in the Great Hall listening to the eloquent proclamations of her loyal subjects during the daylight hours and it was beginning to wear on her. No one mentioned the enemy, which was to be expected, as the act was only to show integrity and to wish greatness to the Pharaoh. Only at night, when she dined with her guests, was it considered a more appropriate time to bring up the rebel's quest in conversation. But,

Anaten was her cousin and felt he was above formality. Besides, was it so bad he wished death to her enemies?

Finally, the Queen gave her nod of approval, allowing the Governor of Upper Egypt his leave.

Mahorse, the Royal Treasurer of God, stood beside her for all the proceedings. As the men arrived, he made a list of their names, including the ones who were unable to travel the distance but bequeathed their loyalty in long flowery letters. By the end of only five days, Tigris had looked upon over two hundred royal officials and received letters from more than eighty. Only five had not paid their respects, which Mahorse noted on a separate list: Two priests, two lords and the Overlord of the Upper Fifth Sepat.

Later that night during the banquet, Mahorse passed this list discreetly to Ibimpetus. By the next day, the Vizier had called upon five lieutenants of the State Police to organize troops for their mission. He handed the Lieutenant of each party a parchment with a destination and a name. Before the royal policemen would return to the palace at Henen-nesut, five men would hang in their home towns with the royal emblem posted to their chests.

The night after the last of the loyalists left the palace, Tigris met with her full Council in the Great Hall. In attendance were the Great Ten, the *Braves of the King* and the Overlords of the most cherished sepats.

The Pharaoh sat on her high throne looking at the two rows of men who lined the aisle; seats faced parallel to each other. The reality of the situation finally began to settle in.

"It has been reported his rebellion has moved out of Abydos," Mahorse was saying, "and his numbers amount to eight hundred men."

"Only eight hundred?" Tigris laughed. "We can run circles around his pathetic little army."

Her attention was drawn to the door as a Lieutenant of the State Police entered the Grand Hall and bowed. "Sorry to disturb, but a word with Tjat," requested the officer.

The Vizier stood, went to the Lieutenant whom he had sent in search of one of the offending priests. They quickly exchanged words and then Ibimpetus turned back to the Council as the officer bowed to the Pharaoh and exited.

"Don't undermine your enemy. His numbers are increasing," Ibimpetus stated. "A reported six hundred more are moving to join his forces." The Vizier walked up the centre aisle, which parted the two rows of men. He stopped in front of his seat at the head and faced Tigris. "Two hundred are being led by Nathashut," he added.

Tigris' eyes grew wide. "Nathashut?" she repeated. "He was just here but a few nights ago declaring his loyalty."

"Not all those who pledge allegiance speak in honesty," said Anaten. "Death to the enemies," he preened as if to gloat on his point made to her several days earlier.

Tigris ignored him. She looked at the Vizier. "Send an army of five hundred to stop him. I want his head. As for the other four hundred rebels, double their numbers and block their travels." Tigris stood. "But, I want Nathashut's head. How dare he bow it down to me and make a toast while holding a knife at my back."

XVII

ALLEGI STEPPED OUT of the Queen's chamber with a scroll to be delivered to the enemy. He walked down the hall towards the back door. Although, he wouldn't set out until morning, he did not want to spend his night at the palace.

The young messenger left the royal grounds and rode into town. He dropped his things off at the guesthouse, went to the tavern and sat watching the door, hoping *she* would come. But, after several hours of seeing only the regulars arrive, he lost hope and left.

Allegi strolled down a narrow street towards the guesthouse. Disappointment followed him. He rounded a corner. Stopped.

At the other end of the block, someone headed towards him, head bent over. Allegi studied the distant figure. It had to be a woman from her size and stature. He moved forward, his heart fluttering with hope.

Why would a woman walk the streets so late alone? he wondered as they neared each other.

The woman raised her head. Allegi froze. He stared blankly at the girl he thought so much about since the first day he set eyes on her. He almost didn't believe his own eyes.

She stopped before him, stared back.

For a long breath-taking moment neither moved. *Say something*, Allegi coached himself before he managed to mutter, "Pleasant night."

The girl blushed. "Yes," she replied.

"I was actually hoping to find you," Allegi blurted without thinking. He immediately regretted his words. Their truth made him feel uncomfortable, exposed.

"Really?" She lowered her head, looked up shyly.

"My name is Allegi."

"Deshyre," she introduced.

"A pleasure." Allegi greeted her with a small bow. "Where are you headed?"

Deshyre smiled innocently. "Can you keep a secret?"

Allegi nodded. She motioned for him to come closer, leaned in, whispered in his ear. "I've been going to the tavern in hopes of seeing you again." She stepped back, lowered her head in the same shy manner as she had before.

Allegi had to repeat her words in his mind to believe them. "I would have never thought the way you ran out that first night."

"I got scared when you caught me looking," she shrugged.

Allegi held out his hand. "Then let me hold your hand so you can't run off again." He was shocked at his own boldness. Shocked, but he didn't care. It was worth the risk of rejection.

Deshyre moved her hands behind her back, bit her lower lip.

"I promise I won't scare you."

She giggled, stretched out her hand and placed it in his.

For a moment Allegi didn't believe it. But, then he looked. *I'm holding her hand*, Allegi thought in disbelief as he began to lead her down the street with no destination in mind. He was just happy to walk beside her, *the girl*—Deshyre.

"Do you like to dance?" she asked breaking the uncomfortable silence they had fallen into.

Allegi shrugged.

"Let's go to a different place. I'm tired of Sechemech." She spun and began to lead him.

Hand-in-hand they walked through the narrow streets chatting, laughing. Allegi was ecstatic. No matter how many times he reminded himself this was all real, he still could hardly believe he was holding the girl's hand. What were the chances? he wondered. He looked at Deshyre's hand again—a web of fingers weaved together with his.

Deshyre caught him. "You're a noble. You shouldn't be holding my hand," she said, trying to pull away.

Allegi glanced down at his attire, which gave away his class. He clenched her hand tighter. "These are just clothes. They don't change me, I change them," he smiled.

"But, I am not of your class."

"Really? I only noticed that you're beautiful and intriguing."

"Do you always say things to make women blush?" Deshyre smiled. She didn't wait for the answer. She pulled him through a doorway where steps led down under ground. Sounds of laughter, music and voices climbed up the stairs to greet them. At the bottom of the steps, a large chamber glowed bright with torchlight. All over the room, people danced, chatted, drank; there wasn't one man of nobility among them.

When they entered the room, several people greeted Deshyre with nods and smiles but they showed their subtle contempt for Allegi's presence.

"So, this is where you've been hiding," Allegi pointed.

"This is the place to be if you want to escape your worries."

An older man called out Deshyre's name. She let go of Allegi's hand and went to him.

Allegi followed.

"Eritum!" Deshyre exclaimed over the noise of the crowd. "I want you to meet Allegi."

Eritum looked Allegi over. "You shouldn't be bringing the Pharaoh's subject in here," Eritum scowled.

Deshyre smiled. "He's not a noble. He knocked one out, stole his clothes, which makes him a thief, so he fits in perfectly." She laughed as she leaned in close and whispered, "He's assured me he won't speak of our secret place." She kissed the bearded man on the cheek.

Eritum stood. He was tall, thin and his face was hard, which even his long curly beard was unable to conceal. He took Allegi's hand, pulled him close so he could speak in his ear. "Beware young messenger, I am watching you," Eritum warned. He moved back, gave Allegi a discerning look, squeezed his hand hard. His expression turned to a smile as he looked at Deshyre. "Now, you two kids go dance and have fun," he said, slapping Allegi hard on the back.

Deshyre took Allegi's hand and led him out onto the dance floor.

"Who is he?" Allegi asked.

"He's known me since I was a child. He's a little protective."

"A little?"

They began to dance to the music, which the musicians played on lutes, harps, drums and bells.

"You must be special," Deshyre winked. "He didn't bite off your head and eat it." She laughed as Allegi spun her around.

Deshyre and Allegi continued to dance, enjoying the night and each other's company as the hours raced by. It seemed as if they had only been together for minutes before Deshyre suddenly gasped.

"How long have we been here?" she asked anxiously jumping up from where they sat watching a woman who just finished singing.

"I don't know—"

"I have to go." She took off towards the door, pushing her way through the crowd.

Allegi followed her to the steps. He raced up the stairs behind her. "Let me walk you home," he said as they reached outside.

Turning, Deshyre walked backwards. "Please, it's better you don't." She smiled softly. "Will I see you again tomorrow night?"

Allegi stood still, watching her back away. "No, I have to deliver a message to Upper Egypt."

"Then I will look for you at Sechemech every night until you return." She stopped walking backwards and ran back to kiss him on the cheek. "I had fun," she whispered.

"I should never have let go of your hand," Allegi said as she stepped away.

Deshyre giggled. She turned and ran off down the street leaving Allegi holding his cheek.

XVIII

ON THE DESERT, not too far from the city of Zawty, the Pharaoh's army spanned across the land like an impenetrable fortress wall. Some seven hundred feet away, Nathashut swallowed his heart after it had rose into his mouth from seeing the royal battalion appear from the earth outnumbering his men. He had hoped to join forces with Euphrates before having to fight, but today his fate lay before him as if the end was already written.

The battle did not last long. Before the hour had gone the Pharaoh's army defeated the rebellion with almost no casualties on the royal side. Nathashut's head would be brought to the Great House and laid at Tigris' feet.

~~~

ACROSS THE LAND, at almost the same hour, the 4th battalion of the Khnum Infantry caught up to the second rebellion led by the Lord of Bisteq. However, the second rebellion was prepared to fight and although outnumbered, their disadvantage did not stir them. They fought long and hard slaughtering twice as many men as the Pharaoh's army and forcing the Commander of the Fourth Battalion to retreat.

Snofru, Lord of Bisteq, was determined to join Euphrates' army. He had sent word that he was coming from far in the north and by the gods, he would show.

~~~

THE SUN DIPPED below the horizon offering its final light. Cheti broke pieces of bread and handed it to his company.

"We have food," Storithen grunted, refusing the bread.

"Suit yourself," Cheti shrugged as he handed the piece to Nefret, who accepted.

A low fire burned in the middle of the group helping to attract bugs away from them. They sat quietly eating their food, studying each other with grim faces as they had done for the past two days.

It wasn't until they were almost finished eating, did Montu break the silence. "When we reach the bottom of the mountain, Cheti and Iritu will leave to get the others. They will meet us at the destination."

"Why don't we all go to join them?" Storithen asked, suspiciously.

Iritu spoke before his comrades could reply. "We can if you'd like."

Cheti sent him a darting look but Iritu wasn't worried. He had overheard Storithen complaining to Nefret that Euphrates would soon leave their meeting place. Certainly, they would not want to delay their travels.

Iritu sighed. "Though, it's five days back the other way."

Storithen didn't respond. Nefret looked at Storithen knowing it was not an option.

"We'll keep moving," Nefret decided. "But, the destination will only be given when Cheti and Iritu are departing." He looked at the two men. "In privacy. Away from the group. The rest," he said, turning his attention to the others, "will have to rely on our guidance."

Early the next morning they reached the bottom of the mountain. As planned, Nefret followed Cheti and Iritu a safe distance from the rest of the group where their voices could not be heard. He revealed the locations Euphrates would be--Wasebet, the Fortress of Ipu--then they said their good-byes.

XIX

$\mathcal{W}$HILE THE REST of his men waited on the outskirts of town, Euphrates and his accompanying party rode into Wasebet.

Children ran out of their homes to watch as the twelve men raced by creating a spectacle in a town that was generally quiet.

Euphrates was dressed in a traditional white pleated kilt, a strengthened head-dress, folded behind his ears with the golden heads of the vulture and the royal cobra on the forehead, and an artificial goatee. He had decided to dress in royal regalia when presenting his position to men in order to help them see him as King.

Leading his party towards the inner part of Wasebet, Euphrates rode in front on horseback while his men followed on camels. Being just after sunset, it was a good guess that many of the town's men would be enjoying their evening at the town's bar before heading home to their wives from a hard day's work.

Wasebet was a town made up of tomb and monument builders, which meant the men were physically strong—just the type of men Euphrates needed on his side.

Euphrates dismounted his horse, headed towards the bar. He instructed his men to wait outside unless needed, save for Somiset, who would help guard against any angry loyalists. Walking forward, Euphrates and Somiset stood inside the doorway, sizing the room.

Inside the plain mud brick walls of the building, men slumped on kilims on the floor. Old boxes and chairs offered a mix-match of seating around worn down tables. Some men played board games while others talked or argued. Although filled with patrons, there wasn't a woman in sight.

Thick walls separated the enclosure from the outside world except for the non-existent roof exposing the sky above. Beer was served from behind a half-wall where the owner, perched on top of a high stool, peered miserably out at the rowdy men. At his side he had a small bow in case anyone decided to get out of hand.

Stepping further into the room, Euphrates brought the men to a silence. Their heads turned towards the door as they noticed his presence standing in the room, looking imperial in his attire. They had heard of him, and now he was there.

"My name is Euphrates," he began as he peered around the room. "I have proclaimed war on Egypt. And, I *will* succeed to my rightful place on the throne." He held his arm out in a gesture for them to take his offer. "Join me in my quest. For Egypt deserves a true Pharaoh at its reign."

None of the patrons in the bar moved, including the old owner. Everyone remained rigid, stunned at the presence before them. Euphrates continued to examine the room, taking in all the men.

"We have a true Pharaoh on the throne of Egypt."

Euphrates looked over at the man who dared to speak out.

The man made his move on the board game he was playing then gestured for his opponent to take his turn. The opponent, however, was not as bold. He sat dumbstruck or perhaps afraid for his friend who spoke out.

Rumours made their rounds through Egypt. Some described Euphrates as a god, others as a beast, depending upon which side the person who told it supported. Nonetheless, all rumours noted that the self-proclaimed King could kill any man no matter his size or skill of weaponry, for it was agreed by all, that Euphrates had the strength of an immortal.

Euphrates sized the man who had spoken out. He was large and muscular with broad shoulders and powerful arms. He wore a short tunic, belted at the waist with a dagger secured at his side.

The man looked over at Euphrates, tensed his brow. "Perhaps you've heard of her—her name is *Nitiqreti, Tigris of Egypt.*"

Euphrates threw his head back to laugh. "A woman? Is this who you call Per'a? The seed of a treasonous murderer?"

The man spun in his seat. "She is an honourable Pharaoh!"

"Yet, she comes about the throne dishonourably!"

The man's eyes narrowed. He leaned forward in his seat. "What makes you so righteous?" he asked, not taking his eyes from Euphrates.

Euphrates looked around at the faces of the men in the bar. They all watched in silence, taken aback by his presence and now by his pronouncements. Slowly, he delivered his answer. "I am the true son of Egypt—"

"We've heard it but why should we believe it?" another man challenged, cutting him off.

Euphrates turned his attention towards the voice then he gradually looked at everyone. "Because I've come from nothing and gained so much in such little time. Because Eset protects me as Horu leads me to redemption of the wrongs I've endured," he said with conviction.

The man who spoke initially urged his comrades with the same sincerity in his tone. "Our Pharaoh keeps her people happy and maintains peace in Egypt," he reminded them before he peered back at Euphrates. "What do you offer but war?"

"I offer *truth* and *justice*—"

"*Whose* justice?"

Their eyes met. The two men studied each other for a still moment before Euphrates responded, allowing each word to roll with impact off his tongue. "Egypt's justice."

Euphrates hadn't expected to meet with such a loyalist this far away from the Pharaoh's capital, especially in a town that erected statues and monuments for a female Pharaoh. A female on the throne was entirely against their Egyptian ideal, most of the people quietly frowned upon it. Euphrates believed that these men--who built monuments to glorify a woman as Pharaoh--would have been the easiest to convince. But loyalty often followed kindness and Tigris had made her mark on her kingdom as a kindly Pharaoh.

Moving forward, Euphrates stopped in the centre of the bar. "My fate has been chosen for me," he explained. "I was born of Wadjkare. I am the son of the goddess Eset and she has seen to it that I grew to become a warrior even though I was taken far from my home. I have heard her voice in my head since I was a boy, saying, 'Take the throne of Egypt, it is your destiny.'" He glanced at his aggressor. "*She* has placed this battle axe in my hand," he said raising his axe. "And, in the name of Oser, her son Horu leads me to avenge my father's death!"

〰〰

AT THAT MOMENT, not too far away, the Lord of Wasebet, Overseer of the Builders, rounded up thirty of his police officers and raced with them towards the town's bar. Word had reached--Euphrates had come to convince men to join his forces. Negada could not afford to lose his workers. The temple in which they were building was to be completed by the end of the month and they were already a month behind. What's more, was the fact that these were *his* men and he would be damned to allow any tyrant to steal them from his command. Besides, Negada thought, if he were to capture the enemy's head and send it as a gift to his Pharaoh, he might be rewarded with a pretty purse and perhaps even land.

The Overseer smiled with the thought. He whipped at his camel to go faster. Behind him, his troop kept with his speed and within minutes they reached the bar.

Riding in, Negada spotted almost a dozen of the enemy's followers standing ready for him.

They must have heard them coming, he thought as he slowed his charge to get a better grasp of the situation. He scanned the area, calculating his opposition. Ten, he counted, finding the last man standing between two buildings. He glimpsed around again. Was this

119

all the tyrant travelled into town with? There had to be more—this was too easy.

Negada felt a surge of anger flood his body as another thought hit him. An insult to my competence for him to think he could have my town at the behest of a handful of men! he grimaced in vain. Filled with anger, he turned his head to call back to his troop. "Fire at will!"

The first arrow to strike came from the enemy, which was shortly followed by another. Beside Lord Negada, two men fell from their camels, first the man on his right, then the man on his left. Negada watched in shock as the stricken men tumbled from their animals to their death.

Rage boiled inside him. "I said fire!" he yelled out again in a heated jolt of madness that made his temples feel as if they would burst. He glanced around his surroundings. Certainly this time his men got some arrows off. They were skilled shooters, trained to ride and shoot arrows towards a target at high speed. But, as two men from his troop pulled up beside him to fill the positions of the fallen officers, Lord Negada watched as they too were struck down in the same manner.

Clearly, the enemies were sending him a message but Negada wasn't about to heed it. "Charge!" he commanded, racing forward so they were too close for the bowmen.

Negada drove his camel towards one of the outlaws with his axe raised above his head. He brought his weapon down into the skull of the enemy, where it stuck. He could hear the man's squeal behind him as he raced on. Negada drew his sword, clashed blades with another rebel as he rode directly into what would become their battleground. He soared past another man, who charged forward, weapon pointing. The man circled on his heels.

A strange noise erupted around Lord Negada—it was piercing, howling, and it echoed up into the night, as if calling out to the heavens. Suddenly, the Overseer of Wasebet realized what it was—his camel was collapsing, making the deafening noise from pain. The animal's two left legs had been sliced from the knee.

Negada sheathed his sword, braced himself for the fall, hoping he wouldn't find himself under the fifteen hundred-pound beast. He hit the ground, rolled, just escaping the crushing body of the camel. Thinking fast, Negada rolled onto his back and prepared himself for a lunge from one of his rivalries. As suspected, a man was already racing towards him, his blade pointing out, ready to slash.

Negada kicked his feet into the man's stomach, thrusting him away, lending time so he could jump to his own feet and unsheathe his sword. But, no sooner than he was on his feet did his assailant attack. His sword crashed against his opponent's, back and forth. The Overseer tried to keep the enemy's blade from reaching him, but he was not as skilled as his rival and soon grew tired. The enemy's blade came towards him in a final blow. Negada held his breath, watched the last moment of his life swing towards him. He closed his eyes, waited. It was the longest moment of his life and it unbearably drew out. He almost wished the sword would strike him faster, end his agony—but no blade came.

Reluctantly, Negada opened his eyes. To his surprise he saw the enemy lying at his feet. Lord Negada panted in relief as he gaped at the dead body. His life was spared! The gods had saved him!

He looked at his comrade who had thrown the knife which saved his life and nodded with gratitude. As Negada observed his surroundings, took in his dead camel and dead rival, an uncanny feeling wisped over him.

It must be certain I am to take Euphrates' head, he thought as he glanced towards the stone wall of the bar that separated him from his reward. What other reason would I have been spared?

He glimpsed towards the entrance. Two of Euphrates' men guarded the door, fighting off the policemen that tried to get past them. Already three bodies lay slain.

With the front entrance not an option, Lord Negada searched the area for a camel that had been separated from its rider during the fight. Spotting one, he rushed towards it, got onto its back. He rode around to the rear of the building, brought the camel up against the wall. Negada stood on the camel, pulled himself up onto the top ledge of the thick wall and peered down into the bar below.

〰〰

INSIDE, EUPHRATES STILL tried to convince the men. He had to stir them—drive their spirits to crave more in order to inspire them to fight for his cause.

121

"This woman you call Pharaoh may keep peace in Egypt, but quiet peace kills a country. We are conquerors living in the greatest Kingdom on earth. When we are quiet for too long, the world forgets this and they build great armies with the desire to rule our land." Euphrates turned to glare at the man who outwardly opposed him. "So, what do I offer?" he asked pointedly. Raising his battleaxe high above his head, he spun back to face the room and roared, "A greater Egypt!"

Some of the men banged their cups on the table to show their desire for his promise.

"Join me," Euphrates yelled out over the noise, "and I promise as we gain riches, the men who follow me now will be rewarded lavishly—"

"The men who follow him will hang from the gates!" a heavy voice cut in.

Euphrates looked towards it.

On top of the far wall a man clothed in battle uniform, wearing a white kilt covered with a leather tunic and purple sash bearing his symbol looked down with a long sword gripped in his hand. Euphrates recognized the symbol as one he had seen marked at the gates of town.

Somiset stepped forward but Euphrates waved him off.

"And you are...?" Euphrates probed, stepping closer.

"I am Negada, Lord of Wasebet and Overseer of the Builders, and you have not only crossed my territory but you have crossed me!"

"Quite the introduction. Did you rehearse that?" Euphrates mocked. He bowed his head without taking his eyes from the man. "A pleasure to meet you." Straightening, Euphrates added. "But, I'm afraid this meeting will have to be short lived."

Negada jumped from the wall onto a table then onto the floor. "I agree. My men need to get home to rest so they can finish our Pharaoh's temple."

"If that's your concern then there's no need to worry and no need to complete it," Euphrates retorted. "Your Pharaoh won't have the throne for long."

"She will not only have her throne but she will have *your* head as a gift from me!" Negada held his sword forward. He lunged towards Euphrates. But, before he made it more than three steps, Euphrates pitched his axe. It landed in Negada's stomach, stopping him short in his tracks. The Lord of Wasebet fell to his knees, gasping for air.

Blood spilled from his mouth as he looked down at the axe that tore into his gut.

Euphrates walked over to him, took hold of the axe handle. "I'm sorry my friend," he said, placing a sincere hand on the man's shoulder. "But, I warned this would be short lived." Euphrates grabbed his dagger from his waist side and as he pulled the axe from Negada's stomach, he pierced the dagger into the man's heart—a stomach wound could take up to twenty minutes to find death and the poor man didn't need to suffer.

Euphrates removed the blade. Negada collapsed.

Euphrates closed his eyes briefly; exhaled. He did not want this but he knew it was part of the trials he would have to face at times.

Slowly, he looked up at the room. "I believe you are all free to make your own decisions now. Who will join me?"

Euphrates' opposer stood up. "I choose loyalty," he said as he marched towards the door where Somiset stood with his arms crossed. The large man took powerful strides across the room. He stopped within an inch of Somiset, daring Somiset to even try to stop him. Both men were of equal size.

"Let him go," Euphrates commanded, admiring his allegiance.

Somiset stepped aside.

Euphrates turned to the room. "All those who want to leave with him, go now."

Several men stood, took their leave but most remained. When the last man made his exit, Euphrates addressed those remaining.

"Welcome," he began, holding his arms out in an embracing gesture. "Those who know of any man who is not present here tonight and who would be willing to return Egypt to her glory, go and inform him their new King releases them from their corvee duty and grants them entitlements as his soldier." Euphrates spun, headed to the door.

As he exited, Somiset stepped forward. "Tomorrow, at the second hour of light, we will be assigning men to positions within the army. All those interested, find yourselves here."

XX

$\mathcal{T}$HE NEXT MORNING just before the second hour of light, a long line already began to wind its way down the street.

Euphrates rode in from the outskirts of town where he and his men had made their camp. The three men who were lost in the rampage of last night were already put to rest underground.

Instead of royal garments, Euphrates wore a standard linen tunic with a leather belt at his waist, which held his weapons. His claim as King was received. The men were lining up to show their acceptance of him as their leader.

Behind Euphrates seven men followed, including Somiset and Tuthiken. They rode in a slow canter alongside the line that curved down the street towards the bar. As they passed, men yelled out, "A King for Egypt!" while boys ran beside their horses.

Euphrates dismounted his horse, went into the bar. He selected a table near the back and sat facing the door. Somiset stood beside him and Menna—a man they discovered could scribe—sat in the seat next to Euphrates and began setting up his writing tools. Once they were all settled, Euphrates called out to Tuthiken who was at the door. "Start letting them in."

"Let them in," Tuthiken echoed to the men who were positioned outside to manage the crowd.

The bar owner marched in. He was the first man to arrive that morning and most probably had slept at the bar. He took it upon himself to contain the crowd outside all morning until Euphrates arrived.

Euphrates looked up at him. "Name?"

"Harkum."

Menna wrote it down.

"Weapon?"

Harkum lifted up the small bow, which he had kept by his side the night prior. "I am skilled with this short bow and I enjoy using it," he proclaimed with passion.

Euphrates nodded. "Make him a Standard-Bearer in Tuthiken's company."

Harkum grinned, pleased to be given a decent rank.

"Next!" Euphrates called out.

The next man stepped up.

"Name?"

"Pathor."

"Weaponry?"

"Whatever I have in my hands," he replied with what appeared to be a sinful smile spread across his lips.

Euphrates looked at Menna. "Hathor Company," he instructed.

The day continued with the long line of men stepping up to the table to give their name and skills and to receive their post. The army was broken down as it always was in Egypt. Officers were in charge of small squads with Lieutenants in charge of slightly more men. *The Greatest of Fifty* was the lowest commander in charge of a platoon of fifty men. Above him was the Standard-Bearer, in charge of two hundred men and the Adjutant in charge of 250 men. They answered to the Captain of the Troop. Organized into companies of five hundred soldiers strong, the Battalion Commander led this company and reported to the General, which in Euphrates situation there was no need for.

The Pharaoh, however, would have multiple divisions each numbering several thousand men. Her army was divided into the northern and southern corps, totaling over thirty thousand dedicated soldiers before calling regular men out to duty. Fortunately, these companies were spread throughout Egypt and would take time to come together. Nevertheless, Euphrates needed to get as many men on his side as quick as possible.

Euphrates glanced over Menna's list, which had already taken up several papyri. By late afternoon they had seen over three hundred men with still many left to go. Euphrates hadn't considered how many men it took to build a monumental temple. There had to be over a thousand, which of course he was glad for since in war, more was always better.

"Next!" Euphrates called out, not taking his eyes from the list.

A young boy stepped up to the table. He peered confidently at Euphrates. "I want to fight," he said.

Euphrates gazed up from the parchments and sized him. "You're too young," he stated as he turned his attention back to the list.

"But, I am fearless and ready."

Euphrates looked up again, eyed him for a moment. The boy stood with his bare chest pushed out, his chin tipped up high in an attempt to make himself look bigger. He was thin—if not, scrawny—and he looked like he wasn't much older than an infant.

"Do you know the cause for which you wish to fight?" Euphrates asked.

"Yes," answered the boy. "So, Egypt can have a King."

"And, what is wrong with your Pharaoh?"

"She's a woman and women shouldn't be Pharaohs. They are too weak."

"Just as little boys shouldn't be warriors," Euphrates pointed.

"But, I am fearless!" begged the boy.

"So may be your Pharaoh Queen. Perhaps you should open your mind before you ask others to do so."

The boy slumped, understanding Euphrates' point.

"How old are you?" Euphrates questioned, intrigued by the boy's spirit.

"Eleven," he mumbled.

"Your name?"

"Barin."

"Well, Barin, if we're still at war in three years, come and see me then." Euphrates glanced up over the boy's head. "Next!" he called.

A large man stepped up in front of the boy. Barin squeezed his way back to the table.

"But, no war lasts three years!" he complained.

"A great many wars have lasted three years. But, I pray you're right that this one will be settled long before I ever see you again. Now, get out of here." Euphrates turned his attention back to the man standing over the boy. "Your name?" he asked.

"But, I can use a sword," Barin declared. He held up a sword almost equaling his height. His expression pleading.

Somiset stepped up to the boy. "You heard him," he said, guiding him with a powerful hand by the shoulder. "Come back in three years."

Barin moaned in defeat. He shrugged Somiset's hand off his

shoulder and stormed out, dragging his sword behind him.

Euphrates chuckled as he watched the young boy leave. "You got to give it to him," he said, looking at Somiset, "the boy's got heart."

By the first hour of darkness, Euphrates was exhausted. He ordered Tuthiken to send the rest of the men off until morning. Tuthiken stepped outside the door and relayed the message.

Euphrates stood, stretched. "How many so far?" he asked Menna.

"Seven hundred and forty-nine."

"Not bad for a day's work," he smiled. He headed towards the door. Somiset followed. Menna gathered his parchments and trailed behind.

Stepping outside of the bar, Euphrates gleamed. "Seven hundred and forty-nine," he informed Tuthiken and the four other men.

Their faces lit up.

"And, still more to come," chimed Tuthiken, looking around at the crowd of men who were turned away for the night.

Euphrates mounted his horse, the smile still tacked on his face as he took a refreshing breath. "I like this town."

He dug his heels into his stallion and rode off. Behind him, his men did the same.

Twilight began to lose its cast to darkness as they rode out of town and back to their campsite.

In his thoughts, Euphrates calculated his numbers—almost two thousand men and still not enough to contest the Queen's army. Most of his men were unskilled fighters—workmen, supporters, believers but not soldiers. However, Euphrates did not care. He would train them and they would fight. Besides, desire and passion made strong fighters and his men had much of both in their want for a king.

Euphrates straightened himself on his horse. Yes, he thought. Desire and passion—victory will be mine. *He could taste it.*

Before long, the riders reached their camp, which seemed unusually still and quiet. Euphrates looked around uneasily. Throughout the campsite small fires burned unattended. The campgrounds almost seemed abandoned with empty tents and beds laid out but no one on them. Yet, before worry could settle in, a drifting noise greeted the riders and urged them to follow.

At one end the campground, music soared up into the starry night sky. Men gathered around a large fire, cheering and whistling at whatever was taking place inside the ring. Curious, Euphrates and the others galloped down towards them and dismounted. Euphrates headed to the circle. He slid through the onlookers to the front, losing Somiset and Tuthiken amongst the crowd of men. As he made his way forward, he was able to see why the men flocked together.

Inside the middle of the circle, five beautiful women—scantily dressed in short gold chain skirts with jingling jewellery around their wrists, ankles and in their hair—moved seductively, teasing and taunting their audience. A group of men from Euphrates' army sat together playing instruments, adding music to their dance.

Euphrates examined the group and spotted Menenthop strumming his lute. He began to make his way over to him, but before he made it half way, two of the women caught him. They danced over to Euphrates, took him by the arms, pulled him further into the middle of the ring. Euphrates tried to refuse but the women wouldn't let go and the men cheered him on.

All five women surrounded him, sliding their bodies against his as they moved to the beat of their dance. With the onlookers rooting in good jest, Euphrates began to dance with one of the women. Everyone cheered. Some men heckled for him to take her as his prize.

Euphrates eyed her. She was beautiful and yet he didn't want her. The woman flirted, begged with gestures for him to take her. Yet, despite her beauty and sexual attraction, the instant Euphrates found his opportunity to make his escape he spun the dancer around and stepped away.

Euphrates headed over to Menenthop. He sat down on the kilim next to him, giving him an inquisitive look.

"They arrived at nightfall insisting on giving us a dance for bravery," Menenthop chuckled as he looked back over at the belly dancers.

"Somehow I think it's a dance for more than that," Euphrates laughed. He watched as a dancer rubbed her body against her prey. "And, now I have a problem—only five beautiful women and a slew of horny men!"

They laughed.

Menenthop looked at Euphrates. "They can save their frustrations for battle," he jeered.

"They?" Euphrates questioned.

With a champion's smile, Menenthop pointed towards one of the women. "Yes—*they*—because she is mine." The dancer caught him pointing, blew him a kiss.

Euphrates chuckled as he turned his attention towards the woman he had danced with.

The woman winked, allowing a sultry smile to almost curl her lips just before she licked them.

Euphrates returned a small nod then looked away.

Two of the women picked up long wooden poles. They pushed them into the fire. The ends burst into flames. They waved them around in the air so the burning ends drew a pattern of light through the night sky. The three other dancers moved in to dance around the flames, bending and contorting their bodies just in time to miss the sweeping fire.

The men watched enraptured. The sounds of gasps and sighs filled the air as the flaming end of a pole came within an inch of a woman until the dancer was safe. The entertainment was exactly what the men needed to boost their spirits and to make the long days and nights of their campaign not seem so long for at least one night. Even Euphrates permitted himself to forget about his troubles to enjoy the dance, glad for its arrival. He leaned back on his elbows, his legs stretched out in front of him, captivated by the moment. Beside him Menenthop strummed on his lute, accompanying the other musicians in an upbeat song.

The night seemed perfect with the stars brightly shining down from the clear black sky, the cool air absent of a sandy breeze, and the warmth of the fire glowing against the striking bodies of the maidens. The lively sounds of the men blended with the vibrant music, creating a peaceful atmosphere in its noise.

Yes, thought Euphrates, glimpsing the joyful faces of the men, the night was just what they needed.

Euphrates spotted Somiset pushing abruptly through the circle, causing a commotion and breaking the lightheartedness of the moment. Somiset emerged from the crowd of men with a stern look on his face and peered around the fire. Locating Euphrates, he marched forward, brushing off a dancer as he stomped by.

Euphrates sat up. He knew something serious must have charged Somiset as his steps were full of purpose.

Somiset stopped at the foot of Euphrates. "A horse rides in from the west," he informed.

A horse? Euphrates thought as he leapt to his feet and tried to look up over the heads of the men. He was unable to see anything; nonetheless, he knew what it meant.

Horses were rare in Egypt. Only a small number were imported into the country by the Pharaoh, which were stabled at her palace. Even the few Euphrates owned he had brought in from the land of Syria. *A horse*, Euphrates thought again as he drifted into his memory:

HE WAS SEVENTEEN. He was being sent on a quest by his guardian Menes, to find a man by the name of Tushratta in the foreign land of Syria. Even though it was an empire that was regarded as one of Egypt's enemies, Euphrates was told he must go. His entire childhood was geared towards preparing for battle and Tushratta was known to be a master of many weapons. Euphrates begged Menes to allow him to stay, but the man insisted it was out of his control.

"Consider it a special gift," Menes said to Euphrates the morning before he left. That was the last day Euphrates had seen Menes. He spent ten years with the man and had come to revere him like a father; then, it was over.

Obediently, Euphrates journeyed from Buhen, a city in the land of Wawat at the northern most part of Egypt's fortified region, to Syria, which was far beyond Egypt's southern border. When at last he arrived in Syria, as promised, Tushratta was expecting him.

"You're here to learn, not to make friends," the older man snapped after Euphrates greeted him with a smile. Once that was clear, Tushratta opened the door.

For three years Euphrates remained in Syria, learning from his strict master in a country enemy to Egypt. Many times he inquired about whom would sponsor such an act but Tushratta never gave an answer.

It was during that time Euphrates first laid eyes upon the beauty and power of a horse with its carved body and lightening speed. He fell in love with the majestic creature and desired one for himself.

One day, Euphrates came home to find a horse waiting for him. When he went to thank his master for the gift, Tushratta only glanced up and said, "It's not me you need to thank." But, again no name was given.

Although in the desert the camel with its ability to endure days without water was much more practical, Euphrates vowed, when he became King, he would adapt the horse to Egypt.

※

"HE RIDES WITH a flag," Somiset informed, breaking Euphrates' memory. "It's her messenger."

The Pharaoh-Queen of Egypt, Euphrates thought as he pushed his way out of the human circle around the fire. He reached the outer ring, looked towards the west and sure enough, not too far in the distance a rider approached, holding the flag of a messenger to signal he rides without threat.

A message from the Pharaoh. Euphrates almost felt anxious. He marched towards the messenger with Somiset in tow. By the time they reached the messenger, the noise from around the fire was a faint murmur in the distance.

They halted as the rider drew his horse to a stop in front of them.

Euphrates glared up at the young man and remembered him as the one who sat to the right of the Queen wearing the emblem of the Gold Scorpion, *Friend of the Pharaoh.*

"I bring a message from the *Neb-taui* King," the messenger proclaimed.

Euphrates chuckled. "So, she calls herself *King?*"

"Indeed. She obtains all positions of a *King,*" Allegi quipped in a sharp, flat tone.

"Really?" Euphrates challenged. "And, when we are at war on the battlefield, what position will she obtain then?"

"Behind her armour, leading the army as a Kings' hereditary title, Commander in Chief, would have pharaohs do."

For a moment, Euphrates thought he heard the young man wrong. He studied the messenger as he digested his words. Did he mean to say she would be at battle fighting with her men? A woman amongst warriors?

The messenger must have read his thoughts. "She is skilled at weaponry, trained since a child from the best masters summoned from all over Egypt and the lands beyond."

The lands beyond? Euphrates repeated to himself.

"She's not your average woman." Allegi's glare intensified. "She is a *King.*"

The image clung in Euphrates' mind and although he stared at Allegi, he looked right through him. A female warrior? he thought. Leading men in battle as *Commander in Chief?*

Euphrates had heard this Pharaoh had gone to battles with her father but he assumed she went as a spectator, staying back, protected by guards.

"The message," Allegi said, breaking Euphrates' thoughts by drawing attention to the scroll he held out.

Euphrates looked at the messenger. "Bring it," he ordered, spinning briskly and stomping off.

Allegi watched after him for a moment before he dismounted. He took Nefer's reigns to follow but Somiset stepped in front. The large man huffed down on him with a gesture to take the horse.

"I believe you already have one of my horses," Allegi spurned. He stepped around Somiset, doubled his strides to catch up with Euphrates.

Inside his large tent, Euphrates took a seat in a chair facing the entrance and waited.

Moments later, Allegi appeared in the doorway. They studied each other scornfully before Euphrates broke the silence. "So, what does your *King* want?"

Allegi stepped further inside, held the scroll out to Euphrates. "She wishes to meet with you again."

"Again?" Euphrates repeated. "For what purpose?" He eyed the scroll in Allegi's hand then waved it off. "Read it to me."

"She did not have me write it—it may be private."

Euphrates considered the messenger's statement. *Private?* He cocked his head. "Read it to me," he insisted.

Hesitantly, Allegi broke the seal on the parchment, unrolled it and read:

> *My great brother and enemy,*
>
> *I can only imagine the weight of grief which you carry in your plight to gain back something as beautiful as Egypt that was once promised to you. And, even though the suns of time have changed your fate, I look to support you.*
>
> *I wish not to bring war upon the people of Egypt and I believe that together we can arrive at a more peaceful arrangement. Before we shed any more blood, I wish to meet with you to discuss this option.*
>
> *Your sister, Pharaoh of the Two Lands, Nitiqreti, Tigris of Egypt.*

Allegi lowered the scroll. He looked at Euphrates who was momentarily lost in his thoughts.

Together we can arrive at a more peaceful arrangement, Euphrates silently pondered. *An arrangement.* He let out a deep sigh and stood. "A meeting." The words seemed only for himself until he looked at Allegi. "What arrangement does she wish to discuss?"

"I don't—"

"There is no arrangement!" Euphrates cut in, not wanting an answer. "Unless she is willing to give up her crowns, there is no arrangement!"

Euphrates moved over to a table. He poured two drinks, carried them to Allegi, and offered the young man a cup.

"I don't really drink alcohol," Allegi said, refusing the beverage.

"Good. Neither do I—*really*." Euphrates pushed the cup into Allegi's hand. "It's grape juice."

Euphrates took a gulp of his drink, went back to his chair, sat down. He kicked a trunk out in front of him, motioned Allegi to sit. "Join me."

Uneasily, Allegi moved to the trunk. He felt a little awkward about joining the enemy but he joined him nonetheless.

Before he was fully seated, the self-proclaimed King bore into him with questions.

"Tell me about your Pharaoh," Euphrates pressed. "What is she like?"

"She's kind—"

"Yes, yes—kind, forgiving; like all Pharaohs. But, I want to know what she is like when the doors are shut." Euphrates' eyes narrowed. He leaned forward on his last word as if daring Allegi to tell.

Without answering, Allegi studied the rebel King contemptuously. Why was he asking this? Did he really think he would divulge secrets about his Pharaoh?

"I really must be leaving," Allegi finally said. "Preferably with your answer." He took a cautious sip of the juice as he eyed Euphrates over the rim of the cup.

"Why has she not wed?"

Incensed, Allegi stood. "Your response?" he demanded, pretending not to hear the question.

"Answer my question first."

"Because her parents died before they arranged her marriage. Your turn."

"Yes. Can she not find a suitor herself? By gods, she is Pharaoh."

Again, Allegi ignored his question. "Very well then, she wishes you to travel to her palace. She promises your protection—"

"Fine. Is she so proud that she fears to lose her power to a husband?"

"My vessel will await you on the Nile, slightly south of here. Bring as many men as you desire. She is honourable; you will not be tricked or harmed."

"Good," Euphrates said with a phony smile. "She realizes her throne is not secured as long as she remains childless?"

Allegi drank back the juice, pushed the cup into Euphrates' hand. He wasn't going to play his game. "Goodnight, sir," he said briskly.

He didn't wait for a response.

Euphrates watched the door flap fall close before he stood and began to pace. "What arrangement," he wondered. "Could it be—"

The door opened again. Euphrates spun to face it. He expected to see the royal messenger but instead the woman he had danced with earlier stepped in.

Slowly, she walked towards him with lust in her eyes. Euphrates remained still. She took the two cups out of his hands, placed them on the nearest chest.

"Your men have sent me to help you relax," she said as she leaned towards him, running her finger up his body towards his neck. She bit his earlobe. "I have just the thing to do that," she whispered, blowing into his ear so a chill ran up his spine. With her finger, she pushed his chin towards her face, kissed him—a soft, luring kiss. She moved away, smiled seductively, ran her tongue over her lips. She took him by the hands, guided him towards the bed. "Come," she breathed, "let me help you to lose your troubles for one night."

Euphrates watched her. She had a beauty any man would want and yet, some part of him didn't want her. He stopped, pulled his hands from hers. "Thank you, but there's no need—"

"I want to," she purred, kissing him again. She drew her words out so they sounded long and soft, "Oh, Per'a—"

Euphrates pulled away. He looked at her as he forced a thought out of his mind. "No, I can't," he said softly shaking his head, his words shocking even himself. "Please... leave."

For a moment, Euphrates thought he lost his mind. The woman was striking. How could he say no? It had been awhile... since he was in the city of Nekhen rounding up men for his cause at least a month ago. He had met a woman during an evening festivity and spent the night with her. The next day, he left with only a farewell kiss. The affair meant nothing to either of them, just a night of enjoyment.

Euphrates eyed the attractive woman standing before him. She had smooth dark skin, voluptuous breasts and thick lips.

This means nothing, he told himself, just a night of pleasure. Still, something held him back. She tried to kiss him again. He found the same thought pushing him away.

The woman stepped back, confused. "Why would you refuse?"

"I'm sorry, I—I just can't for reasons I don't even understand."

The lust diminished in her eyes, replaced by a sour scowl. "You insult me! How dare you!" She raised her arm to slap him but Euphrates caught it.

"Now, you may *definitely* leave," he said in an angry tone, forcefully dropping her arm.

The dancer's face grew red. "You are pathetic!" she hissed. Her lips tightened as she drew in a deep breath. Before Euphrates knew what the woman was doing, she spat in his face, spun, then swiftly stormed out.

Euphrates wiped the spit from his cheek. He shook his head as he watched after her. *Why did he refuse?* he wondered. He denied the answer that came to him, tossing it from his mind. It was only one night. Since when did he have discretion? She was an attractive woman. He was bound to no one.

Euphrates huffed heavily, erasing all his thoughts. He went to his chair, slumped down. He kicked his feet up on the chest he had pulled out for the messenger. He spotted the scroll the young man left behind, leaned forward, scooped it off the trunk.

The Pharaoh, he thought. He remembered the first moment they met. She had raised her head and caught his eyes, capturing him like a fish in a trap. Life seemed to stand still and for a brief instant she had stolen his breath.

Euphrates opened the scroll, read through it.

An arrangement, he thought.

〜〜〜

OUTSIDE, ALLEGI QUIETLY led Nefer through the campgrounds. Most of Euphrates' men were crowded around a fire and seemed to be celebrating, which aided Allegi to go unnoticed. He tip-toed past the tents, trying not to disturb those who did not partake in the festivities by the fire.

Deep within the centre of the camp, Allegi found what he was looking for--a square fenced area containing eight horses. He scanned the pen; found Qare—his large black stallion.

While the camels were left together on the outskirts of the grounds, the horses were caged and closely guarded against desert bandits who would find a lofty pay for the creature. Allegi glimpsed around, knowing someone would be nearby.

He moved cautiously towards the pen. As he approached, Qare caught his scent. The horse snorted, went to the fence.

Allegi let go of Nefer's reigns. "Stay," he whispered. He left Nefer between two tents, somewhat out of the way and somewhat hidden. He moved towards the horses' pen.

Qare grew anxious, making more noise. "Shh," Allegi whispered, looking around to see if anyone had heard the horse's commotion. Qare's ears twitched. Allegi stopped in his tracks to listen.

Someone approached.

"What are you fussing over?" a man asked, nearing the pen.

Allegi dove behind a tent. He observed the man whose attention was on the horses' in the pen.

"Calm yourself," the man said to Qare. He patted the horse down the bridge of its nose. Qare continued to fuss, moving excitedly, grunting, snorting, and shaking his head.

"What is it?" he asked, spinning around to look behind him. There was nothing in the darkness except for the faint light cast by the dwindling fires around the tents. "What do you see?" He examined their surroundings and caught something moving. The man raised his club. "Who's there?" he demanded. He headed towards the tents, peering through the dark. "What the—" he stuttered, confused. "How'd you get out here?" He grabbed Nefer's reigns, led him towards the pen.

Allegi crouched further down, watching with anxiety. It was only a matter of time before the guard would realize Nefer wasn't from the horse pen and he was saddled.

Allegi scoped the area. Scooping up a rock, he rushed towards the man. Before the large man knew what hit him, he collapsed to the ground, unconscious.

"That ought to hurt in the morning." Allegi dropped the rock beside the man's limp body. He grabbed Nefer's reigns, jumped on his back, whistled at Qare. Qare rose on his hind legs and neighed.

"Come on!" Allegi yelled in a loud whisper. He glanced around the area to see if anyone else had heard them. Down by the fire, the group of men were beginning to disperse.

Allegi looked back at his stallion. The horse was trotting around the inner fence of the pen gathering speed.

"Come on Qare. You can do it!" He dug his heels into Nefer and gave the command for the horse to bolt. Behind him Qare raced towards the fence, bounded over it, cleared the wooden rails.

XXI

*M*ORNING HAD JUST woken the earth as Euphrates headed towards the Vessel of the Royal Messenger with five of his men in tow and Tuthiken at his side. He left Somiset to finish enlisting men in the army and instructed him to ride on the morrow out of Wasebet. Somiset would head to Pa-suk and wait for Euphrates who was due to join in just over two weeks.

The self-proclaimed King and his troop of men rode on horseback. Euphrates thought arriving at the Great House on horses would make an impression, proving he was no mere commoner. He wanted the Pharaoh and her palace administrators to see him for what he was—a *King*.

Looking into the distance, Euphrates spotted the ship waiting as promised on the Nile.

An arrangement, he thought. What kind of an arrangement would the Pharaoh want to make with someone who imposed war on her country? Perhaps she sought only to delay his strike while she gathered her army. Yet, Euphrates didn't care. He wanted to see her, discover her intentions and look into her eyes, to determine if what he believed he had seen in them was true.

Reaching the ship, the riders halted, dismounted their steeds and led them up the plank of the boat. Above, Ramska and Allegi loomed over the ledge, watching them come.

Euphrates reached the top first. He presented a small bow to the Captain, then the Royal Messenger without taking his eyes from theirs.

They returned the gesture.

"A great day to sail," Euphrates teased, looking up at the clear blue sky, which was starved of any kind of a breeze.

"That's why we have rowers," the Captain responded with a large smile.

Euphrates couldn't help but smile back. The Captain seemed to be the sort who didn't allow anything to get to him. His eyes sparkled with friendliness and even when his smile disappeared from his mouth, his eyes still beamed on their own.

Instantly, Euphrates liked him.

"Come, I will show you where to stay the horses," Allegi said, turning.

Euphrates followed, giving the Captain a small nod and smile as he passed.

The barge was over fifty feet long with a bow that curved up towards the sky into the head of a cobra. Near the stern, two cabins were stacked one on top of the other. The crew numbered thirty-two men—fifteen oars along each side, one man at the stern to control the rudder and the Captain to give commands.

Euphrates trailed Allegi down the boat's length with his men behind him until they arrived at an open stable where two horses were tied up. Euphrates recognized one of the stallions. He smirked as he shot Allegi a knowing look, trying to conceal his admiration for the young messenger.

In turn, Allegi hid the grin attempting to creep across his face but his eyes gave him away—they were filled with pride.

"I intended to bring seven men with me," Euphrates quipped as he tied his horse to the post, "but I was short a horse."

Allegi patted Qare on the back. "You were always short a horse."

XXII

"WHAT DO YOU mean you invited him here?" Ibimpetus demanded through a heavy breath. "Did you not think it wise to consult me first?" The Vizier stopped at the window again and peered out. A tiny ship grew in the distance as it made its way down the Nile. Soon it would pass Cheti's vessel. The Vizier hoped the enemy would not take it for anything more than another ship travelling the river.

Many boats came and went up and down the Nile each day. There were merchant ships, fishing crafts, ferries that carried passengers and funerary ferries that carried the dead to their final resting place. Seafaring barges imported goods from beyond the Delta and the land of Punt. Transport ships moved cattle, grain and other commodities from city to city including the royal boats, which brought revenues to the royal storehouses. Large ports linked the capitals of the provinces to one another making the Nile a key point of travel and a busy route.

Cheti left the palace that afternoon. He had arrived only a few nights prior to inform Chephren that Euphrates was planning to seize the Fortress of Ipu. This information was immediately delivered to the Council, including the Pharaoh, wherein Tigris gave orders to reinforce the garrison.

Cheti was now on his way to warn the Overseer of the fortress and call upon Dkew-qa clan in the neighbouring town to aid their defence. He travelled on a warrior ship, which stood out from the other vessels—the Vizier hoped it would be overlooked.

Glaring out the window, Ibimpetus felt his temples pulsate with anger. This is not good, he thought. It is never good to let the enemy know what you are doing before you do it. The thought made him more livid. He turned to face Tigris. "What kind of an *arrangement* do you intend?"

Tigris stared at him blankly. She was consumed by her own thoughts and quite frankly didn't care how the Vizier regarded her decision. What *they* had done was wrong and if he had to face his consequences then so be it. To her, his anger seemed to lean towards his own concerns; his own guilt—

Guilt? Tigris laughed to herself. She glanced at the Vizier and wondered if he was even capable of it. One had to have a conscience first.

Ibimpetus glared at her with fiery eyes.

She looked away. No, she thought, he is only capable of fury and self-righteous beliefs. She tried to remember if she had ever seen him laugh. She couldn't.

Tigris peered out the window again, anxious to see her enemy—excited even. Her stomach fluttered with anticipation of the thought that he would soon be here, standing before her, in her presence. She breathed deeply and shifted in her seat.

"I asked, what kind of arrangement do you intend?" the Vizier persisted.

Tigris slowly turned her head to look at him. "To govern the north."

"Are you mad!" Ibimpetus stormed from the window towards her. "You already have a Governor of Upper Egypt. Might I remind you, he is your cousin!"

"I will transfer him to the northern fortification and make him Ambassador of Kush," Tigris replied, calmly.

"Do you honestly think he won't take offence?"

"Do you *honestly* think I care? The further away he is the better. He covets this throne."

"And, do you presume your enemy does not?" The Vizier's voice was loud and strained; tension gripped every part of him. He glowered at Tigris with heavy breaths.

Tigris rose from her Seat of Estate. They were in her audience chamber where he had come to find her. No one else was present. The doors were closed.

Calmly, the Queen stepped down from her raised chair and passed the Vizier as she went to stand by the window. "He won't agree," she said softly as she looked outside, silently wishing he would.

"Then why bother to ask?"

Tigris watched the boat draw closer, allowing a lengthy moment to draw out before she gave her answer, "Because I am a fair Pharaoh. His revenge is just and his claim equally so. Compromise is honourable. And," she added, spinning to look at the long reigned Prime Minister of the country, "it bides me time to secure the Fortress of Ipu."

Ibimpetus smiled.

On the sixth hour of light, when the sun shone directly down on the earth, the palace gates were opened. Trumpets and horns blared, announcing the arrival of the self-proclaimed King.

Tigris had returned to her audience chamber after attending to other court affairs to keep herself busy until Ramska's ship reached the barque station. Now she paced impatiently. She would meet with Euphrates in the Great Chamber of Geb where she would sit on the Great Throne dressed in the fashion of a King so Euphrates would see her for what she was—a *King*.

Already clad in a *shendyt* kilt and *nemes* headdress, Tigris wore a white piece of linen wrapped over one shoulder and around her body covering her breasts but bearing her belly so the kilt would be seen in its full glory as it would on a man. The *nemes* headdress had blue and gold stripes with an *ureaus* on the front—the cobra symbol of the Pharaoh.

Yes, she was Pharaoh. She strived hard to be recognized as such and she would not let anyone take it away from her. In years to come, Egyptians would remember her name as one of the great Kings. Indeed, she would fight for Egypt.

Tigris stopped pacing and eyed the terrace. She tried to keep herself from going out onto the balcony to watch for her enemy. She didn't want him to see her anticipation—her excitement.

Excited to see the enemy? Even the thought was clouded with disgrace. How she hated herself for having it. And yet, she continued to stare at the open doorway unable to tear herself away.

A light breeze drifted in and surrounded her as if beckoning her outside. The terraced balcony extended from the audience chamber giving her a clear view of most of the palace grounds. The high open wall, which led onto the balcony, was columned off to create doorways which supplied light into the room and fresh air in the hot summer months. During the colder times of year, long thick woven rugs were draped from the ceiling in order to help shut out the cold. Large windows offered additional views within her rooms while the terrace off the bathing chamber down the hall provided a lookout on the fourth side of the building. The Pharaoh had a panoramic view of her large palace complex and even beyond its outer walls.

As she stood eyeing the outside, Tigris felt herself giving in. *Argh!* she finally huffed as she stomped out onto the terrace. She couldn't help herself; just a peek.

Tigris eased her way up to the thick stone wall and peered over its ledge.

They were already here. Seven men on horseback arrived with Allegi. *Horses?* Tigris bewildered.

Watching the men dismount, she searched among them for Euphrates. When she found him, her stomach fluttered into her chest. Although he was quite a distance away by the main administrative building, she could make him out nonetheless. He was so perfectly formed: tall, muscular, handsome.

Euphrates must have felt her stare; he looked towards the balcony.

Tigris quickly stepped away from the wall.

"You shouldn't be out there," a startling voice commanded.

Tigris spun like a child caught doing something bad. The Vizier stood in the doorway glaring at her.

She decided not to respond. What could she say? Besides, if she did, it would seem like she was hiding something.

Tigris walked past him into the chamber. She headed out of the room and down the hall.

The Vizier pursued, keeping her pace. "You should keep yourself withdrawn and make him eager for your presence. Do not grant it before its time. This aids to personify your importance as Pharaoh."

"I don't need lessons, Tjat. I've had them many times with my father, I know."

"Then act like it!" he snapped.

Ibimpetus was a few steps behind her, walking with his traditional *mks* staff of office. His irritation engulfed the Queen with uneasiness. She stayed ahead of him, not allowing him to catch up.

They continued down the stairs and out into the main courtyard. Four chair bearers awaited them—two to a sedan, which they held up by poles. A servant waited by each chair holding a large palm leaf to provide them shade.

Tigris and Ibimpetus settled in their seats and gave the signal for the servants to proceed. They headed towards the royal throne room in the main government building. Euphrates was already inside, waiting in the Great Hall to be summoned in to see the Pharaoh. He wouldn't see them before they were settled on their royal seats of estate—Tigris on the Throne of Geb, Ibimpetus to her left in an elaborate chair decorated in gold and Allegi to her right on a chair equally fashioned.

The chair bearers carried the Pharaoh and Vizier through a back route of the main courtyard out of view.

The courtyard was geometrically designed but quite sparse compared to Tigris' private garden. Obelisks extended up into the sky, lining the open space while trees and plants, imported from distant places added their beauty.

The chair bearers moved along a path behind the obelisks, away from the centre of the court. Tigris and Ibimpetus said nothing more to each other.

Soon they arrived at the outer building. The chair bearers lowered the sedans. Tigris and Ibimpetus stepped down. Slipping in through the back door, they made their way down the hall to the Great Chamber of Geb. Tigris led the way into the room and to their seats.

The councillors were already seated aside from Allegi who stood inside the main door waiting. He presented a small bow to Tigris once she was settled.

"He—"

"Have him wait," Ibimpetus cut in.

Allegi bowed his head before he made his way to his seat as a guard stepped outside of the room.

Tigris gazed at the door from her high chair. *Have him wait*, she repeated to herself, so much waiting. But, she knew the Vizier was right. He should wait—especially since he caught her peeking over the balcony.

To wait.

Tigris blinked hard. The large gilded door seemed to move further and further away the longer she stared at it. It stood at the far end of the massive room, directly opposite her seat. Large columns lined the chamber, leading to the royal throne. Yet, the grand chamber felt empty in spite of the eight councillors seated in two rows, which lined the aisle to the throne. The high ceilings helped allude to its emptiness, creating an echo that caused sounds to be heard almost twice. Seats of officials not a part of the Great Ten were left in their vacancy.

Tigris could feel her anxiety grow as she watched the door. The feeling gripped her; she wanted to knead at her stomach to help soothe the sensation but she dared not for fear the Vizier would see. Ibimpetus took note of everything and she certainly did not want him to note such weakness. She discreetly drew in a deep breath, gripped the *was* sceptre tighter in her hand and tried to enjoy the breeze provided by the servants who waved their palm leaves on either sides of the throne. Yet, despite the breeze, Tigris felt her temperature rise the longer she stared at the door, knowing on the other side *he* waited—the enemy; the self-proclaimed King, whom she hated, yet didn't.

Why did she crave to see him? What was it about him that made her feel so giddy inside? She didn't believe her own feeling. How could such a feeling come over her only after having seen him once!

Oh, this is ridiculous, Tigris thought, still glaring at the thick carved door, which held him from her presence. I will not succumb to these absurd feelings, she vowed. *I will not!*

After what seemed like forever, Ibimpetus finally gave the command to allow Euphrates in.

A retainer moved from his position just inside the door. He pulled the door open only enough to slip out.

Again the door was shut.

Tigris' heart beat harder, knowing at any moment *he* would step in. Logic raced into her mind: *Stop it*, it ordered. *You fool! Stop it!*

Tigris knew the voice was right. It was insane to feel this way. Insane and impossible. *I feel nothing*, she forced, obeying her logical mind.

The door opened. Tigris held her breath. A guard led the way to the throne. Euphrates followed. His troop was not permitted in. Two retainers stepped inside the door, took their stand on either side of it.

The guard and Euphrates reached the front in single file. As the guard went to stand in his position at the bottom of the royal platform, Tigris was finally able to fully see her rival. He bore the same *nemes* headdress, a white kilt to his knees, the false beard of dominion and jewellery around his neck and wrists. Her stomach fluttered.

"How dare you wear that crown!" shot the Vizier.

Euphrates stopped at the bottom of the steps, in front of the throne and glared at the Vizier. "Ibimpetus—how nice it is to see you again." His tone was sharp and insincere. He eyed the Vizier coldly. "You of all people should know it belongs on *my* head."

Ibimpetus glared back through fiery eyes but he gave no response.

Euphrates turned his attention towards Tigris. "Was he as strict and horrid with you as a child as he was with me?"

The Queen tried to conceal her smile. Was the Vizier capable of anything else? she wanted to say, but she held back.

Euphrates presented her with a small bow. "My sovereign sister," he smiled, "fair Tigris." He bowed his head again.

Tigris returned a tiny nod but Euphrates' attention was on the councillors.

"Bow your heads in shame, councillors. Your sins have returned to weigh your conscience." Euphrates eyed every councillor but Allegi, with contempt before he spun away.

"Where are you going?" demanded the Vizier.

Euphrates went to one of the empty seats and dragged it behind him. "I see it fit," he answered, "since everyone is sitting, that I should pull up a chair."

The Vizier's eyes narrowed. "What is fit is for you to kneel before your Pharaoh!" He banged his staff against the floor to amplify his demand.

"I am *not* her servant." Euphrates defiantly took his seat. He had dragged the chair out into the middle of the room, directly in front of the Royal Throne of Geb.

Ibimpetus looked towards the retainers standing inside the doorway. He waved his index finger in the air, summoning their service. The two men marched forward, but before they made it five steps, Tigris raised her hand to stop them.

"Leave him," she ordered.

The Vizier sent her a look of disapproval. She knew she would have to explain to him later; however, she did not want the same scuffle as was on the ship—Tigris was certain her guards would lose.

Euphrates let out a deep sigh, bringing the attention back to him. He examined his chair. "A little low, but it will do..." he said as he sized the throne, "*for now.*" Euphrates sat back, extended his feet out in front of him and crossed them at the ankle.

The Royal Throne of Geb was raised on a pyramid shaped platform. It was on the third and highest step as the throne was always above all seats. The Vizier's and Allegi's seats were on the second level. Indeed, Euphrates' point was clear—he considered himself Tigris' equal.

The Vizier huffed with disdain but he withheld his comments. He remained silent until his temper settled. With a disparaging breath, Ibimpetus spoke, "The Pharaoh has considered making you Governor of the North."

Euphrates sprang upright in his seat and peered at Tigris. The look of scorn fell over his face. "*This* is your arrangement? In case you haven't realized, I already govern the north."

"I still have loyalists in Upper Egypt," Tigris retorted.

"Yes, but the majority follow *me*, which makes it *mine*."

"You don't have the force to defend your claim. Even before I call upon my allies in Kush and in Djahy my numbers are too great for you."

Euphrates stood. He took a step towards the throne, delivering his words one at a time with vehemence. *"Never—underestimate—passion!"* He looked directly into Tigris' eyes, breathing deeply.

Tigris stared back. She knew he would refuse. Though, she secretly hoped he would accept so they could meet under different circumstances—allies instead of enemies. But, there was never to be a chance of that and she knew it.

Tigris held his stare. The feelings inside her frightened her—the pound of her heart, the giddiness of her belly. Why? Why with him? *How dare she!*

Tigris wanted to leave the chamber, get away from whatever power he had over her, but she was trapped by court regimen.

She tried to contain herself. Her breaths were short and quick and seemed to have fallen in sync with his.

I feel nothing, Tigris chanted. *I feel nothing!* She continued chanting to help give herself strength as she looked him in his eyes.

Look them in the eye, she could hear her father's voice say. But, her heart beat with fervour and the fear Euphrates could see it overwhelmed her.

Tigris held his stare. Why did it seem to go on so long? Or was it not long at all?

Allegi watched silently but he was more interested in the look on the Vizier's face.

The Vizier studied them—the way they were staring at each other—he didn't like it, but he deliberately observed them with scrutiny before he cut in, "If you accept this offer, you will no longer rule unlawfully. It is a much better position than the one you have now."

Euphrates finally withdrew his stare from Tigris and turned towards the Vizier. "That all depends upon the way one looks at it, Tjat." He cocked his head. "From my perspective," he pointed, *"she* rules unlawfully." Euphrates turned back to Tigris. "Why don't you return the throne to me and see where that leads you."

Tigris' brow unconsciously furrowed. What did he mean by that? Though, it didn't matter. She would not give up her crowns. She would not abandon the Egypt her father had built.

Euphrates responded to her silence. "In that case, we return to war."

He climbed the steps towards her throne—one gradual step at a time--ascended to the top, paused by her feet. He took her hand and knelt, keeping his eyes locked on hers.

"May the best King win," he whispered.

Tigris watched as Euphrates closed his eyes and laid his lips on the back of her hand. Her heart raised into her mouth, stealing her breath. It was the most delicate kiss, warm, sensuous even.

Tigris couldn't breathe; her eyes closed on their own; her body tingled. She felt lost in a feeling she couldn't discern, a feeling she had never experienced.

For what seemed a long time, Euphrates held his kiss, yet when he pulled his lips away, it didn't feel like it was long enough.

Tigris opened her eyes; again caught in her adversary's stare. An unexplained feeling engulfed her and with it fear. She held onto her breath, worried she may tremble if she dared to breathe.

The councillors watched in questioning silence, but in that moment, Tigris didn't care.

Euphrates stood, stepped back slowly letting go of her hand. Tigris softly held on as he pulled away, secretly not wanting to let go but daring not to let him know it. When his hand was at last free of hers, she dropped her arm and for a moment felt sadness. She no longer had the strength to hold his stare.

I feel nothing, she reminded herself, as she glanced away, feeling as if she had let down her father.

Ibimpetus watched her with his eyebrows tensed; Tigris caught his scowl. Embarrassment swept over the Queen, giving her new strength. She turned back to face Euphrates. "May the best Pharaoh win," she replied.

XXIII

TIGRIS FLOPPED DOWN onto her bed. She stared up at the canopy. She was angry with herself; embarrassed of her own thoughts. How pitiful! she thought. Why wasn't she able to maintain control of herself when she was around *him?* She was strong! She never allowed emotions to cloud her better judgement and this should be no different.

Tigris still latched onto the *was* sceptre, her fingers tightly clamped around it as if it provided comfort. She inhaled deeply and closed her eyes.

I must be strong, she reminded herself as she drifted back into a memory:

♒

SHE WAS A child in Men-nefer—seven years old. Her father had seen to it that she was tutored on every topic by eminent scholars he had summoned from far and wide. There was one topic, however, which he felt would be best learnt through him—power and strength of mind.

Tigris remembered being called to his great throne, swallowing hard as she opened the door, feeling nervous as she walked the room's length towards him. They were alone and she thought it odd he wished to speak with her in the Great Room from the Throne of Geb.

As she stopped before him, the King looked down into her intimidated eyes. "Do you wish to please me?" he asked in a powerful voice, which even in a whisper quaked the air around it.

"Yes, Majesty," Tigris answered timidly.

"Then in return you shall have all this and be Pharaoh of Egypt," he said sweeping his arms wide and gesturing to everything he owned.

"But, I am a girl, father. I cannot be Pharaoh."

"I never want to hear those words again," King Qakare snapped. "You are the daughter of a Pharaoh. And, it shall be known that upon this day Amun came to me and declared that when I pass to the Underworld, it is his will that you be crowned Pharaoh of Egypt. I will announce to the royal nobles, the dignitaries, the leaders and all the people of Egypt that this daughter of mine, Tigris, I have appointed as my successor upon the throne with the crowning name Nitiqreti. May Tigris live!"

Tigris stared at her father. His arms were stretched out, his head tilted back so he could look up towards the heavens as if he was speaking to the gods. Then he glared down at her again. Graveness grew on his brows as he furrowed them. "Show everyone you are a

Pharaoh and they will forget you are a woman!" He allowed his words to sink in. "You may be too young to understand this now, but that will all change in due time. Now, you must come and practice." He stood and with him carried a bow laden with gold. It was delicately carved in the shape of a falcon with out-stretched wings. An *uraeus* was depicted on the underside of each wing and carved upon the heart of its chest were the symbols of *was* and *ankh*. "This is for you," he said handing the elaborate bow to Tigris.

The bow almost equalled her in height. She lifted it up. It was heavy but she tried not to show it.

Her father laughed proudly. "Come," he said. "Your will tells me I won't be disappointed."

He led her through the palace and into the courtyard. She followed, struggling with the bow but she did not complain. Tigris noticed a target was set up for the occasion.

"Do you see that target?" he asked grasping her bow in a powerful hand and spinning back to face it. "Watch—"

He held out his hand. A servant, who awaited their arrival, hastily placed an arrow in it. Then, with masculine grace, he quickly drew the arrow on the string of the bow and released it. The arrow shot through the air with great speed. As it flew, the King seized two more arrows before the first made its mark. One after the other, the arrows hit the centre of the target, each one landing just below the other.

"You must aim the moment you've looked at your target not with your bow, but with your mind." He lowered the bow, crouched down to look steadily at his daughter. "I have seen many men fall because they were too busy pointing their bows and squinting their eyes struggling to aim. Time is precious. Know the size of your target; anticipate his movement." He took another arrow. Without taking his eyes off of Tigris he lifted the bow. "Then, you need only to prepare your arrow and let it go at the spot you have already marked in your mind." The fourth arrow blazed through the air and landed perfectly beneath the others. "One continuous movement—fast, swift and confident."

The Pharaoh handed Tigris back her bow and gave her an arrow. "Now practice."

Nervously, Tigris set the arrow in the bow. She awkwardly held it up managing its weight against her chest as she drew back the arrow. The bow teetered in her arms but she selected her target and released the arrow. Clumsily, it flew through the air, wavering as it went. It dropped to the ground far from the target. A rush of disappointment flooded Tigris. She set down her bow, lowered her head.

The King grasped her chin and raised it gently. "Never give up," he said, shaking his head. "A Pharaoh *never* gives in to these feelings."

His touch affected Tigris greatly. It sent a shiver through her body. Somehow it brought with it an understanding of the importance of his words. At that moment, Tigris realized her purpose in life.

I won't disappoint you, father, she secretly swore as she lifted the bow again.

〰

TIGRIS OPENED HER eyes. She lifted the sceptre, looked at it, dropped her arm back to the bed.

"I've disappointed you father," she said softly, remembering the moment she had looked away when her enemy stood before her.

Her father's words echoed in her mind. *A Pharaoh never gives in to these feelings.*

"I'm sorry, father," Tigris whispered as she closed her eyes again.

〰

SHE WAS TEN years old. Three years and she had mastered the bow unlike anyone she knew. King Qakare's patience was plentiful. He was determined to turn his daughter into a renowned warrior, regardless of her gender. The quintessence of it was Tigris was just as determined.

She practiced every chance she had. She trained herself to perform tricks and stunts while she slung arrows. The day she finally felt ready, she went to the King and said, "Come father, let me show you what I can do. I am a great archer—better than any man you have in your army." Tigris tugged his hand for him to follow. She led him out of the palace to the courtyard. She shot each arrow with precision, showing him the stunts she had created, saving her best trick for last. Without hesitation, Tigris shot an arrow through a hole she had cut in a piece of linen and hit a mask between the eyes hanging twenty feet away on the other side. She gazed up at her father and smiled.

151

"That is all well and good," he said, "but, what if your bow is thrown from you during battle or you haven't an arrow left to shoot?"

Tigris stared at him blankly. She didn't expect this reply. She hoped he would be proud, adorn her with praise but instead, he was expressionless.

Her mind scrambled for the perfect response—the answer she thought he would want to hear. She tried to conceal her disappointment. "Show me father what might I learn."

The King smiled, softening his expression as he gestured for her to follow. This time he led her through the palace, outside the protective outer wall and across the Egyptian soil to the Great Temple of Horu. The building loomed high in the sky. An obelisk stood on either side of the giant doorway, which opened into a long, narrow corridor.

The temple was a forbidden place to all but the King and the priest who was responsible for keeping it lit and performing the daily rituals. But today, like a quiet gift, the Pharaoh was permitting her to enter too.

Tigris followed King Qakare further into the sanctuary. She walked behind him in silence. At the end of the long corridor a stairway descended into a great room lined with massive columns. The walls rose forty feet high and the floor was tiled in marble.

Tigris felt a surge of energy sweep through her as she entered the chamber—something about the room felt powerful. She read the inscriptions on the walls as she followed her father to the end of the room, which led to an even greater chamber with even greater pillars. Behind the pillars, weapons and battle garments were donned, and hieroglyphs and drawings on the walls told stories about the great wars. At the far end of the chamber, the gods *Horu, Mut, Montu* and *Neith*, carved in limestone, watched over.

This was the sacred temple of war where she knew her father came to pray before he went off to battle; it was a temple symbolizing strength and courage. Yet, it was a mysterious place, protected by the Pharaoh unlike any other temple.

King Qakare took long strides across the room and stopped before the gods. On the floor in front of the statues was a long narrow pillow on which he knelt.

Hesitantly, Tigris knelt beside him. She watched her father pray, wondering if she should close her eyes and join him. She studied him intently, listening to every word. But, his words were not of a common prayer, they were personal.

"Glorious gods, forgive my sins. I am a warrior and Egypt owns my heart. You give me strength and with it I seek to protect this great nation—my sole purpose here on earth. May you look upon me as a worthy deity. For all that I have done, I have done for Egypt and with that in mind, may you resolve to persuade Maat to usher me into the afterlife."

After a long silent moment, he stood up. "Somehow this chamber gives me strength," he told Tigris. "It helps me to remember why I fight for Egypt." The King blinked hard, which seemed to erase the thoughts, which made him momentarily distant. He began pointing around the room's vastness in a quick attempt to conceal the guilt she did not see. "These weapons and battle garments were once soaked in the blood that pumped life through many gallant commanders. The walls tell stories of the great battles won. And, the Gods of War watch over, bestowing warrior strength, pride and fearlessness unto Egypt's devout soldiers." He drifted off into his memory as if taken in by his own words. "This room holds the spirit..." he whispered, glancing around. He looked at Tigris and his whisper changed, "...the spirit of all the strong, fearless and willing men..." He paused to take a deep breath. The look in his eyes intensified along with his voice. "Men who stormed onto battlefields knowing the risk of death was trivial in comparison to their deed." He grabbed Tigris by the shoulders, pulled her in close and looked intensely into her eyes. "It is *that* honour, which never dies, for it changes the world—when the risk of death is trivial in comparison to the deed," he repeated.

Tigris held her breath as her father let her go. He seemed to explain the power, which she felt radiate within the chamber. She closed her eyes to take it all in, inhaling a long deep breath. She almost believed she could hear the faint cries and clanking swords that once roared from a battlefield. The spirits of the room engulfed her and she absorbed their energy.

"Take this." Her father's voice broke her from her spell. Tigris opened her eyes. Before her, he had laid out three weapons.

Tigris glanced around and wondered how long she was lost in her trance. She hadn't heard her father move to retrieve the weapons or place them at her feet.

"You will learn how to master all weapons," he said, picking up the sword, holding it out in front of him. He studied its long sharp blade, turned it back and forth in his hand, which caused the torch light to glint off its surface. "Mastering all weapons also teaches you how to defend against a mastered force." He studied her. "Know that your greatest enemy is always the master more skilled than you."

♒

TIGRIS' EYES SHOT open. Euphrates had spoken the truth. Her father's prayer all of a sudden made sense—fifteen years later. He had murdered the Pharaoh of Egypt to save the empire and sealed his guilt from the world by closing the Great Temple of Horu.

Tigris let out an overwhelmed sigh. "Is the temple where you did the deed?" she whispered to the walls as if her father stood in the room.

Slowly she sat up. She pulled the *nemes* crown from her head, held it in her hand with the *was* sceptre. She studied the two objects—symbols of the throne, of power. In some ways they felt corrupt.

Tigris stood. She threw them in the chest with the other imperial symbols: the *deshret* crown of Lower Egypt; the *hedjet* crown of Upper Egypt; the double *pschent* crown of United Egypt; the Blue crown of war; the *atef* crown for religious rituals; the *heqa* sceptre of the great ruler; the false beard, sign of sovereignty; the royal *flail* of great life; the *ureaus* headpiece, protection from enemies....

Symbols, thought Tigris. She slammed the lid shut, went back to her bed, flopped down again. Breathed. She had inherited her father's guilt, his sin. *Oh, what sin.*

Tigris spread her arms across the cool linen sheets and closed her eyes.

♒

NOW, SHE WAS fourteen. She was returning from Syria where her father had sent her for three years to learn under a gifted master of weapons. Although she had perfected the spear and the mace, the sword was still a challenge—its heavy weight easily tiring her arms.

"One day you will grow into the sword," her master said, handing Tigris a box as he walked her to the door. Tigris stopped to open it.

Inside was a stunning Syrian sword. Unlike the short dark bronze blade of the Egyptian sword, his was made from a shiny metal. She pulled it from the box and held it up. It was much lighter than the Egyptian sword too.

Tigris examined the weapon, noticed his symbol on the blade—two snakes intertwined with one another. "Thank you," she said softly, admiring his beautiful craftsmanship. "With this, I shall defend my throne."

A month later, Tigris returned to the Great House in Egypt. She went directly to her father to show him how well she had learned weaponry. But, he did not care to see it.

"You have only just begun. Practice is important in retaining skill and for improvement," he stressed before dismissing her.

The King arranged for her to continue training under the General of the Armed Forces. Each day, Tigris rode out of the palace confines, to Ankhtify's camp at the edge of Men-nefer to practice as he trained his men for combat. She fought with passion, with ferocity, determined to become a warrior and gain the respect of the soldiers and most of all, her father.

"My great student," called the General, "with blows like that at the mere age of fourteen it shall be no time before you will be able to challenge men of war and pose a threat."

Offended, Tigris replied, "My great master and grand uncle, not only at this age—which you call mere—do I speak more languages, know more land and understand more politics than you, but I also, old man, move twice as quickly." She raced towards him with her axe raised high above her head. She wielded it fervently at his armoured and padded form, bringing it down hard. It crashed into his shield. She continued swinging her axe. "Thus, I make up for my lack in strength--surely to come in time," she managed through deep grunts and breaths.

Tigris swung with all her might. The General blocked it and within a beat turned the situation around, knocking her through the air. Tigris crashed down hard on her back. Before she had the chance to move, Ankhtify brought his axe down to her chest, pinning her against the ground.

"Nevertheless," the General responded, "you are still as light as a feather." He laughed loudly as he stretched out his hand, offering to help her up.

Tigris looked at him angrily. She didn't move.

Ankhtify grinned. "And," he jeered, "all that knowledge you so keenly brag about may do well in office but on the battlefield, knowledge is weak when might must prosper."

Snubbing his hand, Tigris jumped up on her own, filled with disappointment. She realized she had fooled herself to think she could overcome his strength. It was impossible—she was half his size.

"Agh!" heaved Tigris. "Why do I bother? Why learn all this?" She threw down her weapon. "This is pointless!" she scoffed, looking down at her outfit of armour intended for a man. "Why does he make me do this? I am *only* a girl."

Ankhtify shook his head in disbelief. "This is not the Tigris I know."

She looked up with a defeated glare. "I will never be able to lead an army! Look at me! I'm a girl and I am weak!" Tigris dropped her head in shame. "I wish I was born a boy!" Tears began to flood her eyes.

"Ah, come now princess." Ankhtify placed a large hand on her back. He guided her across the sand to a small pond. Around them, men fought against each other, yelling, growling, while others rooted as spectators. Tigris was the youngest soldier and the only female at the camp.

They reached the pond and stopped. Silently, they stood looking down at their reflections. Tigris watched her tears fall from her cheeks into the water, causing small ripples.

"What do you see?" the General asked at length.

"A fool," Tigris pouted.

"That's not what I see." Ankhtify's eyes smiled as if remembering something. "I see a brave young girl who is more brilliant than anyone her age, who courageously takes on any challenge thrown on her path, and who, at the age of ten, slung arrows better than men who had practiced their whole lives." He pointed at his army men, daring her to compare but she didn't look over. Dropping his arm, Ankhtify crouched down to her height. "I see a girl who does not know the meaning of giving up." He lowered his voice as he turned her to face him. "You know, at one time this girl wouldn't have allowed her lack of physical strength to defeat her mental power." He leaned in, softened his voice even more, as if he was confiding a secret. "What's more, I believed this girl would have made a legacy for herself. Somehow the position imposed upon her seemed more natural than the sun itself." Ankhtify pointed at her reflection in the water. "*She* is tougher than any *boy* her age and I for one, would follow her to the field of battle and proudly fight under her command."

Tigris remained still, her head bent over, tears rolling down her cheeks.

"He makes you do this because he believes in you," he added, softly.

Tigris looked up into the General's hardened face at the softness hidden somewhere beneath. He was a warrior, reputable for his strength and bravery. He had led many battalions in war, unmercifully forcing his men to push themselves past their limits. His soldiers were expected to fight to their deaths until movement was impossible in their bodies. Yet, despite his harshness, every soldier desired to fight directly under his command and was honoured when called upon to do so. Although he rarely showed it to his men, he was known to hide a gentle streak behind his rigid stature.

The General kept a small memorabilia of every man who died under his command. After each battle, he was seen tramping through the bloody grounds of the slain until he found all his missing soldiers and rescued a piece of their armour to honour their deaths. What he did with it, no one knew.

Tigris shook her head. "I don't think I can, Uncle," she whispered, tears still flooding her eyes.

"Well then, that settles it." The General stretched up to his full height and turned to walk away.

Tigris let out a small gasp of disbelief. "Where are you going?" she stammered. She gaped at him, shocked he would so readily dismiss her. How could he so easily give up?

Ankhtify turned back. "Off to train my men. There is nothing more I can do here."

Her eyes widened, she strained to speak through her tears. "Then you truly must not believe in this *girl*, and all you say is a lie since you so quickly turn away."

"On the contrary, princess," defended the General. "However, there is one thing I have learned through my many trips to battle, and that is: no matter how much you train a man and no matter how well he can fight, if he doesn't believe in himself then all is lost. For only the men who decide they *can* have ever prospered."

Tigris weighed his words.

"I have not become the most decorated warrior because I thought I *could not*. There was never a doubt in my mind, had there been, I don't think it would be me standing here before you today." His expression grew intense. "Do you know why I return from wars unscathed by death?"

Tigris remained silent.

"Because my reputation has yet to introduce me to a man who believes he *can* defeat me. It's simple for me to conquer all those who think they can't."

Silence surrounded them; even the noises of the men yelling and clanging their weapons seemed to fade away.

Tigris was moved by her uncle with heightened respect. When she finally spoke, she did so with integrity. "No General. It shall be I, when the time comes, who will proudly fight by your side."

"Ah!" Ankhtify beamed, slapping his thigh and breaking the sombreness of the moment with a smile. "There's the Tigris I know! Now, remove those tears, princess." He stepped closer to her, his expression now serious. "There is one last thing you must heed in order to be a true warrior." His eyes penetrated hers with potency. "Never show weakness or fear. You can lose all in so doing—respect, power, everything. Strength is your dominance. Never let it go even in your most trying moments." He allowed his words to set in for a moment. Then he took a breath, blowing more power into his voice. "Hide your tears and pain no matter its cause. And, know this: a true warrior's strength is most powerful when he has first mastered internal strength."

〰〰

TIGRIS SPRANG UPRIGHT. A knock on the door broke her from her memory.

"Per'a?" called a soft voice. "Per'a?"

Tigris rose to her feet and straightened her clothes. She recognized

Allegi's voice on the other side of the bedroom door. It was the middle of the day and she did not want him drawing any conclusions as to why she took to her bedchamber, especially since she had abruptly left the Throne Room the moment Euphrates had left.

"Per'a?" Allegi knocked again.

"I will be out momentarily," Tigris answered. "Make yourself comfortable." Desperately, she looked around the bedroom trying to find an excuse. She needed a purpose for being there; she did not want him to know she was lying down. Perhaps she could say she had a headache? No, too obvious, she decided, trying to think.

The bedchamber consisted of her bed, several chests and a writing desk. Tigris looked at the desk. She had set two parchments down on top of it earlier in the day when she had returned from dealing with matters of the court as she waited for Euphrates to arrive. Perfect, she thought. She went to the desk, scooped them up, turned to the door. Tigris inhaled a deep breath then blew it out slowly, trying to relax as she stood for a moment to regain her poise. She had long since become skilled at hiding how she really felt. She could cry on the inside while keeping a smile upon her face and a pleasant tone in her voice— the art of illusion.

Tigris breathed again, opened the bedroom door. She stepped into the audience chamber and looked at Allegi who stood by the seating arrangement, waiting.

"Court business is dreadfully boring to read," Tigris said, holding up the parchments. "They almost put me to sleep." She smiled, went to her low bench. Sitting down, she gestured for Allegi to join.

He studied her for a moment; his brow furrowed with concern. "Per'a, I've come to see if you're alright?"

"If I'm alright?" Tigris laughed. "Why wouldn't I be?"

Allegi shot her a serious look as he sat down. "Because of *him*."

"*Him?*"

"Euphrates." Allegi eyed her. "Something seems to change in you when you're around him. I've seen it both times—"

"Nonsense! Perhaps you shouldn't look so hard."

"One does not have to look hard at all. Even the Vizier has seen it."

Tigris' heart dropped. *Tjat? Great gods, no.*

Allegi calmed his tone. "As your friend, Tigris, I ask you for no other reason than concern."

Tigris looked away. She was being defensive. He was only concerned and it wasn't his concern she needed to worry about.

"Yes, Allegi, I'm alright." She turned back to face him. "But, I wish not to have this discussion again."

Allegi didn't respond; he watched her. Tigris moved to lie down. She stretched across the cushion, stared up at the ceiling.

"He asked me what you were like behind closed doors."

Tigris sent him a puzzled look.

"He also asked why you have not wed."

Why I have not wed? Tigris repeated to herself. Why would Euphrates ask such questions—what I am like? Why I have not wed? Sure, he would inquire about her, but not with *these* questions.

Tigris returned her gaze to the ceiling. "Strange," she replied. She wouldn't take Allegi's bait by showing it interested her.

Allegi studied her. She made it apparent she wouldn't discuss Euphrates in this manner. Although he wanted to, he knew it best to change the topic. "When do you plan to go to war?"

"Tomorrow," answered Tigris. "Chephren's ships are ready and Ankhtify's men await his command." Tigris turned. "We will stop him before he reaches the fortress."

Allegi stood. "You seem to have everything under control then."

"Did you think otherwise?" Tigris smirked.

Smiling, Allegi shook his head. "Never." He moved to leave, hesitated. She wasn't herself. He decided not to press her about it. "If you're fine, I will leave you to your privacy."

"I am."

Allegi bowed, walked out.

Alone again, Tigris rolled onto her back. She pushed Euphrates' image from her mind. She didn't want to think about him. Instead, she closed her eyes, allowed herself to drift back to her childhood memories:

〜

SHE WAS AT Ankhtify's camp. Sixteen years of age. By now, she had gained respect from most of the warriors. She had developed ways to make up for her lack of muscle strength by charging low, rolling across the ground, jumping high to avoid her contender's blows and advance her own. Whenever the soldiers were home from their marches she would challenge them to a match, pester them to show her their techniques with their swords. No one could sail a bow better than she and most often she would succeed her opponent in all other feats by outwitting him.

At night, Tigris would join their parties staying close to the man she vanquished during the day, until her charm and humour appeased his anger.

The men grew to enjoy her company even though they teased her about her size. Tigris found humour to be an effective weapon, achieving revenge with her quick-witted tongue.

Tigris always joined the feasts held for the soldiers upon the army's first night of return, and their last night before marching off again. It became ritual for the men to bang their goblets on the table, compelling her to stand up and speak. When she did, Tigris would pick on her audience, commemorating and teasing them, but always sparking a flurry of laughter and cheer throughout the room. Soon it became a superstitious belief that her speech sent them off with a fortune of good luck.

One night, as the cups were banging, growing louder as each drunken man found his mug and slammed it against the low table imploring the princess to speak, Tigris stood up sending a roar of cheer across the room. The young princess raised her cup. "Mighty soldiers, brave and strong; tomorrow you will descend upon our borders and force the enemies from our glorious Kemet. I wish I could march with you but alas the Great Pharaoh claims tomorrow is not my day—"

"Nor should it ever be!"

Tigris turned her head to glare down the line of low tables at the commander who had shouted out. Her face tightened with despise as she stepped onto the table and stomped towards the speaker. The diners, sitting on carpets behind the low tables, pulled their plates out of her way. She stopped in front of the commander as if daring him to say more. "You have something to say, Dalwi?" she hissed.

Dalwi leaned back and frowned.

After a heavy moment, Tigris spun to face the crowd of men, who watched from their tables. "I hear Dalwi, among others, believe I shouldn't be allowed to war since I am a woman—"

"A child," spat Dalwi.

Tigris glimpsed over her shoulder at him. "Very well, a woman-child," she compromised—her tone very matter of fact. "Understandable. It bothers me too."

A supportive murmur raised and died amongst the soldiers.

Tigris shrugged. "However, I *am* female. Unfortunately, it is a fate I cannot change." She spun to face Dalwi. "So, what must I do, Commander, to gain your acceptance? Apparently, you do not like women."

"Not unless they're in the bedroom," he retorted, receiving sounds of agreement from the men.

"That's not what I've heard, but that is your business."

The men laughed.

Tigris glanced over at the soldiers as if she and Dalwi were vying for their support and she had won a point.

Returning her attention to Dalwi, she probed him further. "Do tell why you can't accept me? Have I not proven myself?"

Dalwi remained still. The princess glowered at him until he felt compelled to answer.

"Simply because you are of *female gender!*" He pushed back from the table in a furry and stood. "Men are to be led by men! The fields of battle are to be embraced with strength and fearlessness of which only a man can command. The Commanders and Chiefs of other armies will look upon Egypt in disrepute for having a woman on the throne!"

"They will look in *disrepute* only for a moment," Tigris shot back. "For once they see I can lead and command and fight like the best of men, they will be obliged to regard me with respect!"

"You fool. You're a woman! They'll have an easy advantage over you."

Tigris forced a chuckle. She took a deep breath to calm her anger. Slowly, she shook her head. "On the contrary, *noble* Dalwi." She adjusted her voice to a sultry tone. "I shall have easy advantage over them due to the fact that I *am* a woman." Tigris turned to face the army men. She struck a feminine pose, dramatically batted her eyelashes. Some of the men whistled in support. She winked and blew them a kiss.

Dalwi sat.

"Come," she continued. "Do you really believe such convictions?"

He was silent.

"Here's what I believe." Tigris paced the table. She paused briefly to study the men. They had stopped eating and were now watching quietly, tension stamped on their expressions. "I believe men fool themselves into thinking they cannot be led by women when throughout their lives it has been women who have led them successfully—mothers, for one." She stopped, raised her cup as if to salute them. "Cleverly, they train you from birth to fear them so when your strength outdoes theirs they still have control. Ask Ahmet." She pointed to the unsuspecting soldier across the room. "I have never seen a man move so fast as he when his mother calls him home to do a chore."

Everyone including Ahmet laughed.

"Or, Ramous, who cannot be called out of his house by a thousand men when his wife tells him he may not go."

Again there was laughter.

"You name fear. Fear men seem to lose when out on the battlefield, yet, quickly find when they are home with their *women?* Perhaps we should send an army of mothers and wives out to the deserts for who would contest the hastened results of these women?"

The men snickered with a note of false agreement.

Tigris began pacing the table again. "Or, what about the power of a woman, which weakens men in other ways, causing them to behave like boys and attempt ridiculous deeds only for its reward?" She stopped and threw her hands up. "Say, was it not but a month ago a man lost his head for that very reason?" Tigris nodded, answering her own question. "Yes, I believe so; it was this power which led a man to treason. Funny, I think we can all agree only a woman could convince a man so easily to plot against himself."

Men groaned in agreement.

"Your speech is weak!" Dalwi cut in, frustrated by her babble. "It's not the same—"

"Oh, but it is. You see, the power of which I speak is of natural law, which the gods granted women to make up for their lack of muscular strength. That which *you* define is taught and learned, hence, anyone can achieve it—including *women*." Tigris took a breath. She looked around. The harshness left her tone. Her voice became impassive. "However, since society dictates that we don't, we have come to believe women simply cannot."

"Women are not built for fighting. They *are* weak," he argued.

"Weak? In what way? That we do not take pain like a man? Nonsense! Need you witness the pains of birth? Unless of course you mean physically? Well, I look around this room and see men of all different shapes and sizes. Do you mean to say only the largest should go out to fight? Why then our army would only consist of nine men and you would not be amongst them!"

There was a chuckle from the men.

Tigris breathed deeply to control her anger before she was able to continue. "What about Ashop who feels shamed here tonight because I—a mere *woman-child*—defeated him at day? He is still an extraordinary soldier." Tigris' eyes narrowed. "So, what does that make me?" She glared at Dalwi, daring him to answer but he said nothing.

The chamber fell into such a deep stillness it seemed empty of life.

Tigris cut into the silence. "You fool yourself to believe forte lies in gender when it is more than apparent to anyone who has not set his mind so narrow, that if strength were to lie anywhere, it would be in the heart." Her eyes narrowed again. She glowered with disdain. "I shall one day be Pharaoh. A woman on the throne, called upon by the gods who believe women can be warriors like *Neith* and *Mut*, our *female* gods of War!"

"They are gods! You do not compare!" Dalwi defended.

Tigris crouched down to Dalwi's level. She looked steadily in his eyes, bending slightly forward to bring her body closer to him. She spoke directly to him, no longer for the entertainment of the onlookers. Anger blazed inside her, stinging with redness on her cheeks. "I shall prove your belief false. In all the days to come, when I set foot on the battlefields, I command you to fight by my side so you may witness me in battle." Their eyes locked. "I *am* strong and fearless and you will recognize it!" She stood, spun towards the spectators. "A wise man once told me a warrior's strength is most powerful when it is first mastered within. Physical strength means nothing when fear blocks its way." Tigris paused for a moment; then, she drove a voice out of her chest that shook the room. *"I am fearless!"*

The men stared, bewildered at her behaviour. Some proud. Some unsure.

Her voice calmed. "I promise you this—when the time comes, I shall lead you like the bravest of men!"

"Here, here!" Ankhtify knocked his cup against the table, in support.

"Talk is petty!" Dalwi persisted. "When the time comes, weakness will find you in a bath of blood!"

"As it does any man!" Tigris spat with disgust. "Why must you insist only because I am a woman I shall fail?"

Dalwi's eyes narrowed. Hatred boomed in his voice. "Because I cannot accept Egypt to be sacrificed to a female heir. Women are not to be Pharaohs!" He slammed his fist against the table.

"Do you forget with whom you speak so freely!" warned the princess.

Tigris and Dalwi glared at each other full of rage. Uneasiness choked the air. Men shifted in their chairs.

"Alright," Tigris said, breaking the tension. "If you feel I am not best suited for Egypt because I am incapable of fighting men, then come, choose your weapon and let us fight. May fate decide: if you win, then witnessed by all those here today, upon my father's death, I grant you the throne."

Gasps came from every table. Tigris ignored them.

"And then, may you bare Egypt a son." Tigris' deep, low tone sent a horrid tremor across the chamber. She continued to glare at Dalwi with eyes that pierced him like daggers.

"Princess," came a protest, "you cannot—"

"Is that the sound of fear?" Tigris spurned, spinning around to find the protester.

Ankhtify stood with horror on his face.

"This choice is mine. I will fight today. And, when I become Pharaoh, I make the laws for all men. My promise will be honoured!" She peered around the room into the faces of the soldiers who were stunned by her words. "Today, fate takes Egypt into her hands and let us behold the outcome—which gender shall your future Pharaoh be?" Tigris spun back to Dalwi. "I command you—*choose a weapon!*"

A wry smile curled his lips. "Alright," he finally replied, "the sword."

Men shifted uncomfortably, aware the weapon he chose was Tigris' worst. However, Tigris did not flinch.

"Bring us swords!" the princess called out. She jumped off the table into the centre of the eating arrangement.

The tables were lined together side-by-side forming a square that created a large open space in the middle. The High Commanders sat around the outside of the square leaving the middle of the arrangement empty while the lower ranked army men sat at tables spread throughout the large room. Tigris stood inside the open space where all the upper rank commanders could watch.

As they waited for a servant to retrieve the swords, Tigris gave her warning. "I order all of you to not interfere in this affair. He who does will be regarded treasonous and when I come into power I will not seek mercy for his life."

The servant slowly approached carrying several swords, unsure of his lot in this matter. Tigris cocked her head towards the weapons. Dalwi grasped a sword.

The servant held Tigris' Syrian sword forward. Tigris strode to the table, leaned across it, took hold of the sword. She moved aside, gestured for Dalwi to enter. Dalwi stepped onto the table and down into the centre of the table arrangement.

Tigris led him to the middle and turned to face him. "I bid you well," she bowed, not moving her eyes from his.

"As do I," he replied, doing the same.

Holding up their swords, Tigris waited for him to make the first strike. The moment drew out before their blades began to smack together.

The metal clashed and banged as they slashed through the air. They grunted and yelled with each attack and defence. No one else made a sound. The soldiers gaped, fearing the princess would lose.

Although Dalwi was stronger, Tigris was more agile. She was well aware that if he pinned her down she wouldn't have the strength to lift the pressure of his sword.

Dalwi swung with full force, which to his surprise, Tigris managed to block. Anger raged through him knowing his advantage of strength hadn't yet prevailed. He needed to tire her out, trap her, something. His reputation was at risk.

Dalwi's eyes darted around the room. He carefully chose his

manoeuvre and began backing her up against the table as their swords crossed back and forth against each other.

Tigris noticed his eyes lose interest in her for a brief moment and realized his plan almost before he did. She defended his strikes, calculating her distance from the foreseen trap.

The soldiers watched nervously but no one dared to stop them.

The table was almost behind Tigris and Tigris knew if Dalwi tripped her, he would have the upper hand. Taking one last step, she leapt backwards onto the table.

The commander lunged at her with full force trying to reach her before she got her ground. He raised his sword in the air.

Tigris stepped back. She didn't see the plate behind her. Her foot landed on top of it, causing her to slip. She fell backwards, sending cups and plates smashing to the ground. In a desperate move, she tried to regain her balance but it was impossible; she was caught in momentum.

Falling, Tigris crashed down on her back. Dalwi seized his opportunity. With a sudden charge, he brought his sword towards her.

The princess watched as the shining metal came directly at her throat. The soldiers gasped in horror.

Without a second to loose, Tigris rolled towards Dalwi just missing the blow of his sword as he slung it into the table. She was behind him, on her feet swinging her weapon towards his back.

Dalwi quickly freed his blade and spun to block the attack of her sword. He caught her on an unsuspected angle, sending her sword sailing across the room.

The soldiers' gasps resounded with their horrors.

Tigris followed her sword as rapidly as it left her hand, diving in its direction while Dalwi turned to catch her. She slid between two tables, scrambled across the floor towards the sliding sword. The sword stopped as it hit the wall on the outer side of the table arrangement. Tigris glanced back. Dalwi jumped on top of the tables and ran along them towards her. He would be on top of her within seconds and at his speed she knew her arms would not be strong enough to defend his blow, nor could she roll out of his way in time. Any direction she chose he could follow with ease.

Tigris looked at her sword lying next to the wall. There was only one defence and she prayed it worked.

Dalwi jumped from the table. He raised his sword high above his head and shouted out as he attacked.

Tigris felt her heart pound. She reached out, grabbed her weapon, cocked the sword so the tip pierced into the wall and the handle was wedged tightly against the floor. Then, using the sword as a shield she scurried behind it.

Dalwi's sword was in full swing and he had no choice but to allow it to complete its motion. Against her protection, his angle was wrong. In a vicious swoop, his weapon came clanking down on Tigris' wedged sword, resonating a deafening noise through the air but not shifting the sword in the slightest.

The ring of the metals could still be heard as Tigris kicked the tip of her blade out from the wall. While it timbered towards the ground, she briskly took hold of the handle, scooped it up and swung it at her assailant. By the time he realized her action, it was too late. Her sword cut into the flesh of his calf.

Dalwi jumped back grimacing in pain.

The soldiers rooted her on surging her with power.

Tigris bounded to her feet, sword in hand. She pressed its tip against Dalwi's throat with a new strength attained from triumph. "Throw down your weapon!" she puffed. "Accept what stands before you now." With a bellowing force, she declared, "A *girl!*" The young princess stood tall, daring him to admit his loss. She glanced around at the soldiers before she returned her focus to Dalwi. "You shall remain alive so when I am crowned, you will be there to appoint me as Commander and Chief of Army for Egypt." Tigris pressed the blade against his neck. "Do you accept?" Her eyes tensed. "Anything other than yes will cost your life." Tigris could not bring herself to slay him. Compassion compelled her to find an excuse to grant his life as she glared into his merciful face.

Before her, Dalwi gripped his wound, shocked by his defeat. *How?* It wasn't possible. The image standing before him seemed so small and fragile. Yet, the longer he looked into her eyes he began to see something completely different; something new; something he hadn't seen before: *Power.* Indeed, she was a worthy Pharaoh, perhaps chosen by the gods, thought Dalwi. With a rush of emotional confusion he didn't know whether he admired her or hated her.

The defeated commander stared at the princess in silence. Each passing moment, as his anger calmed, something fell in its place—respect. Dalwi relaxed his fingers allowing his sword to fall in disgrace. "Please, your graciousness, seek pity on my ignorance," he cried, falling to his knees and kissing the floor at her feet. "I—I did not see what I see now. I speak in honesty. I had despised you for Egypt but I was blind. Please, let me live to defend your land in war and regain your honour in shame. I shall be—"

"Enough!" The door swung open and a roaring voice bellowed into the room. Men scrambled to position themselves into a low bow. Everyone bent his head except for Tigris and Dalwi who froze gaping towards the figure marching into the chamber.

"Seize him!" ordered the Pharaoh. "Your life shall be the repercussion of your treachery!"

"No!" both Dalwi's and Tigris' voices rang out together. Dalwi looked at Tigris, stunned she would defend him.

Fear clung to the room as King Qakare Iby stepped further inside. Retainers emerged from behind him, marching briskly towards Dalwi. No one noticed the servant who had brought them the swords, slide back into the chamber.

"Please have mercy, your Majesty!" Dalwi cried as the guards grabbed him.

Tigris spun to face the two large men. "Let him go!" she commanded.

The guards hesitated, looking from the princess to the King.

The Pharaoh glared at Tigris in disbelief. His daughter, who was always so timid around him, was opposing his authority.

"Please father," Tigris begged, "I provoked him. He is a noble commander. Forgive his sin of doubt." She gestured down at herself, desperately trying to convince him. "Look at me. It is only his love for Egypt that begot his treason. He did me favour by his actions." Tigris fell to her knees. "Release him—I beg you!"

Qakare frowned with disgust. "There is only one option in such a matter and that is death!" the King's voice thundered. "Let his blood mark a lesson to all those who dare to threaten the crown!" He glared around the room. The soldiers remained bowing.

Hearing the King's words, Dalwi began to fight against his arrest. The two retainers struggled to hold him as they dragged him across the room.

Tigris stared at her father. A rush of guilt flooded into her chest. She raced towards Dalwi. "No! Stop! I beg you! Stop!" She tried to unleash the guards' hold but they were too strong. Guilt for her part in his death overwhelmed her. "Stop!" she cried.

Dalwi looked regretfully at Tigris. "Let me go," he said, softly. "For this, I deserve." He gently squeezed her hand. "Forgive me."

Tigris stared at him blankly. She persisted to fight.

"Restrain her!" ordered the King.

A guard took hold of Tigris. He held her back. She kicked and fought against him.

Qakare Iby strode to the centre of the room to peer down at Dalwi. "Tomorrow at mid-day, you will be hung at the gates of Men-nefer and every man is required to witness!"

Dalwi's cry of fear, echoed eerily as he was dragged from the chamber.

King Qakare turned to his daughter. "Bring her to my chamber," he commanded the guard.

Inside the King's chamber the Pharaoh glowered at Tigris with rage pumping his veins. Tigris stood by the door; her head bent low, daring not to move.

"You cannot allow your emotions to affect politics! You will be easily overtaken if you do!" Anger loomed on Qakare's face as he looked Tigris up and down. "Look up when I speak to you!" he seethed. "Your position does not grant you the privilege of hanging your head—*ever!*" His last word lanced the air.

Uneasily, Tigris raised her head, biting her lower lip, fighting back her tears. She kept her eyes fixed on the floor—she was afraid to look at him.

"*Strength* is what you must administer with all matters. Confine your heart or it will be your ruin!" Silence followed the low ring of his voice and clung to the air with uneasiness.

Tigris hung onto the lump, which pierced inside her throat. She could feel her father burning her with scorn but her guilt overtook her.

She wanted to stop herself, wished she could, but she found herself raising her eyes to meet his. "Please don't kill him father," she begged. "It was my fault." A tear escaped her eye, rolled down her cheek. She saw his scorn deepen. How she wished she could have silenced her request. But, there it was, out there, making him detest her.

"Then what do you propose I do? Let him walk? Do you not realize to spare a man means to spare yourself?" The King pointed at her, his voice strained with gravity. "*This* was the very weakness he fought you for. You both fool yourselves to believe it lies within physical strength." He shook his head with the same graveness in which he spoke. "Tigris, before you can become Pharaoh you must understand pity and power do not go hand in hand." He stepped towards her. "The reason why men make better warriors is not alone because of physical strength, for plenty of women if taught to use a weapon could fight a man." His eyes narrowed with earnestness; his voice became solemn. "But, it is this, which from your kind you must—*in the name of the crown*—devote yourself to shed...." His expression hardened. "*Emotion.*" The air seemed to shake as he delivered the word. The Pharaoh studied his daughter searching to see if she comprehended what he said. "You see, women lament within themselves while men do not care. That is why we keep them from battle—their emotions run too deep; they feel too much. Men are hard." He watched the tears stream down Tigris' face, justifying what he said. Frustration tightened inside him. Briskly, he moved to her, grabbed her wrist, yanked her towards a mirror on the wall. "Look at yourself!" he commanded, pushing up her chin.

Tigris kept her gaze on the floor, her eyes almost shut, embarrassed by her tears.

"Look!" he insisted. "You cry for some man you barely know, who despised you for your gender, who tried to murder you! A man who dishonoured your position and yet you cry! Why?" Qakare shook his head, still glowering, his anger growing with each tear that fell from her cheek. "*This* is the weakness within a woman. Here is what he was looking for. Go show him!"

Tigris turned her head, pulling away from the grip he had on her chin, trying to stifle her tears. How could she not feel? How could she shed herself of the person she was?

171

She suddenly felt angry. She stepped away from her father, looked up at him, self-pity overwhelming her. "Then what must I do!" she cried. "I am a *girl*, father. I cannot help that. I have tried—the gods know how I have tried to please you. But, I cannot help but *feel*." She unconsciously placed her hand over her heart as she gasped for a breath through a fury of tears. "Why?" she pleaded. "No matter what I do I cannot please you or make you proud!" She wiped her tears with the back of her hand. She hated their ugly presence on her face but she couldn't stop them from pouring out. "I love and honour you. I want nothing more than to become the son you want me to be. But, fate forged a devious path because *I am your daughter!*" Her last words belted with single demeanour.

Qakare Iby stood in silence. When he trained her, when she listened as he taught, he never realized the severity his request had upon her. But, although she was his daughter, he believed in the strength she had always shown. What's more, he believed in time and with age all of this would be irrelevant. She was all he had to continue his bloodline and carry the crown.

Concern gripped his anger. His teeth clenched. "Yes, you are my daughter, a woman born but not bred. Pick yourself up and decide what you want because I have little time to make a King." He stomped from the room, slammed the door behind him.

Tigris' cry erupted the moment the door was shut. She hunched over in self-sorrow and crumbled to the floor. "Why can't he love me?" she sobbed. "Just for a moment." She gasped for air. She lay on her side curled in a ball, her body shaking. Her cry broke into sobs as she tried to stop her tears. But, they continued, bringing the deep seated sound of pain along with them.

Emotions are weak, she thought. She needed to stop crying, regain her strength, pick herself up. She was strong. There was no need to cry. A man would never be found curled on the floor crying to himself.

Tigris held her breath but her chest still shook. "Stop it," she mumbled out loud to coax herself. "I have no emotions. I don't care," she gasped. She forced herself onto her hands and knees. "I don't care," she repeated, finding strength in the words. Her body trembled. She tried to suppress it. "I don't care." Tigris struggled to her feet. She fought the weakness that made her want to crumble to the floor.

"I don't care." She wiped away her tears, stumbled to the door, left the King's audience chamber and made her way to her room. She managed to hold in her cry--the entire way, she held it. It hurt. It caused her chest and stomach to shake in spasms, but she held it in. Only, when she reached her bedchamber and closed the door did Tigris allow her tears to flow—painful, hurtful tears. She made her way to the bed, barely able to walk—shaking, trembling, her knees desperate to cave in below her. "I don't care," she persisted, drawing strength from the words.

Tigris collapsed onto her bed, panting for air. She repeated the three words until she had cried herself to sleep.

〰

THE QUEEN OPENED her eyes. Tears had welled up in them from the memory but she blinked them away. She stood and went to her bedchamber to retrieve the red and white *pschent* crown of United Egypt.

The Vizier had sent news into Henen-nesut that the great Pharaoh would be at her Window of Appearance this evening. The window was cut into the outer wall of the palace and looked out from above the main gates, allowing the Pharaoh to appear in front of the people to accept the gifts they laid at the front gate and to bestow honours to worthy recipients. This eve, Nitiqreti of Egypt would welcome gifts offered as hope for victory over her enemy. Egypt would soon be at war against Egypt, and more than ever, it was the time to instil loyalty.

Tigris placed the *pschent* crown on her head. She was in no mood to show herself. Regardless, it was her duty.

The Pharaoh of Egypt walked from the room and sighed. *Duty*, she thought. She would smile, appear to be happy, though secretly knowing nothing was as it appeared.

XXIV

ALLEGI WALKED TOWARDS the tavern doors. He thought about Deshyre every day since they met, wishing time to hasten to the

173

day he could see her again. It had been over a week since he left Henen-nesut to escort Euphrates back to the palace. As he approached Sechemesch tavern, he worried whether Deshyre would keep her promise.

Pushing the door open, Allegi walked into the establishment. Men and women stood around chattering over the music. He stepped further inside, moving around the patrons so he could view the room unobstructed.

Across the room, Deshyre spotted him. She leapt from her seat and raced towards him. Before Allegi knew what to expect, she covered his cheeks with kisses.

Laughing, Allegi pulled back to look at her, a little stunned.

"You don't know what torture it is to come to a place every night and watch the same door for days, hoping every time it opens you'd walk in," Deshyre pouted.

Allegi smiled. "I'm sorry," he said, gently stroking her face. They stood locked in a stare unsure of where the moment should lead. But, before it became uncomfortable, Allegi took her hand and led her out of the bar.

The outdoors offered fresh air and privacy at this late hour and both preferred anything over the rowdiness of Sechemesch. Together they strolled through the narrow streets hand-in-hand, talking, laughing and learning more about each other. Time sailed by so quickly, they lost track of it. For the first time, Allegi felt as if he was floating on air. When he was with Deshyre, nothing else mattered—the war, Egypt, the Pharaoh—none of it seemed to exist.

Allegi looked at Deshyre, admiring her smooth complexion and long hair. "Where are you from?"

Deshyre's smile disappeared. "What do you mean where am I from?" Her voice turned serious as if bothered by the question.

Allegi shrugged. He didn't mean to insult her, it was just she didn't appear Egyptian. "You're not from Egypt?" he probed.

Deshyre stopped, letting go of his hand. Her expression changed from its soft and gentle nature to one that was cold and offended. "I am Egyptian," she stated before she spun and stormed off.

Allegi froze, taken aback by her abrupt behaviour. But, when he registered that she was fleeing, he went after her. He took hold of her shoulder to prevent her from getting any further away. "I'm sorry," he said, surprised the question would spark her with such fury. "I didn't mean to offend you."

Deshyre stopped walking. She allowed Allegi to spin her to face him but she kept her head bent low.

"It wouldn't matter," Allegi said, softly. He pushed her hair behind her ear. "I still admire you."

Deshyre lifted her head, searched his eyes with a small smile that she tried to conceal.

Allegi smiled back, stroking her hair affectionately. "And, you're beautiful," he added.

Deshyre's smile grew. It flooded him with desire. He didn't care where she was from. He was happy to just be with her.

Allegi bent towards Deshyre, slowly moved in to kiss her. But, as he leaned forward, something caught his eye over her shoulder. He was unable to make out the image but he was certain it was a person.

Someone was watching them.

Allegi redirected his kiss from her lips to her cheek in order to steal a glimpse without being obvious. He pulled Deshyre in close, hugged her, discreetly peering down the alleyway over her shoulder.

In the distance, a tall figure cloaked in black, peeked around the corner.

Why would someone spy on us? he wondered, becoming uneasy. What concern would we be of his?

Allegi straightened. When he did, the figure stepped back behind the wall out of sight. A bad feeling came over Allegi. "Come," he said, taking Deshyre's hand and leading her down the alley away from the prowler.

They rounded a corner. So did the man. Allegi glimpsed back—his feeling confirmed—they were being followed. Allegi increased their pace.

"Where are we going?" Deshyre asked as he dragged her down the street.

Allegi didn't want to alarm her. He forced a smile. "Let's get out of here," he said, pulling her faster so they were in a run.

Deshyre thought it was some sort of game. She giggled.

Allegi glanced behind again. The man was now running too. Panic set in. Allegi wanted to turn, fight, but he didn't want to put Deshyre in danger.

Instead, he tried to lose their pursuer through a series of turns. He rounded a corner, then another. He rushed along the narrow streets and dark allies trying to think of who would want to chase after them. The only person he could think of was the man from Sechemesch, whom he had squabbled with the first night he set eyes on Deshyre. But, that was weeks ago, why now?

Glimpsing back, Allegi sized him—the man seemed so much taller than what he remembered; thinner even. Nothing made sense.

Allegi turned another corner and stopped. He had steered them into a dead end. A wall blocked the path a short way down the alley. Nervously, Allegi looked around.

"What's the matter?" Deshyre asked, still smiling.

Allegi forced a smile, trying to conceal his worry. A man followed them but he wouldn't tell her. No. He wouldn't scare her with that knowledge. "Nothing is the matter," he lied, giving her a playful wink.

Along the building several doorways created small alcoves. Allegi pulled her towards one of the entries and pressed her against the wall. They were hidden in the tiny recessed doorway. As long as their pursuer didn't come down the alley, they would be safe.

Deshyre was laughing again, enjoying Allegi's sudden playful nature. "What's got into you?"

Allegi didn't answer. Her smile was innocent, unaware of their potential danger. He loved the sound of her laughter but he needed to stop her; stop her from laughing; stop her before they were heard. Allegi sealed her mouth with his--kissed her passionately—it was the only thing he could think of to silence her without causing alarm.

Deshyre pulled him closer. Their kiss grew more passionate and for a moment, Allegi forgot they were in danger. But, then he remembered and despite his desire to kiss her longer, he pulled away. Allegi smiled shyly before he leaned back to peer down the alleyway.

It was empty. The man would have been at the alley already but all was still. The alley was vacant. Allegi felt the tension leave his body, knowing they were safe.

"What are you looking for?" Deshyre asked, pulling him back towards her. "No one will see us here," she whispered, kissing him on his ear and down his neck.

Allegi returned her kiss, sending them back into a heat of passion. They began touching each other, feeling each other's bodies. Allegi grew excited and pressed up against Deshyre.

She could feel him wanting her and her body tingled excitedly for his. Caught by intense desire, Deshyre lifted his kilt, welcoming him.

Lust overtook them. Allegi raised her against the wall and thrust into her. He listened to her moan by his ear as he felt her warmth. They kissed, groaned, panted with heavy passion, loosing themselves in their lust. *Magnificent lust.*

When they were done, neither spoke. They barely moved.

After a quiet moment, Allegi moved to lean against the wall beside Deshyre. He looked out into the alleyway where Deshyre had already fixed her gaze. Neither could turn to face the other as they waited for the feeling of shy embarrassment to subside. They stood, catching their breath in the awkwardness they had created.

At length, Deshyre slid down the wall to sit on the ground.

Allegi looked down at her, did the same. He took her hand and kissed it. "So," he said, in an attempt to break the uneasiness, "what do you want to do now?"

Deshyre almost laughed, giving him a darting glance; but she felt more at ease looking into the emptiness ahead. "I should go home," she said, moving to stand up.

Allegi pulled her back into his arms and held her. "Please, don't run off tonight," he begged. "Just stay with me for a little while." His plea destroyed all the embarrassment that engulfed them a moment ago.

Deshyre, relaxed, looked at him tenderly. His expression seemed genuine.

"Okay," she finally said, kissing him on the cheek before she leaned back into his arms.

XXV

EARLY THE NEXT morning, the Queen ordered for her transport barge to prepare to leave to Men-nefer where she would stay three nights. She would set off to war on the fourth day.

While the palace servants hustled to prepare, Tigris went to the bathing suite to bask in the large pool of water while she waited.

The large room was tiled from floor to ceiling in colourful, elaborately designed tiles and the ceiling had a celestial scene painted over it. In the middle of the room, a square bath was sunk into the floor, encased by steps, which led the way into its watery depth.

Removing her robe, Tigris stepped into the warm bath where two maidens, wrapped in linen dresses stood waist deep in the water. They used clay vessels to pour water over her back. Incense burned from small pots set around the pool and perfumes scented the water, leaving their fragrance on her skin.

A breeze blew in from the open terrace carrying the scent of the garden below. The Queen leaned back against the steps of the inset pool and closed her eyes. She felt confused—torn between reason and duty. To fight this war....

She decided to travel to the palace in Men-nefer, where its rooms held memories of her father. Being there made her feel closer to him and she needed him right now—to find the fortitude to go justly into a battle, which was based on a perception of rights.

For quite some time, Tigris lay basking in the water, thinking about her fate until a servant arrived to inform her ship was ready.

An hour later, the barge manoeuvred its way out of the barque station, through the causeway to the Nile where they set sail down the river towards the old capital.

The river was already busy with merchants and fishermen who had long since begun their day. They hailed their Pharaoh and waved as the royal vessel passed.

Tigris was standing by the low wall of the boat looking into the water when Allegi came up beside her.

"Strange you want to go to Men-nefer." He glimpsed her up and down. "Especially, since yesterday you had planned to set out for war today."

Tigris remained quiet, unmoving. Allegi didn't press any further. Instead, he followed her stare. He watched the water splash against the vessel as the oars dipped into the river's darkness to pull the boat along.

He thought back to the last time he had watched the same movement. His feelings were so different back then, so filled with sorrow and yet so filled with hope. Now, they were filled with excitement. He had met *the girl*—Deshyre. He knew her name. He had kissed her, touched her. The memory made his stomach flutter.

Allegi thought about the poem he had written the day he sailed to the enemy's camp as he lost himself in the river. *To cast the spell of great desire, Then steal one's strength away*, he had scrawled on the page. How things change. At last, he found his strength and with it, the girl.

"I sent for you last night," Tigris said, cutting off Allegi's thoughts.

Allegi looked at her.

"I was told you left the Great House."

Allegi turned to lean his back against the wall, grinning as he remembered last night.

Tigris studied him.

"I've met a girl," he said, quietly. He glanced over at Tigris, his grin broadening. "I think I'm in love."

Tigris burst with surprise. "*You? Allegi?* My gentle messenger who never seemed quite sure of his life—in *love?*" Tigris beamed. "I am happy for you." She leaned in to kiss him on the cheek. "What's her name?"

"Deshyre."

"What's she like?"

"She's beautiful but... " his voice trailed off. He looked away from the Queen, casting his sight down onto the deck floor.

"But what?" Tigris' smile slowly faded as she studied Allegi's sombre expression.

Allegi let out a heavy sigh. "But nothing," he finally answered.

Tigris took his hand, cupped it between both of hers. "This isn't the look of nothing," she said. "Tell me Allegi, I am your friend, perhaps I can help."

Allegi considered it. He looked at her. Concern covered her face but he was unsure of the response she would give him even as his friend. At length, he decided to tell her. "But, I don't think she's Egyptian."

"Not Egyptian?" Tigris repeated.

"She says she is but only her makeup is fashioned in the Egyptian way. Everything else reveals she is not."

Tigris remained quiet for a short moment while she thought. Then, linking Allegi's arm, she began to stroll along the ship with him. "Do you love her?" she asked.

He nodded.

"Then don't let anything stop you. Love is a gift from Hathor; it knows no rules and has no boundaries. Embrace it," she smiled softly. Reaching her cabin, she stopped in front of the door, letting go of Allegi's arm. "You have my blessing."

Allegi bowed, gave her a kiss on each cheek.

As Tigris watched him walk away she thought, *If only I could heed my own advice.*

XXVI

BY LATE AFTERNOON they reached the channel that was cut into the land up to the old palace. The horns and trumpets blared to send warning to the palace keeper that Her Majesty had arrived. Having not been informed ahead of time the Pharaoh would be visiting, it was certain the old palace keeper would be scrambling to make everything perfect by the time the gates opened.

Allegi disembarked the royal ship first. He rode ahead to notify the keeper and his wife of their plans while the Queen was carried up the steep towards the palace. Behind, the Pharaoh's entourage made its way up the hill carrying food and some of Tigris' personal effects for her three day stay.

Before they neared the palace entrance, Tigris reached outside the palanquin drape and signalled for her troop to stop.

The guards behind the royal chair saw the signal and ordered everyone to halt. A servant peeked into the small compartment.

"Fetch me a horse," Tigris commanded.

Only four horses were brought for the journey with four retainers sitting atop, guarding each corner of the royal chair.

The servant dashed to the guard who had ordered the halt and quietly informed him of the Pharaoh's request. The guard eyed him quizzically but when he turned his attention to the Pharaoh, who stepped from the palanquin, his expression instantly lost its questioning look.

The royal guard rode up to the Queen, dismounted his horse. "Per'a," he bowed, handing her the reins.

Tigris had made sure to wear a masculine kilt that day so she could sit comfortably on a horse. She took the reins, mounted the stallion and looked down at the guard. "You may continue to the palace," she said before she dug her heels into the horse and jaunted off.

The senior guard snapped his head around to look at the two retainers at the front of the palanquin and signalled for them to follow for her protection.

Tigris rode along the outer wall of the grand palace until it ended. Beside the Great House the large Temple of Horu rose out of the desert. The distance to the temple was further around the fortress' outer walls than through the dark passage cut beneath the earth. But, Tigris didn't care. She hated using the passage. The narrow corridors made her feel uneasy. Besides, outside she could admire the temple's grand architecture set against the blue Egyptian sky. The first pylon seemed to hold up the heavens while guarding the courtyard and the main building behind its enormous wall.

Tigris rode through its great entrance, into the sacred realm and up to the temple. She slowed her horse as she approached the steps leading up to the forbidden door of the Temple of Horu, which was once filled with mystery. Out of respect for her father, the Queen continued to keep the temple closed after his death. But, now she understood what she was respecting.

Tigris dismounted the horse, hesitantly made her way up the steps and through the entrance. The retainers remained outside, guarding what was believed to be the only way into the temple—the secret passage known only by a select few.

Inside, the temple was lit by torchlight. Tigris walked along the first hall towards the stairs, which descended down into the Great Hypostyle Hall. A soft scent of incense floated through the air. Closing her eyes, Tigris felt as if her body was being pulled forward by some unseen force; as if she were in a dream. She moved steadily down the length of the hallway, remembering the first time she was permitted into the temple—it seemed so long ago.

A door opened and the temple priest stepped into the hall, jarring Tigris from her memory. The priest stopped in his tracks the moment he saw his Pharaoh. Smiling broadly, he bowed to kiss the floor. His smile was filled with pride. He had attended to all his duties even in her absence and now the Pharaoh was there to witness his work.

Tigris gave him a gesture of approval. "I would like privacy," she requested before she continued on.

The priest waited until she passed before he went back into his chamber and closed the door.

Moving forward, Tigris reached the steps and descended them into the Great Hall which was lined with massive columns. She walked to one side, touching each column as she passed. *War. Death. Victory.* They were all painted on their surfaces. And, although nothing had changed, the room seemed strange to her as if suddenly she didn't know it.

"Oh father," Tigris whispered, "what have you done?"

She made her way towards the Great Room and stood at the doorway, looking around. "Is this why you shut everyone out of here?"

Tigris entered the chamber and shuddered. A cold feeling wisped through her.

"You had to do it. Anyone in your position would have if they loved this sacred Kemet." A lump formed in her throat. She closed her eyes, continued forward with her arms stretched out behind her, her head tilted back allowing an unexplained force to pull her in. The further she went into the chamber, the more the air grew chilled.

The Queen stopped before the gods. They seemed to look down on her with angry eyes. Tears trickled down Tigris' face. "Why like this?" she cried. "What do I do?" She crashed to her knees on the cushion she had once knelt on with her father. The lump grew in her throat, tears stung her eyes. "What do I do?" she whispered, bowing over until her forehead rested on the pillow with her arms spread out across the floor in front of her in a full bow before the gods.

Then the tears came streaming down her cheeks with desire and frustration. And, the mighty Pharaoh, *King* of Egypt allowed herself to cry long and hard.

ON THE TENTH hour of night, a short time before the sun would wake the earth, a message was delivered to the guard at the palace gate. He quickly carried it through the palace grounds and into Allegi's hands.

Allegi waited for the guard to leave, then broke the seal. Opening the scroll, he read the letter. Before he reached the last word, he sprang from his bed and dressed. He rushed through the hallway and up the stairs towards the King's quarters. Slipping into the audience chamber, he went over to the bedroom door and banged against it.

"Per'a? Per'a?" Allegi called out in a loud whisper as he opened the door and peered into the darkness.

Across the room, Tigris sat upright in bed with an arrow drawn on her bow, aimed straight at her messenger's head.

"Allegi?" she questioned a little disoriented as she set her bow down.

"I'm sorry Majesty, but I have news I thought you would want to hear before the sun rises." He walked further into the room, knelt at the end of the bed, peered at his Pharoah through the darkness. "The enemy marches on Lower Egypt. His army has grown and he is expected to cross the southern border within three days."

"What? Into Lower Egypt?" Tigris felt panic. "But he was to attack the Fortress of Ipu! I have sent Ankhtify to reinforce it. We will never get a message to the General in time." The Queen's face clouded with concern as she scrambled to think.

〰
〰

THE SERVANTS WERE woken on the eleventh hour and ordered to pack for their return to Henen-nesut. The drapes, cushions and rugs were gathered in chests and taken down to the ship but the food and lights were left to the housekeeper for his troubles.

At precisely the shift to day, the Pharaoh's vessel left the barque station.

XXVII

"WE WALK ON the path of our gods! Oser, slain by Set, thrown into the Nile River to become the ruler of the dead, guards us. His wife, Eset, the Great Mother Goddess who raised their son to avenge his father's death, protects us. Horu--who fought many battles against his father's murderer, until at last he defeated Set and became the ruler of the land of Egypt--guides us. Indeed, we walk on the path of our gods. For much is the same as my father, Pharaoh of Egypt, a deity as man and like Oser, he was slain by his 'brother.' And, I, raised by the good Goddess Eset to avenge his death, hold up my battle axe like Horu and lead us into combat in the name of justice!" Euphrates held his axe high above his head. He rode on his horse up and down the line. Over two thousand men stood in front of him and he yelled so every one of them could hear. "Like Horu, we may have to fight many battles but we will defeat our enemy. And, by the will of the gods and in honour of Oser, I will regain my rightful position as ruler of the lands of Kemet!"

The men roared, thrusting their weapons in the air. "A King for Egypt!" they hollered. Clubs banged against shields as they cheered for Euphrates.

"Tomorrow we will march to war with the gods at our side! And, let us remember," Euphrates thrust his axe towards the heavens, "we walk on the path of our gods!"

Euphrates lay on his bed staring into the darkness. He couldn't sleep. Tomorrow would be their first battle. All these years of preparation and he had brought men together who were not ready to fight. He wanted to go to the Fortress of Ipu to train his men behind the garrison's protective walls but since learning the Pharaoh had received word of their plans and had sent her General to reinforce the fort, Euphrates decided to change his course and march into the south. He knew Tigris would react the moment she discovered his action—it was the only territory in Egypt she still had under complete control. Euphrates' presence in Lower Egypt would greatly threaten her power and crown. As he expected, in defence, the warrior Queen gathered an army, which was en route to prevent his entry.

Euphrates sighed heavily. Tomorrow, he thought. He wasn't sure if he wanted it to hurry up or take its time to arrive. "Tomorrow," he whispered in the silence, the thought tensing his brow. He pushed his hand into his forehead.

Tomorrow he would see the Tigris again, if she did go to battle as her messenger had said.

The Pharaoh.

He remembered their last meeting—she was dressed in male clothing sitting on the Great Throne of Geb. She was beautiful, strong and held a power unlike any woman.

Euphrates sat up in bed and hunched over. He pressed into his temples where the pressure built inside his head. This was not how he had planned to go to war. His true enemy lay in Saqqara for all eternity with his life made glorious on his tomb walls. And now, Euphrates was forced to face the murderous Pharaoh's daughter in order to keep his silent promise to his father.

Rubbing his head, Euphrates groaned. He had to see it through. He couldn't forsake his promise because of unimagined circumstance; his aim was strictly to win back the throne and restore his father's bloodline. And, by the will of the gods, he would.

Euphrates tensed. *Restore the bloodline,* he repeated. Tigris' face appeared in his mind. He thought about how she made him feel when he was in her presence. Could he dare say the feeling was *blissful?*

Euphrates pushed the vision away, continued massaging his temples. The pain inside his head pounded harder. If things were different, he thought. If they were not enemies—she was the type of woman he wanted: strong, confident, beautiful. He shook his head not believing his own thoughts. But, whatever it was that drew him in and made him want her seemed only to grow stronger each time they met.

Euphrates huffed. "What cursed fate," he grumbled, emptying his mind of a thought as he collapsed back down onto his bed. He closed his eyes, let out a long deep sigh.

Tomorrow, he thought.

XXVIII

$\mathcal{T}$HE BEAT OF the Pharaoh's drums was heard across the desert even before her army was seen.

Euphrates' men were lined up in rows. Everyone except Euphrates was on foot.

Sitting on top of his stallion, Euphrates stared out over the land waiting for the Royal army to appear. But, the sound of the drums came first, sending warning with a steady, heavy beat echoing each step of the warriors' march.

Euphrates watched and waited. His moment was drawing near—the moment Euphrates envisioned ever since he was a boy.

At last, the royal army rose up into view and halted. A horn blew the call of war. Then, everything fell to a dead silence.

Euphrates peered through the bleary wave of heat at the massive army ahead of them. Although they were only a small line in the distance, it was apparent the royal army was not small—their numbers tripled Euphrates'.

The land remained hushed as the two armies assessed the situation. Then, the drums rolled out again and the royal soldiers began to march forward, closing the distance.

Euphrates turned his horse to face his men. "Before us, the Queen's army marches in fearsome size. But, do not shy from their numbers for we walk on the path of our gods!"

The men fixed their attention on their chosen King. They needed motivation to be able to battle confidently. The royal army out-numbered them not only in size but also in skill.

Shouting loudly, Euphrates gave his men a reason to believe they could win. "We fight for a cause, which is just and noble. And, warriors with passion and desire and belief behind their weapons always prevail despite numbers, despite skill, despite size!" Euphrates allowed his words to carry over the rows for a still moment before he held up his axe and roared, "By Oser we will prevail!"

The men agreed with cheer.

"Look upon that army," Euphrates hollered over their yells and the banging of their weapons. He pointed to their rivals who grew as they came towards them. "Know just as one small man can kill a lion twice his size and many times his strength, we *can* defeat that army!"

The men's cheer grew louder.

"In the name of Oser!" yelled out one of the men.

Other calls followed:

"In the name of justice!"

"In the name of our King, Usermaathor!"

Euphrates studied the Queen's army and devised his plan. Her number was too great and his men not yet trained. He knew his best option would cause doubt from his men or even anger by sparing their egos. But, ego was dangerous and often made bad choices. Wise men never based their choices on pride. Euphrates knew sometimes pride must bow to logic.

The only strategy for the weaker opponent was to out-think his opposition and Euphrates' plan spared ego to do so.

He turned to the men and gave his instruction. "When we march to battle, I want you to be chaotic in your fight. Do not look to winning. And, when I call retreat every man is to do just that."

The men's expressions were appalled with Euphrates' unprecedented scheme.

"We might as well lay down our weapons now and admit to loss!" scoffed one of the men.

"Loss is when you give up," Euphrates corrected. "And, by our retreat, we are *not* giving up." He began riding in front of the line. "Have no doubt. This course of action I command not in vain. Trust my leadership for I *will* lead us to nothing but victory!" Euphrates raised his axe above his head.

He was dressed in a short kilt covered by a thick leather warrior apron and he wore a leather corselet over his chest. In his hand he held his axe and at his side was his sword. The men were clothed in whatever they had. Most wore knee length kilts, some had helmets. They clung to spears and shields with additional weapons fixed at their waists. Those who had armour wore it.

The front two lines gripped bows—archers first, spearmen second and everyone else behind.

Riding to the middle of the front line, Euphrates stopped.

The royal drums gave their final beat as the Queen's army halted.

Once more everything fell silent. The Royal Army was in position, waiting, watching.

Euphrates turned his horse to face his opponents. His day had come—tomorrow had arrived. The war he longed about finally came to head. And yet, this was not his fantasy at all.

Euphrates looked at the army before him, disappointed that Qakare Iby did not stand amongst the soldiers; that he would never get his chance to strike him down. Regardless, he still fought for a cause, and he vied for it just as much. Yes, he would win back his rightful throne.

For some time neither force made a move, then, from the Royal side, a horse rode into the empty battle ground between the two armies.

Euphrates squinted, trying to make out the rider but the distance blurred his vision. He waited until the rider almost reached the middle before he dug his heels into his stallion and galloped out.

The hard desert ground was flat all around them before it took up towards the sky over the dry cavernous mountains. Its rocky earth surface was much more conducive to battle than the soft sands in the west.

As he neared the rider, he noticed the blue crown of war and suddenly felt his stomach flutter.

Tigris.

Riding in, he examined her, slowing his horse to give himself more time to look. She was dressed in masculine armour with a bow on her back, a sword at her side and a dagger in her belt. She looked beautiful. Stunning. Sparkling in the sunlight. She sat high on a white horse, fully fashioned for the occasion while Euphrates' black horse bore only a saddle.

Tigris slowed her steed to a walk. They drew in closer. A tingling sensation laced the pit of Euphrates' stomach and grew when they stopped head-to-head.

Euphrates sized the Egyptian Pharaoh. "Nitiqreti," he said flatly, nodding his head to greet her.

"Usermaathor," Tigris replied, keeping her head held stiff, her voice sounding as if it almost groaned the prenomen name with disgust.

Silence gripped the moment as the two eyed each other. Then, Tigris took a breath. "Withdraw. You do not have enough men to contend with my army."

A sarcastic grin curled Euphrates' lips. "Wait until you see them fight."

Tigris eyed his force ruefully. "They won't even have the chance." She pulled on the reins of her horse.

Euphrates watched the Queen gallop away. A feeling rushed over him and he suddenly didn't want the moment to end.

"Tigris!" he yelled before she was able to get very far. He didn't know why he called to her or what he would say. It was as if her name flew from his mouth on its own and by the time it hit the air, it was too late to take it back.

Tigris halted. Euphrates rode to her. He circled her horse, drew up to her side. He examined Tigris' face, searching her expression for the look he had found when he had kissed her hand. He was certain he had seen it, *felt* it even.

Tigris remained with her stare fixed forward on her army, waiting for him to speak, not giving him her attention.

Euphrates was quiet, studying her. He wanted to see it again—the expression that revealed how she truly felt—he needed to know if what he saw was real. Euphrates took her hand, looked into her eyes. "May greatness always rain upon you and may the gods watch over you. I wish you luck, good Tigris." He moved to kiss her hand but Tigris pulled it away.

"Keep your luck," she retorted curtly. "You will need it more than I." Whipping at her horse, Tigris raced back to her army, leaving Euphrates facing his.

As the Queen fled, a feeling of loss fell over Euphrates and he hadn't even yet begun to fight.

Euphrates sized his men—almost three thousand. He took a deep breath. "Alas, it is war," he whispered.

〰

THE QUEEN'S HORSE galloped across the desert leaving her enemy behind. Yet, moments from now they would face each other again, this time with their weapons raised. Tigris took a deep breath trying to soothe the tightness in her chest.

Why did he behave with such seduction? Why did he insist on

looking at her with longing and kissing her so sensually?

This time she pulled away before he was able to lay his lips on her hand even though it pained her to do so. But, she would not go to battle with confused emotions. She needed to keep her head clear and remember today she faced her *enemy*.

Tigris sucked in another deep breath. What will become of this day? she thought. Certainly, it would not take long to defeat him—and then what? What will be when the dust has settled? Will everything go back to the way it was?

Tigris cringed at the idea then almost felt to laugh. *Impossible.* How could anything go back when everything had changed?

The *King* of Egypt, Pharaoh of the Two Lands, reached her army. She pulled her horse to a stop. Before her, her army men looked imperial standing ready for combat; ready to fight for *her*.

"Good noble warriors, I have fought with you since I was a child," she said, addressing the men. "Many of you at one time helped train me and I have made it my life's purpose not to disappoint you. I am your Pharaoh, a woman born but not bred. Now, in the second year of my reign, I lead you into combat as any Chief of Army would do!" Tigris turned, pointed to Euphrates' army. "Ahead of us a man claims his rule over Egypt. He promises you a Pharaoh *King*. He replaces the supreme deity, our royal god Re with Oser. But, if it was the will of the gods that he be Pharaoh then it would be him, not I, at the head of the royal army today." Tigris pointed to the heavens. "The gods removed him!"

Tigris began to ride along her front line. She yelled out with power behind her voice. "Today let it be written for all eternity, Nitiqreti, Tigris of Egypt, is a divine being. That which has happened was meant. I am a god of men, King of Egypt, chosen by Amun. Like all Kings before me, I bravely lead you into battle to restore peace in our great Kingdom of Kemet!" Tigris rode to the centre of the front line. She jumped from her horse, slapped its rump to send it away. She lifted her bow from her back where she had it strapped and grabbed an arrow. "In the name of Amun-Re let us return Re to Upper Egypt and reunite our lands!"

Tigris set an arrow in her bow. "Archers ready!" she yelled out.

The command was echoed through the companies by the Battalion

Commanders and then repeated by the Captains of the Troops. The two front lines got down on one knee and set their arrows in their bows.

"*Fire!*" Tigris ordered.

Before she finished the word, Euphrates' army ran forward. They divided in half, running apart, leaving a large open gap in the middle of the battle ground.

The royal arrows, already released, soared through the air, failing to strike their target as they fell into the barren middle. Only the ends of her battle line were able to succeed as Euphrates' army raced in those directions.

Dividing rapidly, the self-proclaimed King made it awkward to use the bowmen. Much of the Queen's army would have to reposition. Euphrates' militia now stood waiting for her in two separate forces.

Tigris analyzed the situation. She unsheathed her Sumerian sword, held it forward. "*Charge!*" she commanded.

Her army charged forward, splitting in two in order to align themselves with their opposition. As they did, Euphrates' archers rained arrows down upon them from both sides. Royal soldiers were struck down to their knees and trampled on by the men who followed behind them.

Tigris continued forward, holding her bronze shield above her head. Most of her soldiers carried wooden shields with a leather covering but the Pharaoh's was made of metal with Set, the God of War, carved and painted on the front.

As the royal battalions persisted, Euphrates' two forces suddenly began to run back towards each other fencing in the Royal Army from both sides.

Tigris halted. Men raced passed her while those who noticed Euphrates' plan, stopped to hold their ground. The Queen looked around, calculated. If they held ground, regrouped, they would be surrounded, trapped in the centre of the rebel force. She needed to keep Euphrates' army separated; they would be weaker that way.

Frantically, Tigris spun. "Push out!" she ordered, signalling the men who stopped to hold ground. "Push back out!"

Desperately, Tigris searched through the rush of men until she spotted one of her commanders. She ran to him. "Push out. Keep the army separated. Don't let him lead us into a trap!"

The commander nodded, yelled an order to his men.

Tigris looked around again. She darted to another commander. "Push out!" she pointed. "Our numbers are greater. He won't survive if we keep his army divided."

Before Euphrates' forces had the chance to close in the Royal Army, Tigris' soldiers were driving them back, pushing them out, keeping them divided.

Relieved, Tigris eyed the two battles and wondered which one Euphrates fought amongst.

The coalition and the Royal Army collided. The battle ensued with angry weapons soaring. Battle axes and clubs banged together, swords slashed violently and spears flew through the air. Roars of men rose up, covering the battleground like a blanket.

Tigris held her shield in her left hand, her sword in her right. Like every other soldier, she fought hard, slaying men.

Beneath their feet, the desert seemed to drink the blood of the slain; yells and cries shrieked across the land, inviting the vultures circling the sky waiting for their turn. But, the gruesome fight did not go on for long.

Euphrates' men fought chaotically. No one seemed to be in charge or give commands as they faltered. They failed miserably in a poor attempt at combat.

Finally, Tigris heard Euphrates order their retreat. Men pulled out, away from the battlefield. Euphrates remained. He continued to ward off soldiers until his men were free from the fight. Then, he fled to join them.

The royal army watched their enemies scurry away defeated. The soldiers rejoiced in victory, holding their weapons above their heads in cheer. But, Tigris did not feel like she achieved victory yet. Somehow she knew this was only the beginning.

The bloody remains of the slain and the whimpering cries of the wounded surrounded them.

Tigris peered into the distance, thinking, questioning. She was still watching the enemy retreat when Intify, who commanded in Ankhtify's absence, came up beside her and waited for his orders.

"Kill the dying, help the suffering and collect the booty," Tigris commanded before she stomped away.

An hour later, the corpses were burned.

XXIX

ЄUPHRATES AND HIS men reached their camp where the doctors, cooks and men of other duties had remained behind. The camels and donkeys lazed about the desert in a group while the horses were confined to a make-shift pen. Everything remained packed on wagons in case they needed to leave immediately. But now, they would unpack and stay the night.

Euphrates climbed on top of one of the wagons and banged his axe against his shield in order to get the men's attention. They gathered in front of him, chattering noisily, still angered by the embarrassment of their retreat.

Tuthiken came up beside the wagon where Euphrates stood. He inhaled an enormous breath and used it to bellow out, "Quiet!" His voice was so strong it seemed to shake the earth beneath their feet, bringing the men into silence. Looking up at Euphrates with a grin, Tuthiken gave him the floor.

The self-proclaimed King glanced around at the men who gathered; more still moved in, taking their time in their annoyance but Euphrates didn't bother to wait.

"Do not dwell in anger, my good men," he began. "Sometimes it is necessary to make difficult choices in order to succeed. But, only those who are strong enough to concede to making these choices find their success."

The sour expressions of the men conveyed they were not convinced.

"Today, we retreated from battle but we return to our camp with very few casualties—a triumph in itself. I promise when we return to the battlefield tomorrow you will find yourselves with a different confidence." Euphrates jumped down from the wagon and made his way through the crowd. He would say no more; he would let them see for themselves.

The men began to disperse, complaining about their fight.

Euphrates decided to leave them alone to brood. He felt exhausted, dehydrated. He wanted nothing more than to fill his gut with water and lay out on his bed in solitude.

Looking up at the sun, Euphrates calculated the time. It was just after mid-day and yet, the day felt long. Sweat dripped from his brow. He swiped it away.

Euphrates walked through the grounds, turned a corner and stopped short. The boy who had attempted to enlist in his army was at his camp. A rush of fury went through him. He marched up behind the child. "What are you doing here!" he snapped, startling the boy.

The boy spun around with a frightened look on his face.

"How did you get here?" Euphrates demanded.

"I—I followed your troop," he quivered.

Euphrates glared down at the child in anger. "I told you, you could not join my army!"

"But, I killed a soldier today."

Disbelief engulfed Euphrates. "And, you're proud of that?"

The boy looked up at him dumbstruck.

Euphrates couldn't believe it—an eleven year old boy in his army. How did his men not see him and prevent it? Euphrates huffed heavily, his rage adding to the heat. "How am I supposed to get you home?" he scowled.

"I don't want to go home." The boy's eyes were begging but Euphrates didn't care.

"Well, you're not staying here," Euphrates turned and walked away. To add to all of his stresses, he now had to figure out how to get the child back to Wasebet.

The boy followed him, almost running to keep up. "Please Per'a, let me stay. I beg you. I promise to be no trouble."

Euphrates stormed to his tent, ignoring him.

"Per'a, I beg you! I want to be a warrior. I will slay a hundred men for you!"

Euphrates didn't answer; his mind was made up. The boy was going home. He would not have the child's blood on his hands.

Marching into his tent, Euphrates threw the flap closed behind him. But, the boy persisted, following him in.

"Please," he pleaded.

Euphrates spun to look at him, shocked the child was bold enough to enter his tent without invitation. He glared at the child. The boy's face looked as if he were about to cry.

"Where are your parents?" Euphrates demanded.

"My father's in jail and my mother doesn't care."

"You probably have your poor mother worried to tears."

The boy shook his head. "I told her I was going to war and she said, 'good.' She only cares about my sister."

Euphrates studied him. He was small and thin and too young. What would he do with a *boy?* Euphrates frowned in contemplation. "What is your name again?"

"Barin."

"Barin," repeated Euphrates. He shook his head. Eleven years old, he thought, remembering the boy's age.

Barin stood with his sword in his hand, which dragged to the ground, the blade still blotted with dried blood.

Eleven, Euphrates thought again. It's a wonder he wasn't killed.

Euphrates shook his head contradictorily to his words. "Alright Barin, you may stay."

The boy's face lit up.

Euphrates tensed his voice. "But, you are *not* to go to battle."

The excitement in Barin's eyes left as rapidly as it had come. "But, I have passion behind my sword and you said, 'despite size!'"

"Though, I did not say *despite age.*" Euphrates studied Barin with admiration; he really liked the kid. The boy had a warrior spirit and he definitely had passion. Still, Euphrates would not have the child's blood on his hands.

"So, do you want to stay?" Euphrates asked in a deep tone.

Barin nodded.

"Then you do *not* go to battle. Do you understand?"

The boy remained still.

"If I see you on my battlefield, I will have you taken back to Wasebet before the fight is even over. Do I make myself clear?"

Through big brown eyes, Barin looked timidly at Euphrates and nodded.

"Good. Now promise me," Euphrates demanded.

"I promise," Barin agreed in a faint whisper.

Euphrates sighed before breaking the tension with a smile. "I will find other noble jobs for you to do to keep your stay. And, if you keep your promise, I will teach you weaponry."

Barin's face lit up again.

"Now, go find Menenthop and tell him he is to watch over you."

The boy spun and ran out of the tent elated to be a part of Euphrates' army.

Smiling, Euphrates went to a large clay pitcher and drank back some water. He lay down on his bed, looked up at the tent roof and sighed heavily. Another night of waiting for tomorrow, he thought. Another night spent thinking about the Queen.

Images of the battle flashed through his mind. She *fought* with her men. The idea of it astounded him. *Strong, confident, beautiful.* And, to know, she was only a stretch away from where he lay now....

Euphrates sprang up, went to his desk. He pulled out a piece of parchment and his writing kit. Crushing pigment with some water he dipped his brush into the ink and scribed:

> *My dearest sister Nitiqreti, Tigris of Egypt,*
>
> *It is my regret that I was unable to face your father in the time of his reign for he is my true enemy. Nonetheless, fate has found me on the battlefield facing you with my desire to restore my father's bloodline, which I had solemnly promised as I watched him die in your murderous father's arms.*
>
> *Today, I witnessed your greatness when you raised your sword and led your men into battle. You are a glorious Queen. And, when I look into your eyes, behind the glory I see the way you look at me.*

Euphrates stopped writing, read back what he wrote. The brush had glided across the page as his thoughts fell onto the parchment in all their honesty. He wondered if he had written too much. Though he didn't care; he just needed to see—to know if that look he had witnessed meant something—if it was real. How else could he find out but to write to her in hopes she would read his true message and respond with the same honesty?

His brush hit the page again:

> *We both fight for Egypt, for greatness, and for the causes we believe in. But, does it not strike you as odd that our names are of two great rivers in Sumer where our fathers at one time campaigned together?*
>
> *Great Tigris, there must be more to it.*
>
> *I know that look in your eyes....*

Euphrates set down the brush as if it were possessed. He rolled up the papyrus and pulled a small glob of clay from a compartment in his writing box. Wetting it, he slapped it on the scroll, took out his seal and stamped the clay with the carved image of the scarab next to his cartouche to seal it close.

Euphrates sat back in his chair for a moment, clasping the letter tight in his fist. Disbelief rushed over him. What was he thinking? What if he imagined what he saw in Tigris to be more than what it was? Standing, he let out a deep sigh, left his tent. He didn't care; he needed to know.

Walking through the tented area, Euphrates found Barin sitting with Menenthop who enthralled him with a tale he sang as he strummed his lute.

"Look," Menenthop pointed when he spotted Euphrates approaching. "There's our Great King now."

Euphrates smiled, stopping before them. He looked at Barin. "Whatever stories this man sings to you, it is a far stretch from the truth."

Barin grinned back at Euphrates. "I believe you were strengthened by the gods."

Chuckling, Euphrates gave Menenthop an inquisitive look.

Menenthop shrugged. "Kids these days, I don't know where he got that."

Euphrates smiled, shaking his head at Menenthop. He held up the scroll to Barin. "I have found a very noble job for you to do. It is dangerous and not a job I would entrust with many."

Barin gleamed with excitement.

"Come and walk with me."

Leaping to his feet, the boy rushed to Euphrates' side, leaving Menenthop singing to himself.

"Does he know he can't sing?" Barin asked.

"No," Euphrates snickered. Taking a few more strides, he looked at Barin, changing the topic. "Do you know how to ride a camel?"

Barin nodded, still with a big grin stretched across his face.

"Can you be trusted?"

Putting his hand over his heart, he nodded again.

"Good." Euphrates stopped at a tall vessel of water and pulled out a ladle. He offered it to the boy.

Barin gulped down the water, handed the large spoon back to Euphrates. Dipping it into the pot again, Euphrates took a drink for himself.

Several vessels were clustered together and filled with water and many of these same clusters were spread around the camp. A team of men were responsible for keeping the water vessels full. The job of the water bearers was honoured; water was their life source and supremely important for survival in the dry sands of the desert.

The rebellions travelled the route of the Nile. When the vessels were low, the water bearers would trek out to the river with the vessels and bring them back replenished. Wells along the desert routes also provided a resource where the water could be refilled.

Euphrates dropped the ladle back into the water vessel and looked up at the position of the sun. It would be a couple of hours before the sun would begin to set. Lowering his eyes, he turned his attention to the boy and looked at him with graveness. "When dusk arrives, I want you to deliver a very important message to the Pharaoh."

Barin's mouth fell open. "To the *Pharaoh?*" he repeated, shocked to be given the opportunity to go before her. It was an extreme privilege, which not many commoners ever had.

"Her camp is set about an hour's ride from here, close to the Nile." Euphrates pointed in the distance. "You will ride with a messenger's flag and be protected underneath it." Euphrates studied the boy.

Barin's expression was still filled with excitement.

"You must make sure it is delivered directly to the Pharaoh and not to her Royal Messenger." He waved the parchment in the air, emphasizing his instruction. "This message is for the Pharaoh's eyes only." Euphrates deepened his voice to give it an inflection of importance. "Can you handle this gallant appointment?"

Wide-eyed, Barin nodded anxiously, his face glowing with eagerness.

Euphrates held the scroll out to him. The boy placed his hand around it, went to take it but Euphrates held on.

"Respect her," the self-proclaimed King added, sending the boy a piercing look. "She is still a Pharaoh."

Euphrates let go of the parchment.

XXX

*T*IGRIS LAY IN her lavish tent listening to the soft music Allegi played. He blew on a double pipe, which gave off a deep yet smooth tone.

The tent was large and filled with decorations. Rugs and furs covered the ground and trunks, chests and statues of protective deities were arranged for visual beauty. There was a table and chair for the Pharaoh to eat at as well as a large low bench. The bench had bronze legs carved in the shape of a lion's paw and held up a rectangular frame with leather tightly stretched across it to make a bed. Cushions and pillows overflowed off the bed onto the floor. Everything was either painted or made from colourful fabrics. Set across the white backdrop of the tent, the rich and vibrant colours indeed made the interior feel like it was fashioned for a Pharaoh.

Lying down, Tigris listened to the tranquil flow of music as she replayed the battle in her mind. She was shocked at how poorly Euphrates' army had fought. It was so unlike what she expected from him that she almost believed she had dreamt it.

Tigris opened her eyes, looked over at Allegi. "What do you think of today's battle?"

Allegi pulled the instrument from his mouth, bringing the tent into silence. He thought for a moment before he answered. "Strange," he said, still thinking.

"Me too. He started off strong, with great strategy but when the battle began his men did not know how to fight."

Allegi shrugged. "He has spent his time recruiting men. He hasn't had the opportunity to train them."

Tigris closed her eyes again, grinned. "And, we will ensure he never gets that opportunity."

Allegi raised the pipe back to his lips and continued to play. The soft low-pitched noise of the instrument was passive, pleasant, perfect.

A while later, a voice called out and the tent flap drew open, revealing the darkening sky outside as a servitor stepped in. The servant bowed and took the tray of food he carried over to the table.

Allegi set the double pipe in one of the chests. He went to grab a chair by the tent wall, brought it over to the table and sat across from Tigris.

"I think tomorrow I will return to the palace," Tigris informed.

A puzzled look spread over Allegi.

"It's too expensive to keep all of the soldiers here, especially when Egypt is facing famine from the upheaval caused by this civil war," she stated. "A single division is more than enough to take the rebel force—" Tigris let out a small laugh. "A company could bring down his army."

Allegi chuckled. There were only five hundred men in a company and three thousand in Euphrates' army.

Tigris lifted her cup. "To a great first day at battle and to many more," she toasted.

Allegi raised his cup. "Or to many less."

They sipped.

The meal consisted of ostrich, vegetables, bread and sweet wine with a dish of fruit for dessert. The soldiers, however, would have fish and beer.

〰〰

OUTSIDE, AROUND THE campfires the soldiers celebrated their victory with food, drinks and laughter. Above, the sun had fallen allowing the light from the fires to illuminate the camp.

Barin rode into the royal camp on camel and steered himself to the closest fire pit. The men fell hushed as they took notice of their unexpected guest.

Drawing his camel to a stop, Barin watched as a soldier stomped towards him.

"Who are you?" the soldier demanded, sizing the boy.

Barin gestured towards his flag. "I am the King's messenger."

The soldier bellowed with laughter, his comrades joined in. "The *King?*" he questioned. "You ride in from the wrong side to be bringing a message from the *King.*"

"I bring a message from *King* Euphrates," Barin said stubbornly, standing his ground.

"Oh," retorted the soldier, stepping closer. "You mean you are the *rebel's* messenger?" The soldier turned to the other men around the campfire. "No wonder the fool can't fight. He's employed children barely off their mother's breast."

The men roared with laughter.

Barin grew angry. "I killed a man in battle today!" he bragged, defending his size and capability. But, as the words rolled off his tongue and the soldiers' laughter ended, Barin regretted his words.

The man who stood next to Barin spun to face him with a vehement glare. "Come, say it again boy," he urged.

Barin hesitated. Tension seized the night air around them with such speed that fear pumped into the boy's chest. But, he wouldn't allow himself to back down. He was a warrior. He pushed out his chest, repeated his words, "I said I killed a man."

"You killed a man?" the soldier repeated. He gestured at the royal camp. "One of *our* men?"

Barin suddenly realized the trap he had put himself into. His heart pumped harder.

"Is this the news you come all the way to *our* camp to deliver?"

The reflection of the fire burned in the soldier's eyes and for a moment Barin thought the soldier was bewitched.

"A warrior by day and a messenger by night?" the soldier growled. He lunged at Barin's camel and took hold of the messenger flag, which was strapped to the animal. "How dare you travel under the protection of peace when you raise a sword!" His voice boomed with rage. He tried to rip the flag from the camel. Struggling, he managed to get the staff loose. He threw the flag into the fire.

Barin gaped, frightened for his life. "I was just made a messenger today," he informed. "I've been forbidden to fight."

The soldier yanked Barin from the camel. "But, you killed a man, right? One of ours?"

Barin struggled, trying to get out of the soldier's hold. "Let me go!" he shouted. "I come in peace!"

"Perhaps we should *kill* you in trade," the soldier spat, lifting Barin above his head. He threw the boy to one of his comrades.

The soldier caught him.

Barin kicked and fought to no avail. "Let me go! I bring a message to the Pharaoh!"

"Perhaps we should throw him in the fire," said the soldier who caught him. Like a doll, he tossed the boy over the flames to one of the men on the other side of the fire.

"Put me down! Let me go!" Barin screamed.

The soldiers ignored him.

〰

TIGRIS SET THE piece of meat she held in her hand back down on the plate and listened. "Do you hear that?" she asked Allegi.

Allegi listened for a moment but before he had the chance to reply, the Queen sprang to the door.

Tigris strode towards the noise. She was certain she heard the screams of a *child*.

"*I bring a message to the Pharaoh,*" the voice cried.

A *child?* Tigris questioned, wondering if she made the voice out right. What would a child be doing here and why did the voice sound like it was distressed?

She turned a corner alongside a tent and came in view of the fire pit. Peering towards the campfire, Tigris could see something being tossed in the air over the flames. She focused in on the figure and gasped in horror. It *was* a child!

Tigris ran towards the group of men. What were her soldiers doing! What was a child doing at her camp! "Put him down!" she ordered as she reached the fire with Allegi at her heels.

Startled by her presence, the men dropped the boy and bowed their heads in shame.

"What kind of way is this for *royal soldiers* to behave?" she scorned, going to the boy to see if he was alright.

Barin stood, dusted himself off with rage frowning his face. He held back his tears; he would not cry. After straightening his clothes, he looked up. His mouth fell open as he gasped—the Pharaoh Queen stood over him.

"Per'a," Barin whispered, falling to his knees stricken with awe. No one in Wasebet had ever laid eyes on her graciousness and now, he was in arm's reach. "I bring a message from the King—for your eyes only."

Tigris looked down at him, taken aback by the situation—angered by her soldiers' behaviour; stunned by the fragile frame of the small boy who belonged to Euphrates' army.

Her mind raced. For a moment she was dumbstruck. It took a moment before she could respond. "Follow me."

〰

ALLEGI LOOKED AT the flag in the fire. He went to it, took hold of the staff, which hung out of the flames, scooped it up and grabbed the battle axe from the belt of the soldier standing next to him. With a single chop, he cut off the flaming end of the pole. He tossed the axe into the fire and stormed to the boy's camel. Grabbing the reins, Allegi led the animal away, leaving the men to their shame.

〰

THE QUEEN MARCHED into her tent. "You bring a message?" Tigris questioned, pulling her chair away from the table and facing the room. Sitting, she eyed the child.

"Yes," Barin responded, lowering to his knees and bowing his head to the floor.

Tigris studied him. He couldn't be any more than nine or ten years old. "What would my enemy want with such a young boy in his army?" she questioned.

Barin kept his head to the ground. "I snuck off with the rebels when they left Wasebet and His Majesty only discovered my presence today."

Tigris strained to hear him. "You may sit up," she permitted.

203

Raising his body, Barin remained on his knees, keeping his head tipped in a slight bow. "I begged him not to send me back to Wasebet," he explained, "so, he granted me the noble duty of messenger."

Tigris sat quietly. The job of a messenger, she thought—so the child would be protected under the flag of peace. She eyed the fragile yet brave boy and nodded with a slight smile on her lips. "And, a very noble duty it is," she agreed. "What's your name?"

"Barin."

"Your age?"

"Eleven."

"You have much courage for eleven, Barin," Tigris said with admiration.

Barin lifted his head. "I want to be a warrior—a General of armies."

Tigris let out a soft chuckle. "You are definitely well on your way."

Her comment brought a pleasant smile to the boy's face. Tigris studied him briefly, suddenly feeling betrayed. "Tell me Barin, why do you choose to fight with the rebels?"

The boy's smile disappeared and his eyes looked to the floor in shame.

"Tell me," she repeated, softening her tone. "Your honesty won't anger me."

Barin said nothing for quite some time before he dropped his chin to his chest and admittedly whispered, "A King for Egypt."

His words dug hard into Tigris but she let them go. Sighing, she stood.

Barin followed her with his eyes.

"A King for Egypt," she echoed. "It is so unfortunate men and women can never be equals." She walked towards the boy, crouched down to his level. "Other than being born a woman," she asked softly, "have I ever done anything to make you not want me as your Pharaoh?"

Barin shook his head, no.

"And yet, I am not good enough." Tigris forced a grin, shook her head with disdain as she stretched her arm out towards the boy. "Your message," she said, gently.

Barin pulled out the scroll and handed it to her.

Tigris took the parchment, returned to her chair. Plopping down, a heavy feeling surrounded her. She was unsure whether it was because of the boy or because she held Euphrates' words in her hand.

Tigris opened the letter and read it. When she was done, she allowed the scroll to roll itself back up. She slumped back in her seat.

He didn't even sign the letter, she thought. His last line abruptly stopped and its words echoed in her mind. *I know that look in your eyes...*

The look in my eyes? Tigris contemplated. She refused to believe he saw anything.

Standing, Tigris went to a chest and opened it. She pulled out a piece of parchment and a writing kit then carried them back to the table. She sat facing the table, pushed the dishes aside and prepared to write. But, as she stared at the empty page in front of her, she found she didn't know how to fill it.

What was he asking? Could he have seen it in my eyes? My secret truth or did he interpret it as something else?

I know that look. Did he really expect her to admit it? She would never admit it—*could* never. They were *enemies*. How could she admit to it? How did *it* even exist? The thought made Tigris bitter. It was weakness and she had pride.

No, Tigris seethed. She would not let that childish feeling lessen her sense of self. She would never give in.

Tigris chewed on the end of the brush. She knew the boy was watching and he would no doubt report her reaction to Euphrates. She forced her composure as she opened the letter to skim over it again.

A glorious *Queen*, she noticed. He had underlined the word *Queen* as if he mocked her title. The sight of it made her blood boil. But, in spite of her rage, Tigris delicately set the scroll down on the table, dipped her brush in ink and wrote:

> *Oh brother, <u>blasphemous King</u> of Egypt, Euphrates,*
> *The only look you see in my eyes is scorn. I often wonder if your drunken father was left to rule our great nation, would there even be an Egypt here for you to claim?*
> *Though, it pleases me that you have confessed to my greatness and have recognized me as the warrior Pharaoh I am.*
> *You say we both fight for Egypt with the same cause, but truly*

our causes are much different. While I fight for peace, you fight
to steal my land at whatever cost. Tell me, which to you seems
more honourable?

Your humble sister, the <u>Neb-taui King</u>, Nitiqreti, Tigris of
Egypt.

Tigris set down her brush and leaned back in her seat for a moment
while she thought about what she had written. She knew mentioning
his father as a drunk was lowly. But, he referred to her father as a
murderer and the sight of the word—maybe more the truth of it—
brought her pain.

Remembering the boy, Tigris glanced over at him. His eyes fell to
look at the floor. The boy's gesture indicated he felt caught, which
meant he noted something about her behaviour. Indeed, he would
report it. Tigris couldn't be bothered to care.

Turning away, the Queen sat up, rolled up the parchment, sealed it
with clay and stamped it with the Royal Seal. She took the scroll to the
boy and handed it to him. "Please deliver this to Euphrates." She
returned to her chair, slumped down.

〰

BARIN STOOD AND went to the tent door. He looked back at the
Pharaoh with admiration. She was so beautiful and so kind. Guilt
struck him. He raced to her side, took her hand and fell to his knees
with his head bowed. "I'm so sorry Per'a for betraying you. Please
forgive me," he begged.

Tigris looked at him. Smiled. Using the hand, he held, she lifted his
chin. "Noble Barin," she said, tenderly. "I do forgive you." Her smile
faded. Her expression became solemn. "But, you must be sure to keep
your honour." The Queen placed her hand on top of his head. "You
have chosen your side. Now, you must be loyal to it." Stroking his
cheek, she pulled her hand away.

The boy looked up into her eyes and she could see he understood.

Barin raised his hand over his heart and whispered, "Honour."

Tigris forced a small smile and nodded towards the door. "Now,
return to your King and deliver that message."

Barin rose to his feet, keeping his head bent. He leaned over and

206

kissed Tigris' hand, which rested on the chair arm. He ran out.

Outside, the boy found his camel waiting for him. Strapped to the animal's back was a new messenger's flag on a shorter staff.

Barin beamed as he climbed onto the camel. This was the best day of his life!

XXXI

EARLY THE NEXT morning, half of the camp packed and prepared to leave. Only Sekhmet division was left to deal with the coalition under the command of Intify.

Seated on her sedan, Tigris was carried towards her ship with Allegi riding by her side. The last of the equipment was being gathered and would follow the procession to the river. Food provisions for the men making their way home would be put on its own vessel and distributed to the cities along the Nile in the name of the Pharaoh.

Famine begun to grow in Egypt under the mayhem of war and the inundation of the Nile threatened to be low. Since many soldiers were withdrawn from the battle, giving food in such drought times to secure favouritism was more important than keeping it. The generosity of the Pharaoh would help to gain support from the people, which would reduce the possibility of more anarchy.

A long caravan rolled towards the ships. Men followed alongside of the wagons, moving towards the small town by the river where the ships were able to dock. It would take them less than an hour to reach the vessels.

The Egyptian sun had not yet shown itself but the sky was growing light. Tigris stared up towards the promising light of morning. Euphrates' words echoed in her mind all night.

I know that look.

His words threatened the wall inside her. How could she have let him see it? Why did it even exist?

The weakness within women, she could hear her father warn. Tigris clenched her teeth. No, she could not allow it to weaken her. She had promised to rule like a man. She couldn't permit that shameful feeling to take control.

You must in the name of the crown devote yourself to shed emotion, her father's voice boomed inside her, his final word delivered with a thud.

Tigris blinked hard at the sun, which peeked over the horizon. She glanced at Allegi, pointed. "By the time the sun reaches the west, I am hoping this war will end." She momentarily lost herself in the radiance of the sky. She forced all feelings away, angered by their existence. Then, she waved one of the retainers forward.

The large man rode up to the side of the sedan. "Your Majesty?" he nodded.

Tigris' voice was unusually cold and hard. "Return to the camp and inform Intify that I want my rebellious leader brought back to me *dead.*"

Allegi whipped his head around and glared at her in horror.

The retainer dropped out of line and took off to the royal camp.

"Why do you want him *dead?*" Allegi demanded, shock apparent in his tone.

"Because he is my *enemy* and that is what you do with enemies of the crown," Tigris defended through clenched teeth.

Allegi shook his head. He couldn't believe she would give such an order. He had seen the way they looked at each other every time they met; he had witnessed how intense that look had grown when Euphrates kissed her hand. One could *feel* it even—it was so strong it overtook a room. Moreover, and for some reason, he did not view Euphrates as an enemy at all.

"I believe your greatest enemy is yourself," Allegi scoffed. He stopped his horse, waited for the chair bearers to get ahead. He didn't want to be next to her. Anger burned inside him.

Allegi watched the army men and wagons pass by him. Fury pushed its weight on him until he felt as if he couldn't move. Why did her order make him so angry? he wondered. But, somehow it just didn't seem right. Of course killing the enemy in war was natural but *this* did not seem natural.

Tigris seethed with rage as she sat in the sedan holding the face of contentment. She wasn't sure if she was angry with Allegi or herself. She *had* to make that order. It was the only way to end this war—to end her thoughts. She didn't sleep last night—couldn't sleep. All night she thought of *him*, his letter—his insinuating words. What did he want? Why did he write it?

Does it not strike you odd that our names are of two great rivers in Sumer where our fathers at one time campaigned together?

Yes, it was odd. Why would the two men name them together? Yet, what did it matter now?

The first of the Queen's procession reached the royal vessels. Tigris' chair was lowered. She stepped off and walked towards the plank. She hated being carried up the steep incline on the sedan.

Beside her, the line of men divided. Five large ships were needed to carry them all back to Henen-nesut but only two could dock at once. While the other vessels waited in the middle of the Nile, the first two ships would load then make way for two more to come into the station. The last ship would carry the extra food and would sail on its own.

Tigris climbed the ship plank. She was glad to be leaving. She didn't want to be anywhere near *him*.

"Per'a! Per'a!" A rider raced towards the vessel. "Great Majesty!" he hollered.

Tigris stopped and turned.

"Per'a! A letter!" The rider reached the bottom of the plank. He jumped down from his camel, raced up the incline towards the Queen and presented a quick bow. "The young boy came to deliver it to you. It's from the rebel King."

Tigris peered across the desert. "Is he reconsidering already?" she leered.

The soldier pulled the scroll out of a pouch and handed it to her. Tigris took the scroll, thanked him with a nod, continued up the plank.

From further back in the line, Allegi observed the exchange. He raced towards the ship. For some reason, knowing the letter was from Euphrates propelled him. He jumped off his horse and soared up the plank towards the Queen almost knocking the soldier over who delivered the scroll. By the time Allegi reached her, Tigris was half way to her cabin.

Tigris darted an irritated look at her messenger as he came up beside her. "What is it with you?" she spurned. "What are you looking for?"

Allegi remained quiet. He walked beside her with his eyes fixed on the deck floor.

Tigris furrowed her brow in frustration. "Do you not understand he is my *enemy*—*enemy to my empire?*"

Allegi responded with more silence.

Tigris let out a long breath. She stopped to face him. "You are five years younger than me. You think like a child. You are chasing dreams—impossible dreams!" Spinning with a huff, Tigris began to walk again. "I don't know exactly what you pretend to see but it does *not* exist."

They arrived at her cabin door, stopped in front of it.

"I want you to be happy," Allegi finally said.

Tigris forced a smile. "I will be happy when this war has ended and everything returns to the way it was." She pushed the door open, stepped inside the dank cabin.

"I don't believe that to be true."

Tigris froze with her back to Allegi. She knew he was right but she would never admit it.

"Nor is it possible for it to ever be the way it was." Allegi almost whispered the words but their reality rang loud, jabbing her like a knife, tearing at her with their truth.

"The question is, Per'a, what do you choose to do with the way it *is?*"

His question robbed Tigris of her breath. The air clung inside her increasing the pain that had sprung up within her chest. She couldn't speak; couldn't reply. All she could manage was to close the door and shut Allegi out.

Tigris dropped her weight against the door and hung her head back. *Why can't I just have a war? A simple war where both sides hate each other?* She looked at the scroll in her hand. She didn't even have the will to read it. She mustered her strength, made her way to her chair, slumped down. For a long time Tigris stared at the parchment as if it was cursed, unable to open it, fearing what lay on its page.

Read it, she urged herself as she picked up the letter and broke the seal.

Sweet Tigris—the first two words made her stomach flutter. *Sweet Tigris.* Why did he have to use *sweet?* Though, she knew he picked his words with purpose. It made her almost afraid to read the rest. With her heart beating fast, Tigris forced her eyes back onto the page:

Sweet Tigris,

You write your letter with deceit. You hide behind the pretence of war—I am sure of it. For I know I did not mistake the look exposed in your eyes for scorn as scorn does not have tenderness to it.

Tigris dropped the letter. Her hands were shaking. How could he be so bold!

In a daze she stood, causing the parchment to roll from her lap and fall to the floor. She went to a container of water in the corner of the room, pulled out the ladle. Her hand shook, spilling the water as she poured it into her cupped hand and doused it over her face.

"I hate him!" she whispered, dropping the ladle. *Why?* Why did he have to act this way?

There was a quick rap on the cabin door before it opened.

A servant stepped in, bowing. He held a tray of food in his hands. "Your breakfast, Majesty," he said, taking the tray to the table and setting it down.

Tigris forgot she had requested to have her breakfast on the ship instead of at the camp. She didn't want to eat. She didn't want anyone around. The servants would be in and out all morning, unloading her furnishings from her tent back into the cabin. She wished to order them to stop. But, if Allegi was to notice, it would only help prove the messenger's words.

"The morning is growing hot. Would you like me to call servitors to fan you?" the servant asked.

The Queen shook her head. She was too troubled to speak but she certainly didn't want anyone in her presence no matter how hot the day—she'd rather sweat.

Bowing again, the servant added, "I wish you a pleasant journey, Per'a." He closed the door behind him.

Tigris went to the food. Sat. Tried to eat. Her stomach felt uneasy. She forced herself to take a bite of the dried fish and bread but she could barely manage it.

Looking over by the Seat of Estate, she eyed the trampled scroll on the floor near its legs. The sight of it caused her grief. Why did

Euphrates insist on bringing impossible things to surface?

Tigris felt confused. She stared at the paper, wanting to read all that Euphrates had wrote and yet, too afraid to do so.

Hesitantly, Tigris stood. *Be strong*, she coaxed herself as she went to the parchment, scooped up the paper and took it to her bed.

Lying down on her back, Tigris unrolled the scroll and found the spot where she left off:

> *Though, before I met you I could only think of Egypt and winning her back in the name of my father. But, since the moment our eyes met, I can only think of you and winning you over in the name of love.*

Tigris gasped. She didn't believe what she just read. How could he use that word—he barely knew her!

Tigris sat up, whipped the letter down on the bed. Such lies! Was this a part of his ploy to seize Egypt? She didn't believe him. She didn't trust him. They had only seen each other—what? Three times? Who ever fell in love that quickly or that easily?

Tigris breathed heavily. She eyed the scroll, even more afraid of it.

A knock. The cabin door opened.

The Queen dropped down on the bed and closed her eyes. Servants entered the room with the chests from the tent and began setting up her cabin. They laid out the rugs and set out the statues while one servant refilled the water vessels in the corner of the room.

Tigris pretended to be asleep. Everyone tiptoed around. Even the servant who placed the pillows on the bed next to her did so gently, trying not to wake her.

As the servant set the last pillow down on the bed, he noticed the scroll. Picking it up, he took it to the table and set it down on top. Then, he left the cabin. The other servitors finished their duties and exited.

Tigris opened her eyes and looked at the ceiling. She felt the bed beside her for the letter. It wasn't there. Her stomach tightened with panic. She sprang up, searched frantically, knocked pillows from the bed as she slid her hands across its surface. She jumped to her feet, glimpsed around the room, spotted the scroll on the table. Relief swept over her. She stood still, surprised at her own behaviour, shocked at how much she feared his words but wanted to read them.

Tigris dashed to the table. She scooped up the letter, unrolled it and read:

> *It doesn't have to be this way. Together we can end this war and unite our lands. Think how strong Egypt would become.*
> *I look forward to your response.*
> *Your loving brother, Euphrates.*

Tigris let out a small gasp. Oh, how evil, she thought. Indeed she didn't trust him. He feigned love to get his way. How conniving! But, she saw right through it. Yes, he sought to trick her into his arms so he could take hold of the rest of her country. No, she would not be deceived!

With sudden anger, Tigris went to a chest and grabbed her writing equipment. She dropped it on the table and sat down. Her hands were still shaking, in fact, her whole body shook.

Tigris tried to steady herself as she touched brush to paper:

> *Errant Euphrates,*
> *You call yourself brother out of respect, yet have no respect for my intelligence. How dare you write such words using love in order to secure your deepest desire—Egypt.*
> *Yes, sinful brother, the look you see in my eyes is indeed scorn. I scorn you for your lies!*
> *We have only ever set sight upon each other thrice, what fool would fall in love under these conditions?*
> *Believe me; I want nothing more than to see you dead and this war done.*
> *Nitiqreti, Tigris of Egypt*

Tigris slammed down her brush. She didn't bother to read it back. Instead, she sealed the letter and left the cabin.

Stepping outside, Tigris examined her surroundings and froze.

Great gods, they were moving! She began to run towards the bow. "Stop the ship!" she yelled. "Stop the ship!"

The ship was over one hundred and fifty cubits long and the Captain could be anywhere. The rowers were down in the bowels and certainly would not be able to hear her order.

"Allegi!" she called still running forward. "Stop the ship!"

Bumping into a servant, Tigris took hold of the small man. "Have you seen Allegi?"

The servant shook his head.

"Go to the Captain. Tell him to stop the ship," she instructed desperately.

Nodding, the servant remained still, staring at the Pharaoh, dumbfounded.

"Hurry!" Tigris barked, breaking him from his stupor.

The servant took off towards the bow. Tigris raced to the ship wall. She peered over, judged how far they had gone. A small sense of relief soothed her anxiety—they hadn't travelled very far.

Tigris spun from the wall, darted along the ship. "Allegi!" she called again, running back towards the stern and along the side of her cabin. She reached the end, turned the corner, collided with her messenger.

"Tigris!" Allegi puffed, worry spread across his face. "What happened?"

Tigris shook her head, panting. She held out the scroll. "I need you to deliver this to Euphrates."

Allegi gave her a questioning look. He glanced towards the moving land.

"I have sent a servant to stop the ship," she said, answering his thought.

XXXII

A YOUNG SPY ran into the royal camp near the southern border.

"Commander!" he called, finding Intify shaving outside his tent. "The rebel is marching."

Intify dropped his razor and looked at the man. "What a terrible hour to start fighting," he grumbled.

The sun was burning red, barely visible over the horizon. Dawn only just begun and would linger awhile before turning into morning. As a matter of fact, Intify would still be sleeping if the Pharaoh hadn't left so early.

"Go and tell my Lieutenant to wake the men," he huffed, picking up his razor and resuming his shave.

〰

THE REBEL FORCES marched towards the middle ground between the two camps. Within the hour, they lined up and waited.

Euphrates rode out in front of his men. "Today we will fight," he said. "We will put our hearts in our hands and swing our weapons with passion!" He looked back across the desert. There was no sign of their enemies. Perhaps he would have enough time to train them.

Jumping off his horse, Euphrates stood before his front line. "You four," he pointed, waving the men towards him.

Four soldiers stepped out. Euphrates moved them into position—at least an arm's length between each man.

"Our objective, of course, is to remain alive while we slay the enemy. Each and every one of you is a vital part of this army."

He pointed to four more men in the front line and waved them forward. The second group lined themselves behind the first.

"Our best defence is making ourselves a difficult target." He raised one of the men's bows, gesturing to the others to follow suit.

"When I yell 'charge,' we will run forward to close the distance. The first few rows will be the safest from the Queen's first launch of arrows." He turned. "You there," he said pointing further back into the crowd. "You will be in targeted range so hold your shields up." He spun back to his example. "I want everyone to spread out."

Euphrates allowed time for his men to take in the arrangement of soldiers.

"If we stand together, we give each arrow a good chance of striking someone down but if we stand apart, we reduce that by half. The Queen's army won't aim at men, they will aim for distance. They will be positioned shoulder to shoulder but we will be spread apart."

Grabbing a handful of arrows from the leather pouch on the back of one of his men, Euphrates strode out in front of his volunteers. He threw the arrows in the air. They fell towards his model group. Some arrows landed in the empty gaps between them while others fell straight towards the men. The men used their shields to deflect the arrows.

Euphrates walked back to the men, making a gesture with his hand to highlight his point—at least half of the arrows fell into emptiness.

He went to the second row. "While the first line shoots their arrows, the second line prepares. Once the arrows are launched, the man behind advances to the front." Euphrates grabbed a man, pulled him to the side, pushed him through the space between the front soldiers, "And, the front line drops behind." He pulled the man who was in front of the soldier he just moved, and pushed him in behind. Then, he turned to face the warriors. "Any questions?"

No one spoke.

"Good." Euphrates whirled back to the men in his set up. "Let's see a little run of a demonstration."

The two soldiers went back to their positions.

"Charge!" Euphrates bellowed.

The eight men re-enacted their war tactic. The front line pretended to shoot arrows and then fell back.

"To the left!" Euphrates instructed as the second line raced forward.

The army men watched their comrades for a short duration before Euphrates called them back.

"The shooter shields the man who is setting his arrow. We run zigzag to make it more difficult to be targets. And, we fight with partners." Euphrates began walking the front line. "When we get into the thick of battle, we fight back-to-back in pairs. If you're facing the wrong direction and there is no enemy to slay your weapon at, consider it a break. Do not be battle hungry. You will indeed get your chance. Consider yourself the tortoise shell of your partner. Having eyes in the back of your head is a blessing in war."

Euphrates pivoted on his heels, paced back the other way. The eight men rejoined the group. He spotted one of them pointing. Euphrates followed the man's finger. The royal army came into view.

"Our wait ends." Euphrates jeered, "...with no time to practice. But, I'm sure you will all do well."

Euphrates stood by Tuthiken, Menenthop and Somiset.

The Royal Army rose into position less than half the size they were the day prior. A sense of surprise swept over the rebel force.

"What happened to the Pharaoh's army?" one of his men questioned.

Euphrates smiled. "Perhaps they don't think we can fight. But, today we'll show them! And, today, *they* will retreat!"

The men cheered.

"Prepare your weapons!" commanded Euphrates. He waited for them to prepare, then ordered, "Spread out!"

The men spread out leaving gaps between.

Euphrates sucked in a deep breath. "First two rows—" he called, "charge!"

The men ran forward. The first row shot their arrows then fell back allowing the second row to move in front.

Euphrates allowed some space before he bellowed out again. "Next two rows—charge!"

The second set of rows followed the first two out.

The royal army fired their arrows and as Euphrates promised, many of them landed in the empty pockets between the men; many were deflected by shields.

Euphrates called for two more sets of rows to venture out before he finally yelled, "Everybody charge!"

The last of the men drew their battle axes, clubs, and swords. They raced forward, their King leading the way. Already the front line was colliding with the royal army. In the heart of the battle, they needed to push together in order to create a line of defence.

Euphrates raced in, weapon raised. "Stand together men!" he commanded. "Stand together!"

The men filled in the gaps, pushed in closer, fought back-to-back to defend in both directions.

"Partner up!" Euphrates yelled to his men that followed him onto the battleground. His appointed commanders echoed the order as they charged in, weapons swinging.

The royal soldiers broke through their line. Blood splattered. Blades clanked. Men hollered. Dust flew. Euphrates slayed men with speed and his men fought strong.

Slashing another man, Euphrates looked up. A royal soldier raced towards him, his club gripped in both hands above his head. Euphrates dove forward, holding his dagger out in front. He launched himself through the air, driving the blade into his opponent's exposed belly.

The man hunched over, blood spilled from his mouth. Euphrates somersaulted to the ground. He rolled onto his back, moved to get up. Suddenly, another soldier was on top of him bringing his long spear towards Euphrates' chest. Euphrates caught the spear with one hand, fumbled for his axe with the other. The enemy's spear almost touched him. He gave up fumbling for his axe, reached up and gripped the spear with both hands before it impaled him. He struggled to keep the point from piercing his body. The soldier pinned him with his weight.

Euphrates yelled out, finding strength in his low growl as he fought off the sharp point of the spear that threatened his life. He didn't know how much longer his arms could hold it off. Already his muscles shook from the extensive force he exerted.

His heart jumped. A shadow clouded over him blocking the sun from piercing into his eyes. A sword swooped down. Euphrates didn't see it coming until it was too late. He was trapped between both weapons. He watched the sword wail towards him, unable to do anything as he struggled to hold back the spear that pushed over his chest. Then, the sword switched angles and struck the staff of the spear, cutting it in half. Again it changed directions. It sailed towards the royal soldier's neck. With his grip still on the spear, the man didn't have time to pull another weapon. His face fell with fright as the sword severed his head.

The shadow drew in. Menenthop looked down at Euphrates. "Partners?" he grinned.

Euphrates smiled. "Ya—" He barely had time to finish the word. He leapt to his feet, drew his sword and used it to block the attack of a soldier charging at Menenthop.

As Euphrates and the soldier battled, Menenthop paired with his leader. They moved together and where one failed to see an attack the other caught it. As a team, they were able to kill many men.

Euphrates glimpsed a man bringing his club down on Menenthop. He spun out from behind his comrade, hacking his axe into the man's side. The soldier collapsed.

Euphrates gave Menenthop a playful smirk.

"No fair," Menenthop groaned, "he was mine. You were supposed to—what was it? Take a break."

Euphrates laughed. "Too slow. Besides, all's fair in war."

"Duck!" shouted Menenthop.

Obeying, Euphrates ducked out of the way just in time. Menenthop jabbed his blade into the attacker, instantly killing him. He looked down at Euphrates who had dropped to the ground and offered a hand. "That's twice I've saved your life."

Euphrates stood. "I owe you one," he jeered before he ran back into the battle.

The fight continued. More royal soldiers crumbled than did the rebels. The rebellion as a whole fought well and achieved the upper hand.

Sand and dust from the hard eastern desert was kicked up causing the air to become cloudy, making it harder to see. Euphrates and Menenthop lost each other in the haze until Euphrates heard Menenthop wail. He raced towards the voice, fought his way through the dirty air and spotted Menenthop on the ground. One of the Queen's men was over top of him.

Charging, Euphrates brought his sword towards the soldier. The man blocked it. Euphrates glanced down. Menenthop was lying on his back, a spear protruded from his chest. Rage surged through Euphrates' body. He wielded his sword at the soldier with vengeance, cutting into his flesh and defeating him with a single blow.

Euphrates hurried to his friend. "Menenthop!" he gasped, looking down on Menenthop's pale complexion. Euphrates dropped to his knees. He took hold of the shaft of the spear and broke it close to Menenthop's chest. "You're going to be fine," he whispered.

Menenthop grimaced in pain. Euphrates left the spear head inside him—it would do more damage coming out.

"God, it hurts," Menenthop choked.

"I know. We'll get you back to camp and look after it. You're going to be fine."

Menenthop's eyes grew wide. "Behind you!" he shouted with what little strength he had.

Euphrates scooped up his sword, whirled around at full force. He slashed through the knee of his attacker. The man crumbled to the ground, screaming in pain. Euphrates finished him off before he turned back to Menenthop.

Menenthop grinned in spite of his pain. "Now you owe me two," he strained through a heavy breath.

Euphrates returned a soft smile. "I will come back for you," he said, rising to his feet. "Just don't die."

"Promise." Menenthop raised his hand as if to swear it.

The battle went on for some time. The rebels grew stronger. The royal forces weakened. Then, through the sounds of men and the clashing of blades, Euphrates heard the Queen's Lieutenant Commander order, "Pull back!"

The royal army retreated, leaving the rebel forces with the dead and the wounded. When the dust settled and Euphrates' army could see the Pharaoh's soldiers scurrying back to their camp, they thrust their weapons into the air and resounded with victory.

Euphrates scooped up a large wooden shield amid the fallen men and rushed to find Menenthop.

"Menenthop!" he yelled, desperately searching around the dead bodies. He found him not too far away. Euphrates dashed to Menenthop's side and dropped to his knees. Menenthop's eyes rolled back.

"Don't die on me!" Euphrates begged. "You promised! You're going to be fine." He rolled Menenthop onto his side, ignoring the man's cry of pain and slid the long wooden shield under his back.

Tuthiken had spotted them and rushed over.

"Help me carry him," Euphrates said as Tuthiken came to a sudden halt beside him. He gasped when he saw it was Menenthop.

Together they lifted Menenthop up, the shield acting as a gurney.

The army made the hour long march back to camp. The strong helped the weak and the wounded. Euphrates and Tuthiken only stopped to give Menenthop water.

When at last they approached the campsite, Euphrates called out, "Quick! Get the *swinew!*"

Moments later, the doctor was racing towards them. He looked at Menenthop's bleeding chest. "Hurry!" he commanded, leading them to his medical tent.

Euphrates and Tuthiken set Menenthop down on the tent floor. The doctor was already rummaging through a trunk, pulling out instruments, ointments and medicinal herbs. He grabbed a decanter off the table, fumbled the items over to Menenthop.

Handing the decanter to Euphrates, he nodded at the suffering man. "Give him plenty of this."

Euphrates lifted Menenthop's head and poured the alcohol down his throat. Choking, Menenthop spat the liquid out of his mouth.

The doctor looked up. He grabbed the clay bottle from Euphrates and chugged it back. Wiping his mouth, he offered the last of it to Euphrates. "It helps settle the nerves."

Euphrates refused.

The doctor raised the bottle to finish it off but Tuthiken stepped in and snatched it out of his hand before he had the chance to get it to his lips.

"Settle the nerves but keep your mind steady, *swinew*," Tuthiken growled.

Huffing, the doctor picked up an ointment. He smeared it around the wound where the spear shaft protruded from Menenthop's chest. He grabbed a wooden stick off the linen where he had laid out his tools and shoved it into Menenthop's mouth. He gave Euphrates a stack of clean linen and nodded.

The doctor took hold of the broken shaft and ripped the spear head from Menenthop's body. Menenthop yelped in pain. Euphrates quickly covered the open wound with the linen and pressed down hard to stop the blood. Menenthop continued to cry out.

"You're fine," Euphrates comforted in spite of the bad feeling he felt in the pit of his stomach. Already the pile of linen cloths was soaked with blood.

The tent flap unexpectedly flew open. Barin ran into the tent and froze.

Euphrates glanced up. "Get him out of here!" he ordered Tuthiken.

Striding to the boy, Tuthiken took hold of him.

"I want to see him!" Barin yelled, trying to squirm out of Tuthiken's grip.

"You can see him when it's done."

Barin defiantly struggled. He stared at Menenthop's limp figure. "Swinew," he cried, "he's going to live, right?"

The doctor didn't answer.

Barin tried to push away from Tuthiken so he could run to Menenthop's side but the large man had too tight of a grip on him.

Tuthiken scooped him up, carried him out of the tent and set him down. "Stay there," he pointed sternly before he stepped back inside the tent. He closed the flap and sat by the door to guard it.

The moment Barin was gone, Euphrates looked up at the doctor. "He's going to live, right?" he asked, echoing the boy's words.

The doctor sucked in a loud breath through his teeth, leaned back to examine Menenthop, and then let out the breath with a long sigh. "I can sew him up and give him medicine for the pain."

"But will he *live?*" Euphrates pressed.

"That depends on how he heals. As long as he doesn't break a fever or get an infection he stands a good chance."

An hour later, Tuthiken stepped out of the tent. Barin still sat outside, waiting. Holding the flap open, Tuthiken nodded at the boy.

Barin crawled into the tent and went to sit by Menenthop. He looked at the blood soaked bandages wrapped around Menenthop's chest. The doctor was putting away his tools. Euphrates sat on the opposite side of him.

Barin looked up at Euphrates. "I'll watch over him," he whispered.

Strolling sombrely across the campsite, Euphrates and Tuthiken left Barin to sit with Menenthop. All around them, the men rejoiced with victory but neither Euphrates nor Tuthiken were in the mood to join.

They remained silent until they reached Euphrates' tent. Stopping outside of it, Tuthiken looked at his leader and said, "I hope Storithen and Nefret are still alright."

Euphrates didn't respond but he agonized internally. Yes, he thought, two more friends to worry about.

Leaving Tuthiken, Euphrates stepped inside his tent and stopped. Adrenalin built in his veins. Someone sat in his chair.

Although Euphrates hung his head, he could see the silhouette out of his peripheral vision. Cautiously, slowly, he made for his dagger.

"I bring a message from Tigris."

Euphrates looked up. The Royal Messenger of the Pharaoh sat waiting for him with a scroll in his hand. Euphrates tried to subdue his anger but between the battle, Menenthop, and thinking about the welfare of Nefret and Storithen, his nerves were too much on edge. He stormed over to Allegi, snatched the scroll out of his hand, tore open the seal and quickly read it.

Euphrates whipped his head up from the parchment to glare down at the Queen's messenger sitting in the chair below him. "She lies!" he snapped, crushing the letter in his fist.

Allegi stared at him, alarmed. He had no idea what was written on the page.

Euphrates moved forward, placed his hands on the armrests of the chair, bent down over Allegi and leaned in close. His eyes narrowed. "You have seen the way she's looked at me. Would you call it *scorn?*"

Allegi was speechless.

"Would you call it scorn?" demanded Euphrates in a hollow voice.

Allegi found himself shaking his head, no.

"No," Euphrates confirmed, stretching up. "What would you call it then?"

Allegi didn't answer.

"Hate? Disgust? Frustration?" Euphrates glowered with anger at the royal messenger—*Friend of the Pharaoh.* "You must know," he pointed. "You wear the honourable emblem *Friend of the King.* So tell me, what truth hides behind her eyes?" Euphrates waited but still Allegi did not speak. Frustration intensified Euphrates' glare. He cocked his head. "You don't know or you don't want to say?"

Not waiting for an answer, Euphrates spun. He began to pace. He spoke to Allegi without looking at him. "Then, I will tell you what I see behind her eyes—attraction, desire and a feeling, which can quickly lead to love." He stopped, studied Allegi, daring him to deny it.

The young messenger said nothing.

"Say if you disagree," Euphrates challenged.

Allegi sat still, staring wide-eyed at the enemy King.

"Say it!"

Only silence gave a response.

The air grew thick and hot in discomfort. The Queen's messenger remained speechless.

Euphrates sighed. "Then you agree for if you didn't you would defend." He began to pace again. The room settled back into its uneasiness. Euphrates slipped into his own thoughts as he walked back and forth; Allegi watched.

After several turns, Euphrates stopped pacing. He shook his head in disbelief. "Stubborn, stubborn woman," he whispered as if thinking out loud. "Does she not believe in love at first sight?" The rebel King looked at the Queen's messenger. "I am not afraid to say I felt all of it—attraction, desire and *that feeling.*" He slunk down on top of a chest. "We could rule these lands together, join our forces—"

"She will never concede."

Euphrates let his eyes focus on Allegi. He was looking at the messenger but his stare gazed through him. "Why not? Even you admitted you could tell she felt the same."

"Yes, but *she* will never admit it." Allegi eyed Euphrates who had sunk into his thoughts. For the first time, Allegi saw something he never thought he would see in the confident, self-proclaimed King: *vulnerability.* It struck him with bewilderment. And, although he should have thought it weak, there was something about it that seemed so free.

"Tell me, what do you think?" Euphrates asked. "Am I absurd to believe we can unite?"

Allegi shook his head. He didn't mean to answer but he found himself possessed to do so as if what the Pharaoh's enemy proposed was right for both Tigris and Euphrates. Something about the two of them together seemed natural—as if it should be. In truth, it felt more honest than the war they faced.

"No," Allegi finally admitted. "I think it absurd for you not to."

For a long while, they sat in silence, staring into the room but looking into their thoughts before Euphrates ran his hands over his head and broke the silence. "I do not have the energy or desire to write my correspondence. It has been a long, hard day. Tell her whatever you want."

Allegi couldn't believe how long he sat in the silence, across from the enemy King, deep in thought. He looked up at Euphrates. The rebel. The enemy. And yet, he didn't see him as an enemy at all.

Finally, Allegi stood, headed to the door, stopped. He turned back to Euphrates. "I will tell her the truth," he said softly. "For I believe this quest is nobler than your war."

Bowing, Allegi departed.

XXXIII

$\mathcal{T}$HE QUEEN'S SPY crawled along the hard Egyptian earth to get a better view of the enemy's camp. He left his camel a fair distance back and now lay on his stomach in order to make it harder for the rebels to see him. In the vast open desert between the capital cities of Ipu and Dkew-qa there was nothing to hide behind except the blurry view of distance.

The spy crept in closer. He peered at the tents and the surrounding area of the rebel's campsite. The camp remained quiet. No one stirred. It was late morning and the spy had been there for quite some time, waiting, watching, but no one stepped from his tent.

The rebels were gone.

Reaching the royal camp, the young spy searched for Intify and found him soaking his feet. "Commander," he called, bowing his head as he approached. "There is no movement at the rebel's camp."

Intify opened his eyes, looked up.

The spy was no more than eighteen. He wore a sand coloured tunic with mud smeared over his skin. Yet, despite his camouflage, the commander could see through the mud and read the concern on the young man's face. The commander, however, wasn't the least bit concerned.

"Too much celebration last night over their petty victory," Intify grumbled. He stepped out of the clay pot. "Find Iby and tell him to inform the men to ready for battle. We won't wait on them. Ra will finish his sail before they get up," he said, looking up at the sun.

By late afternoon, the Queen's army stood at the battle grounds waiting for the rebels to appear but they did not show.

"Are they taking the day off?" Intify griped as he waved his arm for the men to begin marching again.

An hour later, they reached within view of the enemy's camp. Tents and pots were laid out, even linens hung to dry in the sun but there was no sign of life.

Intify and his men tramped into the enemy's campgrounds.

Everything seemed surreal. The camp was lifeless—no sounds, no movements, nothing. The royal soldiers tore into the tents and found them empty.

Intify's face fell with horror. The enemy was gone.

XXXIV

Nefret and Storithen had waited eight days in Wasebet for Cheti and Iritu to return with their troop. Storithen grew anxious. They were another half a week behind Euphrates and it seemed as if they would never catch up.

Wasebet was becoming unruly. With no leader to keep the peace, the citizens squabbled over food and who should take over. Likewise, the tension between Montu and Storithen thickened.

"Let's just leave," Storithen whispered to Nefret as if someone might hear them. They shared a small room in one of the mud-brick buildings in town. Its thick walls and high windows gave them privacy but still Storithen whispered. "We're losing time staying here."

The morning light shone through the small high windows. Nefret was trying to sleep. He was curled on his side with his back to Storithen.

"There isn't a rebellion force meeting up with us," Storithen persisted. "I say we leave without Montu and the others."

Nefret rolled over. He looked at Storithen who was already packing his things.

The two men left the room, almost tip-toeing in the broad daylight. They would escape town without the others. Fate unfortunately was not on their side.

"Where are you going?"

Startled, Nefret and Storithen looked up. Montu had come to look for them in their room and found them in the narrow street out front of the building by their camels.

"We—we were just coming to get you," Nefret stuttered. "We're not waiting any longer for your troop."

Montu eyed them suspiciously. "Why not tell us before you packed so we could have time to prepare?"

Storithen yanked on his camel's reins. "We will be having our breakfast," he barked.

Nefret took hold of his camel and followed Storithen. "We're leaving in an hour."

XXXV

ANATEN WALKED QUICKLY through the palace complex of Waset where he had lived for the past two years under the authority of the Pharaoh. As Governor of the North, he conducted government affairs in the name of the Pharaoh and reported his business to the Vizier. Each month he sent a barque down the Nile to the royal storehouses with the taxes he collected in his jurisdiction. But, today the vessel would not leave port and he no longer considered it the *Tigris'* palace in which he resided.

Everything had turned out perfectly. His lords and ministers agreed with him. They supported his claim; after all, he was blood cousin to the Pharaoh.

Yes, Anaten thought, everything was perfect. He looked down into his cradled arms and admired the white crown of Upper Egypt. He had commissioned it to be made and the tailor had done such a fine job. Anaten held up the crown to admire it more fully.

Soon, all of Egypt will be mine, he thought, stroking the royal crown.

He climbed the steps inside the first pylon of the palace façade, drawing himself closer to the moment he had imagined for a very long time. His lungs puffed under the fatness of his body, but through his heavy breaths, he gleamed.

The last step brought him to the entrance of the *Window of Appearance.* Anaten placed the *hedjet* crown on his head and waited. An anxious smile grew on his face lifting his chubby cheeks under his eyes. He could hear Rekhmira, whom he appointed as his Vizier, speaking.

"...I now give you your new King, Pharaoh of Kemet, the beautiful soul of Re, Anaten."

Anaten stepped onto the balcony and smiled this time for the crowd. He opened his arms, welcoming the applause. For the number of people who watched, the applause was very light but Anaten didn't care. He was Pharaoh. What could the *Queen*, his cousin, do about it? She was too busy at war and his lords had ensured the people of Waset supported him. Those who didn't were deprived of food until they chose to accept their new monarch.

To fund his endeavour, Anaten had cut off the resources he was to send to the south. He raided the Queen's gold and precious stones mined in Kush as they went past Waset down the river. Even the caravans crossing the great city of Waset were plundered and their goods brought to him. Yes, he ruled this land and now he made it known that he *owned* it.

"Good people of Egypt, today is a glorious day," Anaten began. "The great god Amun-Re has made me King of Egypt."

"Blasphemy!" came a shout.

Anaten ignored it. He had his special police force—the *Medjays*—scattered amongst the crowd to keep any hostility under control and he could see them searching out the voice.

"Under my rule you will be rich with bread and beer—"

"You are not our King!" yelled the same voice. The *Medjays* seized the man, dragged him from the crowd. But, the man did not surrender.

"Our fair and beautiful Nitiqreti is our Pharaoh!"

Anaten's smile faded. "Amun-Re does not desire a *woman* to rule his land! He has come to me, her cousin, still with royal blood and asked that I watch over this nation—"

"Liar!"

The people watched baffled.

Anaten's blood pumped with rage. "Bring him forward!" he commanded.

The officers dragged the man to the first pylon by the main palace gates where the *Window of Appearance* was cut into the stone above. *The man was a priest.*

Anaten turned his attention to the crowd. "All those who protest the will of Re will give their life for their sins."

"Then you will die!" spat the priest. "Ammut comes for you!" His voice cracked the air like thunder. The people seemed to hold their breath, believing the words of the priest.

Anaten looked down at the man who was held by the arms by the two officers. Fury and embarrassment fumed inside the Governor. How dare this meagre priest spoil his glorious day!

"I've heard enough!" Anaten roared. "Kill him and place his head as an offering!"

"Ammut will come for you!" the priest cried out again before an officer of the Governor's Special Forces stepped forward, raised his axe and sliced off the priest's head.

The people gasped in horror.

Anaten smirked. "Let him look onto my palace and see in death my Kingdom, which he denied in life."

The officer placed the priest's head on the earth. His eyes still open, his expression frozen in shock, looked in terror at the palace gates. Servants were waved in to carry his body away.

The crowd stepped back, appalled at the sight.

Anaten looked around. This was not how he imagined it. He needed to bring the attention back to him and remind the people he was now their Pharaoh.

Anaten took a deep breath and bellowed, "Let it be written that in the season of *Shomu* Anaten has become the magnanimous Pharaoh of Egypt! And, from this day, I will be known as Achtoy the Great!"

Anaten turned from the window, leaving the people in fear of their new Pharaoh.

XXXVI

BACK IN HENEN-NESUT, the Queen gratefully took to the comforts of her palace. Soon news would follow that the rebel forces were taken down by the Royal Army and Egypt was once again hers. After witnessing the enemy fight so poorly, Tigris believed news wouldn't come any other way.

The Queen made her way through the palace grounds to the office of the Vizier. She walked alone, giving herself time to think.

The sweet smelling flowers poured their scents into the air, which drifted to her. Tigris wished to sit in her garden under the shade of the exotic trees by her pond but instead she begrudgingly went to attend council as duty deemed.

The stresses of war, thought Tigris. It had only begun and she was already tired of it—tired of the fighting, the killing.

The killing, she gasped. A hollow feeling came over her. What if a message arrived stating her army managed victory over the rebels? She had ordered Euphrates' death. He would be brought to her feet and laid out before her *dead*. Tigris' chest grew tight. *What have I done?*

The tension mounted inside of her. It is the only way, she assured herself, the only way to end the absurdity. But, in spite of her reasoning, of all the logical thoughts she compiled to justify her order, Tigris nonetheless, felt pain—a deep wrenching pain. Suddenly, she hoped her forces had lost.

Tigris arrived at the Vizier's residence. She went up the stairs towards his study. This was the first time she would see him since she returned from war two nights ago. Entering the room, she found Ibimpetus, Chephren and Allegi waiting for her.

While Allegi sat off to the side, the two older men stood by a high table, studying some parchments. Ibimpetus despised the young messenger's presence in the council but tolerated it only out of duty. Still, he made a point to exclude Allegi from matters that he specifically handled.

"Good morning," Tigris said, looking at the men but smiling at Allegi. She took a seat near one of the tables.

Ibimpetus looked up at her. "I have received three messages in the last twelve hours," he informed, getting straight to business. "Two were from Intify." He collected the parchments off of the high table and held them up.

Tigris' heart sunk. *Two from Intify*, she repeated to herself, fearing their words.

"The first is requesting more soldiers."

More soldiers? Tigris stared at him, confused.

"Apparently the rebellion was not as incapable of battle as they let on.

Intify claims they killed half of his men and he was forced to retreat."

A sudden feeling of relief shot through Tigris. Her enemy had won! Euphrates was alive! She almost smiled.

"His second message reports the rebel army disappeared into the night and he is unaware of where they're headed."

Tigris sat quietly for a moment. She didn't care. Euphrates was safe. The news brought her so much unexpected pleasure she was even surprised at herself. The tension in her chest dissipated.

"We have dispatched a message informing Ankhtify to join with Intify. Cheti will remain at the garrison with the reinforcements from Dkew-qa."

"No!" exclaimed Tigris.

Allegi eyed her quizzically.

She noticed the way Allegi was looking at her and she knew what he assumed of her response but that was not it at all. "He will head to the Fortress of Ipu," Tigris stated. "Where is your map of this country?" Tigris stood up and looked around.

The room overflowed with scrolls, parchments, books and stelae. She didn't know where to look first.

The Vizier set the messages down on the high table, went to a basket, pulled out a long scroll. He took it to the table where the Pharaoh stood. He spread the scroll out in front of her, placing stones on the four corners to prevent it from rolling up.

Tigris peered down at the map as Chephren and Allegi came over to join them.

"He will continue towards the south as was his intent," Chephren argued, pointing at the border. "He is seeking complete take over and he has already succeeded the north."

Tigris gave her General an incredulous look. Was the man really that stupid? Indeed, Euphrates threatened her border, which was why she had marched north to stop him, but he was certainly not ready to cross it yet.

"Was it not you Chephren who ordered Cheti's mission?" Tigris asked.

The Admiral looked at her puzzled.

"Did he not report two of Euphrates' men were expecting to join him with more forces and meet him at the Fortress of Ipu?"

Chephren didn't respond. He knew what she was getting at and he felt embarrassed by his comment. Even more so he hated the fact that she saw the logic before him.

"He will go to the fortress for two reasons: first, he needs more men to succeed the south and second, he will keep his promise to his two loyalists who hope to find him there." The Queen returned her gaze to the map and studied it. The map was drawn in colour and included all the palaces, temples and fortresses along with caravan routes and oases.

The three councillors and Tigris each stood to a table side with their heads bent, chins almost touching their necks as they peered at the map in thought. If Euphrates was to succeed into the fortress, advance his men, patiently wait while his army increased, the south would be greatly threatened.

As time lingered on, more people swayed with their decisions as to who should reign in Egypt. The drought added to their fears, which made loyalty succumb to desperation. *A King would end their curse*, they preached.

Tigris needed to go into combat, win, destroy peoples' doubts with her victory.

It was the Vizier who broke the silence. "He will meet against Ankhtify's army along the way," he stated resolutely as if they need not concern themselves with the thought any longer.

Tigris shook her head. "You don't give him enough credit." The Queen shot Ibimpetus a look of disgust as she recounted Euphrates' successes: "He kept his coalition from us until he was prepared to make it known; he hid his camp of unknown size successfully in the caverns of the mountains; and, he fought so pathetically I was convinced two divisions were unnecessary." Again, she shook her head. "And now, you think he is going to take the most probable route when he knows Intify needs reinforcements and he thinks we believe he will press the south? He knows Ankhtify has left the fortress, en route. He may as well have made the order himself." Tigris lowered her head and glared at the map. "No, he will take the hardest course away from Ankhtify to keep us thinking he's heading to Lower Egypt."

She ran her finger deeper into the desert area along the surface of the parchment. "He's travelling the back route, away from the water sources." She continued to draw her finger along the map to the fortress.

The Fortress of Ipu was set by the river bank further north of where the battle began. If the rebels marched the course near the Nile, it would take them about four days but through the desert mountains it would take at least eight.

"They won't survive," Chephren blurted, examining the map. "Their numbers are too large to have enough water to make it."

Tigris used her thumbnail to press into the papyrus and to draw a line. "The eastern desert is hard and rocky unlike the soft sands of the west." She slowly dragged her thumb out from the eastern side of the Nile into the barren land of the east. She stopped, lifted her nail off of the parchment, gazing at where she had scratched into the map. "He will survive if he knows about the old river under the earth."

Chephren and Ibimpetus looked up at her surprised.

"There are several." The Queen smirked, "One of the many secrets my father believed a Pharaoh should know in order to have strategy in such matters." She shook her head with puzzlement. "Apparently, someone believed he should know too."

Tigris inhaled deeply. She turned to Ibimpetus. "Where is my uncle meeting Intify?" She hoped she wouldn't get the answer she knew he was about to give.

"At his camp."

Of course, thought Tigris. Closest to the southern border. "So," she huffed, slumping down in the chair, "he's had four days head start while Intify's message travelled here. He'll gain another five days while your message reaches Ankhtify, four days for Ankhtify to get to Intify and then another four days back if we send word for them to change course. That's seventeen days." Tigris exhaled heavily. "Even if we dispatch a message today for Intify to march to Ankhtify, it will still be twelve days before our army returns to the fortress." She thought for a moment. "The back route will cause Euphrates an additional four days' march. That still gives him a minimum of four days to secure the fort."

"Three days," Allegi interjected.

The Queen and the two older men looked at him. The young councillor rarely spoke in council unless called upon to do so.

"He has to dig for water," Allegi explained. "The rocky eastern desert may make it easy for an underground river to exist but it also makes it difficult to break ground. They will dig when the sun is gone and camp at their river for at least a day."

The councillors stood quietly as they considered their situation. Everyone searched their minds for the best course of action. For a long period, the room was hushed before the Queen sat up.

"I am leaving tomorrow. Prepare the fleet, Chephren," she ordered her Admiral of the Royal Vessels. Then, she held up her hand and began to count on her fingers. "Four days for your message to reach here, another four for me to reach Intify and only one day if we port the army by ship to Ipu. We will send a mercenary from Intify's company to meet up with Ankhtify and turn him around." Tigris smiled wryly. "Nine days if we leave tomorrow," she stated, holding out her hands to show her fingers. "We will reach the Fortress at the same time as the rebels. They will have no time to secure it."

The Queen could see the look of please on the men's faces. She pushed her chair back and stood. Their plan was made. Now, she needed only to wait until morning to embark upon her mission. "Chephren, ensure we sail enough ships to transport these armies." Nodding her head to signal she was adjourning their meeting, Tigris headed to the door.

"There is still the third message," the Vizier reminded her, stopping her in her tracks.

Tigris spun around. She didn't like the tone of his voice. She watched as he went over to his high table, picked up the third letter and brought it towards her.

Tigris knew the message was bad—he wasn't telling her, he was making her read it. She moved forward, met him half way and took the parchment. Reading the message, the Queen gasped.

Allegi rushed to her side and grabbed the parchment. He was the only one who hadn't yet seen the letter. As his eyes moved over the page, his face fell in horror.

The Governor of Upper Egypt, Councillor in the Great Ten, cousin of the Pharaoh, Anaten, claimed himself Pharaoh of Upper Egypt. He cut off her supply from the north, which would send the country into poverty, especially during a time of war when riches were needed to maintain a strong army and loyalty from the *sepats*.

Tigris felt stunned. She was losing everything. Even her cousin betrayed her.

She sent the Vizier a piercing look as if to say, *I told you.*

Stress lined his face. What she lost, he lost and he wasn't the type of man to permit loss.

Death to the enemies of the throne, Tigris remembered Anaten pledging. Is that what he considered her—an enemy of the throne—*his throne?* Yes Anaten, she silently agreed, her blood boiling. Death to the enemies of the throne—*my* throne! "Kill him!" Tigris ordered. "Slay my betraying cousin and make his death unbearable!"

XXXVII

*T*IGRIS CONTINUED TO head across the palace complex towards her private garden. She needed to calm down. She wanted to be amidst the beauty of the plants and flowers, surrounded by their soothing fragrances where she could watch the fish swim in the pond and find peace in solitude. But, Allegi chased after her. He now walked beside her in silence and she knew why.

"You bring a letter?" Tigris asked, holding out her hand. *Another message*, she thought. The morning was full of them.

Allegi nodded. "Yes, I bring a message but it was not scribed."

The Queen looked at him questioningly.

"He asked that I tell you what he said."

Tigris lowered her hand. "Good. You can tell me in my garden."

They passed the front door of the royal apartments and headed towards the back of the building where her garden was sculpted.

The Pharaoh's private garden was large and designed with paths and ponds and cages holding her favourite wild animals, which consisted of mostly large cats. Different plants were sectioned together including domestic bushes and trees as well as exotic ones brought in from countries as far east as Asia Minor and as far south as Cilicia. Many were gifts from Kings of foreign lands and from her royal dignitaries.

"I would prefer to tell you in the privacy of your chamber," Allegi insisted. He nodded towards the doorway at the back of the building.

"It is too hard to see what ears listen out here."

Tigris looked around. Allegi was right. There were too many places to lurk in the garden and it certainly wasn't a good place to discuss such matters. Tigris gave in. She tramped up the steps into the building.

They went down the hall, up the stairs and to her quarters. Entering the audience chamber, Allegi closed the door.

The instant the door was shut, the Queen spun to look at her Royal Messenger, *Royal Confidant*. Her expression was hard, urging him to get on with it.

Allegi said nothing.

Tigris quietly eyed him, imploring him to speak but he just looked at her, contemplating, deciding. Tigris could see it in his eyes—his uncertainty. It made her feel uneasy.

After a long silence, she pressed him. "We are in privacy. What message does he have you tell?" Tigris was unnerved. She felt as if the recent correspondence she had with Euphrates was their secret, which he had divulged to her messenger.

Allegi looked her up and down. "Do you believe in love at first sight?" he asked, softly.

"What?" Tigris balked, taken aback by the question.

"Love at first sight—do you believe it exists?" he rephrased.

"Don't be ridiculous, Allegi. That is the fantasy of fools." Tigris walked further into the room and stood. She didn't feel to sit. She couldn't relax.

Allegi stepped in closer. "But if it did exist, what feeling do you think would describe it?"

The Queen glared at her messenger confused. Why did he ask such questions? How was she to know? *She had never been in love.*

Moving to sit down, Allegi shook his head at her little by little, like a disappointed parent, saddened by her response. "Fair, beautiful friend, do you even know what love feels like?" he asked as though he read her mind.

Tigris could feel her cheeks burn. The question made her uncomfortable. She pressed her hand across her forehead and turned away from him.

Allegi quietly studied her for a moment. "Why does it scare you?"

Tigris froze—only for a second but long enough to feel her heart stop, the blood stand still in her veins. *Scare me*, she repulsed, whipping around. "It doesn't scare me! Nothing *scares* me! I don't know what foolish fable you and your new found friend look to create but it does not exist!" She glowered at her messenger, her confidant, her friend. Yet although she yelled at him, she wasn't angry with him. She was angry with herself—angry the feelings did indeed exist and she could not control them. "I've told you before I do not want to discuss this *now or ever!*"

Allegi ignored her request. "He knows the secret you hide, betrayed by your eyes that whisper the truth in the way you look at him. I even recognize it—"

"Keep the message he has you bring, Allegi. I do not want it." Tigris stormed into her bedchamber to get away from him but Allegi sprang from his seat and followed.

"Then I come as your friend and not as your messenger."

"I do not want to hear it!"

"You *need* to hear it!" Allegi barked back.

The Queen looked around her bedroom. Allegi was already inside the doorway. She had no way of closing him out. She felt trapped like an animal in the plains, unable to escape, caught in a net, watching the hunter close in. Her palms sweat, her temperature rose and she actually felt nauseous.

Allegi calmed his voice, spoke to her softly. "Your heart beating fast, your breath being wisped away, your stomach tingling—these are the feelings of love, Tigris. Having a desire so deep you do not know its roots or reason—that is *love*."

Tigris turned away from him again. She fixed her gaze outside the window, tried to shut out his words. She didn't want to hear them. She was trembling; desperately trying to hold still.

"Love cannot be explained. Its existence is magical. Sometimes it lasts a short while and other times it lasts forever." Allegi moved closer. He stood behind her, whispered almost in her ear. "But, love should never be denied."

His words brought her immense sadness. They made tears burn in her nose and behind her eyes but she bit her inner cheek and held onto them. No, she wouldn't cry, not now, not in front of Allegi—she could never let Allegi see her cry, see her so weak. *See the truth stream down her cheeks.*

"He says what he sees in you he feels in himself—attraction, desire and an emotion begging to love you."

Allegi's whisper breezed by her ear, yet moved the floor beneath her. Tigris felt dizzy—nauseous and dizzy. She kept her eyes focused outside the window. She breathed deeply, heavily, quickly, in an effort to fight back the tears that were on the brink of bursting out. She tried to hold herself together—manage as she quivered internally. *Crumbled inside.*

"He wants to unite and rule Egypt *with* you—"

Tigris whirled around. Scepticism covered her face. Anger pushed the tears aside, gave her strength to speak. "Do you not see it Allegi? He looks to possess Egypt any way he can! He seduces me with lies!"

"I believe he speaks the truth—"

"He has you fooled! But he will not—*cannot*—fool me!" She shook her head—short, quick, vigorous shakes. "No—no one can fall in love so easily!" Tigris strode to her bedroom door. She stood beside it, looked at Allegi. "I will not listen to this. I will not give up Egypt. I will not unite with him. And, I will certainly not give into a foolish heart!" She turned her head away from him, breathing heavily. The tears, the trembling—she forced them still. She didn't move from the door. Her gesture was clear—she wanted him to leave.

Allegi remained watching her for a moment, studying the way she stood, the way she breathed. Why did she deny the truth? He couldn't understand it. It frustrated him because intuitively he believed all would be made right if she united with Euphrates.

Allegi went to the chamber door. He stopped in front of Tigris. "You are wrong," he said in a low voice. "True love should never be so *hard*—it just *is*." Allegi left her chambers.

Tigris waited for the last door to close before she stepped back, slammed the bedroom door to release the tension that boiled inside of her. She raced to her bed, flopped down on it. Her whole chest ached but she would not allow herself to cry. No, not for this; not for something not meant to be. Instead, she whispered through her gasps, "I am strong. I don't care...."

〰〰

IN TIGRIS' DREAM, she stood in the desert alone. Scarabs crawled all over her. They covered her completely. Then someone appeared and the beetles scattered down her body, into the sand, revealing the figure before her and leaving her utterly exposed. She looked at Euphrates, suddenly wanting the beetles to return, to cover her again. Silently she prayed to the gods to call the scarabs back and make them shield her. But, the sands hardened under her feet.

Euphrates stepped forward.

His face. She recognized it from a place before. He was younger then. She had stopped in front of him. They had looked into each other's eyes. It was love at first sight. She could not deny it. She would have followed him to the end of the earth if he had spoken to her.

A man stepped between them. He forced her away. Far away. Said her time was done.

Who was this man? She had known him. Where was this place? She had stayed there.

The dream ended.

XXXVIII

*T*IGRIS PULLED HERSELF from the bed and went to the mirror. Taking hold of it, she opened up the passage and slipped into the tunnel making her way through the darkness and down the stairs. Rapping on the door, Tigris pushed it open and stepped into the chamber.

The room seemed more dishevelled than normal. All sorts of items were dumped out on the floor. Tigris found Kafate by a chest emptying out its contents.

Kafate looked up. "I can't find my crystal," she complained.

Tigris eyed the priestess. Worry and stress hovered over the old woman with the thought of the crystal being lost. Seeing her stressed made Tigris feel uneasy. The woman was so old and fragile Tigris feared the priestess didn't have the ability to live through her grief.

Tigris stooped down, put her arms around the old woman and helped her to her feet. "Maybe," Tigris suggested, guiding Kafate to the cushions beside the black pond, "you should let the crystal find you." Tigris helped Kafate to sit.

The priestess looked up at her and smiled. "You're right," she whispered. "It will come to me when it must." Kafate watched Tigris go to the opposite side of the water hole and sprawl out across the cushions. As the priestess studied her, her smile faded into a discerning squint. "I feel uneasiness about you—sadness," Kafate said. "This is not the Tigris I know."

Tigris forced a small grin. "I am fine," she lied. "I just came for the company. I don't feel like being alone."

Tigris had lain on her bed all afternoon trying to escape the misery of her thoughts by napping. But, she had only managed to drift in and out of sleep and the ordeal of it had brought more anguish than ease.

"I take it your battle went well? You've returned early," Kafate asked.

"Went well?" Tigris let out a fake laugh. "He made a fool out of me to gain advantage." The Queen shook her head, shot Kafate a look of warning. "I don't want to discuss *him*," she begged.

Tigris spent the day trying to get Euphrates out of her mind; trying to erase from her memory the words he sent through Allegi's mouth. She had come to the priestess' chamber to escape her thoughts of him. No, she definitely could not bring herself to discuss him, not even with the priestess.

Tigris forced a smile, changed her tone. "Would you please tell me one of your stories instead?"

"Are you not too old for stories?"

"Never! One can't ever be too old for a good story." Tigris made herself comfortable. She tapped her fingers on the ground to beckon Heka. The cat ran to her. She scooped him up, cradled him on her chest.

"Tell me one about the Greek gods. Their stories are so fascinating."

Kafate arranged herself as she stretched out on the cushions. The priestess smiled softly but there was something more behind her smile.

"How about the story of Hero and Leander?" Kafate asked.

"Perfect. I don't remember it." Tigris would listen to whatever would keep her mind away from thoughts of Euphrates.

The old woman closed her eyes and began to tell the tale of the two lovers and how Hero and Leander's love for each other was so great but they were unfortunate to be separated by a river. Still, they would not allow the river to keep them from each other as their love was true.

Each night, Hero would light a lamp in her tower and wait for Leander to swim the straight to reach her. But, one ill-fated night, a storm blew out the light. Leander became lost in the waters. With no light to guide him, the stormy river pulled him into its depths and he drowned. The next morning when Hero found her lover's body washed to shore, she climbed the tower stricken with grief. Unable to live without him, Hero leapt from the tower and plunged to her death in the river where her body was found lying next to Leander's.

As Kafate told the story, Tigris forced herself to focus on the priestess' words to prevent her mind from returning to its recent turmoil. She envisioned everything the old woman described. Kafate always told her stories in great detail, making the listener imagine actually being there. The priestess learned when Tigris was young, if she made the story short, the child would only pester her to tell another. So, she found it easier to drag one fable out.

Tigris looked over at the priestess. Kafate was still rambling on about the lover's doom but her words had become slow with many quiet pauses in between. Tigris realized the old woman was falling asleep. As a child, she would have woken her up to complain she was drifting off to sleep then tell her where she had left off. As an adult, she understood the old woman needed the rest.

Standing, Tigris stretched. The chamber looked like a storm had blown through it from the priestess' quest to find the crystal. Tigris decided to straighten things up before returning to her chamber.

She went over to one of the chests where its contents were emptied out onto the floor around it. She put the contents into the chest, closed the lid, moved to the next pile of mess.

"The ram and fish," Kafate whispered in her sleep. "The ram and fish...."

Tigris was picking a book off the stone floor when she heard Kafate's strange whisper. She observed the old woman as she slowly lifted a copy of the *Am Duat* and stacked it on the two other books piled in her arm.

The priestess whispered louder; her voice very grave and slow:

> *The ram and fish will come to meet,*
> *And their souls they will deceive,*
> *For land and throne both hunger for,*
> *Deprives the heart, which makes them poor.*

Tigris stood up. She hugged the books to her chest as she watched the priestess.

"Deprives the heart!" Kafate spat.

The Queen stared at her in bewilderment.

"Deprives the heart!" repeated the old woman in a growling whisper. Suddenly, she began to struggle in her sleep as if she was in pain. Her breathing became heavy, broken, with panicky gasps.

Tigris dropped the pile of books and ran to Kafate, shaking her awake. "Kafate!" she cried.

The old woman's eyes popped open. "The fish," she whispered.

Tigris pulled back and stared at her.

The priestess scrambled to get to her feet, groaning in pain but not allowing it to slow her down.

"You were dreaming," Tigris said as Kafate hobbled to a table.

"No," Kafate said, shaking her head rapidly, "not dreaming, *seeing*."

The Queen looked at the old priestess, puzzled.

"You are the fish," Kafate proclaimed as she poked around the table.

The fish? Tigris repeated to herself, trying to remember all the old woman had mumbled in her sleep.

"He is the ram." The priestess clumsily knocked things over trying to find whatever she was searching for. She spun, went to one of the chests, opened the lid and rummaged through it, emptying things onto the floor.

Tigris watched. She had just cleaned up the room with only one mess left to tackle and now Kafate was dumping out the chests again. Nonetheless, she didn't care. She was interested to know what spirited the priestess. What had she *seen?*

"Before I came to Egypt, I stayed in Sumer. Some priests there were beginning to chart the sky into twelve houses." Kafate examined the pile of books on the floor, which Tigris had gathered. She scooped one up and opened it.

Many pieces of papyrus paper were bound together by thread. Inside, the pages were filled with drawings and writing.

The Queen moved to stand behind Kafate. She looked over her shoulder, down onto the open pages. The script was foreign. Tigris recognized it as Sumerian—one of the languages her father made her study as a child. But, it was scribed in the old script and it had been such a long time since Tigris read it she had difficulty making out the words.

Kafate snapped the book closed and eyed Tigris. "You were born in *Parmatit*, during the twelfth house."

Tigris listened, uneasily.

"The last house," Kafate informed. She took a breath and shuffled over to a table, scooping up the satchel of etched stones. "He must have been born during the first house of the ram." The priestess looked back at Tigris and peered deep into her eyes. "The beginning and the end," she whispered.

Tigris felt overwhelmed. She didn't like where this was going. An unsettling feeling overtook her. She watched as Kafate spun and scurried to the black pond, using her staff to help her move.

Watching the old woman's strange behaviour, suddenly, made Tigris feel nervous. She wasn't sure if she wanted to hear more. Instead of joining the priestess by the pond, she began to tidy up again—anything to stay away. She picked up the books, put them in a chest, and stepped to the next pile with lingering movement— watching, listening. *Afraid.*

Closing the last of the mess in a trunk, the Queen turned to face Kafate. Curiosity compelled her to peek over at the old woman while she had cleaned but now that she was done, she couldn't help but to fix all of her attention on the priestess.

Kafate was sitting down with the flat stones dumped out in front of her. She flipped them over so the etchings faced the floor.

Tigris remembered what Euphrates said in his letter. With trepid steps, the Queen made her way over to the black pond but she did not sit.

"Kafate?" she asked softly. "Do you know why we were both named after two great rivers, Euphrates and Tigris? Doesn't that seem odd?"

The old woman stopped flipping the stones to look up at her. She shook her head. "No dear, your fathers intended for you to marry."

Tigris' heart dropped to her stomach. A lump grew in her throat. She must have heard wrong. *Must have.*

"They had campaigned together to strengthen Egypt's boundaries— the Pharaoh, Chief of the Army, and, your father, General of the Armed Forces. They were close then—friends."

Tigris began backing away.

"When they reached Sumer and won their battle between the two great rivers, which run side-by-side until they become one, they decided in their victory that the King would name his first born son Euphrates and the General his first born daughter Tigris, so the two could unite like the rivers and be as powerful as water."

Tigris wasn't ready for the answer. *Intended for us to marry.* No, this was too much. Besides, it didn't matter anyway. That was then, this was now.

She continued to back up, almost tripping over a pot. She no longer wanted to be in the chamber—it no longer offered comfort.

Kafate picked up a stone with the symbol of water etched on its flat surface and held it out towards Tigris. "Water—the source of life."

"We are enemies now," Tigris muttered, still stepping backwards. Her eyes locked on the priestess as if Kafate was an enemy and her words a weapon.

Tigris desperately tried to erase this knowledge but one truth clung in her mind. *Supposed to marry.* The idea of it brought her pain. *So much pain.* Why did it have to be like this? What curse doomed them to become enemies?

Tigris reached the mirror, pulled it open.

"Listen to your heart," she heard the priestess say before she escaped into the tunnel.

I have been listening to my heart! Tigris responded in her thoughts. It tells me to guard Egypt; to honour my father. It causes me sorrow and I am beginning to hate it!

The Queen raced up the steps unable to move fast enough. She panted heavily—not from running but from the pressure inside her. Her chest was so tight with pain she felt as if the world crushed her beneath its weight.

Reaching the bedchamber, Tigris closed the mirror behind her. She held it closed, fearing it would open on its own and whisper Kafate's words.

She looked around, gasping for air. The chambermaids had lit the lamps in her chambers during her absence. They burned amber against the stone walls. Outside the stars glimmered in the night sky giving light to darkness.

Tigris felt lost. She didn't know what to do with herself. She wanted to run away—away from her thoughts; away from the war; away from everything. But, there was nowhere to run and no one to run to. Her mind raced with anguished thoughts and she fought back the tears. *Why?* Why was she doomed to such a fate?

"Oh, Eset," she whispered into the heavens.

Tigris rushed to her desk. She sat, picked up her brush and wrote. She was barely cognisant of what she scribbled onto the paper. The words poured out of her as if they could not be controlled. *"Dearest Euphrates,"* was all she remembered writing when she had finished and sealed the scroll.

Tigris dropped the parchment down on the desk and pushed away from it. She couldn't even look at the tightly rolled paper with her words divulged inside it without fear pumping through her blood.

Her hands were still shaking when she pulled the last letter Euphrates had written to her out of a small box and carried it to her bed. She lay down, curled onto her side and held the letter in her fist under her nose, hoping it would smell like him.

He wants to unite and rule Egypt *with* you, she remembered Allegi saying. How ironic, she thought. At one time they were meant to rule together.

Tigris began to cry. Quiet tears streamed down her cheeks. She closed her eyes, hugged Euphrates' letter against her chest—this was the closest she would come to holding him. Knowing that, made her cry harder.

XXXIX

ALLEGI STOOD DESPERATELY in the tavern. He had been gone so long he feared Deshyre would question his return. The last time they were together, he promised to meet her the next night—that was nineteen days ago. Already it had been an hour since Allegi arrived at Sechemesch—long past the time they had usually met.

Allegi moved from his seat to stand by the door. Anxiously he waited, peeking outside every so often to see if she was coming. But, each time he looked, the alley pierced him with its emptiness.

A concubine inside the tavern approached him. Allegi was not in the mood to deal with her. He began to walk away but she caught up with him, "She stopped coming two nights ago," the maiden informed as she strolled past.

Allegi halted, registered what the woman said. When it sank in, he raced to her side. "Who stopped coming?"

"The girl I've seen you meet in here." The woman turned to face him. Pouted. "She came every night for a long time. I guess she gave up. *Men*," she added with disgust.

The maiden moved to walk away. Allegi grabbed her. "Do you know where I can find her?"

She spun, sized the Pharaoh's messenger. Her eyes flickered then peered at him with a seductive glimmer. She slowly ran a finger across Allegi's stomach as she sulked, "What's she got that I don't got?"

"My heart," Allegi said flatly.

The maiden removed her finger, gave him a discerning look.

"Do you know where I can find her?" Allegi repeated, desperation penetrating his words.

"Perhaps." The woman began to walk away.

Allegi took hold of her again, this time by the hand. He placed a small sack of *duben* in her palm.

The concubine opened the sack. "Wow. You could have paid this and had much more fun."

Allegi went to grab the pouch but the maiden snatched it back.

"Alright," she said, shoving the sack between her bosoms. Her eyes narrowed, her voice lowered. "You know she's really one of those

Asiatic Bedouins?" She looked at Allegi as if the information would shock him but he didn't care. He just wanted to find Deshyre.

Disappointed she didn't get the reaction she was hoping for, the woman continued, "Their camp is said to be north of town, near the tower." The woman walked away.

Allegi rushed out of the tavern, jumped on his horse and raced out of town. He found the campsite as the maiden said, near the tower and rode to the edge of the camp. He jumped off Qare, cautiously made his way through the tented community, looking.

Fires burned where men gathered to drink and where women gathered to keep each other company as they made necklaces and rugs. Children ran naked around the goat skin tents as if they didn't have a bedtime and a group of old men sat around a board game. As Allegi passed by each group, they stopped what they were doing to gawk at him. He felt out of place in his royal clothing, guiding his horse through a foreign camp. He walked precariously by the small packs of people, hoping to find Deshyre amongst them.

A drunken man approached him with a sour expression cut onto his face. Allegi slowed his pace.

"You've no business here!" spat the man in a thick accent. The drunken man halted in front of Allegi, blocking his path.

Allegi could see by the man's stance his desire to fight. Allegi stepped back, tried to walk around him but the man side-stepped to block him again.

Around them, a crowd began to form as if they already knew what was coming.

"I am looking for Deshyre," Allegi stated.

"You've come to the wrong place. You're not welcome."

Again, Allegi tried to step around him but this time the man pushed him backwards.

Allegi stumbled. "I just want to speak with her."

"And, I said you're not welcome here!" The man charged at Allegi.

Fists swung. They threw each other around. The crowd edged them on, stepping out of the way when one of them was tossed. Allegi ducked out of the thrash of the man's fist. Although the man was bigger, Allegi knew how to fight. He swung, connected with the man's face.

The noise of the commotion stirred by the fight drifted through the air towards a tent not too far away. Deshyre stepped out to see what was going on. She spotted the rowdy spectators and moved towards them to get a better look. As she approached the crowd, she found it odd that the spectators moved aside to allow her through. She eyed them quizzically until she reached the front. Deshyre stopped short and blinked hard. *Allegi?*

She was momentarily stunned with disbelief and when she was sure it was him, she didn't know whether she wanted to turn to run away or to stop them from fighting. But, as the drunken man punched Allegi in the stomach, knocking the wind out of him, Deshyre found herself tramping into the ring and shouting, "Stop it! Stop this!" She pulled the man back. "Go rest your head, Senuret!"

The man backed away, suddenly more interested in Deshyre's presence than his fight.

Deshyre continued to march forward past Allegi to the other side of the ring. She pushed her way through the crowd.

Allegi raced after her. "Deshyre!" he called, but she continued on, away from the spectators, away from him.

"Deshyre!" he shouted again as he broke through the crowd himself.

"Go back to your palace, Allegi. You shouldn't have come here!" Tears began to stream down her face as she stomped past the tents away from Allegi. Then, the tears broke from their silence and she burst out crying.

Allegi could hear her crying. He increased his pace. "Why do you hide your home from me?"

"Can you not see, Allegi?" she shouted back to him through her sobs. "You're a royal noble. What would you want with this place?"

"You," Allegi answered in a soft tone but it was enough to stop Deshyre. She kept her back to him.

Allegi was several steps behind. He stopped walking when she did. "I don't care about your blood," he added.

Deshyre spun around. Her face was streaked with tears. She wiped them away with the back of her hand, stormed towards Allegi and pointed hard on his chest. "For seventeen days I went. Seventeen days! Why has it taken you so long to figure out what you want?" The question made her cry again, made her angry. She marched away.

"Deshyre!"

"Go away, Allegi. I'm not the girl you call upon when it pleases you. You may have met me in Sechemesch but I am not a harlot."

They had marched out past the tents into the darkness of the desert. Behind them the campfires spilled their light into the emptiness beyond the camp.

Deshyre quickened her pace, forcing Allegi to jog in order to catch up to her. He tried to grab her arm to stop her, but she shrugged him off.

"I'm a servant to the Pharaoh, my time is not so free," he said with frustration. Didn't she see the ships depart down the river? Didn't she know his duty robbed him of choice? Her anger sparked a fury within him. How could she be so unfair? But, as Allegi watched her storm away, flustered with the thought of never seeing her again, he knew his frustration was petty in comparison to losing her altogether.

He called after her, "I would have been there the next day if it was possible. I would have been there every day!" Still, she stomped away. It tore at his heart. Then the words leapt from his lips. From deep within they came. "Please don't leave me. *I love you.*"

Deshyre froze. Even Allegi was surprised by his own words. But, he knew he meant them.

He slowly walked up to her, turned her to face him. He looked at her affectionately, wiped a tear from her cheek. "All I think about is you."

"Do you mean that?" she asked, softly.

"That I love you?"

She nodded.

Allegi nodded back, his smile loving, genuine.

Deshyre jumped into his arms, kissed him passionately.

Allegi's smile grew. He took her hand, led her to his horse. "Let's go somewhere private," he said.

Approaching Qare, Deshyre looked at Allegi. "You have a horse?" she asked, surprised.

Allegi smiled. He patted Qare on the nose. "He belongs to the Pharaoh, but he gives his loyalty to me."

Deshyre glimpsed at Allegi, shyly. "I don't know how to ride that."

"It's no different than a camel."

"I never rode a camel." She pointed to the campsite. "We walk."

"Then, I'll teach you." Allegi lifted Deshyre onto the horse and climbed up behind her. They sped through the desert and he gave her the reins.

She laughed with excitement, the wind refreshing her face. For a long time they rode before Allegi brought the horse to a halt. He steered them over to a large rock grouping, jumped from the horse and helped Deshyre down. Digging into his bag, he pulled out some wooden sticks.

"You came prepared," Deshyre teased.

"I always travel with fire and water." The fire took flame. "And, of course, my writing kit."

"What do you write?"

"Letters and royal documents for the Pharaoh."

Deshyre put her arms around Allegi, speaking gingerly to him as she caressed his body. "I mean, what do you write for yourself?"

"Poetry," he shrugged.

"I knew it!" she grinned as she circled his heart with her finger. "I knew you had a romantic heart." She kissed his ear. "Read me one."

Allegi shook his head, uncomfortable with the request. "Let's lie down." He pulled her towards the fire. "I have to leave tomorrow to go to the Fortress of Ipu." He lowered himself to the earth, guided her down towards him. They lay on the ground, wrapped in each other's limbs. Allegi leaned over her and began to caress her arm. "I don't know how long I'll be gone." He pushed her hair from her face. "You've heard—"

"About the war?"

Allegi nodded.

"Is it dangerous for you?"

"Me? No," he laughed. "I hold the safest position—I'm a messenger. And, luckily for me, everybody wants the last word."

They both laughed.

Deshyre's expression grew serious. She looked into his eyes. "Just as long as you come back to me," she said, pulling his head down so she could kiss him.

"I will always come back to you, Deshyre," he whispered, kissing her lips.

Deshyre rolled on top of him. "I still want to hear one of your poems."

Allegi looked at her. She was smiling, her eyes pleading.

"Please?"

Allegi laid her down on her back. Slowly, he began to remove her clothes. He kissed her ear, whispering,

Like a lotus blossom,
In the murky waves

He kissed her neck, made his way down her body.

'Your beauty blooms to capture me,
To be rescued from the slaves.

He kissed her breasts and belly.

'Then, in my tender arms you sleep,
After I promise a happy life.

Allegi kissed her neck again, made his way back towards her ear where he whispered his last line,

'And, down on bended knee I beg,
For you to be my wife.

He pulled away, looked affectionately into her dark brown eyes.

Deshyre was speechless.

"Marry me," Allegi begged.

Her eyes grew wide. Unable to speak, she nodded. Deshyre kissed him passionately. "I love you," she was finally able to say.

They lay naked under the blanket of the sky with their clothes spread out like a sheet beneath them. This time they took their time as if every moment was to be savoured. They fell asleep wrapped by each other's arms and for the first time, Allegi was truly happy.

XL

$\mathcal{T}$HE QUEEN TOSSED in her sleep. She was dreaming— dreaming about her past. She was at battle with her father. They were fighting the *Tejehenu*. Swords were clashing. Men were dying. Tigris finished off another man. She looked around to determine where she was needed next. She saw her father, fighting, ferocious. How she admired him. He was so strong. She wanted to be like him. How she tried. They couldn't say she didn't try. She fought men. She went to war. She inherited his inner strength—or at least she liked to believe so.

Tigris watched her father swing his blade. His muscles tightened, glistening under his sweat. She wondered if he had ever watched her with the same admiration. If he had ever thought, *yes, my daughter, she has lived up to my expectation.*

How she loved him. How she clung to the moments when he spared his work to give her some attention. Just a little, always a lesson, but she coveted it with pride.

He had brought her to the battlefield; allowed her to march with his army into war. She had waited all her life for him to call her out to battle. Alas, the day had come. She wanted to make him proud. Slay a thousand men so he would announce at the feast: *This is my daughter, heir to my throne, a glorious warrior.*

A man roared towards her, stopped when he realized he held his axe over a woman. Tigris seized her opportunity, cut him down. She looked for her father again. She wanted to stay close to him. Let him see. Yes, let him see that she was a great warrior.

An arrow soared past her. Tigris followed it with her eyes. It blazed through the air towards its target.

Her eyes darted. Her mouth fell open. The arrow aimed for her father. She couldn't breathe. Her chest felt like it ripped open. God, she couldn't breathe.

If only she could do more than watch. Scream. *Something.* But, she could only watch. Watch as the arrow found its mark. Watch as it shot into the King. Watch as it pierced her father's chest.

The King took a step. Collapsed.

Tigris froze for only a second before the reality of the moment hit her like a club. Pain. *Crippling pain.* No, this couldn't be.

"*Father!*" she screamed, racing towards him. Panic gripped every part of her body. She began to sob uncontrollably as she rushed to the King's side. Everything around her faded into a blur—the fighting, the noise, the danger—none of it seemed to exist.

Reaching him, Tigris fell to her knees, held the Pharaoh in her arms, her head pressed against his chest. How she had always longed to hug him like this but not like this. She had imagined that when it happened, he would hug her back and it would have been he who reached out to draw her in. But instead, his arms were loosely spread out at his sides.

"Father!" she cried. Tigris opened her eyes. The arrow had gone through his armour and into his chest. Blood trickled out from where the arrow protruded. His face had lost colour.

Anger spread over Tigris. She began to shake him. "Father! Father! Open your eyes! Do not die on me!" Tigris looked up towards the heavens. "Oser, do not come for him! Protect him great Eset!"

The King began to cough blood. His eyes opened. "Egypt is yours," he mumbled in a weak voice.

"No! No! I don't want it! Great Per'a, do not die!"

King Qakare Iby smiled gently. "My royal daughter, I die in peace knowing this great nation will be safe in your power."

Tigris sobbed. "No, I don't want it," she begged, shaking her head again and again.

Qakare grabbed her face, held her still. He found some strength and used it in his voice, his tone, his grip. "Know you are a *King*. They will only try to take the throne from you if they believe they can." He coughed, bringing up more blood. "Never let them believe it. Remain strong. Protect the throne of our bloodline." He gulped for air. "Don't let anyone take Egypt from you." The King choked. *Gasped.*

"No!" Tigris cried, shaking her head non-stop. "Do not die!"

"Promise me," Qakare whispered.

Tigris couldn't stop crying or shaking her head or saying no.

"Promise me!" The King's voice was suddenly powerful. It broke Tigris out of her state of shock. "Promise me and let me die in peace."

Tigris could only stare at him. How could she concede to let him die?

"Say it!" The King coughed, blood spilled from his mouth.

He was dying and Tigris couldn't prevent it. Her body trembled from the core. "I promise," she finally gave in so he could hear the words before it was too late.

As the words hit the air, the Pharaoh's eyes rolled back. His coughs and gasps ceased and the Egyptian King fell still.

Tigris was in shock, not wanting to believe the day she longed for greeted her like this. She hunched over the King; her Pharaoh; her father. She cried; cried until her uncle came to carry her away.

THE QUEEN SPRANG up in bed and looked around the darkness. Her body was wet with sweat. Her heart was beating fast. In her hand she still clutched Euphrates' letter.

Promise me, she heard her father say as if the chamber was haunted by his voice.

Tigris whipped the scroll across the room as if it were poisoned and fell back down on the bed. She began to cry, tears of anger. Yet, as angry as she felt, she wasn't sure what her anger was for.

XLI

$\mathcal{A}$ DAY HAD passed since they left Wasebet. The tension between the two parties was unbearable. It would still be a few more days before they would reach the fortress and food was becoming low.

"How do you know your King will still be at the next location? He wasn't at the last and we have been traveling a week now."

Storithen looked over at Montu. They were resting in the shade of their camels while the sun was at its hottest point of mid-day. "*Your* King?" Storithen questioned.

Montu glared at him for a moment.

"You said, *your King*," Storithen pointed.

Montu didn't respond.

"If he is *our* King, then who is *your* King?"

Arman and Seti looked at Montu worried. Their faces revealed their secrets.

Nefret glanced at Storithen.

"Who is your King?" Storithen pushed. "What clan are you from?"

Montu didn't respond.

Storithen looked at Nefret. "We are fools!" he exclaimed, rising to his feet. "Why did we not ask them this question? We know what rebellious clan comes to meet us." Storithen spun on his heels to face Montu. He pulled his sword from his belt, pointing it. "The question is—do *you?*"

Montu rose to his feet. He did not know the answer to the question. He left the royal ships at the beginning of this war and had no contact with anyone from whom he could find out. He only conversed with his companions and the two rebels, save for some men at the foot of the Wadi Hammamat. Cautiously, Montu drew his sword.

"I knew it!" Storithen bellowed. "Infiltrators of the Queen!" Storithen lifted his sword.

Arman and Seti leapt to their feet and moved to stand beside Montu. Nefret joined Storithen. Everyone's weapons were drawn.

"Take us to Euphrates or you'll find your death torturous," Montu commanded.

"Never!" bellowed Storithen.

"You do not stand a chance. It's three to two and Nefret is only half a man," Seti quipped.

"Wrong," retorted Storithen. "It's six to three and I haven't even counted Nefret."

"The desert will swallow your traitorous blood!" Montu seethed, cutting his sword through the air. The five men fought.

The sun beat down mercilessly on them as they expended all of their energy in battle. Swords clanked. Sand kicked up, dusting the air.

Consumed by the fight, no one noticed the army of men ride in on camels until they had them surrounded.

When the five travellers realized their danger, they lowered their weapons and looked with astonishment at the clan, which seemed to have magically risen out of the sand.

The leader narrowed his eyes and studied the five figures. He jumped off his camel, walked towards them. Spitting into the earth, he glanced at the faces of all five men. "We are looking to join forces with

Euphrates. Do any of you know where he is?"

"We are with Euphrates," Montu was quick to answer.

Storithen and Nefret gave him a darting look.

"These two men are assassins of the Pharaoh," Montu pointed.

"Liar!" spat Storithen.

The leader of the militia stepped towards Storithen.

"We just discovered it now, which is why we fight," Arman added to Montu's argument.

The leader of the army studied Storithen. Storithen's fumed with anger but he bit his tongue.

"Assassins?" the leader questioned. "These two?" He spun, walked behind the line of five men and sized them. He stopped behind Storithen again, drew his dagger, and laid it on Storithen's throat. "Last words?"

"None." Storithen said in a low growl.

The leader looked at the front row of his men and nodded his head. Two men raised their bows, drawing their arrows on the string and pointed them at Storithen and Nefret.

Montu smiled.

The Commander of the Troop pointed, signalling his men. Without delay, the two men let go of their arrows, adjusting their aim. As the arrows sped through the air, the leader grabbed Montu and slit his neck from ear to ear. The two arrows struck Arman and Seti simultaneously. All three men dropped to the earth.

Storithen looked at the leader of the clan. "How did you know?" he asked.

"I doubted Euphrates' comrades would be so quick to lead me. Besides, he who speaks first has the most to hide." The leader smiled. "Snofru," he nodded, introducing himself.

"You don't look like you've abandoned your Pharaoh," Nefret cut in, pointing to the Lord of Bisteq's regal garb.

"Easier to travel the desert this way." Snofru went to his camel. "But, if I'm going to fight a war, I choose to fight for a king."

"Your clan?" Storithen challenged. He wouldn't make the same mistake twice.

"We are from Utes-hor. I am the Lord of Bisteq." Snofru pulled a sash from a sack tied to his camel and held it up, his emblem stitched to the fabric.

Storithen smiled, relieved. "This is Nefret and I am Storithen," he introduced. "You don't know how grateful we are to see you."

Snofru looked at the three dead bodies. "I think I do," he chuckled. He climbed onto his camel. "Take us to the King," he called out.

XLII

𝒯HE MEN STAGGERED from the heat. They were low on water and had been rationing what was left of it for the past couple of days. What remained wasn't enough for everyone to have a drink.

The men grew hostile; anger burned with the heat of the sun. Their anxiety drew them into fights with each other and their morale was low. They needed water; they needed to regain their strength.

Euphrates guarded what was left of the water, saving it for Menenthop, the wounded and the men who would volunteer to dig. Only he knew they would have water soon and everyone would be refreshed. They had reached the underground river.

Stopping, Euphrates examined the barren surroundings. He was taken out here once when he was a teenage boy by Menes and told to study the land.

〰

"BENEATH THIS SPOT runs a river," Menes had informed.

Euphrates knew everything Menes told him was a lesson that bore special importance in its knowledge. No sooner than the words left Menes mouth did Euphrates kneel down in front of a rock to mark it.

Menes looked at him as he carved into the stone, saying, "First you must know where to find the rock. Second, you should never rely solely on markings, for they can be destroyed."

For four days and four nights, they remained in the desert. Menes allowed Euphrates the time to take in everything from the sky at night to the landscape at day.

〰

ALMOST FIFTEEN YEARS later, Euphrates stood in the familiarity of the scene. He felt a connection to the surroundings and knew it was from the days spent there so long ago.

As Euphrates stood observing the landscape, an uncanny feeling drew over him. *Had Menes foreseen his future?* At the time, marking the river seemed like every other lesson with the same guiding theme of preparing to regain the throne of Egypt. But, now as he relied on the underground river for survival, it felt as if Menes had known all the trials he would face.

Euphrates glanced around trying to remember which stone was his. Below the rock the river ran under the earth. Locating the rock would make their quest easier. But, even if he didn't find the engraved stone, Euphrates knew he found the location of the river. Those four days he had spent here as a young teenager, complaining it was a waste of time, now ranked amongst the most important days of his life.

Euphrates scoped the land. He told Tuthiken and Somiset to search for the hieroglyphic symbol of water on the western side of a large rock—the side facing the Nile. The men tramped the area searching.

Euphrates turned to his army. "We will rest here overnight and I promise before the sun rises, you will be refreshed with more water than you can drink."

As the men sprawled out to rest, Euphrates went to scour the area with Somiset and Tuthiken. Unlike his two comrades who examined the ground for the stone, Euphrates observed the landscape in case the rock had been destroyed. He moved across the earth trying to recall the exact location in which Menes had made him sit, not allowing him to move for those four days. He eyed the mountains, which couldn't move in his life time, and he looked at the sun's position against them. Turning, he walked out to where he memorized the invisible line to run across the desert at that special spot. Euphrates stopped when everything appeared exact—the time of day, where the sun touched the mountains, the direction, the distance, and then he calculated the season. Everything seemed to line up perfectly. Euphrates looked at the ground. A few steps away a fair-size rock protruded from the earth. He went to it, squatted down, and looked at the western side of the rock.

Four rows of zigzagged lines were carved into the side of the stone. Euphrates whistled. Tuthiken and Somiset looked over before they rushed to his side.

Euphrates ran his finger over top of the etching in a moment of awe. It seemed so long ago when he had made the mark. He never imagined then, almost fifteen years later, he would depend upon that river, and even more bewildering, that its existence would save his life.

Euphrates looked up at Somiset. "This is where we dig."

XLIII

SNOFRU AND HIS clan neared the Fortress of Ipu with Storithen and Nefret. The garrison was gated and watchmen paced the wall walk. When they spotted the militia approach, the guards stopped and tried to determine who they were.

Closing in, Snofru noticed their sashes. "Euphrates isn't there," he said, bringing his troop to a halt.

Storithen eyed Nefret who in turn looked at Snofru confused.

"They wear the royal sash of the Pharaoh." Snofru nodded in the direction of the guards. With slow steps, he led his men forward, giving himself time to think as he closed the distance.

Nefret grew pale. "We are in time," he claimed. "Besides, Euphrates would have waited an additional week to see if we'd come." Nefret turned to Storithen. "Euphrates..." he whispered. "Is it over?"

"He hasn't been here, yet," Snofru assured as he assessed the situation.

"But, he *said* he would be here."

Snofru looked at Nefret's worried face. "Don't cast down your weapon, yet. If Euphrates was dead, the world would know. Word travels faster than man. Even you would have heard out here in the desert alone." Snofru returned his attention towards the fortress.

"Euphrates is a man of his word," Nefret insisted.

"Maybe so but he hasn't been here yet." Snofru peered at the guards. "They are expecting someone."

As they neared the fortress gates, a guard yelled down to them, "State your position and purpose."

"I am from the city of Pa-suk. I received an order from the Pharaoh to help reinforce the fort. The rebel forces are reportedly marching forth." Snofru pulled a scroll from his pouch and held it up.

Storithen and Nefret eyed him, suspiciously.

"You don't look like Dedu," the guard yelled down.

Pa-suk was one of the neighbouring towns of Ipu. It was very probable the Pharaoh would send an order for any town within close proximity to supply their forces to help protect the fortress. Snofru knew of the town but forgot the name of the Lord who governed it.

"I am his cousin, Hatep. Dedu is very ill and asked I go in his honour."

The watchman studied Snofru for a moment and noticed he and his men were clad in noble attire. "Lower the gate!" he ordered.

The gate began to lower. Snofru smiled at Storithen and Nefret. "That was easy."

The Bisteq clan rode in through the fortress gates and stopped in the main court on the inner side of the garrison's walls. Snofru waited until all of his men were inside the wall before he bellowed, "Attack!"

Drawing his weapon, he charged forward taking the Queen's military by surprise. The rebellion raced through the fort like a sand storm while the royal army scrambled for their weapons unprepared for battle as they waited on their Pharaoh. A message arrived that day stating both the Pharaoh's army and rebellion were on their way to the fort. Surely the Queen would have sent reinforcements. Indeed, the watchmen were not expecting *this*.

Snofru's men had beaten the imperial forces, which outnumbered them in the desert and now, with the advantage of surprise, Snofru's offence would certainly reap victory at the Fortress of Ipu.

The Bisteq clan charged through the garrison both on camel and on foot. Storithen stuck with Nefret so he could help defend the small man. When he needed to move, he grabbed Nefret and dragged him with him so as not to lose sight of his friend.

Glancing around, Storithen spotted Cheti moving along the allure. Fury blazed through him as everything began to make sense. Cheti did not go back to join his rebellious forces, he used the information given to him to move in on Euphrates' destination and prepare for his arrival.

Storithen grabbed Nefret by the arm, raced to the stairs and soared up them. Cheti saw them coming and began to run. He disappeared into a tower at the end of the walk. Storithen pursued. Reaching the doorway, he slowed his pace. He let go of Nefret and cautiously entered the tower's rooftop terrace. On the other side of the enclosure, Cheti swung swords against Snofru who entered the tower from a second doorway.

Rage still pumped through Storithen's veins, yet, at the same time he was happy to meet with Cheti. "This one's mine," Storithen said to Snofru as he approached.

Snofru stepped back. Cheti turned to face Storithen. Storithen eyed him coldly.

"So, these are your forces," Storithen scoffed as he lifted his blade.

Cheti stepped sideways and Storithen matched his movement. The two men moved in a circle, waiting for the other to make the first move.

"How nice of you to bring them to our destination. I hear the Queen's army is on its way. Are you ready to fight against them?" Storithen mocked.

"You are an abhorrent anarchist. How dare you turn your nose up at me when you have forsaken your Pharaoh."

"My Pharaoh is Euphrates and I have not forsaken him!"

Storithen brought his blade down. Cheti blocked it. The two men began to battle. They charged back and forth from wall-to-wall, pinning each other down but escaping in time.

Cheti stepped forward, swung his blade with violent force, knocking Storithen's sword from his hand. Kicking Cheti in the gut, Storithen afforded himself time to get to his weapon.

Cheti hunched over to catch his breath. Anger burned his cheeks. He peered at Storithen and charged. He kicked Storithen over before he was able to pick his sword off of the ground. Cheti stepped back, raised his blade, and brought it down.

Storithen was on his back. Before Cheti had the chance to finish his swing, Storithen sacked him in the knee, cracking it.

Cheti yelped in pain, stumbled back. He hobbled on one foot, bent over, grasping his knee cap in one hand and using the other hand to balance himself on his sword like a cane.

Storithen scooped up his weapon. Stood. He walked over to Cheti, raised his sword. Stopped. Blood poured out of Cheti's mouth and the man fell forward. For a moment, Storithen watched perplexed. But, as Cheti's body caved to the stone floor, it revealed Nefret standing behind him with his axe in Cheti's back.

"I didn't think it fair you have all the fun," Nefret jeered.

Snofru came up beside them. "Grab the body," he commanded. He headed to the stairs.

"You killed him," Storithen smirked, walking away.

Nefret struggled to drag the body from the terrace.

The three men reached the bottom of the tower and stepped out into the court. The battle was over. Snofru's clan had won. Men were dragging the bodies of the dead out of the gate and laying them in a heap, preparing them to burn. The stench and disease that would follow would prove more deadly than the battle itself if they didn't get rid of the carcases.

Nefret added Cheti's body to the pile and returned to Storithen's side.

Snofru looked at his new comrades. "I believe this fortress is ours!"

XLIV

*C*HE ROYAL SHIPS pulled into the port closest to Intify's camp. It was late evening when they arrived and they still had an hour's journey to the campsite.

Tigris sat in the cabin staring at the letter she had written to Euphrates. It was sealed with clay—a thick hardened blob imprinted with the royal emblem of the scarab. She eyed the seal, which prevented her from reading the letter and debated whether she should just break it open and read what she wrote. She had written the words in a state of emotional turmoil and couldn't remember what she had put to page. Now that she was calm, she agonized over whether she should send it or read it.

Tigris glared at the scroll. There it was: across the room, on top of the table, calling out to her. She knew if she read the letter, she would never send it. Inside its curled edges, her feelings were all rolled up on that sheet of paper and the idea of it scared her. A part of her wanted her words delivered to Euphrates. A part of her did not.

Tigris stood, walked to the table where the scroll lay taunting her. She bore down on the parchment as if it were poisoned.

Send it, a voice inside her whispered. But, no sooner than the whisper spoke, was it interrupted by a more powerful voice ordering the letter's destruction.

Tigris felt her heart pound hard against her chest, begging. Something within her resolved to give way. She scooped up the parchment and raced out of her cabin before she could change her mind.

The Queen found Allegi near the plank gazing into the river, his dark eyes cast down, pouring their doubts into the Nile. He looked as if he were lost.

"What's wrong?" Tigris asked, approaching him.

Allegi glanced up at her. He shook his head. "Nothing."

"That isn't the face of nothing." Tigris leaned over the ship's wall beside Allegi. She stared down at the two men who were preparing to ride to Intify's camp to inform him of their plans.

Allegi noticed the scroll in her hand, gestured towards it.

Tigris almost forgot but as soon as Allegi reminded her, her heart began to pound again. She wasn't sure if it was from fear or from hope. For a moment, she had the urge to drop the letter into the river below and allow it to be washed away. If only a strong gust of wind would come and steal it—what could she do then but deem it was the will of the gods to have removed it from her control. However, there was no wind—at least, not one powerful enough to take the parchment from her grip.

Tigris looked at Allegi. With all her will, she hastily held out the scroll to him. "Take it from me," she said, thrusting it in his hand.

Allegi gave her a curious look.

"Just deliver the letter to Euphrates at your best opportunity." Tigris walked away. She mustered all of her strength to leave him with the letter, to not tear it open or to even tear it up.

263

THREE DAYS LATER, the royal mercenaries intercepted Ankhtify. His army was led to the ships. They boarded and continued towards the fortress.

XLV

*W*HEN DARKNESS BEGAN to drop over the land, Euphrates rose to his feet. They had rested all day under the Egyptian sun. Men sprawled out on their mats or on the dirt ground itself. They hadn't set up tents or unloaded the wagons since they would only stay the night and moreover, lacked the energy for it.

Euphrates walked out into the centre of the large group of warriors and stood on his marked rock. "Good men," he began, stirring them from their rest. "I know these last days of our journey have been difficult since our water has been low. But, as I promised, we will break ground this eve and be refreshed by the river, which runs beneath us." Euphrates' voice carried easily across the open air of the desert, intriguing the men to pay attention as they heard him claim a river. "I need volunteers. Ten men to dig down into this hard Egyptian soil. Those who volunteer will receive two cups of water each for his labour."

The men began to chatter, weighing out the choice of whether the water they craved was worth the energy they would have to expend.

"We will dig in shifts of one hour stretches." Euphrates walked to the wagon loaded with water vessels. Almost all of them were empty. Tuthiken and Somiset guarded the wagon from desperate men who tried throughout the day to seize it.

Reaching in, Euphrates pulled out a large clay pot and a cup. He poured water into the cup and held it up. "Who will be the first to drink?"

Tuthiken stepped forward, grabbed the goblet of water from Euphrates. He drank it back. Euphrates poured him another. Finishing the second cup, Tuthiken marched over to the rock, opened the goat skin bag, set beside the stone earlier, grabbed out a shovel and drove it into the ground.

Somiset followed suit. He drank the water then joined Tuthiken.

Gradually, men rose to their feet and joined in the dig. When there were ten at the rock, Euphrates gulped back two cups himself and lifted a large pick. With full force, he cracked it into the ground.

When the hour had passed, the next ten stepped up, took their drinks and began to dig. Euphrates did not take any breaks. He broke the earth, loosening the hard ground for the men to shovel away. Tuthiken and Somiset did not stop either.

Four hours later as the men began to lose hope and doubted Euphrates' promise, water swelled up into the hole. Those digging dropped their tools and rejoiced with excitement.

Everyone had his turn to drink—almost three thousand men. They continued throughout the night, making their way to the water hole. Even when the sun made its appearance on the horizon, men still waited their turn.

The rebellious forces remained by the pit for the entire next day. The men drank, washed and rested until the sun, once again, lowered. Then, with their skinned pouches and water vessels full, the small army set off to the Fortress of Ipu.

The Fortress of Ipu stood by the Nile like a massive pillar of guarded rock. Its thick outer walls were fifty feet tall with ramparts twenty feet thick. Cornices, towers and loopholes helped in protecting its outer walls against attack. The only way to besiege the stronghold was to force the gates or scale the walls.

By early afternoon, on the ninth day, the rebellion came into view of the structure. Euphrates eyed its high walls and sealed gates, which loomed down onto the desert with intimidation. Breaking into the garrison would be a challenge.

"Prepare the siege shelters and ladders!" Euphrates ordered.

Retrieving the equipment, the men began to piece them together. The siege shelters offered a protective roof against the fortress' high advantage, which enabled an easy rain of weapons down on its attackers. The shelters would help move the army close to the fortress where battering rams could be used to break down the gates.

When everything was prepared, Euphrates gave the command for the men to move forward. They marched their way towards the fortress across the open desert, closing the distance at considerable speed. The caravans followed for now, but they would stop at a safe distance until Euphrates seized the garrison and they could transport the cumbersome supplies in with ease.

Barin sat with Menenthop in one of the wagons. Menenthop was getting worse. He had broken into sweats and spoke frantically in his sleep. The boy did his best to keep him comfortable, wiping his face and chest with a wet cloth every so often. But, Menenthop was failing quickly.

Before long, the wagons stopped. The warriors continued. They approached the garrison. Everything was still and quiet.

Euphrates found it odd they did not meet with the fort's defence. No bows were slung or spears lunged. The fortress seemed as if it slept. Even in the towers and behind the cornices no life moved.

Could it have been abandoned? Euphrates wondered. He knew his men were suspicious too—they were looking at him for answers.

"Forward!" Euphrates commanded. Regardless of what lay in store, they were going into the fortress.

The rebellious forces of the coalition moved in close to the fortified building and still no weapons fell from the upper levels. The air remained hushed, still. Even the sounds of nature seemed not to exist.

Then, in the distance behind them, a trumpet blew. Euphrates froze.

The Queen's army.

Slowly, he turned to peer across the desert. Sure enough the royal military grew out of the sand. As he watched, a second army moved in from the east. Euphrates looked back at the fortress.

The rebellion was caught in a trivial position—the fortress threatened them from one side and the massive army prepared to storm them from the other. Outside the garrison walls, Euphrates had to make a decision of where to aim his defence and he prayed the fortress continued in its present slumber.

"Front line with me!" Euphrates ordered as he headed to the back of his army, making it now the front. He shouted for the men to move out of their way to allow his first wall of defence with their bows and arrows through. His army spun on their heels to face the two royal battallions, which positioned themselves in the distance.

"Men at the back, keep your eyes on the garrison!" Euphrates shouted, knowing the fortress still posed a threat.

Euphrates quickly sized the Queen's forces—tremendous by comparison to the rebellious King's three thousand men.

Euphrates spun to face his soldiers and shouted with conviction. "We have faced these numbers before and have been victorious. We will prevail again! Under the truth and justice of Maat, she will protect our cause! Raise up your battle axes to triumph! By the great god Oser, we will not go into the Underworld today!"

Behind his military, the gates of the Fortress of Ipu began to open. Euphrates watched dreading what would follow. *God, they were trapped!*

A Commander of Fifty, who led a troop at the back, cried out, "The gate opens! Raise your spears! Ready your weapons!" His men dropped to their knees and prepared to fire.

Yet, when the gate was fully open, only emptiness greeted them.

Euphrates didn't understand it.

A single camel rode out. Euphrates' men parted to allow a path for the rider to pass.

As the lone rider approached, Euphrates blinked hard to make sure his eyes didn't deceive him.

"So, are you coming in or are you going to stay outside and fight them?" Nefret asked.

Euphrates was baffled.

"We were going to let you scale the walls but..." Nefret pointed to the Queen's army, "...when she showed up, we thought to invite you in."

Euphrates beamed with relief. "How nice of you to reconsider."

Nefret bowed his head.

Without hesitating, Euphrates shouted to his men, "Into the fort! Quickly, into the fort!"

From across the desert the command of the General of the Royal Armed Forces roared, *"Fire!"* Arrows soared through the air chasing men into the gates.

Euphrates looked to his caravan. "Into the fort!" he yelled. Left by themselves, in the safety of the desert away from the attack of the fortress, the wagons were now in great danger.

"Abandon the wagons!" Euphrates shouted. He needed to get his men into the protection of the garrison. Trying to manoeuvre the wagons across the desert now would be too slow. Arrows had already begun to shower them. Men were being struck down. And, even though his fighting soldiers moved into the safety of the fort, the men who held other positions within his army—such as the doctors, the cooks, the water-bearers—were still at risk. They had remained with the caravan and now had a fair distance to sprint before reaching the fort.

Euphrates glanced at the gate. The siege shelters were the first to go into the fortress. He would have called for them to help protect these men except his soldiers crowded the gate as they pushed their way in, making it impossible for the shelters to get back out.

Frantically, Euphrates rode further into the desert. He grabbed the *swinew*, launched him onto his horse, drove him in close to the fortress, set him down and raced back to help another.

Some of the men cut the camels loose from the wagons, jumped on their backs to ride in faster. Barin remained in the wagon with Menenthop. Their driver hadn't abandoned them; he knew the boy and Menenthop relied on him to get them to safety. Arrows dropped down around them. Barin held onto Menenthop who groaned in pain as the wagon bumped along the hardened desert towards the gates.

A sudden jerk made Barin look up to find his wagon turning. The wagon was driverless. The driver had been torn from the wagon by an arrow and rolled to his death in the desert. With no one to guide them, the camel ran wild. The animal turned, bringing them towards the royal enemy.

Barin raced forward. He scrambled into the driver's seat and looked around. The reins dangled off the back of the camel to the ground. Barin stretched his body across the post joining the animal to the wagon. *Too far.* His small hands couldn't reach them. He pushed himself further along. The bumping movement swung him around the post nearly throwing him off but he held on. He dangled upside down with his knees and arms locked around the wooden beam. He could see in the sky, arrows like lotus, flying overhead.

Using all his strength, Barin struggled to get himself upright. Twice he almost fell but he managed to hold on. He was now on top of the post. He slid his way to the rump of the camel, reached out, grabbed the hump, pulled himself up. He found the reins, slapping the earth where they dangled. The boy caught them, tightened his fist around the leather strap and yanked on the reins. He steered the wagon back towards the fortress.

Ahead of him the gates were closing. Everyone who survived was now inside; the supplies left behind.

A new panic gripped the boy. "Open the gate!" Barin screamed. "Open the gate!" He whipped at the camel, drove the animal faster. Screamed, "Open the gate!"

The large gate drew upwards, rising off the ground. There was no way for Barin to get the wagon into the fortress but he still whipped the camel, forcing it to speed. If the gate closed, they'd never hear him; never see him from the other side of the thick garrison walls.

The wagon bumped along behind. Water jugs fell off the back, breaking into pieces as they hit the ground.

"Euphrates!" Barin called as he neared the gate. He stood on the back of the camel, steered the animal in closer. Fear pumped inside him but he had no choice. At the last possible moment, Barin jumped, launched his body forward over the door that continued to rise off of the ground. The boy hit the wooden gate with a thud and rolled down the steep incline into the fortress.

"Open the gate!" he yelled in pain.

Euphrates ran to him repeating the command, "Open the gate!"

Tuthiken and Somiset saw the boy and knew immediately Menenthop was still on the other side of the fortress. They raced out amidst the danger of the falling arrows and retrieved the wagon.

The gate was closed again. The Queen's army ceased fire. The rebellion gained the protection of the fortified building.

TIGRIS STARED AT her fortress. She ordered her men to cease fire and move back when the gate began to close. They needed to organize their attack and until they did, they would keep out of the range of their enemies.

Ankhtify rode up to her side.

Tigris' face still glowered with bitter astonishment.

"I left Cheti in charge," the General informed as he halted next to her.

"Can anyone be trusted!" Tigris seethed. "I am surrounded by a nation of traitors!" She continued to glare at the Fortress of Ipu. "Prepare the siege shelters and scaling ladders!" she shouted.

∿∿∿

INSIDE THE FORTRESS, Menenthop was laid down in a chamber. The *swinew* looked him over with a grave expression. Menenthop had a severe fever and his breathing was so heavy it sounded painful. Each breath grew further apart and they were now so far apart it was a wonder how he lived to the next one.

Swinew looked up at the five men—Euphrates, Storithen, Tuthiken, Somiset and Nefret—who bore down on him with hope and worry tangled together on their brows. Then, he glanced at Barin who sat by Menenthop's side. At length, the doctor shook his head, "Any time now."

Barin began to cry. They all watched in grief waiting for the dreaded moment. Finally, it came. Menenthop's eyes fluttered as he gasped desperately for his last breath of air. Then, he was stiff.

Somiset pulled the crying boy closer to him, offering him comfort. "He is at peace now," he whispered, "out of this painful world."

The *swinew* covered Menenthop's face with a linen shroud.

The five men stepped out of the chamber and met with frantic commotion. Soldiers ran about shouting orders and heeding them.

Snofru walked towards them, bowed when he reached Euphrates. "Snofru of Bisteq."

Euphrates nodded.

Snofru looked questioningly towards the chamber behind them.

Euphrates shook his head. "Into the *Fields of Peace*," he said, sadly.

"By the will of Oser." Snofru returned. He allowed a moment of silence out of respect for their deceased friend before he jumped into the matter at hand. He gestured to the men who raced about.

"The Pharaoh's army has begun to attack," Snofru informed. "We've already made many preparations over the past couple days while we waited for you."

The group began walking through the front courtyard towards the gate.

"My personal favourite," Snofru pointed.

Behind the large gate, men pushed a wooden wall with spears protruding out towards the entrance and placed it behind the door. Large stones were being stacked behind the makeshift wall to prevent it from being knocked over when the royal soldiers barged in. When they did, the first of them would impale themselves on the spears.

"Our second wall of defence," Snofru added.

"Impressive."

A heavy bang could be heard on the other side of the fortress' gates. The Queen was attempting to break the door.

"How does it look from up there?" Euphrates pointed. They glanced up to see men scurrying the battlements, taking cover behind the cornices. Burning arrows launched over the wall and men hurried to put them out. Boiling pots of water were passed through an assembly line of men to the top where they were poured down on the soldiers who attempted the scaling ladders. Through the loopholes men shot arrows down on the royal army.

"They won't get in today," Snofru assured.

The attack continued until late into the night when the Queen called off her army so they could rest and recuperate. The royal military retreated to their camp, which was now set up in the desert just far enough out of the range of the rebellion's archers.

〰

EUPHRATES CLIMBED THE tower to the rooftop to assess the situation. Much damage had been made to the thick wooden gate. Many of the Queen's men were killed but still not enough to make their numbers even. By tomorrow, the gate was sure to be penetrated.

Euphrates stared at the Queen's camp in the distance. Searching among the tents, he tried to see if he could make out which tent was hers.

How close she slept tonight—under the same sky, the same stars, he thought.

A feeling of longing grew inside him. How odd that he warred against someone he so desperately wanted. He imagined being in her tent, holding her, kissing her, touching her.... How strong Egypt would be if they stopped fighting; if they united and ruled the country

271

together—*King and Queen.*

Euphrates spun. He descended the tower; his steps determined; his pace unwavering. He went to Barin who rested in a chamber within the centre building--better protected from the battle surging outside the fortress walls. Opening the door, Euphrates peered through the darkness. The boy was sleeping. He stepped over to him, crouched down and shook him awake.

"Barin," Euphrates whispered. "Where is the messenger's flag?"

"With the water vessels," the boy answered still half asleep. His eyes rolled closed as Euphrates stood.

Euphrates found the wagon in the court and the flag inside it like the boy had said. He grabbed the flagstaff, found a camel and strapped the pole to the animal's back. Jumping on the camel, he raced towards the gate, shouting, "Open the gate!"

Somiset and Nefret ran into the court to see who was making such a demand.

"Open the gate!" Euphrates repeated.

Confusion and dismay held them still. They noted the messenger flag cast above Euphrates.

"I said, open the gate!"

Without asking questions, Nefret set off to round up men to help move the spear wall.

Euphrates watched. His mind raced. He looked sternly at Somiset. "Don't stop. I want that gate open when I get back." He rode towards the centre building, dismounted the camel, rushed inside to his chamber where he dug through a chest and grabbed a linen sheet. He dropped the linen over his head, wrapped it around his neck and across his shoulder to help conceal his face.

Moments later, he was outside again. He climbed on the camel and galloped towards the front gate. By the time he reached the entrance, the stones had been moved from behind the spear wall and the gate was almost lowered.

Somiset sent Euphrates a questioning look but Euphrates said nothing. He rode out of the fortress, across the battlefield towards the Queen's camp. Guards lined the outskirts, creating a protective wall of defence, keeping watch on the garrison.

Euphrates reached the royal camp and halted as a soldier approached.

He gestured to the flag. "I bring a message to the Pharaoh."

The soldier reached out to take it.

"I have orders to directly deliver it to Her Majesty," Euphrates said, refusing to hand over a letter.

"On this side of the battlefield I supersede your commander and your orders are to give it here." The soldier held out his hand again.

Euphrates looked past him. He kicked his camel, tore past the line, charging into the tented area of the royal camp.

"Shoot him!" yelled the guard to one of his men who was holding a bow.

The man looked at him helplessly. "We can't kill a messenger—he carries the flag."

"Well, stop him!" the head guard erupted with frustration.

Three guards scrambled to catch Euphrates.

Euphrates drove his camel through the camp, turning sharp corners, trying to lose the guards. He knocked down tents and crates as he made his way along the narrow pathways towards the centre of the campsite. He knew the Queen's large tent would be placed in the centre, safely surrounded by her military.

〰

INSIDE HER TENT, Tigris oiled her skin. She wore a loose fitting tunic with no jewellery or wig. She came from a bath set for her in another tent. The hot bath was just what she needed to relax enough to sleep. For once, she thought about nothing.

Sitting on her bed, Tigris rubbed the oil onto her leg enjoying the silence of the tent and her mind. But, the silence didn't last long. The tent flap ripped open. Someone rushed in.

The Queen reached under her pillow and grabbed her dagger. She glared at the tall stranger, covered in a dark shroud, standing in the middle of her room. Cautiously, she rose to her feet and pointed her dagger out towards him. Outside, Tigris could hear the voices of her guards shouting, "*Into Her Majesty's tent!*"

Without speaking, the stranger showed his weaponless hands and slowly brought them towards his head.

"I will kill you before you have the chance to touch your weapon," Tigris warned in a low and definite tone.

"I come in peace." The man lowered his hood revealing himself.

Tigris gasped. She blinked hard to make sure she saw the figure correctly.

Euphrates! How? Why? Her thoughts whirled.

The guard's shouts drew closer. "He's in the Pharaoh's tent!"

Tigris hid her knife behind her back as two guards barged in.

They froze just inside the door seeing their Pharaoh cornered by the messenger. The two men gave a quick bow.

"Many apologies, Per'a, we told him to hand over his message but he charged the line." Both guards stood behind Euphrates, unable to see his face.

Euphrates eyed Tigris—at her camp he was at her mercy.

Tigris didn't move; couldn't move. What was this feeling? *Fear.* Yes, fear.

The guards waited on the Pharaoh to give her command. She looked from the guards to Euphrates and back again, uncertain. She wasn't in danger but his presence was foreboding.

Oh, Hathor, Tigris deliberated internally. Did she have the strength to hear his words, to stand in his presence alone?

Tigris finally nodded at the guards. "It's fine. Leave him with me."

The men bowed. Exited.

Euphrates didn't hesitate. The moment they were gone, before the tent flap smacked the ground, he moved towards Tigris. "It doesn't have to be this way," he whispered, taking small, slow steps.

Fear. Such fear. Tigris tried to find her strength. She narrowed her eyes, brought her arm forward, pointed her dagger out at him again.

"Clearly, you do not wish me dead or you would have had your soldiers drag me away," Euphrates stopped with his chest against the tip of her blade.

"Perhaps I wish to kill you myself." She lifted the knife to his throat.

Euphrates shook his head in disagreement. He stepped closer and Tigris let him come. "Your eyes deceive your tongue."

Tigris shook her head no, unable to speak.

"Then, look me in the eyes, tell me you don't want me and I will leave and never look back." Euphrates looked deep into her eyes, raised his hand, gently took hold of her wrist which held the knife.

Tigris felt her knees weaken. There *he* was, standing in front of her.

Euphrates. She wasn't sure if it made her happy or scared but she knew it made her weak.

"Speak the truth. Tell me what you want," he was saying.

"I don't want *this!*" Tigris hissed, finally finding the courage to speak.

Euphrates studied her. He stepped in closer, the knife still at his throat. Their bodies slightly touched. He could feel her warmth. "No, tell me you don't want *me.*"

Tigris shook her head but she couldn't say the words. Her breaths were heavy. Her heart pounded so hard she was certain he could feel it.

They stared silently at each other, their breaths quivering until Euphrates pulled her in tight against his body, and kissed her passionately.

Tigris lost her breath. *His soft wet lips. His tongue.*

The knife fell to the floor. She touched his face.

Their kiss was filled with longing, desire. They stumbled back over the chests stacked beside the Queen's bed, knocking a small statue of the goddess Sekhmet to the floor.

Tigris arched backwards on top of the large wooden box, breathing, panting. *Fear of what she felt.*

Euphrates leaned over, kissing her neck, holding her waist. His hard muscular body pressed against her—how she wanted him!

"End this war," Euphrates whispered, working his kiss up her neck. "Unite with me. Together we can rule this country." He kissed her ear, sending chills along her spine. "Be my Queen," he softly begged.

Sudden anger flared within Tigris. She pushed Euphrates off of her. "*Your* Queen?" she questioned as she straightened on her feet. "And, you as my *King?*" Tigris slid away from him. "Clever," she sneered. Her voice turned deep and powerful. Her words viciously lashed out. "Egypt is *mine* and I will *not* be ruled!"

"How will you ever bear an heir reigning this country alone? Your line will end here!"

"My line will flourish with a noble whom I will make a prince! But, I will not give up the crowns of Egypt. I *am* Pharaoh!"

"You are stubborn!" Euphrates walked away, stopped when he heard her speak.

"Why is it that a woman is expected to give up everything for a man? A boy born under the title prince grows to become a King, and no marriage, no love can take that from him. But, a woman is told to remove the crown and hand it over. Well, I won't! If it truly is me you want then unite as my *Prince*."

Euphrates spun. He stomped back to her. He stood close, leaned in. "*Why*—you ask. Because, it is the will of the gods—a woman was never meant to wear the crown and..." he moved back, peering hard at her, "my birth given title was to be *King!*"

"You are just as stubborn!" Tigris stepped away from him. Even in her anger, she couldn't handle being so close to the warmth of his body. It caused strange feelings inside of her, feelings one should not have for an enemy.

Coldly, Tigris glared at Euphrates. "It seems clear the will of the gods and what was meant to be, for the crown rests upon my head and you have long since lost your title—to me, Nitiqreti. *Pharaoh* of Egypt."

An uneasy silence hovered as they locked eyes. No one moved. But, inside, Tigris trembled. *Why?* she thought. *Why like this?*

After a long moment, she took a step forward, changed her tone, spoke softly. "You are right. It doesn't have to be like this, Euphrates." She moved closer to him, took his hand. "Please, end this war. We can sign a treaty. I will give you land. Be my Prince and I will cherish you."

Euphrates studied her, lifted her hand to his face, felt it against his cheek. "I have never felt for any woman the way I feel for you. I cannot think but to see your face. And, though it may sound foolish, I believe my heart has fallen in love with someone I do not even know." He changed his tone, whispered, "as if you were meant for me." Euphrates lowered her hand from his cheek, deliberately shook his head from side to side, ever so slightly. "But, you ask the impossible. I cannot be your Prince." He leaned into Tigris so his lips rested on her ear. "Be my Queen. I promise to be fair."

Tigris closed her eyes. Why? Why like this? The question whirled in her mind, over and over. It brought her pain. But, there was only one choice she could make, one choice that was honourable.

Tigris turned her head away.

Euphrates pulled back, looked at her, wanting to find the truth in her eyes that couldn't lie. But, her head was turned and her eyes were to the floor, refusing him. He knew she would never concede; that wasn't who she was. It was the very thing he admired in her and the very thing he right now hated.

Letting go of her hand, Euphrates turned, lifted the linen shroud over his head.

He was gone. The flap fell behind him, pushing a wave of thick air into the tent.

Tigris' face cringed. The pain inside her swelled. She covered her face with her hands, gasping repetitively for air.

"*I don't care*," she whispered through her gasps. "*I am strong.*" Tigris stumbled to her bed. Her legs were numb. Her body trembled. The pain pierced inside her chest, causing her gasps to become more frantic. She could barely walk. She reached out for the stack of trunks beside the bed to help steady herself.

"*I don't care*," she repeated. She allowed herself to slide down the wooden boxes to the floor. She sat with her back against the chests, her head leaned backwards, trying to calm herself with deep breaths. Quiet tears rolled down her cheeks, burning her flesh.

Why? It was the only question she wanted answered. *Why* did he make her weak? *Why* did he cause her pain? And, the fear. *Why* the fear? So much fear! Hathor, why did she feel this way? But, there were no answers.

Tigris remembered his last words. They made her feel warm inside; how different compared to how she felt now.

She cupped her face, thought about what she said to Allegi. *That is the fantasy of fools. No one can fall in love so easily!* How could she think Euphrates was crazy when her own heart was just as foolish?

Tigris took a deep breath, wiped away her tears. She wouldn't allow her heart to control her. She could never step down from the throne to become Euphrates' Queen and him—her enemy, the man who sought to take her country—made her King. What shame! How weak the world would see her! But, if he became her Prince to unite the land again, then the world would view her as a conqueror—a leader of men; a true deity.

No, there could only be one union. And, no matter how much her heart yearned for him, she would not give in. There would be no crown matrimonial. She would fight to keep Egypt in her control. She was *King* and no one's Queen!

Tigris rose to her feet. She found her strength. She ignored the pain within her chest. Yes, she was strong.

The Pharaoh climbed into bed, closed her eyes. She tried to block out all thoughts of Euphrates. *Tried.* But, he stood in her mind, appearing gallant. She remembered how he moved towards her and slowly leaned in. How he kissed her passionately. How his kiss did not lie—there was feeling in it; a feeling that sucked away all of her scepticism with its warmth and honest embrace.

Tigris opened her eyes. Gasped. The letter! Oh gods, what did she write!

Leaping from her bed, the Queen raced to her messenger's tent. It was dark; he was sleeping. She found her way to his bed and shook him. "Allegi! Allegi!"

The young messenger stirred from his sleep, dazed.

"Allegi!"

He opened his eyes, blinked, registered it was the Pharaoh, bolted up. "Tigris?" He scrambled to light a lamp. The tent came into a dim glow.

"Where's the letter?" Tigris asked, her voice desperate.

Allegi looked puzzled.

"The letter. The one for Euphrates. Where is it?"

"I delivered it."

Tigris let out a whimper. "When?"

"This night, when the battle ceased."

"To whom?"

Allegi was sitting upright in bed with a sheet covering him below the waist. His expression grew worried. The Queen's behaviour was panicked, odd.

"To whom?" she pressed.

"Euphrates could not be found and of course they wouldn't open the gates. The letter was tied to a rope and pulled up to the sally-port. I believe it was his man Somiset, who swore to deliver it."

Tigris cupped her face, looked at her messenger. "I need it back!" she cried through clenched teeth.

Allegi shook his head. His eyes were wide with pity. "Per'a, it's too late."

EUPHRATES HAD TAKEN the high chamber in the inner building. Steps led up to a rooftop terrace where he had a 360 degree view of the Egyptian landscape. He stood on the terrace looking towards the Queen's camp. The starlight sparkled above and the air was still.

Euphrates found himself pacing, stopping at the wall to look towards the royal camp, pacing, and then back again. He seethed with anger— *hatred* even. Yet, his hatred wasn't for anyone—it was for his unfortunate plight.

Her Prince, he thought. He was a warrior. He had conquered half of Egypt. He had convinced men to follow him. He could not lay down his head at the foot of a *woman*. What warrior, what man would give himself up to such shame? No one would respect him.

Euphrates glanced over the wall but kept his pace.

It was so much easier for her. She was a *woman*. No one expected her to rule the country and most did not even want it. Never before had there been a woman on the throne and people did not like change. Yes, it was *she* who should step down.

Euphrates stopped at the wall again, peered out over the desert at the Queen's camp.

There she slept, he thought. If only she said yes—he would be beside her right now.

"Euphrates?" Somiset called out to announce his presence.

Euphrates looked towards the staircase. He watched Somiset come into view.

"This came for you tonight." Somiset held out a scroll.

Euphrates eyed it. "When?" he asked, *hoping*.

"While you were gone."

His hope died. Euphrates took the letter.

Somiset descended the stairs.

Euphrates glanced again at the royal camp before he made his way down the stairs and into his chamber. He sat by the window, the moon casting a soft light into the room, the stars sparkling in the sky. He slowly ripped the seal, watched the clay crumble to the floor. He hesitated for a moment before he flattened the parchment and held it up so the moon light shone on the paper. He read:

Dearest Euphrates,

I don't know what to write you. My brush strokes this parchment and I allow it to speak. But, to say how I feel, to put it on paper is to make it real; to make it known. And, once it is known I cannot undo it. Yet, I cannot stop my hand from writing.

I do not know this thing you call love at first sight for I have never known love at all. My loyal messenger claims one can find it in a beating heart, a stolen breath and a giddy stomach. If this is so, then that is to put lightly the way I feel when you are in my presence. Even in my quiet moments I am possessed by these feelings and by you in my thoughts—capturing me and stealing my strength. Is this love? I dare not say the word. It seems laced with weakness. Though, I can say, if things were different, I would race into your arms, begging your fidelity. But alas, my position—my fate—holds me from this desire, which has caused me so much pain in its want.

I was raised to be a King and I will die a King.

You've made your promise—which I respect you must keep—but I have also made mine.

Oddly, it is our father's deeds, which have placed us in this ill-cursed fate, and now it is our promises to them, which binds us to it.

Sweet Euphrates, the look you see in my eyes is longing.

May the Great Amon help us to find our way. All I ask is if you succeed me in this war, you give me an honourable death. Cast aside your feelings, look onto me as if I were a man, then strike the blood from my body and let me die like a warrior King.

I wish it wasn't so.

Nitiqreti, Tigris of Egypt.

XLVI

By LATE MORNING, the royal military was marching towards the Fortress of Ipu. Sand dusted over them, carried up on the eastern wind. They trekked forward to the beat of the war drum, bringing the fortress closer with each step.

Today would be a success.

The battering ram led the way towards the entrance. The high gate was damaged from the beating it took the night before. Today, it would be brought down.

The Queen rode beside her uncle. He had remained on the battlefield last night after the fight ceased, tramping through the dead, looking for his men and pulling a piece of their armour from them as he was known to do. It wasn't until the late hours of night when darkness began to fall away from the sky did he finally give orders for the corpses to be burned.

The battleground had been cleared of the fallen soldiers; their bodies placed in a pile; torches set them to flame as it returned them to dust.

Cinders and smoke still crackled into the morning sky as the last of the fire died. The soldiers marched past the darkened ash without looking. It could be them tonight, lying in a heap. The morbid scene sent a hollow chill through the hot Egyptian air.

"We will surely break through today," Ankhtify said to Tigris as they rode on. "When he is found do you want him dead?"

Tigris did not respond. She already gave the order to Intify a couple weeks ago, when her uncle was not present. What was she to do? Was she to call back the order? Under what pretence? That he *kissed* her? That she felt for him unlike the way one should feel for an *enemy?*

The Queen stared at the fortress wall. She could see the tiny figures of men scurrying behind the battlement along the wall walk preparing their defence.

Euphrates had kissed her. She never dreamt it possible and yet, she had dreamed of it. How sweet his lips and soft his touch—she wished she could feel him again.

The desire brought a sudden bout of anger. Resentment scorched her veins.

Why torture me Hathor when you know I cannot have him! she screamed inside herself. How evil the gods to place this feeling in my heart! Of all the men, why *him?*

Tigris' chest ached. It had ached all night. It felt ripped and torn and beaten. She looked over at the smoke drifting into the sky out of the ashes of human flesh.

Lucky, she thought. For them it was over.

"Halt!" Ankhtify's voice boomed across the desert, pushing the air like a powerful wind and breaking Tigris' inner contemplation.

The soldiers came to an abrupt stop. The General halted them just out of the range of the garrison's defence. They waited on the command of their Pharaoh, Commander and Chief of Army.

Tigris sat on her horse clad in leather armour, wearing the blue crown. War was about to begin; blood was about to spill. She looked at the sun looming in the sky, piercing down from above, timing the end. By the time it sets this night, a win would be gained and a loss would be succumbed. Yet, as long as she or Euphrates lived, the war would continue. No terms would be met; their fight was to the death—for land, for power and for all of Egypt.

Tigris took a deep breath. "Battering ram forward!" she bellowed.

The men jogged forward holding the thick tree trunk in one hand and their shields above their heads in the other.

"Siege shelters forward!" Tigris commanded.

As the men pressed towards the fortress, enemy arrows began to sail from behind the crenels.

"Archers move up!"

The soldiers obeyed their command. They stepped into the dangerous battleground putting them within distance of their shot.

"Ignite your arrows!" Tigris yelled.

The ends of the arrows burst with flames.

"Positions!" Ankhtify ordered.

The men raised their bows, pointing them into the sky so they could get a high arc up and over the fortress wall.

"Fire!" Tigris roared.

A blaze of arrows sped through the sky: some soared past the enemy's arrows; others were knocked out of flight as they crashed into them. The royal army continued to launch their attack as the battering ram and siege shelters moved towards the fortress.

On the inside of the garrison's walls, the arrows rained down setting fire to all they hit. Screams from the rebel militants sliced the stony air as they were struck dead.

"Call in the spearmen," Tigris ordered Ankhtify.

The General waved his hand in the air, which was seen across the stretch of men. His commanders noted the gesture and called their spearmen forward. Ankhtify pointed his finger forward, lowered his arm in a fast motion that gave the command for the men to strike.

The spearmen charged towards the fortress. The battering ram was already at the gate crashing into it. Men from behind the siege shelters stepped out and began to swarm the walls. Ladders were raised, soldiers scrambled up them. They were knocked back, shot down but the men persisted. The spearmen propelled their spears toward the parapet taking down militants who hid behind the safety of the wall.

The Queen looked at her uncle. "Hold back with the reinforcements until the gate comes down," she ordered before she whipped at her horse, raced towards the fortress, shooting arrows from her steed without missing a target.

Tigris looked up, spotted a rebel lower a spear down the side of the wall to push a ladder away from where it leaned. Tigris pointed her bow at the rebel and shot. The man was hit but he managed to knock the ladder out before he collapsed. She watched her men fall as the ladder toppled over.

"Reset the ladder!" Tigris called out to the soldiers as she reached them. "Carry it up to the wall!" She jumped from her horse, ran in to help lift the ladder back against the fortress.

Not too far away, the gate was beginning to crack, bowing in where the battering ram continually slammed into it.

The Queen shot arrows up at the rebels who dared to send projectiles down on the soldiers scaling the wall. Behind her, Intify ordered the bowmen closer to the garrison to shoot at free will.

Large stones were cast down from above onto the royal army. Many of them targeted the battering ram but where one man fell, another rose in his place.

The ram drove into the gate. The sounds of breaking helped give the soldiers strength. They charged the door with full force again and again. Each time they pulled away, the gate cracked and crumbled more. Then, the weakened point snapped. The centre caved in. The corners of the door collapsed in on itself.

Watching the gate come down, Tigris yelled, "Into the fort!" She grabbed her sword, held it in the air. "Into the fort!"

The spearmen charged while other men took hold of whatever weapon they had and advanced the gate. Inside, the spear wall pushed forward, lancing the first line of soldiers.

Tigris looked over at it. The wall blocked their entry. "Push it back!" she commanded.

The Queen helped her men try to shove back the wall. Behind the defensive structure, a force repelled against them. They struggled with the tall wooden wall, unable to make it move.

Tigris stepped back. "Clubs and maces tear down the wall! Tear it down!"

Men moved aside allowing soldiers holding the weapons the Queen had called for to run in. They hammered them into the wall, breaking off the spears, tearing out holes. The royal soldiers speared their daggers through the broken wood, cutting men on the other side.

The wall weakened.

Within a matter of a short time, the Pharaoh's army succeeded in ripping apart the spear wall and pushing it back.

Across the desert, Ankhtify watched and waited for his perfect timing. When he found it, his voice ripped across the sky, "*Charrrge!*"

The Royal Army broke into the Fortress of Ipu and the true battle began. Throwing sticks whipped through the air, taking men down on both sides. Swords clashed. Maces pounded. Clubs cracked bones and skulls.

Tigris swung her sword, pressing further into the protective walls that were besieged by her men. Ankhtify's reinforcements reached the fortress gate and fought close behind. Blood spilt and splattered while shrieking pain cried out.

The imperial forces slowly gained inside. The gate had fallen; the walls were breached. Tigris looked up. She could see her soldiers battling on the wall walks above.

They were in.

BARIN CRAWLED ACROSS the floor of the chamber towards the window. He could hear the noises outside, down below. Hollers from the strong, cries from the weak—they all came to him with terror.

The boy's heart pumped against his chest. Fear surrounded him. He knew the Pharaoh's army was inside the walls and the protective fortress no longer provided protection, but he wanted to *see*—to know the danger.

Barin rose to his knees. He put his fingertips on the windowsill. Slowly, he pulled himself up, peered over the ledge.

A head flew—severed from its body. Barin gasped. He ducked back down. The image replayed itself in his mind. So many men; so much blood; and, the *head*. The boy pulled his knees to his chest and hugged them. He was told to stay in the chamber. He wasn't allowed to leave.

Barin began to rock, comforting himself with the motion. Around him the chamber was dank and dreary and it no longer felt safe. He kept his eyes peeled around the room, every corner, every shadow now seemed dangerous.

The head continued to flash in his mind. He could see the man's face so vividly—the eyes opened, then the mouth, *"Leave!"* it screamed to him. Barin tried to block out the dreadful image. He blinked hard in order to focus elsewhere but the man's head kept reappearing, moaning to him, *"Leave."*

A *bang* shot through the chamber. The door flew open. Barin jumped. He pulled his knees in tighter, drew back against the wall, his eyes wide, his body tingling with fear.

Just inside the doorway, one of the Queen's soldiers stood. Barin recognized his face.

"Well, look who it is," the man beamed. The soldier stepped into the room. Smiled. His teeth were rotten.

Barin watched him. He was the soldier who had torn him from his camel, tossed him in the air. Now he was alone in the chamber with the horrid man. Barin's chest panged from fear that swelled inside him. He didn't know what to do. He remained still, keeping his eyes on the enemy soldier.

"The messenger boy?" the soldier questioned. "Or are you the combatant who killed my brothers as you have claimed?"

Barin didn't respond.

"Not so bold now, are you?" The man took another step towards him.

Barin looked at the open door. There was a clear path to it—an opportunity to escape. Eyeing the door, Barin dashed forward. The soldier stepped back, slammed the door closed.

The boy froze.

"Don't leave. We have so much to discuss." The soldier smirked seedily as he began to walk forward. "Though, I have a question. If you are such a warrior, why do you cower in here?" His voice was as rough as his face and as evil as his smile.

Barin felt his body unlock from its paralysis, sparked with the sudden will to move. He raced on all fours across the room and under a table. His heart beat fast. He needed to get out of the chamber but the only way was through the door and the big boorish soldier blocked its path.

"Come out and play with me," the soldier called, partially singing the words. He stepped up to the table, bent down. "Where's all your bravery now, *coward?*"

Barin grew angry. His cheeks flushed with heat as he stared into the soldier's ugly face. He was not a coward! "Give me a sword and I'll show you!"

The soldier's smile disappeared. He reached under the table, grabbed the boy by the arm. Barin kicked and fought but the large man held onto him.

"You want to play soldier?" he barked, picking Barin up and restraining him under his arm. "Then let us play!"

The soldier stormed towards the door, flung it open.

Barin kicked and screamed but it was useless.

〰

EUPHRATES FOUGHT ALONG the wall walk helping his men keep the Queen's militants from coming over the wall. Already many had succeeded only to find their deaths on the other side.

Small fires ignited around the rebels as burning arrows landed inside the building. Some blazed up with such fury that their threat of burning everything to the ground was more dangerous than the Queen's men storming the wall.

"Water!" roared a cry as a fire blazed out of hand.

"Water!" echoed another man almost simultaneously from the other side.

Orderlies raced around with water bags to douse out the flames.

The Fortress of Ipu was set beside the Nile. An underground piping system brought water into the massive structure. The team of Hapi were responsible for supplying the water as needed. They raced back and forth filling bags and pouring them over fires to keep the building from burning.

"Water! Water!" cried one of the rebel soldiers, frantically.

Two men ran in with water bags.

Euphrates stepped back to let them by, spotted a man steal over the wall and race towards the tower steps. Euphrates flew to the staircase in pursuit. He descended the stairs, exited the tower onto the court where the Queen's army had broken into the fortress and now battled his men inside the once protective walls.

Losing the soldier in the crowd, Euphrates looked around. The royal army continued to flood the gates. Snofru's clan did well at holding them off. Those who managed to get by faced some of Euphrates militia in the forecourt. More of his men protected the wall walks, preventing the Queen's soldiers from gaining the upper levels. The high ground was always a stronger position as there were more places to take cover and the bird-eye view provided better aim. If the Queen's army was to breach the upper levels, then all would be lost.

Observing his surroundings again, Euphrates spotted a man slip into the inner building. His men who fought outside of it did not see him go in. They were fighting too far from the door, giving stealthy soldiers access to the tower. Euphrates ran to the building, into the whirl of blades. He sliced his sword through the air, cutting into the back of a royal soldier, sending the man to the ground, which left Euphrates standing in front of Somiset.

"Move back! Guard the entrance!" Euphrates ordered as he rushed towards the building's doorway.

Inside the large building, Euphrates glimpsed the man rounding a corner. He went after him at full speed. The man ran up the stairs with a bow tied over his back and a sword in his hand.

Doubling his steps, Euphrates lessened the distance between them as he raced up the stairs.

The soldier looked back, realized Euphrates was catching up. Unable to out run him, he spun to face Euphrates on the steps.

Euphrates charged forward, lifting his sword. He swung. Their blades came together with a deafening crash. They wielded their weapons again and again, their arms ridden with power. Euphrates pushed forward, forcing the man further up the steps towards the landing where they could be on level ground.

The soldier tried to prevent it. He knew if Euphrates reached the landing he wouldn't stand a chance. He had to keep Euphrates on the stairs and maintain the upper hand.

Forcefully, the soldier moved down the steps. He swung his blade against Euphrates', tried to push him back but Euphrates didn't move. He stood his ground, resisted the natural instinct to step backwards away from the threat of the weapon. Euphrates allowed the soldier's blade to close in, blocking it with rapid defence.

The sword tore by him. Euphrates waited for his moment. As the soldier took another step, Euphrates reached out, grabbed the man's corselet. He pulled him forward, cutting him with his sword as he launched him down the stairs.

The soldier tumbled hopelessly to his death.

Euphrates inhaled, giving himself the chance to regain his breath before heading back downstairs to aid his men outside. Then, he heard the cry:

"Let me go! Put me down!"

Euphrates stopped. He recognized the voice. *Barin!*

Spinning, he soared up the steps to the upper level. A soldier carried the boy under his arm towards the open roof top terrace.

"Let him go!" Euphrates yelled after him as he hastened down the hall.

The man stepped onto the terrace, turned. He carried his sword in one hand, the boy under the other. Raising his blade, he placed it under Barin's neck and stepped backwards.

"Put him down," Euphrates warned, holding out his sword, taking long, slow strides towards the soldier. "He's only a boy. Are you too cowardly to fight a man?"

The soldier grunted. He dropped the boy onto the stone tiles, held his sword out to Euphrates.

Barin grimaced in pain from the fall, his heart beating fast. He didn't know what to do. He remained curled on the ground, watching.

The soldier charged Euphrates. They brought their weapons down on each other, blocking, advancing, striking blade to blade.

The soldier's sword grazed Euphrates' shoulder, drawing blood. Euphrates only looked, but it didn't stop him. He sailed his sword, pushing the soldier back.

Although the man was larger than Euphrates, his blows were not stronger. Euphrates was more skilled. He swung his sword with impeccable power and skill. Again and again their blades clashed back and forth trying to tire the other out.

The soldier eyed Euphrates' gash, seeking his opportunity to strike the wound again. When he found his moment, he cut deeper into Euphrates' arm.

Euphrates groaned in pain. Against his will, he dropped his weapon. He saw the soldier prepare to swing at him again. He bent over, reached for his sword but the soldier kicked it away, bringing his blade down towards him.

Euphrates dove out of its path. The soldier spun. He charged at Euphrates. Euphrates scrambled for his sword.

He wouldn't make it in time.

He snatched his throwing stick from his belt, flung it at the man. The stick struck him in the stomach, doubling him over for only a second. His leather corselet protected him and the man was made of muscle.

The soldier drew up to his full height, growled in rage, lunged forward.

Barin gaped in fear. The vision of the head flying through the air returned except this time the head was Euphrates'. The thought made his heart sink. He watched as the soldier loomed over Euphrates, raising his blade.

Barin jumped to his feet and ran towards the man. "No!" he screamed as he reacted instinctively: He saw it in the soldier's belt, the dagger he now gripped in his hand; that he shoved into the man's back. He pulled down hard, ripping flesh, tearing muscle.

The soldier cried out in pain. He spun on his heels to look behind him. He wielded his blade through the air as he turned, slicing the boy's bare chest.

Euphrates watched in horror. It was too late to do anything.

Barin looked down at himself. He pushed his hands over his wound as he gasped. *The feeling of warmth.* He held out his hands. His mouth dropped open at the sight of his own blood, which covered his small hands like gloves.

Before him, the Queen's soldier collapsed to his knees, choking on his own blood before he toppled over.

Barin looked at Euphrates. He took a step backwards, collapsed to the ground.

Euphrates rushed to the boy's side and covered his gushing wound with his hand, trying to stop the bleeding. *So much blood.*

Barin looked at him, his mouth still open in shock, his breath shaking with a fearful cry. "I—I kept my promise," he whispered. "I stayed in the chamber. I didn't go to fight. I kept my promise."

Euphrates gently looked at him. "I know," he replied. "You're a noble boy." He glanced down at his blood soaked hand. He couldn't stop the bleeding and there was no one around to help.

Euphrates sucked in a breath, all that his lungs could hold, and bellowed out, "Swinew! Bring the swinew!" His call echoed down the tower so loud, one would swear it shook the rock.

He looked down at the boy again, shaking his head in a daze. This couldn't be happening. He could feel Barin's small body quiver beneath his hand.

"It's so cold," Barin whispered.

The Egyptian sun beat down from the sky; the fires added to the unbearable heat.

"It's so cold," chattered the boy.

Euphrates examined Barin's pale face. "It is," he lied as he ripped his cape from his neck and laid it over the boy's body.

Barin swallowed hard. "I wanted to be a great warrior like you." Tears rolled down his cheek.

"You are," Euphrates whispered, barely able to speak. He choked on his words. His eyes began to tear. *Why the boy?* Of all men, why the boy? He wanted to save him but to move him would be more fatal than letting him lie still. He had to press the wound, stop the bleeding—if only the cut wasn't so deep.

"Swinew!" Euphrates bellowed again.

Somiset reached the terrace doorway and froze. His steps were slow as he went to Euphrates' side and looked down in disbelief. He stood in shock before he finally managed to say, "Swinew is coming."

The boy was still quivering. His breaths became more desperate.

"You are a noble warrior, Barin," Euphrates said, his voice solemn. He held the boy's head up to make it easier for him to breathe. "The bravest I had in my army."

Barin looked at Euphrates and tried to smile. "I am happy." He inhaled, but his breath did not come back out.

Euphrates waited, waited to hear him breathe. *Waited* as a knowing grief grew inside him. He glared down at Barin, not wanting to believe the truth.

No, not the boy! he silently prayed. *Please, Oser, not the boy!* He began to shake him. "Breathe!" he yelled. "Breathe damn you!" He shook him with fury, trying to force his last breath out again but nothing came. He shook him harder and harder. "Breathe!"

Somiset placed a strong, gentle hand on Euphrates' shoulder to stop him.

"No," Euphrates whispered, laying the boy down to rest.

Barin looked so peaceful. A slight smile frozen on his lips. Indeed, he looked happy.

Euphrates could not believe it. The boy had barely lived a life. He was not supposed to be here. Euphrates remembered him dragging his sword up to his table in Wasebet. How he admired him. Full of courage. The bravest in his army of men.

Euphrates took the cape that covered his small frame and delicately pulled it over Barin's face. He sat for a moment in silence, praying for the boy's protection on his journey into the afterlife. Then, he wiped the tears from his eyes and finally stood. Beside him, Somiset's eyes were also filled with tears—the one man Euphrates thought he would never see cry.

The two warriors stood side-by-side, gazing down at the small draped body. Euphrates' thoughts raced. His feelings seemed strange and so confused.

The killing—what was it for? For a second, he couldn't remember. If those he cared about died, would it be worth the crown? He thought about Tigris as he looked up over the garrison's walls at the river, which cut through Egypt dividing the land. He almost laughed at their quirk of fate.

The swinew finally arrived. Seeing the small draped figure, he dropped his sack and gasped, "Barin?"

He received no answer.

Euphrates spun, scooped his sword from the ground and ran from the terrace like a raging bull.

♒

TIGRIS WAILED HER sword. The rebels were successful in keeping the royal forces from swarming the fortress. They had been fighting for a long time and still they hadn't been able to push past the forecourt and into the upper levels. The men were growing tired and the pounding heat didn't help. The sun burnt their flesh, drying them out. All around, shouts came from both sides as commanders ordered their men.

"Behind!" came a shout.

Instinctively, Tigris knew it was for her. She twirled, cutting her sword through the air, slicing the enemy in half. She stepped away, caught sight of another man as he lunged towards her. She grabbed the dagger from her belt, thrust it forward into his gut, jumped back and swept her sword down on him.

Tigris looked around in a momentary daze. So much blood. So much fighting. What was it for? Oh yes. *For Egypt. For honour. For victory.*

An arrow soared past her. She watched it strike one of her men. She looked in the direction from where it came. Up on the wall walk a rebel aimed his bow. She followed his aim. *Intify.*

With speed, the Queen shoved both dagger and sword into her belt and grabbed the bow from her back. She drew an arrow out of her pouch, set it on the string and released it. The arrow sped into the enemy. But, before the enemy fell, he released the arrow already set on his bow. The weapon shot through the air. Tigris barely had time to think. She ran towards Intify screaming at him, "Move! Move!" but her voice was muffled beneath the other calls and yelps and cries.

Tigris squinted at the arrow overhead, blazing down. She dove into the air, flung her body at her commander, knocked him out of the way.

292

She watched as the arrow struck the ground beside them.

Intify looked at her with gratitude.

Tigris nodded, rolled onto her knees to stand up. But, she only got to her knees. Shock paralyzed her. She couldn't move.

Great gods, no!

Disbelief strained over her body as panic set in.

Ankhtify.

She didn't want to believe what she saw: the sword pierce into him, through him. Its point protruding from his back, glinting in the sunlight. She blinked hard, hoping she had seen wrong, that it wasn't her uncle who had dropped to his knees. But, when she opened her eyes, she did indeed see his face. His rough face that held a gentleness beneath his cracking skin. The face that had taught her, inspired her. The face that had promised she wasn't left alone in the world after her father had died. The face that went pale—so pale; so quick.

Tigris willed herself to move, scrambled to her feet, running, screaming, "*No!*" The word echoed out of her mouth for as long as it took her to reach the inner building.

Outside the doorway, the Great General of the Royal Armed Forces timbered over. Above him, a man pulled his sword out from Ankhtify's chest.

How? Tigris gasped. It was impossible! He was Ankhtify! The Great General. No man was ever born brave enough to defeat him!

Tigris drew her blade, raised it in the air. With all her strength, she cast it down onto the man.

He blocked her strike.

Tigris pulled her weapon back, lifted it up again to cast another blow. She looked at her enemy. Saw his face. *Gasped.* Her blade was already in full swing.

The two swords came together with a *clash* then suddenly stopped. Both blades were held still—crossed against each other, perfectly still.

Tigris could barely breathe. Everything was happening so fast. The world was spinning. *Why?*

Stunned, she looked down at the weapons where the metal, once hot with fury lay frozen with feelings.

It was then that she saw it—and, what she saw, she wasn't ready for: On his sword, the same symbol of two cobras entwined together was engraved—a Syrian sword made identical to the one she held in her hand.

Tigris heaved in air, trying to force it past her throat that momentarily closed up. Tears sprung into her eyes. Beside her, her uncle lay dying and she could not bring herself to slay his murderer.

The Queen stepped back, looked into Euphrates' eyes. His expression too was stunned. She dropped her sword and fell to her knees next to Ankhtify. "Uncle," she cried.

Euphrates stepped forward. He reached out to touch her.

"Go!" Tigris yelled.

Across the court, royal soldiers ran towards them, Intify amongst them.

Tigris glanced at her men, then at Euphrates. "Go!" She looked back at her men again. There were ten of them, maybe more. It was certain they would rip apart the man who killed their General like a pack of hungry wolves.

"Quickly!" Tigris screamed, her eyes soaked with tears.

The soldiers closed in. Euphrates glimpsed them, turned and took off into the building.

By the time the Queen's men reached, Euphrates was gone.

The men chased after Euphrates, fighting their way to get to him. Only Intify and three others stopped beside the Pharaoh. They looked down in shock at the General, lying in a pool of his own blood. Sorrow stung the air. The men removed their helmets, bowed their heads in prayer.

"Uncle?" Tigris whispered. "Great Ankhtify."

The General opened his eyes. He looked up at Tigris. A smile glinted on the corners of his lips. She recognized that smile since childhood. It was filled with tenderness; love. He was all she had left in this world. *He couldn't die!*

She remembered the days when he trained her to be a warrior. He believed in her like no one else. He offered unwavering loyalty, support, comfort. *Oh gods, he couldn't die!*

Who would defend her? Who could she trust? It was Ankhtify who had announced after her father's death, if anyone tried to take her throne they would not live out the night. He promised she would not be alone in this world; he had promised he would be at her side. *This couldn't be happening! He cannot die!*

Tigris took his hand and clasped it. "Please uncle, I need you." Her sobs over took her; she couldn't control them; she couldn't stop them.

"Don't cry for me good Pharaoh," Ankhtify whispered.

"No uncle," Tigris begged. "You cannot die on me. You are strong. Fight it!"

Ankhtify smiled gently. "Beautiful Nitiqreti, there's no better way for me to die." He winced in pain as he drew in another breath to speak. "By the hand of a great warrior—someone who believed--" Ankhtify coughed. His eyes closed.

Tigris could feel the warmth of his blood trickling against her knees. She cried harder. "Please don't," she begged. *Oh great Amun, this can't be!* First her father. Now her uncle.

The General's eyes fluttered open. He could barely force the air from his lips but he mustered what little strength he clung to so he could speak to her, tell her one last thing—tell her the truth. With the last bit of his strength, Ankhtify reached up, pulled Tigris' head down towards him and whispered in her ear.

His words brought a profound feeling of revelation and at the same time confusion. Tigris listened in shock, listened to all that he said in his last moments—his final confessions of truth. Her mouth gaped open, not believing what she heard, or at least not wanting to. When his last word reached her, his hand fell and a strange groan sounded his death.

Tigris couldn't move. Her body felt numb. Ankhtify's words hung in her mind. She pushed them out. For the time being she needed to forget what her uncle had told her. Her men were at war, her General was dead, and she had to deal with the situation which surrounded her.

Slowly, the Queen sat up. She looked at Intify through tear streaked eyes. "What can you report?" she managed, regaining control of herself.

Intify responded with a sense of defeat, "We have lost many men. Our numbers are plummeting. The men are growing tired and weak from the sun." He looked at her resolutely, "They need water."

Tigris inhaled deeply. They had been fighting for many hours and her soldiers were unable to secure the fortress. She would lose more if she kept them in battle instead of pulling them out. They needed to recuperate.

Tigris forced herself to make the order, forced the words from her mouth. "Sound the retreat," she said. Tigris almost shuddered. *Retreat,* she cringed.

XLVII

"ON THIS NIGHT as Amun-Re looks down from the heavens, you shall be known to Egypt as our glorious warrior, General of the Armed Forces." Tigris placed her hand down on top of Intify's head. "Bring us glory."

Kneeling before the Pharaoh, Intify looked up at Tigris as she removed her hand. "And, with it, victory," he added. He took both of the Queen's hands and kissed them.

Tigris pointed to her soldiers who gathered to watch. "Stand and greet your army."

Intify stood, turned. The army saluted.

Tigris climbed into her sedan and motioned for them to go. Her ship was already being prepared to leave. In front of her, Ankhtify's body was wrapped in linen and carried high on a gurney towards the ship.

Intify returned a salute to his men. He looked towards the Pharaoh. Later he would address the army as their new superior, but for now, he had other concerns. He caught up to the Queen's sedan and came to a walk beside the chair. "Will you return?" he asked.

Tigris was quiet. She felt emotionally drained. *Return?* she questioned herself. *To meet with her enemy again?*

She looked at her new General. Sadness hung its veil over her face and with all that happened in the past twenty-four hours, she wasn't able to hide it. "I don't know."

Tigris gestured the chair bearers to halt.

Intify stood beside her.

With a commanding and definite look in her eyes and her tone sharp and sincere, she ordered, "If you succeed in taking the fortress, I want Euphrates brought to me alive."

Intify frowned. She had previously instructed him to kill the self-proclaimed King and now she revoked the order.

"*Unharmed*, Intify," Tigris said with assured importance. She waved another gesture and the chair bearers took off.

XLVIII

*T*IGRIS DREADED THIS visit. Last night, after six days of rowing the Nile, her ship had reached Henen-nesut. Ankhtify's body was taken to the Great House to be mummified while the funeral preparations were being made. The ritual would take seventy days before his body would be laid to rest in his tomb.

Now, Tigris made her way through the capital to Ankhtify's home. The chair bearers carried her on her elaborate palanquin, retainers rode on horseback, protecting her on every side and a small entourage of guards followed behind. Children ran next to them screaming, "Per'a!" with their hands held out to the guards who passed out small keepsakes in the Pharaoh's name. Several men and woman also raced along side of her enclosed chair, trying to peek past the retainers, begging for her to hear the injustices made against them. The guards worked at keeping everyone back while they kept their eyes peeled for any signs of danger amongst the crowd.

Alone inside the enclosed palanquin, Tigris was trapped with her thoughts. Ankhtify's last words still gripped her with unbelievable heaviness. She didn't understand it; she didn't want to think about it; and yet, she couldn't help it.

The chair bearers stopped in front of Ankhtify's large mud-brick home. The house stood three stories high with both a front and back courtyard. Tigris looked at the foreboding door and inhaled deeply. She waved for two of her retainers to go and knock while she stepped from the palanquin.

Standing for a moment, Tigris willed herself to move forward along the walkway to the house. She watched as an older lady came to the door and looked questioningly at the two royal guards who had summoned her with a rap. When she spotted the Pharaoh her questions were answered. Her knees buckled in shock. "*No!*" she wailed. A painful cry erupted inside her, causing her to stumble back. She tried to reach out for the wall to hold herself up.

Tigris raced to the older woman. She grabbed her before she was able to fall. Hugging her, Tigris could feel her own tears burn in her eyes. "I'm sorry Aunty," she whispered. Tigris guided the shaking woman into the house.

The retainers turned their backs to the door and stood guard while the two women disappeared inside.

Entering the reception chamber, Tigris led her aunt to a long bench to sit down. The morning sun cast its light through the long open windows making the room bright. Incense burned on a small table filling the room with its soft fragrance.

Tigris looked at her aunt. She had never seen her cry before. Mernieth was a strong-minded lady, strict at times but always caring despite her rigid ways. Tigris allowed her time to cry. She gazed through her own tears at the large mural painting on the wall across from the bench. It was of a lotus pond, and its soft colours offered a sense of tranquility.

Mernieth wiped her tears away and took a deep breath. "I always knew this day would come but you can never prepare for it." She forced a knowing smile but it was broken with sorrow.

Tigris pulled a thin string of flat copper scales from where she had tucked it into the wrap of her dress. She held it out, allowing the string to dangle in front of them.

Mernieth took it. "Cartouches," she said, looking at the names engraved on one side of every scale. "Ankhtify made thin sheets of copper and cut them into these small rectangles. He gave one to every man who was enlisted underneath him and had his scribe carve the soldier's name into the metal. Every man who fought directly under your uncle's command was expected to wear his cartouche in battle at all times." Mernieth stood. "Come," she said, walking from the room.

The older woman led Tigris through the length of the house and across the back garden to a small enclosed temple styled building. Stopping briefly, Mernieth held the length of the string out and studied it with concern. Then, she piled it in one hand, climbed the steps to the door and went into the small chamber. Tigris followed.

Small cut squares in the roof allowed sunlight to shine down into the room. The light glinted off the walls in an almost blinding way. Tigris looked around, amazed. Strung from ceiling to floor on all four walls were small copper scales. In the centre of the chamber was a table where Ankhtify would have banged out the sheets of metal.

Mernieth looked around as well. "He never wanted to forget their names." Finding what she was looking for, she grabbed the ladder, and carried it across the room. Near the top of a wall on one side of the room, a small empty space remained. She climbed up the ladder to the spot. A long string already ran from one corner of the wall to the other. Many more were strung in lines all the way to the stone floor. Lines of copper scales were tied across these strings displaying their cartouches to the room. Aside from the small space, which Mernieth had climbed to, the walls were full.

"It was Ankhtify's wish to die a warrior's death before this room was filled." She tied one end of the string of copper Tigris brought to the line on the wall and stretched the other end across, tying it taut. Then, she moved back to look. Mernieth burst into sad laughter as tears streamed down her cheeks.

Tigris gazed at where her aunt tied the string. Only a small space remained.

Climbing down the ladder, Mernieth went to stand next to the Queen. She linked arms with Tigris, guided her out into the sunlight, and strolled across the courtyard to the house.

"He died a warrior's death," Tigris assured her. "He even said there was no better sword of which to be slain."

The Great General's widow glanced up at her niece. "Good," she whispered. "And now, he will be remembered for all time as a Great Chieftain."

XLIX

*C*HROUGH THE TORCH lit streets, Deshyre made her way home from the tavern. She knew Allegi had promised to see her as soon as he returned but it had been so many days—twenty days since he had left to be exact. Deshyre began to doubt if he would come back to her. She wanted to believe his words but she feared them, feared disappointment.

He said he loved her—of course he meant it, he didn't have to say it. She would believe him. Even though the Pharaoh's ship was seen docking two days ago, Deshyre was certain Allegi anxiously waited for the moment he could escape the palace and run into her arms.

Turning a corner, Deshyre pulled the linen sheet she had draped across her back up over her head. She hastened her pace to rush down the alley and past *the door*. Why had she chosen to take the short cut? She knew of its danger and still she chose its route.

Deshyre eyed the door with caution. Her heart began to beat rapidly. She became angry with herself. She had vowed to put an end to the agreement she had made; to never return to this door; and, now, she walked the path like a fool.

Just get down the alley, she coaxed herself.

Deshyre fixed her eyes on the ground, took quick strides and neared the door. Danger felt as if it seeped into the alley from behind the ominous entrance. Quietly, she stepped by the doorway—two steps and she was past. She quickened her pace, eyeing the last of the row of buildings where she could turn the corner and be out of sight. She almost reached the end of the alleyway where the turn promised safety before a heavy hand gripped her neck. Deshyre gasped. She reached up, tried to unleash the fingers that pressed into her throat.

The hand pulled her back down the alley and into the door. There were no lamps burning inside the small chamber, just sudden darkness.

Deshyre wheezed for air under the crushing power of the hand. She was dragged to the middle of the dank room before she was let go and pushed aside. She felt as if the fingers still pressed into her neck. She rubbed at where she could feel them, coughed to open her airway as she turned to look at the silhouetted figure blocking the open doorway.

"I have nothing to report and I will no longer assist you," she hissed. Deshyre held her head up high, took powerful strides towards the door.

The man grabbed her, roughly threw her back into the room. Deshyre fell hard onto the floor. She looked up at the man as she climbed to her feet.

"You will continue to get information from that messenger," he spat.

No, thought Deshyre, she wouldn't help him anymore. She stood, looked at him unflinching. "I am done," she insisted.

"You have already been paid."

"The animals are still alive. Take them back."

"And, what will your clan eat in this time of famine?" The man stepped further into the room but Deshyre did not cower.

"We are desert people. We will survive." She stormed towards the door again, head held up, hoping. The man stopped her. He gripped her face, crushed his fingers into her cheek as he held her below the chin. He stepped forward, forcing her back. The moonlight from outside the door caught his face, revealing him in the darkness, but Deshyre already knew who he was.

"You have made a deal and there's no going back on it," Eritum said. "Besides, whose country are you faithful to? Ours or theirs?" He pushed Deshyre down.

Her hands smacked hard against the stone floor as she braced herself. She climbed to her feet, determined. She would not let him overpower her nor would she crumble under his threats. "I am faithful to my heart," she spat, defiantly trying to walk from the room.

Eritum raised his arm, belted her across the face with the back of his hand, sending her flying. She crashed into the wall, slid to the floor, winced in pain. She wiped the blood from her lip, forced her trembling body up.

"You will extort information from the Pharaoh's messenger and bring it to me. I want to know when the Queen and self-proclaimed King will be in an exposed surrounding." Eritum pulled out his dagger. He stepped in close to her, leaned over, whispered in her ear. "Cooperate, or I will burn your people to the ground. And..." he ran the tip of his blade over her bleeding lip, down her chin and along her throat, "I will add your messenger boy to my list." He pricked her with the point of the blade.

Deshyre grimaced. Blood trickled down her neck.

Eritum spun. He headed to the door. "Do not disappoint me, Deshyre," he said before he left.

The moon seemed to laugh at her from the sky. A rush of guilt engulfed her. Deshyre watched the door, biding the time she thought it would take Eritum to disappear from the alley. Tears streamed down her face, her body shook. What arrangement did she make? Deshyre burst out crying. She wanted to see Allegi more than ever now. She wanted him to hold her and tell her everything would be alright. But, how could he? She could never tell him the truth—that their meeting, their relationship was all based on lies.

L

$\mathcal{T}$IGRIS WHIPPED THE letters down on the floor and grasped her forehead. Everything was falling apart around her and she couldn't stop it. She was losing control.

Two letters—one from Lord Khenti of the Sais sepat and the other from Lord Ako of the Djeka sepat both declaring they were unable to support the war. They justified their reasons with the granaries and food sources being low, which caused hostility in their regions, and claimed their soldiers were needed to maintain control of the people. Both Lords bequeathed their regrets and promised to hang charms at the gates of their towns to favour the Pharaoh's victory. Oddly enough, their letters were almost identical, as if they decided together—strength in numbers.

Tigris spun and walked to a table. She picked up a small carved wood figurine of a soldier and twirled the figure around in her fingers. Fifty of them were lined in rows on a board, each holding a spear in the right hand and a long leather shield in the left. They were meticulously painted with eyes, hair, helmet and white kilt; no two were carved alike.

Tigris was in the Vizier's study. Behind her, she could feel Ibimpetus' presence like a heavy weight in the room. He had given her the letters the moment she entered his chamber and hadn't said a word since. Instead, he sat at his high table writing on a parchment, waiting.

Tigris set the soldier back in its place on the board. She turned to face him. "So, two more sepats refuse to support me." The statement was rhetorical. She knew he had read the messages.

"You are losing Egypt," he stated nonchalantly as he dipped his brush into the ink.

The words made Tigris cringe. "I *will not* lose Egypt," she hissed.

"The Lord of Nekheb sepat with two thousand soldiers sacked Intify from behind and joined the rebellion."

Tigris gasped. She stared at the Vizier unable to speak.

"Intify was able to retreat with three thousand men. His message arrived late last night informing the enemy still dwelled in the fortress and that he needs more soldiers."

"Then I will take ten thousand men to his aid," she snapped.

"We cannot afford it."

"We need to!" She spun and glared at Ibimpetus with disbelief. How could he be so calm?

The Vizier continued scribing as he spoke, as if what he was saying was unimportant, "The country is breaking down, operations are being abandoned, petty warlords are rising up all over and the inundation threatens to be meagre this year." He turned on his stool. "The people need reassurance you still govern the land outside of this war."

Tigris turned away from the Vizier. She couldn't believe all this was happening. Each day everything seemed to get worse. She glanced at the board of soldiers. Why was she failing when she had numbers on her side? It was as if she was doomed. *Cursed!* she thought.

"You must attend the Coming of Sopdet," Ibimpetus added.

"I must end this war!" The Queen spun to face him.

"You have commanders to march to battle for you but there is no one who can take your seat on the throne at the great festival. You must go and build your allegiances or your absence will turn more people from you." The Vizier had set down his brush and stood by his table glowering at her.

Tigris turned away. She felt hot with rage. Egypt was slipping through her fingers. She was unable to seize control anymore. Nonetheless, she would not see defeat—*could not*. She had to do everything possible to hold onto the country. *Everything.*

She knew the Vizier was right. She had to carry out the inundation ceremony, let the people see she was still *Pharaoh.*

〰︎

IBIMPETUS WATCHED THE Queen fidget with the toy soldiers.

When her father, Qakare, had insisted he would raise his daughter to be Pharaoh, Ibimpetus pleaded against it. Yes, she proved capable of taking on the role, but there was one undying problem, a problem which couldn't be solved through teachings or training—she was a *woman*. And now, when Egypt faced chaos, this problem only worsened. The people became less inclined to follow a female. They blamed her reign for Egypt's upheaval. *The gods are angry*, they said in the streets.

Ibimpetus cared only about the well-being of Egypt. He had worked too many years to keep the country strong. Powerful. He had spent his time doing whatever it took to prevent the destruction of the nation. *Whatever* it took.

He had served under three Pharaohs—Euphrates' father, Wadjkare; Tigris' father, Qakare Iby; and now, Nitiqreti. He had overseen everything. *He* had made Egypt great. And by the gods, he would not allow his hard work and dedication to be destroyed. Not for the likes of any Pharaoh. This was his Egypt—all its glory was because of him. He had made her strong; he had revived her after the country's downfall under Wadjkare's rule. Yes, Egypt was his and he would ensure no Pharaoh would destroy this great nation as long as he lived.

"You must marry," Ibimpetus finally said.

Tigris set down the figurine in her hand. She had been lining them up meticulously on the board to just manage the energy that brewed inside her. She turned, looked at the Vizier.

"The Kushite King's eldest Prince has been promised to you."

Tigris burst out laughing. She couldn't believe what she just heard.

"If you marry him, the Kushites will sign a treaty, Egypt can move her frontiers further north and the King will send his army to support this battle."

Tigris still stared at the Vizier baffled. "The eldest prince?" she questioned. "You mean the eldest prince who is all but twelve years old?"

"It doesn't matter," the Vizier snapped. "You must marry and make your marriage crown matrimonial."

Tigris let out another gasp of laughter. "Crown matrimonial?"

"The people need to see a male on the thrown. Joining with Kush will strengthen Egypt not to mention, expand our borders."

Tigris' smile of shock turned sour. "I am not marrying a twelve year old Kushite boy and giving him the crowns of Egypt!"

The Vizier glowered at her. *Vanity*, he thought. "You have had your time of being Pharaoh. You are the first female ever to sit upon the throne. Be content with the blessings you've had but in the name of Kemet do what's best for this country and put the crown back on a man!"

Tigris shook her head with disgust. "You would have me marry a *boy* who is not even *Egyptian*. What am I to do with a boy?"

"I don't care what you do with him!"

"Of course you don't," Tigris retorted. "It's not your life you're sacrificing."

Ibimpetus could feel his anger singe his cheeks. *Greed*, he thought. Greed and vanity. Tigris had to see the logic, she was sensible but greed kept her hands clenched around the crown. He would not let her hold onto it at the detriment of Egypt. She had to marry. There was no choice for her as Pharaoh. It was the only way to save Egypt and bring the people's faith back to the Great House and the Head of State.

Ibimpetus studied her and suddenly realized her deliberation. "Do you honestly think as Pharaoh you get to marry for love?" He let out a sarcastic chuckle. "That is the luxury of a commoner but as royalty all you get to marry for is land and country and power. Be satisfied with your other luxuries."

Tigris spun away from him. The Vizier continued to study her. He could not believe her—*Love!* The fantasy of a woman, he thought. Men did not care about these things—they had harems to satisfy these needs—another reason why women made dire pharaohs.

The Queen turned back to face him, pausing briefly before she spoke. "What if I marry Euphrates?"

Ibimpetus was speechless. For a moment he thought she was joking but as he looked into her eyes he realized she was sincere.

"Would you not get what you want? The war ended, Egypt united, the forces joined and a crown on the head of a man whom the people are turning to love."

Inwardly, the Vizier scorned her. How dare she even suggest it! he thought. He could feel his ears growing hot, his cheeks beginning to burn again. His face hardened. "You cannot!" he spat.

"Why?"

"Because I will not have it!"

"But, it is not yours to have. It is my decision as Pharaoh. You do not own this country, Tjat. You oversee it for *me*."

The Vizier narrowed his eyes, piercing her with intensity. A callous grin curled his lips in a sinister warning. "You *need* me," he said coldly. "Do not make an enemy out of me Tigris. It will not fair you well."

Tigris returned his glare. "Or what?" she dared. "You will have me murdered as you did his father?"

He did not answer. He turned away, walked over to a chest, and opened a covered bowl sitting on top of it. Inside was his amulet on a string. He picked it up, covering the gold pendant with his hand so Tigris could not see the symbol carved into the circular piece. The amulet gave him strength, reminding him of his purpose.

Slowly, evenly, he finally responded, "That blood lies on the hands of *your father*." He pulled the string over his head, tucked the amulet into his tunic.

"Perhaps," Tigris retorted. "But, *you* mastered the plan."

The Vizier did not look up at her. He wouldn't admit to it even though she pretended to know. He returned the cover to the bowl. "Only a woman would think to marry her enemy," he callously insulted.

He walked towards the door, glanced at the Queen as he passed her by. "I will make the arrangements tomorrow for you to go to Mennefer to carry out the Coming of Sopdet," he calmly said before he exited.

Later that night, the Vizier returned to his study and went to his table. He took out a fresh piece of parchment, picked up his brush. Dipping the hairs into the ink, he wrote:

> *Great Brother, General of Glorious Egypt, Intify,*
> *Our beloved Pharaoh Nitiqreti, Tigris of Egypt has given orders to send to your aid the requested soldiers. She has also ordered her enemy, Euphrates, be destroyed and his head brought to her as an offering of victory.*
> *Ibimpetus, Tjat, Overseer of the Two Lands.*

LI

$\mathcal{T}$IGRIS PACED IN her room. She had been pacing all day—it helped to settle her nerves, helped her to think. She couldn't believe she suggested to Ibimpetus that she marry Euphrates. The words had escaped her mouth by their own power. She knew she couldn't. It was insane to even think it.

Marry Euphrates. What was she thinking? Where was her pride? *He is the enemy.* The disgrace of it!

Tigris poured herself a cup of water and drank it back. She suddenly felt exceptionally hot. She poured some water in a bowl, splashed it on her forehead.

The Vizier's expression was carved in her mind; she couldn't push it out. The look of shock, disappointment and contempt had all been contorted into one sinister scowl. Everything he noted in his first meeting with Euphrates was now confirmed and it showed its disgust on his face and in his eyes.

How could she be so careless?

Tigris began to pace some more. She couldn't stand still. She couldn't relax.

A sudden knock on the door startled her. She looked at the water clock; it was late, well into the night. Who would knock at this hour? She had given her chambermaids leave for the night.

The knock came again.

Warily, the Queen made her way to the door and opened it. "Allegi?"

"I must speak with you. I cannot sleep."

Tigris stepped back to allow Allegi into the room. "What is it?" Her tone was genuinely concerned. She closed the door and leaned against it.

Allegi spun to face her, tension straining his brow. "I want to marry the Bedouin girl," he blurted.

Tigris moved from the door. "Are you asking me?" she questioned, confused.

Stepping up to her, Allegi took her by the hands and dropped to his knees. "I need your approval." His expression was desperate. He looked like he hadn't slept in days. Dark circles were beginning to make their faint appearance under his eyes. He seemed drained.

Tigris studied him, a little taken aback by his behaviour. He didn't *need* her approval and yet he sought it out in desperation.

Smiling gently, Tigris raised his hands to her lips and kissed them. "If you love her then of course you have my blessing." She probed into his eyes. Behind them, she could see doubt. "Though, it seems more to me you come to look for a reason why not to marry her."

Allegi was stung by the truth of her statement. "But, she is a *Bedouin—Asiatic,*" he proclaimed as if the words were cursed.

Tigris squeezed his hands and sighed. "Allegi," she said, softly, "you have the good fortune to listen to your heart. Be blessed and let it guide you where ever that may be."

For a quiet moment, Allegi considered what she said. Then he kissed her hands. "Thank you, Per'a," he whispered. He stood, started to the door, stopped. "You will come to my marriage?"

Tigris lowered her head. "You know I can't."

Allegi didn't respond. He knew—a pharaoh participating in a ceremony at a Bedouin camp would be frowned upon, dangerous even.

"Besides," Tigris added, "I've decided to travel to Men-nefer to carry out the Coming of Sopdet." She looked at him as a thought hit her. "Bring her. The festival is not for another sixteen days. That should give you enough time for your marriage and for both of you to join me at the Great House in Men-nefer." Tigris went to him and took his hand again. "I'd love to meet the girl who has stolen your heart from me."

They both stood quietly for a moment.

"Are you sure you won't need me during that time?"

"Need you? No. Miss you? Indeed." Tigris smiled.

He returned a smile, leaned over and kissed her on the cheek and went to the door.

Tigris felt a wrenching pain sneak up and rip at her own heart. To some degree, she was envious. Allegi had the fortune to follow his heart—*freedom,* she thought. In many ways, she was as much a slave to her country as her servants.

"Per'a?"

Tigris jumped. She thought he was gone.

"What bothers you?"

She spun to look at him. "I'm not bothered," she lied.

"I know you better." Allegi closed the door and turned back.

"Please Allegi, go and get married and be happy—"

"And, what about you?"

Tigris turned away. "Me? I am Pharaoh. That's more than enough." She walked out onto the terrace. She knew where this conversation was going and she didn't want to go there again. "Please spare me of this discussion, Allegi."

"I can't." He followed her outside.

"Why?"

"Because above everything else, I am your friend and I will not abandon you even if you order it."

Tigris faced him. "I cannot live the fantasy you dream for me."

"But, you are Pharaoh. You make the laws—"

Tigris let out a burst of laughter. "I am Pharaoh, which means I am confined to expectations and governed by ideals. I am not as free as you believe."

"What about listening to your heart?"

Tigris walked away from him. She ran her hand along the thick ledge of the balcony wall.

Above them, the stars shone brightly in the black sky and around them the earth slept soundly.

"That is for the common people. I must listen to duty," she finally replied in a flat tone.

Allegi stepped up to the balcony beside her. He groaned in defeat. "Agh! Your plight makes me angry."

Tigris eyed him quizzically. "*You?*"

"Yes." His face furrowed as he explained, "In your chamber, I painfully watch you mourn what you want, but will not permit yourself to have—and what you want is Euphrates."

Tigris stepped back. She was taken off guard by his comment. She wanted to stop him from talking but she couldn't speak.

Allegi pointed over the balcony across the desert. "And, in his tent I painfully witness the look of a desperate heart that knows it cannot have what it wants—and what it wants is *you.*" Allegi stepped forward. "He is not an enemy. You both fight for the same things."

"I will not listen to your absurd little fantasy!" Tigris walked away but

Allegi pursued. He grabbed her arm, pulled her back so her ear was by his lips. "Do not walk away, Per'a. It is not my fantasy. It is yours and it is his. I am just the messenger."

Tigris yanked away from him. "Stop it!" she hissed.

"I won't. As your friend I will not let you sacrifice yourself."

"Stop it!" she insisted, storming back into the audience chamber.

"Imagine, Tigris. You can have a future together. Things will be better. He'd be your saviour, and you, his. Admit it. At least to yourself."

"I beg you to stop!"

"Then tell me I am wrong."

Tigris turned back to face him, threw her hands up in the air. "What do you want to hear, Allegi? That I feel for him? That I think about him endlessly? That my chest pains except for the moments he is in my presence? I won't admit it. I can't!"

Allegi stepped in close to her. "You just did," he whispered.

Tigris knew but she couldn't help it. She was unable to hold back the words. They burned inside of her, begging to be heard. Saying them out loud released them from their painful prison. Yes, her heart throbbed for him. She was almost glad she somewhat admitted it.

Closing her eyes for a second, Tigris let out a heavy breath. "It doesn't matter, nothing will come of it." She held Allegi's hands, resolving to plea. "Please Allegi, as my friend I beg you to leave this alone."

He studied her. Her eyes flicked away. He saw beyond them. The truth. Slowly, he shook his head, no. "Sometimes, Tigris, our lips say one thing but our souls beg for another. It is because I am your friend that I cannot leave it alone." He stopped shaking his head and peered into her eyes, saw her pain. "Between us, I am the only one who speaks your truth." He raised her hands to his lips, kissed them. "And, because you won't, I am listening to your heart, which begs me for help."

Tigris pulled her hands away. She went back onto the terrace and looked out over her land. The tears burned behind her eyes but she would not let them spill.

Allegi watched her for some time. Tigris could feel his presence but she said nothing. She bit her cheek, calmed her tears with feelings of hatred and anger and strangely found comfort in her rage.

After Allegi left, Tigris went into her bedchamber and through the passage to Kafate. She pushed open the panel at the bottom of the stairs, stepped into the room. Although it was late in the night, lamps still burned in the chamber.

Tigris looked around the room before she made her way to the short hallway, which led to Kafate's bedroom.

"Kafate?" she whispered loudly as she stopped in front of the drape, which shut off the doorway into the bedchamber. "Kafate?"

"I am here."

Kafate's voice came from behind Tigris. Tigris turned. "Don't you sleep?"

"Don't you?" the priestess quipped with a smile. She nodded towards the main room, suggesting they move from the small hall.

Tigris followed.

When they reached the sitting area around the black pond, Kafate stretched up to look at Tigris. "I suppose I wouldn't get sleep tonight anyway." She handed Tigris the cup she carried.

The cup was filled with warm milk and some kind of herb floated on top of it. The aroma was calming. Tigris took in its sweet scents as Kafate lowered her body to the floor, using the staff to help ease herself down.

"One of these days I fear I won't be able to get back up," the priestess grunted as she sat. Reaching up, she took the cup from Tigris. "What plagues you to seek me out so late?"

Tigris didn't know where to begin. All her recent problems brewed inside her and she felt as if they would cause her to burst. "Everything!" she blurted.

Kafate gave her a warm smile. "Why don't you start with something."

Start with *something*, Tigris thought as she felt the tribulations of all that weighed upon her right now suddenly leap to the surface. Tigris walked away. "Where do I begin?" she groaned. "How about with the fact that I am losing Egypt, I barely trust my Vizier who insists I marry a Kushite boy, my people are turning away from me and my dear messenger pains me with his childish quest to save me from that which

I do not need saving." Tigris dropped her arm and turned to face Kafate. The old priestess still held that warm glowing smile between her cheeks.

"Come and sit, dear," Kafate said.

"I can't. I'm too wound up."

Kafate sighed. She glanced away and spoke quietly, "It appears to me one choice would put an end to all your troubles."

The Queen looked at her confused. *One thing?* Intrigued, she slowly made her way to the sitting circle and sat down.

"But," Kafate said sharply. "This choice, you are unwilling to make." The old woman allowed a moment of silence to enable her words to sink into Tigris' thoughts.

Although confusion tightened on Tigris's brow, in the back of her mind she could hear the answer calling out to her. One voice. *One thing.* But she refused to listen. She pushed it further away. She listened to a louder voice that threatened: *Do not listen to that quiet voice. You can't!* it warned. Tigris obeyed. She stared at Kafate, pleading with her eyes for the priestess to give her the right answer. But, Kafate just shook her head.

"It doesn't matter what I say, Tigris," the old woman finally said. "You are not willing to change your mind."

"I need an answer," Tigris begged.

Kafate took a long sip of her milk. Her bangles clanked together as they slid along her arm. She seemed to ponder something. She looked over the rim of her cup, glaring into the darkness of the precious black pond. At length, Kafate set her cup down on the floor beside her. She was shaking her head again.

Disappointment swelled within Tigris even before the old woman spoke.

"You already know the answer."

The priestess' words didn't register. Tigris was more focused on the fact that Kafate refused her. She desperately moved around the black pond to Kafate and laid her head on the priestess' lap. "Please Kafate, I am so confused."

The old woman stroked her hair with tenderness. She looked at Tigris with pity and resolved to say, "That faint voice you hear inside your mind speaks from the heart, Tigris." Kafate sighed. "But, you are not ready for anyone's advice, including mine."

Tigris sat up, moved onto her knees. "Yes I am," she swore. Her eyes were glassy from the tears she clung to. "Please, tell me."

The old woman's face turned hard, serious. She sat quietly, studying Tigris and debating whether she should appease the young Queen, until finally, she gave in. "Marry Euphrates."

"What!" Tigris gasped, jumping to her feet. "You are as crazy as Allegi!" She walked away from the circle. "I cannot marry him—I *cannot*—nor do I wish to." She lied. She couldn't admit the truth, not to Allegi or even Kafate. As a matter of fact, she couldn't even admit it to herself.

Kafate remained still, watching the Queen.

Tigris went to a table, began picking things up. She didn't know what she was touching; she just needed to do something to distract her mind.

Marry Euphrates, the priestess' voice repeated in her mind. *Marry Euphrates*, her own voice echoed back, remembering what she said to Ibimpetus. Tigris pushed the words away; she wouldn't hear of it. She picked up another object from the table, opened her hand, examined it. She needed to focus her mind on something else—*anything else*.

A rock. She fidgeted the stone in her hand.

"He is my enemy," Tigris whispered.

Kafate shook her head. "An enemy is someone who hates you."

Tigris weighed Kafate's words. She changed the topic. "Tjat wants me to go to Men-nefer to carry out the Coming of Sopdet but I think I should return to battle." She kept her back to Kafate.

The priestess closed her good eye, peered into the black pond with her blind eye. Under the torchlight the water seemed to move like waves rippling across its surface. The waves appeared to speed up as the old woman glared deeper into it.

"Go to Men-nefer," Kafate responded in a flat tone. "There are things there you must do and experiences that will only find you there."

Tigris stopped fidgeting the stone. She was surprised the priestess would advise her to go to the festival of the inundation. To return to battle would put her closer to Euphrates. Wasn't that what the old woman wanted?

Tigris set down the rock. She moved to the sitting area and sprawled out on the cushions. "So, you think I should leave the battle?" she asked just to make sure.

Kafate opened her eye, looked at Tigris. "There are certain things you must face and your opportunity to meet with them lies only in Men-nefer." Her voice was deep and assured and held a sense of importance in its tone.

Tigris knew better than to ask Kafate what they were. Besides, deep inside she knew Men-nefer was where she needed to go—she *felt* it.

LII

*T*HREE DAYS LATER, Allegi rode into Deshyre's camp on the outskirts of Henen-nesut. He had seen her every night since he spoke with Tigris and today they were to wed.

Allegi pondered that thought for a moment. Before nightfall, he would be married, Deshyre would move into the palace with him and he would have a wife to go home to. The thought seemed almost unreal, but it made him happy.

Their marriage union would follow Egyptian custom; in a witnessed agreement, he would promise all of his possessions to his wife if he was ever to mistreat her and it resulted in a divorce. Then, Deshyre would move in with him to complete the marriage.

Thinking about it, Allegi felt disappointed. A new wife moving in with her husband was the most important part of the union and yet, Deshyre would not move in this night. Her people were throwing a celebration and tomorrow they would leave for Men-nefer to join the Queen at the Coming of Sopdet. The traditional move would not happen for several weeks. Allegi feared it to be a bad omen. Even worse, there was something he needed to do before he went to Men-nefer, which he hadn't yet mentioned to Deshyre. And now, on the night of their marriage, he would have to tell her.

Allegi cleared his mind. He did not want to think about it. He would enjoy this day before he would spoil it with such discussion.

Nearing the centre of camp, a nervous yet excited feeling replaced his disappointment. He would be married soon and Deshyre would be his wife. No more stealing into the night to meet with her, no more watching her race off—they would be together.

Allegi slowed his horse and glanced around. Ivy was strung on posts around the empty fire pit where the celebration would take place. Gifts were spread out on a kilim. Flowers were also spread about and some were laid down as a path, which the couple would cross together. At one end of the path a small desk was set up for writing the contract. It was decided that Allegi would write the marriage contract as none of Deshyre's people knew how to scribe, and Deshyre would provide two witnesses.

Since both Allegi and Deshyre were orphans, only the people of Deshyre's clan would be present. The clan chief, however, demanded a price for Deshyre's hand, which Allegi had gladly paid in gold and silver.

Allegi was amazed by the extravagant decorations for a marriage. Aside from the Pharaoh, Egyptians generally didn't have marriage celebrations. The decorations made him more nervous. He didn't want to be a spectacle.

Allegi pulled Qare to a stop. Women and girls ran up to him to give their respect. When he dismounted his horse, they fought to kiss his hands. He laughed at the attention.

Allegi looked around for Deshyre. Many people approached the fire pit but there was no sign of his soon-to-be wife. He felt a brief fluster of worry until an old woman gave him a toothless smile and patted him on the hand as she led him to the little desk. She mumbled something in her language. Allegi didn't understand her words but he understood that she was telling him to be patient.

More people began to gather around the fireless pit, causing Allegi's uneasiness to grow. The marriage union was supposed to be a private occasion between the husband, wife and witnesses but here at Deshyre's camp, everyone was invited to watch.

Allegi eyed the growing crowd. Why anyone would be interested to view two people sign an agreement was beyond him. Although he thought it strange, he didn't protest. He stood silently by the writing desk, willing Deshyre to hurry.

After a short while, Deshyre stepped out of a tent in a white linen dress, draped in ivy and lotus blossoms. Stretching up from the tent door, she smiled at him, taking his breath away. Her makeup was done in the Egyptian style and she wore a braided wig, encumbered with jewellery.

She took slow steps, approaching him with that timid smile, which had stolen his heart the first night they met. His heart pounded as she stopped in front of him.

"Forever yours," Allegi said, taking her hands.

"Forever yours," Deshyre repeated, softly.

Allegi kissed her and then bent down to the writing desk. Picking up the brush, he dipped it into the ink, glided it across the page. He bequeathed all of his worldly possessions to Deshyre if he should cause them to divorce; his money, furnishings and his house and land in Khem, which the Pharaoh had granted him. Before Allegi rolled up the scroll, he dipped his brush in the ink again and wrote, "You are my most beloved gift. I would sacrifice everything to have you. Forever yours. Forever love." He signed his name.

Allegi set down the brush, delicately rolled up the scroll. He stood and handed it to Deshyre. She took it and passed it to the witnesses who crouched down to the writing desk to sign their names.

Deshyre picked up a small perfume vase off of the table and gave it to Allegi. He looked at it quizzically, not knowing what to do with it. Tipping her head, Deshyre guided his hands up to pour it over her hair. The perfume trickled out of the bottle. The women in the crowd let out a deafening shriek. Allegi jumped.

Deshyre giggled as she looked up at him. "They're congratulating us," she whispered.

The two witnesses stood and bowed to the newlyweds. They handed the contract to Deshyre as another shriek ripped through the crowd from the women. Deshyre linked arms with Allegi. As husband and wife, they walked down the petal path together. Music began to play. The tribal song engulfed them with its melody. Allegi glanced around unsure what to do next.

"My people like to find any reason to celebrate," Deshyre said, noticing his awkwardness. She shrugged. "Who doesn't like festivities? Enjoy it." She kissed him on the cheek and spun off in a dance.

The burning sun descended from the sky casting a soft orange glow across the land. As night grew, fires began to spark up. A cow was sacrificed for the occasion. It was cut into pieces and cooked over several small fires. The people became intoxicated from beer on empty stomachs, waiting for the cow to cook. Musicians continued to enchant the air with their tunes.

Allegi found his opportunity to dance with Deshyre. He held her close. The day was perfect—the most perfect day of his life. The girl from Sechemech was now his wife. Then he remembered what he had to tell her and the perfect day clouded with heaviness.

Feeling a piercing energy at his back, Allegi looked around to find a familiar scowl. Eritum stood off to the side, watching. Despite the other couples who danced around, Eritum's stare distinctly followed them.

"Why does your friend still seem to not trust me?" Allegi asked. "I've married you."

Deshyre glanced over Allegi's shoulder to see. Her heart sank. Oh gods, *Eritum*. She ducked her head, hid behind Allegi's body. "I don't know," she said softly, trying to hide the worry that crept inside her voice.

Eritum stood, his arms crossed against his chest, his long curly beard and hair perfectly arranged and his attire boldly stating his Sumerian origin.

"Let's escape this," Deshyre said, taking Allegi's hand, leading him from the main fire pit.

"But, isn't this celebration in your honour?"

Deshyre looked around. "It's an excuse to party. We won't be missed." She continued forward almost dragging Allegi with her.

Behind them, Eritum pursued.

A familiar feeling surrounded Allegi. His memory took him back to the night when he pulled Deshyre through the streets of Henen-nesut away from the stranger who followed. He looked back at Eritum and realized it was Eritum's presence that must have made Deshyre want to leave. How different from the first night she introduced him to the man. "Deshyre, what is--"

Eritum gripped Deshyre's shoulder, pulled her to a stop.

Deshyre turned. "Eritum—how nice of you to come." Her tone was insincere and hinted at uneasiness.

"I wouldn't miss your marriage to this Royal Scribe and Messenger,

Friend of the Pharaoh, for anything." A sinister smile ended his statement.

Deshyre returned the smile, bowed her head. "Enjoy the night." She spun to walk away but Eritum's large hand gripped her shoulder again.

"A word?" he insisted.

Deshyre gave Allegi an apologetic look, and then stomped away. She led Eritum into a still area of the camp, empty of people. She didn't stop until she knew Allegi couldn't hear. She whipped around to face Eritum. "I told you I was done," she snapped.

"And, I told you we do not accept returns." He looked over towards the fires where the cow was being cooked—a leg here, another there, half a rib hung over a low fire... "It looks to me like you've already cashed in on one of your payments."

Deshyre willed herself not to look. "I will get you another cow."

His laugh cut her like a knife. "I don't want another cow, I liked that one." His smile disappeared. "Besides, do you think your people will let you walk out of here with their livestock? Our agreement is sealed." His eyes narrowed. "You *will* bring me the desired information and you *will* help orchestrate the desired situation." He turned his attention to Allegi who watched them in the distance. "Or, you will find your beloved husband hung at the front gates of the palace with his heart torn out of his chest."

Deshyre held onto the tears that came with the thought.

"Now," Eritum spat with his callous smile returning to his lips, "don't you think betraying his trust is sweeter than surrendering his life?"

Deshyre didn't respond.

"I will give you a month only because it takes time to sail the Nile and our two Pharaohs have placed themselves at an awkward distance from each other." He eyed her for a moment. "Three weeks," he reaffirmed. "And, at the end, someone will die." He looked over at Allegi, gave him a wave goodbye.

Allegi waved back.

Eritum spun, walked back towards the campfires.

Deshyre remained still, fighting the tears that sprung to her eyes and burned in her nose. She watched Eritum through blurry vision with hatred.

Eritum walked towards one of the spits and pulled his knife from his belt. Cutting off a piece of the cow, he turned as he bit into the meat and grinned.

Deshyre closed her eyes and turned away.

Allegi watched Deshyre come towards him. Something was wrong; she almost slumped as she walked and her face looked incredibly sad. "What's the matter?" he asked as she reached him.

Deshyre almost collapsed against his chest as she hugged him tight.

"What's wrong?" Allegi persisted, softly. He pushed Deshyre off of him so he could look into her tear-filled eyes.

"I'm okay," she lied. "It's just Eritum does not approve of my marriage to an Egyptian. He is an old thinker and he believes strong countries are made of pure blood. He denounces our future children." Tears fell from Deshyre's eyes with the hate she had for Eritum and more so, herself. That was her first lie to her husband; already their marriage was cursed and she was the one who had decreed the spell by casting lies.

Allegi studied her for a moment before he pulled her into his chest to hug her. "Let's not think of this tonight." He held her close, searching for Eritum by the fires. Allegi watched him--he didn't fit in.

"Let's go to my tent," Deshyre whispered. She didn't want to celebrate anymore, or eat the cow or be anywhere near Eritum.

Neither did Allegi.

In the tent they could still hear the music, laughter and voices outside but at least they were alone.

The tent was decorated for their marriage night. Several lamps burned, lighting the darkness with a soft glow. Incense scented the room. Flowers added their sweetness and rose petals were sprinkled across the bed.

Deshyre eyed Allegi. She plucked the ivy and lotus blossoms off her dress. Allegi lay on the bed, watching her undress. The happiness that had pumped through them not too long ago, was gone. Sombreness doused the young couple's excitement. They each had their own reason—Deshyre hated her lie; Allegi hated his truth.

"Forget our worries, husband," Deshyre said as she crawled into his arms.

Allegi stroked her cheek. "As long as we're together, I'm not worried." Rolling onto her, he kissed her.

Later that night as they lay quietly in each other's arms, Allegi struggled with the pressure of informing her of his decision. Already he had put it off many times, not wanting to spoil the moment. He found comfort in staring into her big brown eyes, holding her hand, lying with their noses almost touching.

You must tell her now, his thoughts whispered. He pushed them aside to spend a few more moments in this tranquil heaven. But, as the moments passed and time waned on, Allegi felt the burden of his decision pressing its immediateness.

"Promise me you will understand," Allegi finally said.

"Understand?" Deshyre didn't like the tone of his voice. She moved back to study his face.

"There is something I must do, which may come to you as bad news."

"Please, no more bad news tonight, Allegi. Let's lie in each other's arms and save this talk until tomorrow." She nestled in close to him, placed her arm over his body.

Allegi rolled onto his back and looked up at the peak of the tent. He figured it would be easier for him to tell her if he wasn't looking at her. He willed himself to speak, force out the words, "I cannot wait until tomorrow, Deshyre. I must leave tonight."

Deshyre gasped. "Tonight? *Leave?* This is the night of our marriage, Allegi. What heartless Pharaoh sends you on a mission on this night?"

Allegi closed his eyes. He inhaled deeply compelling himself to admit the truth. "The Pharaoh does not send me."

Deshyre sprung up onto her forearms so she could look him in his eyes. "Then who sends you?" she demanded.

Allegi could feel Deshyre's dark eyes burn into him. He took a breath, slowly forced the words from his mouth. "I do," he said, facing her.

"You do?" Deshyre jumped from the bed, grabbed a long tunic, threw it on. "Why?" she begged. "Does this night hold such little importance to you?" She turned and frowned at him.

His chest pained—seeing her hurt, knowing he caused it.

"Why?" she huffed. "Why must you go tonight instead of tomorrow? Why not marry me yesterday instead of today?" Tears streamed down her face. Her body trembled.

Allegi sat up, reached out, and grabbed her. He pulled her down onto the bed and into his arms. "I love you, Deshyre, and this is the best day of my life—"

"And, you choose to spoil it!"

Allegi said nothing.

Deshyre cried harder. She turned to kneel on the bed. She took Allegi's hands and begged, "Please Allegi, my love, my husband, do not leave me tonight. It means so much for you to choose to stay with me as a symbol of how much you truly love me." Her voice was broken by her sobs. "Any night but tonight."

Allegi's heart broke. He didn't want to leave but he knew if he didn't carry out his plan he would regret it and possibly resent her for it. "Allow me to explain to you, Deshyre. I need you to understand that my plan is reliant on time and to see its success I must leave tonight—"

"If you leave tonight, I will not be here when you get back!" Deshyre pulled her hands from his. Stood.

"Then I will search the world until I find you."

"Then you will seek loss; for even if you find me I will always remember there is something more important than me." Deshyre stormed from the tent.

A blend of painful emotions erupted inside of Allegi. He looked around, grabbed the first thing he could reach and whipped it across the room towards the door. The object hit the thick woven goat hair flap and fell to the dirt ground. Allegi looked at what he had thrown and almost laughed; the amulet of *djed*—symbol of stability.

Climbing from the bed, Allegi dressed. He scooped up the amulet and left the tent.

Outside, the people still celebrated. No one seemed to notice the newlywed couple was missing.

Allegi glanced around, hoping to see Deshyre. *I hate this camp*, he thought. It seemed to shroud separation over his relationship with Deshyre. Both times he had been at the camp were the worst moments they shared together. And yet, the camp also held his best memories. It was here they spent their first night in each other's arms and it was here they were married.

Reaching Qare, Allegi led him through the Bedouin camp, to the outskirts.

"Allegi?" Deshyre's voice called.

His heart skipped. He turned to face her. She was walking towards him.

"I cannot let you go like this."

Allegi went to her.

"I was thinking about it, and realized I don't even know where you're going or why. I think if I did, I would understand."

He leaned in and kissed her. "I love you," he whispered, grateful she was giving him a chance. Allegi took her hand, looked around the open area, led her to a large rock to sit.

"A boat awaits me on the Nile," he said as they reached the rock. They sat on the ground and leaned their backs against the stone. Deshyre pulled her knees up to her chest and hugged them.

"It will take six days to sail to Upper Egypt and seven days back to Men-nefer, which is only enough days to reach in time for the Great Festival of the Coming of Sopdet." Allegi stopped. His expression changed to plead with her. "Meet me there."

"Into the palace without you?"

He removed the Gold Scorpion from his skirt and placed it in her hand. "Take our marriage contract and show them this at the gate. They will let you in and take you to my quarters. I will be there the night of the Great Festival."

"But how—"

"I have also arranged a boat for you. It waits for you on the Nile and it will remain until you arrive." Allegi pulled her hand from her knee and began to caress it. "To be honest, I don't know why I feel compelled to make this journey, but I know if I don't, I will never sleep again." Allegi gazed into the heavens. "It feels as though the gods send me—as if tonight I am their messenger."

Allegi fell into his thoughts. They remained quiet for sometime before he began to tell her what he was doing and why. When he was done, they returned to the silence.

They both cast their stare up into the sky, freckled with stars. Sadness draped the silence. Deshyre closed her eyes, turned her head away from him and whispered under her breath, "I wish our love moved you as much."

Allegi looked at her. Her words slapped him. How could she doubt it? How did she not feel it in his kiss, his touch, or see it in his eyes? He threw his arm around her and roughly pulled her in. He whispered in her ear. "Know it does my wife. The difference is, ours is realized. We are blessed, for there is no better love than one that is known and shared." Allegi let her go. Stood. Her words cut him deeply and they still stung. "I must leave." He opened his pouch and pulled out her amulet. "Here. I found this in your tent." He held it out to her.

Deshyre eyed the pillar with three cross bars, carved out of horn. "Keep it," she said, softly.

Allegi shook his head, insisting, "You need it more than I." He bent down, placed the string over her neck. The amulet fell to her chest. "Let it be a symbol of my love for you so no matter where I am or what I do, you know that it's forever." He stretched up, went to his horse.

He mounted, looked at Deshyre, galloped away.

Deshyre stood watching him with tears in her eyes. In one hand she held the Gold Scorpion and in the other, she gripped the amulet.

LIII

SIX DAYS LATER, Allegi reached his destination around the time when the night sky had reached its full darkness. The hands of time pressed its worry on him. He needed to leave this same night in order to make it back to Men-nefer in time for the evening celebrations of the Great Festival.

Allegi disembarked the vessel and gazed up into the black sky, praying Re would sail his *Mesektet* boat slower tonight. He had to leave before the sun returned to the sky and wondered if it was even possible. Anxiety swelled in his stomach. *Time*, he lamented, sometimes an enemy, sometimes a friend.

Allegi drove Qare forward at full speed towards Intify's camp, holding his messenger flag up so the sentries would know he posed no threat. Behind Qare a closed wagon bumped along strapped to the horse.

Intify stood waiting for him at the campsite by the time he arrived.

Allegi halted his horse and bowed his head. "Imhotep."

"Imhotep," the new General returned. He didn't wait for Allegi to dismount before he started in. "You bring a response?" he stated more than asked.

Allegi darted a confused look. The General caught it.

"I dispatched a message requesting more men over a week ago. Tjat promised reinforcements."

"I'm sorry," Allegi said, taking Qare by the reins. "I do not come with a message for you; I come with a message for Euphrates." Allegi looked towards the fortress. Even in the distance it stood tall and foreboding.

"What about me and my men? We've been watching them rebuild that door for days. All our efforts wasted! The longer we wait the more chance they have at strengthening their weak points and undoing what we've done!"

Allegi glimpsed at him before leading Qare forward. "I am sure the Pharaoh is making arrangements. Her interest strongly lies in seeing the rebellion brought down."

Intify followed him. The glow of rage on his face could be seen despite the darkness. "You're *sure?*" he mocked, repeating Allegi's word. "I need *certainty!*" He pointed towards the Fortress of Ipu. "They out-number us. If they wanted to march out of that fortress tonight and storm towards Lower Egypt they could, for I do not have enough men to stop them!"

Allegi halted abruptly. He gave the General a contemptuous look. "Funny. When your numbers were greater than his, *he* stopped you." His eyes hardened, piercing the General with disgust. "He did not give up so easily." Allegi strode forward, leaving the General twitching. He moved through the site, led the horse drawn wagon past the tents.

The General broke his stance, doubled his strides to catch up. He eyed the wagon suspiciously. "What message do you bring the enemy?"

Allegi did not respond.

"Why would the Pharaoh dispatch a message to him?"

Allegi continued forward, still not answering.

"Has she abandoned this mission?" he demanded, his voice strained with accusation.

Allegi stopped to look into Intify's eyes. "The message is neither of your concern nor business, but I can assure you the Pharaoh's primary concern is *this* mission." He studied the General for a moment. "If you would like me to take a message back to the Pharaoh, give it now. I won't be crossing through the camp on my return but circling its perimeter."

Intify examined the wagon. "That is a large message you carry." He walked to the back and reached for the door.

Following, Allegi grabbed the General's hand. "As I already mentioned, General, this is not of your business." He let go of Intify's wrist, went to Qare, climbed on the horse's back. "If I were you, I would look more to concerning myself with how to regain control of that fortress." Allegi dug his heels into his horse, drove it forward. He held up the flagstaff and rode to the garrison.

On the gatehouse roof, protected behind the parapet, men watched him ride in, their arrows pointed, suspicious of the wagon trailing the messenger.

"I bring a message for your King," Allegi yelled up to the men standing above. He pulled Qare to a halt.

"Give it here," one of the guards responded, dropping a small pail tied to a rope over the side of the thick stone wall.

Allegi watched the pail hit the ground. "No, I need to see it is delivered to him immediately."

"I assure you, it will be." The soldier's voice was ruff and impatient.

Allegi stood his ground. "I must take it to him myself."

"And, how do you suppose you will do that?"

"I *suppose*, you will let me into the fortress and show me to Euphrates."

The man laughed. His comrades joined in.

"Do you hear that?" the rebel asked the other watchmen who stood with him. "We will let him into the fortress." The guard looked down at the messenger. "Why don't we lower the gate and you can ride in. As a matter of fact, how about you invite your army in with you? We will have a little party."

"I *must* speak to your Lord."

"Then place your scroll into the pail." The watchman's tone was final.

"My message is not written."

The guard's voice turned angry. "Let me guess, your message comes on the tip of a knife."

"I pose no threat!" Allegi persisted. "I must speak with Euphrates. I insist you bring him to the gatehouse and let him make this decision."

"And, I insist you scribe your message and drop it in the bucket or your voice will not be heard."

Allegi's frustration heightened. Time was speeding by and right now it was his enemy. He needed to sail tonight in order to make it back to Men-nefer in time. He pulled back on Qare, moving further out from the wall. "Euphrates!" he bellowed at the top of his lungs. "Euphrates!" He drove Qare along the fortress wall yelling Euphrates' name for a long time. His voice carried across the open sky.

Euphrates peered over the parapet. Spotting him, Allegi drove Qare back towards the gate.

"Good, Euphrates," Allegi called out, "I must speak with you in confidence."

Euphrates didn't respond. He eyed the young messenger and the wagon behind his horse.

"The Pharaoh doesn't know I have come but I urgently request your audience."

Euphrates stepped back, out of sight.

Silence followed. Stillness.

"I beg Euphrates; I come for the good of both you and Tigris!" Allegi shouted. He looked up and saw no one. Everyone had stepped away. Desperation crept through him--this wasn't what he envisioned.

Just when he was about to give up, a rope dropped over the wall and the watchman appeared. "Tie this to your waist and we will pull you up."

"Can you not go any faster?" Allegi asked Ramska, peering out over the bow.

This was their seventh day of sailing; the night of the Great Festival. The evening darkened on them quickly.

"How much longer?" Allegi asked again.

Ramska smiled. Even the lines around his eyes seemed to have aged through softness, opposed to hardships. "I promised I would get you there on the eve of the Festival and by Hapi, I will." His smile brightened. "Now, go and relax. The night has just begun. We have plenty of time." Ramska dismissed Allegi with a friendly shove.

Allegi left the Captain. He walked along the ship to the cabin, thinking about Deshyre, hoping she was waiting for him at the palace in Men-nefer. Their argument left him feeling uncertain and all he could think of now was holding her in his arms.

Allegi opened the cabin door. He stepped into the room, looked at the form sitting in the dark. Lighting a lamp, Allegi turned to the figure. "Why sit in darkness?" he asked.

"I thought I was supposed to be inconspicuous."

"You've been aboard for seven days. The Captain knows you're here," Allegi said, stating the obvious.

Euphrates stood and stretched. "Actually, I was thinking I must not have been in the right frame of mind to agree to this insane plan of yours."

A grin curled Allegi's lips. "Maybe—but you were in the right frame of heart."

The door opened. Ramska stuck his head in with his almost permanent smile still stretched across his face. "Prepare to disembark the ship. We will be docking shortly."

Confusion flooded Allegi. He was just out by the bow with the Captain and there was no end in sight.

Ramska read his expression. "Sometimes when you look too hard, you overlook the obvious."

A short while later, Allegi drove Qare up the incline towards the palace gate at full speed. Behind his horse the wagon bumped along the uneven ground.

The Great House at Men-nefer was well lit and the sounds of music and voices rose up from inside the walls. The reception of the Festival brought many royal dignitaries into the palace. But, with war and anarchy stirring Egypt, security was heightened.

Slowing Qare, Allegi reached the first pylon of the high gate where six guards were positioned outside. Above them, six more walked the top of the gatehouse holding bows.

Allegi jumped from Qare and went to stand in front of the horse where they could see him fully. The head watchman bowed, recognizing Allegi.

"I am sorry, brother; but, we are checking everybody tonight, even the Friend of the King."

Allegi remember his Golden Scorpion and looked down at his kilt where it was missing. "Did a girl—"

"Deshyre?" the guard interrupted.

"Yes." Allegi could feel relief settle through his body.

The guard nodded. "She's inside."

As fast as his worry dissipated with the thought of Deshyre waiting for him inside, it was replaced with a sudden strike of fear. The guard moved to the back of the wagon. Allegi followed, watched as he opened the door. His heart nervously rose inside his mouth where it began to pound.

Inside the wagon, a chest stood alone.

The guard looked at Allegi.

"A gift for the Pharaoh," he said, trying to keep his voice from quivering with his nerves.

The guard analyzed the large chest. It was carved out of wood with a colourful pictorial painted on all four sides as well as the lid. Allegi stepped back as the guard pulled himself up into the wagon.

"Open it," the guard said. No one was above suspicion. Everyone who crossed his gate was inspected thoroughly including the royal messenger.

Allegi slowly stepped up into the wagon beside the guard. His heart beat faster. He felt nauseous as he took hold of the lid on the chest, lifted it. He held his breath.

The guard peered into the empty box. Just peeked, didn't look. He turned his attention to Allegi. "Enjoy the Festival," he said as he jumped from the wagon.

Allegi let out a sigh of relief. If the guard had really looked at the chest he would have noted how shallow its interior was. The false bottom was obviously placed half way.

Allegi closed the lid, jumped from the back of the wagon. By the time he settled on his horse, the gate was fully opened. He steered Qare forward wanting to rush from the guard in case something triggered a realization.

Allegi rode along the back of the palace away from the main court where the celebration was taking place. He went straight to the royal apartments, around the building by the Pharaoh's private garden and halted. Dismounting his horse, he raced off to retrieve two servants to help him. Due to the celebration, a servant was not hard to find. They were everywhere, waiting to be summoned for a menial task the summoner could have easily done himself. Before long, two men followed Allegi back to the wagon and helped him with the chest. Together, they carried it into the building, up the stairs to the King's apartment.

"This is fine," Allegi said once they entered the audience chamber. The servants left. Allegi closed the door. He checked the adjacent rooms to make sure no one was around before he went back to the chest. He flung open the lid and reached down to the false bottom. Pulling at the sides, he removed the board, exposing Euphrates curled below.

"I cannot believe I am doing this," Euphrates huffed as he stretched up and stepped out of the box.

"You've come too far to turn back," Allegi reminded him. He went to the door, stopped in front of it and looked back at Euphrates. "But, if you do, Ramska is waiting for you on the river. You may leave whenever you want. Though, you have little time to change your mind." Allegi opened the door and paused. "If you choose to cower, you will have no problems exiting the Great House, but know, you will not be able to return." With that, Allegi was gone. He closed the door, leaving Euphrates with a choice: the plan they discussed; or walking out with no turning back.

The music played, the dancers danced and the entertainers entertained in the main courtyard where the celebration of the Coming of Sopdet was held. Exotic animals were brought in for the occasion and stood confined in their cages for guests to admire. Dinner had ended awhile ago and the guests had left the banquet hall to continue outside where they could lighten their bellies with fresh air.

Allegi entered the courtyard. It was robust with guests, live with energy. He looked around. Before he left the royal apartments, he checked his bedchamber for Deshyre and found it vacant—but, at least he knew she was here.

Allegi made his way through the people, stopping to greet them out of politeness but focused on finding his wife. He felt as though he was floating—happy his scheme succeeded as planned, and happy to be back with Deshyre.

Spotting her, Allegi stopped. Deshyre stood across the court leaning against a pillar. She looked beautiful but sad. He hastened forward, bumping his way through the palace guests to go to her. She began to walk away. His mind flashed to the first night he laid eyes on Deshyre—*the girl*. Her beauty had captured him but before he had found the courage to go to her, she had disappeared. The same feeling fluttered inside him now, except this time it was secured by the knowledge the girl was his forever.

Allegi reached out, grabbed Deshyre's shoulder.

Startled, Deshyre spun. Her face softened—relieved to see Allegi—then it grew tense again.

"Tell me you will stay and dance with me?" Allegi smiled. He linked his arm with hers and guided her back into the party.

"Where have you been?" she demanded in a loud whisper as she walked with him.

"No kiss?"

"I have been waiting on you all night, worried something happened."

Allegi laughed. "Something happened? I told you—"

"Everyone's looking at me as though I don't belong."

"They're admiring your beauty."

A smile almost crept over her lips, but vanished quickly. "I don't belong here, Allegi."

"You're my wife. You belong with me and thus, you belong here." Allegi turned through the crowd and headed towards Tigris. "We'll dance when you're in better spirits," he winked. "Come and meet the Great Pharaoh."

Deshyre glanced at the Pharaoh who was perched on a platform and sat guarded from her guests. She stopped abruptly, pulled her arm from Allegi. "No husband, I can't address the Pharaoh."

Her face looked frightened. Allegi soothed her with a gentle smile. He linked arms with her again, pulled her along. "Of course you can, she has asked to meet you."

On the other side of the grand court, steps raised to a large patio, roofed by a cabana. Four thick, richly carved wooden posts held up the flat roof. Underneath, a long chaise sprawling with pillows was centred for the Pharaoh to lounge on where she could retreat from her guests but still enjoy their company.

Tigris was stretched out on the flat leather chaise, propped up by pillows and sipping wine. A prophet kneeled by her feet poetically prophesising the inundation of the Nile.

Allegi pulled Deshyre to the steps. He looked up at the two retainers who side stepped and crossed their staffs to stop him. One of the guards glanced over his shoulder at the Queen.

Looking down, Tigris smiled. She waved her approval. The retainers stepped aside, allowing Allegi to pass.

The smoke of the incense rolled down the steps almost choking Allegi with its suddenness. He resisted the urge to dust the air in front of him. Beside him, he could feel Deshyre pulling away.

"Relax," he whispered, tugging at her arm.

"The great Nile River shall rise up to swallow your enemy..." the prophet was saying as Allegi and Deshyre reached the top step.

"Allegi!" Tigris exclaimed, happy to see him.

Allegi bowed. Deshyre dropped to her knees, leaning over with her arms out in front of her. She placed her forehead on the ground in full bow.

Tigris looked down at her. "The beautiful wife of my fair Allegi," she smiled, swinging her legs off the chaise to sit. "Rise, and tell me your name."

Deshyre lifted her head, slowly sat up. She remained on her knees. Her voice was faint, almost inaudible. "Deshyre," she replied.

"Deshyre," Tigris repeated. She glanced at Allegi who stood beside his bride. "So, it is you who has stolen the heart of my most valued nobleman."

Deshyre dropped back to the steps in a bow, embarrassed.

Tigris laughed. "No need to be ashamed if you intend to keep it safe." Stretching out her arm, she gestured with her fingers. "Come."

Deshyre obeyed, looking at Allegi for support, finding comfort in his coaxing smile. When she reached the foot of Tigris, Deshyre took the Queen's outstretched hand and kissed it as she knelt.

Tigris smiled. "I am happy for you. Live, love and be blessed with many children."

Deshyre kissed the Queen's hand again and returned, "Thank you, Great Per'a, I wish you the same."

Tigris' smile faded. Sorrow glinted in her expression but only Allegi noticed.

"Enjoy the festivities," Tigris said, her tone confirming the sorrow Allegi had seen.

Allegi looked at his Pharaoh. He leaned in close to her ear. "I have left my gift for you in your bedchamber. Please don't wait until the end of the night to go and see it." He kissed Tigris on the cheek, took Deshyre's hand and led her down the steps. Before Allegi disappeared into the crowd, he shot Tigris an enticing smirk, gestured towards the royal apartment building and smiled.

LIV

$\mathcal{T}$IGRIS STARED OUT over the court from her cabana watching her guests have fun. The festival was a success. Five days of preparation—the food and wine, the entertainment and the optic pleasures such as the animals and statues—had all been enjoyed. Many dignitaries and noblemen had sworn their support. The Vizier was pleased. Yet, Tigris did not find any pleasure in it. She did not want to be at the Great Festival or even in Men-nefer for that matter. Her heart was at the battlefield many days north of where she sat. And, although she was Pharaoh, god of men, highest ruler in the Egyptian Empire, she was still not privileged to be where she wanted to be.

Allegi's smile lingered in Tigris' mind. A gift, she thought—sent to her bedchamber instead of to the court with all the other offerings she received.

Tigris peered towards the building. It was a good excuse to escape the party.

The Queen made her way through the crowd, trying to avoid being trapped in conversation. When she made it to the inner building, she quickly glanced around to be certain no one was paying attention, before she hurried around to the back building.

Tigris stood by her private garden, which was off limits to her guests. The music and chatter from the courtyard softened, muffled by plants and trees, blocked by the building.

Tigris felt a sense of relief to be away from the bustling crowd. She glanced around the garden to make sure she was alone in case any lovers had snuck away from the party to find privacy in the restricted area. Everything was still. All that crept through the garden were her childhood memories.

Tigris had spent a lot of time here as a child, mostly schooled by her tutors. But, the memories Tigris enjoyed the most were sitting amidst the foliage with her father, listening to his stories. She looked towards the bench they used to sit on together; it brought warmth, yet, sadness—sadness to see it empty, knowing she could never sit with him again.

Tigris felt like lying across the bench under the canopy of the warm Egyptian sky, feeling the light breeze blowing in from the river dust across her, but curiosity for what Allegi brought drew her up the steps and into the building. She strolled along the wide hall, narrowed by thick columns. She passed the door of the queen's chambers and remembered her mother—how much she hated her, how much she wanted to love her. Tigris shuddered at the thought of the queen's chambers. They held too many unpleasant memories. She avoided going into them. She only forced herself to pass through when she went down the secret passage to Kafate's chamber during her long stays in Men-nefer, as it was the only route. Kafate always came during the Coming of Sopdet. It was an important time, plus Tigris remained in Men-nefer for over a month and she didn't like being away from the priestess for that length of time.

When she visited Men-nefer, Tigris stayed in the King's quarters and slept in her father's bed. It made her feel closer to him. She had removed all of her mother's belongings from the palace—everything that reminded her of the hated queen. The only thing remaining was the mirror in the queen's audience chamber that hid the passage to Kafate.

Reaching the main staircase, Tigris climbed the steps to the second floor. The royal apartment building was dreadfully empty. Everyone was in the courtyard enjoying the party. Not even a servant passed in the hallways. Suddenly, Tigris no longer wanted to be alone. The idea of it made her feel as empty as the building. She would view Allegi's gift then return to her guests.

Tigris moved along the hall, beginning to feel wary of what might await her. Why did Allegi put it in her room? She paused in front of the chamber door, took a breath, before she pushed the door open and peered across the room.

Inside, a beautifully carved and painted chest sat in the middle of the floor. Tigris shut the door behind her and went to the trunk to admire it. The picture on the lid was of her sitting on the Throne of Geb with servants—or were they children by her feet? On the longest sides, the pictures represented Egypt—north and south; on the shortest sides the carvings exemplified her riches.

Tigris crouched down and ran her hand over the smooth wood. The scent of cedar perfumed the air around the chest. Tigris breathed in the fragrance as she took hold of the lid and lifted the top open. Peeking in, she found it empty.

"You won't find your gift in there."

Tigris jumped. The lid slammed shut. She spun to face the voice. Her mouth dropped open.

"I like what you've done to the room."

No, this couldn't be, she thought. *How?* Tigris couldn't move.

Euphrates stood in the adjacent bedroom doorway watching her. He leaned against the wall, a slight smile glowing on his face.

Tigris' heartbeat hammered inside her, her body trembled. Although, she didn't fear him, she feared everything about him. "How did you get in here?" she finally managed to say.

His smile broadened. Euphrates straightened off the wall, stepped forward. "I am your gift," he said, sweeping his arms to gesture.

The Queen's face fell in shock. *Allegi?* She looked towards the door. She suddenly felt dizzy. *Her gift?* Her chest tightened. She felt hot, flushed. "You shouldn't have come," Tigris panted as she stood and headed to the door.

"Why? Because Egypt means more to you than your heart?"

Tigris froze, spun. "The very pride you mock me for, you are just as guilty of!"

"It is different." He moved closer. "Egypt would never accept their Queen marrying her adversary and calling him a *Prince*. Even your loyalists would frown upon you."

"But, they would accept me calling him my *King?*" Her eyes narrowed, blazing with resentment. She turned from him with disgust. "You are like all the rest. You cannot bear the authority of a woman." Tigris continued to the door.

Euphrates followed. He took hold of her arm and stopped her. He tried to turn her to face him but Tigris shrugged him off.

"No, Tigris, I respect you more than you know," he said in a low, honest tone. "I'd even be your humble servant."

His words made Tigris' stomach flutter. His presence made her weak. They stood in the silence—tense silence. To Tigris, it was deafening.

Euphrates stepped back, his quiet movement rattled the air, easing the tension—only a bit. He studied her. Tigris turned, not all the way. Instead, she stared across the room, setting her gaze outside the window, her striking profile offering him her ear.

Euphrates shook his head with pity. "You refuse to see it."

Tigris walked away. She went to the window where she could peer out over the court. She watched the people below enjoying the night. She didn't want to watch them, but it made staying in the room a little easier.

"Egypt wants their Pharaoh, *King*."

Tigris glanced at him. Her cheeks stung with anger. "I am their *King*."

"Not in the way they want. It's a man they want on their throne, Per'a." He spoke gently, like a father who didn't want to disappoint his child.

Tigris bit her cheek, glared out the window.

"People turn from you to me for that reason, not because they care for my cause." He gradually moved towards her, speaking softly. "For me to be your Prince would turn all of Egypt against us for I would be the one who betrayed the promise of granting them their King and you would be the serpent who lured me." He stopped behind her, settled his sight amongst the guests outside. "Those who follow you now— your loyalists—want an heir more than they want you upon the throne."

Tigris tried to shut out his words. She knew they were true and that truth ripped at her gut. She didn't have the will to defend, nor did she believe she could. The truth in Euphrates' words made her want to storm from the room to get away. And yet, as much as she wanted to leave, she didn't.

Tigris was torn between two realities—one, which she wanted to prove wrong and the other, which she was too afraid to give in to.

"You as Queen and me as your King not only unites this broken Egypt but gives hope for a son. That's what they want—"

"Enough!" Tigris burst, spinning from the window and stepping away from him. Tigris couldn't bear it anymore. She could feel herself trembling, fighting back the tears. "Egypt wants a *Pharaoh* and I have proven a woman can grant them that." She glared at him, burning him with disdain. "You expect me to bow down to that which I've fought my whole life against!" She moved to walk away but stopped herself. She looked him square in the eyes. "Like you, I have made a promise." She struggled to hold back her tears. She would never let him see her cry. "Why must you ask so much of me?"

"Because the first day I set eyes upon you, my heart began to beat."

Tigris breathed heavily. She tried to calm herself. He was walking towards her and with each step that brought him closer, her body weakened. She stepped backwards, away from him, until she hit the wall.

He bore into her eyes as he approached, seducing her with his dangerous eyes. He was still speaking softly, gently, "I admire your strength and passion and I worry when you hold up your weapon to storm the field."

He was standing in front of her, looking at her the way he did the first time they met. Tigris pressed further into the wall, her breath now shaking.

Euphrates continued to move in closer, leaning his face towards hers as he spoke. "I even sometimes forget my cause when I march to battle for it's stifled by my greater desire to glimpse upon your beauty."

His lips were almost touching hers. She could feel his breath on her face. Her body tingled with desire, trembled with her gasps for air.

Suddenly, Euphrates kissed her—his soft lips locking against hers.

Tigris couldn't hold back any longer. She reached up, held his face, kissed him back. With striking passion, she kissed him back. His tenderness sucked away all the anguish she felt these last days, leaving a sensation of warmth.

"I don't want to dream about you anymore," he whispered as he kissed her ear.

Pulling back, Euphrates looked into her eyes again. She knew he was seeking their depths; all the secrets she tried to keep from him were visible in this weakened moment. But, Tigris didn't care. She wanted him and he knew.

Euphrates picked her up, carried her into the bedroom. He laid her on the bed, leaned over her. Tigris brought him down into her arms and kissed him again. She could barely believe this was real. Her fantasy, her desire, now hung over her within reach. She had to look to be certain.

Euphrates' strong body was propped above her. She touched him to make sure he was real—placed her hand on his face, her finger brushing his cheek. Yes, he was real. This was real. *She was touching him, kissing him; he was in her arms. Euphrates, the self-proclaimed King of Egypt—her enemy.*

There was nothing she wanted more.

Euphrates kissed her neck, her shoulder. He ran his face down her arm and into her open hand, kissed it, looked at her, removed her dress. He kissed her breasts. She could feel his warm tongue running against her skin bringing her pleasure. Her voice escaped her throat—she couldn't hold onto it and it caused her to moan. Oh, how he caressed and touched and kissed her with tenderness—such tenderness that it scared her.

Fear.

It means nothing, Tigris told herself as she opened her eyes to look at him. He was naked now, climbing his way towards her, pressing his muscular body on top of hers. She could feel him inside her. And, beyond every other sensation, for the first time she felt complete.

"Euphrates," she whispered, unable to hold back as his name erupted from inside. She looked at him stunned, hoping he didn't hear.

He was lying down on her, stroking her hair, looking into her bewildered eyes. "I am in love with you, Tigris," he said softly, as he kissed her lips.

Tigris stiffened. She tried to push his words out of her mind. They filled her with fear. Incredible fear.

It means nothing, she told herself. But, in her chest, her heart pounded, pounded hard, so very hard, as if it were trying to break free. She forced herself to ignore it. *It means nothing*, she repeated.

Euphrates was making love to her and Tigris could feel it was nothing less than love—actual *love*. She lost herself in the moment, giving way to her emotions. She couldn't hide behind her fears in their heat of passion. The way she touched him betrayed her secret and told the truth of what he had seen in her eyes since that first day.

She was exposed. What was she going to do? Oh gods, what next? But, she wouldn't let herself think about it now. No, now she would live her fantasy, her desire, her dream, her impossible dream—later she would run. Yes, she had to. He was the enemy. She could never let her subjects know her sin.

♒

THE VIZIER LOOKED up at the inner building. He had seen Tigris steal away from the festival to retreat to her chamber. All of her guests still lingered in celebration—she needed to grace their presence as host and Pharaoh and yet, she escaped her duty.

He looked towards the window. Could it be? he wondered. Ibimpetus slipped through the crowd to get a better look. The glowing lamps spilled out of the King's chamber into the night sky. The Queen stood in front of the window looking down at her guests.

The Vizier squinted, peered through the distance. Did someone stand behind her?

"Tjat?"

Ibimpetus turned around.

Allegi stood with Deshyre. "I would like you to meet my wife, Deshyre."

Deshyre bowed.

The Vizier grunted with contempt. *An Asiatic in the Great House.* It disgusted him. He moved to walk away.

Allegi knew he was headed for the royal apartment building. He had seen him examining the window.

338

"Chephren is looking for you," Allegi said, stopping the Vizier in his tracks.

Ibimpetus glanced towards the King's window. It was empty. He looked back at Allegi. Why did he not arrive with his wife? The Vizier was informed she had come alone into the palace last night.

"He says, it is urgent," insisted Allegi. "He's in the library."

Annoyed, the Vizier begrudgingly went to seek out the Admiral. He would deal with the Pharaoh's poor behaviour another time.

〰

EUPHRATES SLEPT QUIETLY against her, holding her hand. Tigris' heart beat rapidly inside her chest; it hadn't stopped. She felt so alive, so happy, and yet, so sad. Her wish was an impossible reality.

If only this moment could last forever, she thought. If only....

Tigris shook away the thought. She studied Euphrates' sleeping body, admiring him. She had been watching him sleep for some time, afraid to close her eyes lest she wake to find him gone, or even worse, that it was all a dream. But, the night grew old and she found it harder to remain awake. Her eyes rolled back and unwittingly she whispered, "I love you."

〰

EUPHRATES OPENED HIS eyes, looked at Tigris. He was certain he heard her say it but she was sleeping. She looked so peaceful; so beautiful. Her voice echoed in his mind. *I love you.* He knew he hadn't dreamt it—he was sure of it—she had whispered the words. Euphrates pulled her closer, wrapped her in his arms, fell back to sleep.

〰

SEVERAL HOURS LATER, Euphrates sprang from the bed and began to get dressed. His sudden movement startled Tigris awake. Her worst nightmare met its moment.

"It's almost morning," Euphrates said, stopping to look at her.

A profound sadness filled Tigris. Standing, she wrapped the linen bed sheet around her body like a classic Egyptian dress. She didn't speak. What could she say?

They just looked at each other, their pain crushing the air between them. Tigris couldn't bear to watch him leave. Her heart that pounded with happiness earlier now sank to the pit of her stomach. But, what could she do?

It's for the best, she tried to convince herself. *I am Pharaoh.*

Tigris tried to remain composed, find her strength, ignore the pain. Her father's voice entered her mind: *Don't let anyone take Egypt from you.*

Ankhtify's last words pushed the late King's voice aside: *Your father had found Euphrates. The boy had witnessed his sin. The Council demanded the prince's death. Qakare took on the deed, said it was done but sent the boy to the northern frontier. It was he who paid for him to be raised a warrior so he could avenge his father's death. Your father vowed if Euphrates grew strong enough to fight and win back Egypt from him then the scale would be balanced.*

Tigris couldn't breathe. She felt so confused.

Euphrates moved towards her, dropped to his knees and hugged her waist. He pressed his head against her stomach. "Tell me you will marry me. Tell me and I will stay and face whatever we must face."

Tigris moved to touch his head. Her hand shook as she brought it forward. She wanted to comfort him, to say yes.

Don't let anyone take Egypt from you. You are Pharaoh, the voice boomed.

Tigris pulled her hand away before she touched him. "I can't," she whispered. A lump swelled in her throat. "I can't throw away all I have built." Tigris cringed from her own words. Tears burned in her eyes and nose but she prevented them from escaping. She could feel Euphrates hold his breath as her words hit the air.

Slowly, he stood. Tigris forced a nonchalant expression on her face. He kept his eyes to the floor.

"I must go," he said. He turned, went to a passage door, which he knew existed since childhood.

Tigris walked with him. She led him out of the building and into the private garden. Their silence was tense, it begged to be broken, but they said nothing.

Tigris managed to steal small glances at him as they moved through the narrow pathways. Her heart broke. He looked so hurt. She wanted to say something. Give in. Believe everything would be okay. But, she had pride. It was what made her strong. She had to stay strong.

I am strong, she coaxed herself in spite of her pain.

Turning a corner, Tigris led him down the walkway to the back of the garden. A large obelisk pointed to the sky in front of the outer stone wall of the palace. Tigris stopped in front of it and turned to face Euphrates. She kept her head bent, unable to look him in the eyes. She fought back her tears with the lump in her throat. They threatened to fall if she did anything; so, she did nothing. For a long quiet moment they stood before each other.

It's for the best, Tigris tried to convince herself. *You can't let your heart get in the way of reason. The people will laugh at you.* The voice resounded in her head with such conviction, she believed it.

Tigris willed herself to look up at Euphrates—just a glance, it was all she could bare. "There is a door behind the obelisk, in the thicket. Once it closes, you cannot come back."

"I know," Euphrates whispered.

Of course he did, the palace was once his. Tigris' chest tightened with guilt.

"Come with me," Euphrates begged, taking her hand.

He can't be serious! Tigris forced herself to look into his eyes; they showed he meant it.

You are the first female Pharaoh to ever sit upon the throne. Defend that honour! Change the world! Maintain your pride! the voice in her mind hissed with fear. *You are nothing without it!*

"Come with me," Euphrates pleaded. "Together we will tell all of Egypt—"

"Tell all of Egypt what?" Tigris pulled her hand from his. "The Pharaoh they followed has submitted to the enemy?"

Euphrates studied her, anguish crushed his brow. "Who cares what *Egypt* thinks!" He shook his head in disbelief. "Do you not love me?"

In the sky the moon was full. Tigris found her escape in its glowing light. She fixed her eyes on the moon trying to shut out his question, which ripped at her chest. Inside, she felt as if her heart was bleeding. She could even hear its once quiet voice rising up, shouting to her, *You love him! Why are you doing this? Tell him you love him!* But, her pride held her back, fighting against her heart. *Be strong. The heart is weak! Don't give into it!* it warned.

Tigris' head began to hurt.

"Do you love me?" Euphrates asked again.

But, Tigris could not answer. She was too afraid to tell the truth, too afraid to lie. She struggled internally--pride warring against love--tearing at her insides with such cruel pain.

Euphrates shook his head again, sorrow shadowing his movement. "I am not your enemy, Tigris." He pointed his finger, pressing it into her chest. "Your enemy is much closer than you realize." He dropped his arm, stepped back.

Tigris felt dizzy. A lump grew in her throat giving her pain. Tears burned behind her eyes. Her chest felt as if someone tore it open. She looked at the moon—it was somewhere to set her eyes, anywhere but him.

I am strong, she said to herself. *I am strong*. Yet, as much as she tried to force the words, they kept giving way to the ones she didn't want to hear. *Tell him you love him! Tell him and everything will be fine.* But, she feared those words. Feared them beyond anything else in the world.

Euphrates shook his head, not wanting to believe her decision. "Alright," he finally said. "You win." He spun, made it as far as the obelisk. Stopped. He turned back to face her.

Tigris felt her eyes slowly lower from the moon. They darted around. She saw him standing there, silently pleading—*hoping*. She glanced at his face—it was too hard to look. But, she saw his anguish and could tell he was waiting--giving her the chance to change her mind.

A silent voice called her—maybe his soul—begging her to run into his arms. It was powerful. Yet, she couldn't move. She wanted to—how she wanted to go to him but her pride was so much stronger. *Don't let anyone take Egypt from you.*

I am Pharaoh. I am strong. I am strong, she chanted to will herself the strength.

Euphrates slowly walked back to her. "Goodbye, Great Per'a," he whispered. He leaned in, the warmth of his lips igniting her skin all over her body as he gave her a soft, lingering kiss.

Tigris felt everything crumble inside of her. Her knees weakened. Her body shook. She strained to remain on her feet.

She opened her eyes.

Euphrates was at the obelisk, looking back, giving her one last chance. *One last chance.* But, Tigris could not move or speak. Her gaze returned to the moon, away from the torture of watching him leave.

Save me! she yelled. *Save me!* But, he couldn't hear her for the words never left her mouth.

Euphrates was gone.

Tigris' legs unlocked from beneath her. She ran towards the obelisk, stumbled around it to the hidden door in the thick outer wall. The vines were pushed aside. The door was closed. He was *gone.*

The Queen gasped for air. Her lungs were crushing beneath the pain. She gasped and gasped and gasped. She rested her forehead on the door and cried. "No," she whispered, not wanting to believe he was gone. Or was he? She could still run to him.

Open the door. Open the door and go to him, her heart pleaded.

Tigris stepped back, peered at the handle. She lifted her trembling arm and reached for the knob. Something stopped her.

You can't! You can't let him see you cry, see you weak! He will take advantage of it. *You are Pharaoh.*

Tigris dropped her arm and stepped back, crying harder.

Don't let anyone take Egypt from you, the voice of her father roared in her mind.

Tigris held her breath, held onto her cry. She wiped her face with the back of her hand and managed to fight back her tears with rapid quivering gasps.

"I am strong," she whispered.

She couldn't stand to be near the door any longer. She ran through the garden towards the royal apartments. She rushed through the main hall, slipped into a secret tunnel. There were no lamps lit but she didn't care, she knew the route.

Tigris felt as if she were suffocating. She rasped and panted for air, to push out the crushing feeling inside her chest. "I am strong," she cried, to give herself strength. But, her legs felt so weak. Every part of her wanted to crumble, to collapse in despair. Nevertheless, she ran—ran until she reached the exit and pushed against the wall.

Tigris threw the door open. She stepped into the Temple of Horu— *Temple of War.*

The eternally burning torchlights led her to the Great Chamber. She moved forward. Tears escaping down her cheeks. She couldn't hold onto them anymore. Her breaths became desperate sobs. Her sorrow turned bitter with each step that carried her forward. Each step grew faster with anger until she was running down the Hypostyle Hall into the Great Chamber; running with hatred; running with fury. She didn't stop until she reached the middle of the room.

The Queen looked around at the walls, which were painted with so much death, blood and treachery—glorifying the Pharaoh's battles.

She was filled with rage, unable to hold back. From deep within, her cry erupted with resentment and hatred. *"Father!"* she bellowed, letting out all the pain trapped inside her chest. *"Why did you make me your son!"*

Her words echoed back. She cried harder, gasping for air. "I don't want this cursed Egypt!" she wailed as she crumbled to the floor, crying. *Crying with everything she had.*

In the Temple of War, the Great Pharaoh of Egypt lay on the floor for a long time. She cried until her tears ran dry. When she could cry no longer, she laid in the silence, not thinking, not feeling, too emotionally exhausted to muster the strength to stand up. Inside, Tigris felt empty, dead.

"I am strong," she whispered. "I don't care."

LV

*T*IGRIS DESCENDED THE steps from the second level in the royal apartment building at the palace of Men-nefer. Already it had been over two months since she was with Euphrates. She had ordered the destruction of the Temple of Horu and remained in Men-nefer to see it through. One-by-one the stones were cut from the temple to be used in another construction. The Great Temple of War would exist no more.

For the past months, Tigris felt as if she ceased to live. She didn't have the energy to do anything more than what was necessary. But, life went on regardless. Her court officers remained in Men-nefer with her; the Vizier continued to conduct government affairs and see to the army. Tigris agreed to all of his decisions without really hearing them. She ate her meals alone instead of in the hall with the nobles who lived within the palace. And, since the night of the festival, the normal lifestyle of Pharaoh entertaining guests ended. Each day that passed became harder for Tigris to get out of bed and even to eat. If the Vizier didn't expect her daily attendance, she doubted she would even leave her chamber. For Tigris, life had lost meaning.

The Queen gazed out the window. The sun was high in the sky--mid-day--and she was still in bed.

The door opened. A chambermaid stepped into her bedroom. "It's past noon, Your Majesty," she said, stating the obvious. The woman bowed, retreated from the room and shut the door.

Tigris forced herself out of bed. With sullen strides, she made her way along the corridor to the bath and later, the dressing room.

In the dressing room her attendants waited. The jeweller and wig-maker stood by their carts stacked with containers and the chambermaids held her dress, which would need no adjustment. Tigris had ordered she only be given long loose tunics to wear. She no longer cared about beauty or appearances and the loose tunics were her most comfortable attire.

Removing her gown, the chambermaids pulled the tunic over the Queen's head. The wig-maker opened a reed basket to pull out a wig, but before he had the chance to reach in, Tigris gave her approval. Pendua nodded, took the short classic bob out from its basket.

No one spoke. And, in their discomfort, no one dared to look the Queen in her eyes.

Tigris fixed her stare forward. She didn't care about what they showed her, least of all what she wore. She felt numb to the world and dead inside.

As the wig was placed on her head the jeweller pushed his cart forward. He moved to grab a box but Tigris pointed. He looked to where her finger aimed and picked up the small wooden container. Opening the box, he pulled out the gold necklace with calcite fringe and matching earrings.

Tigris nodded. She remembered first seeing the jewellery set the day Allegi brought her the message regarding Euphrates. The calcite, mined from the river, tacked so plainly on the gold necklace was ugly by comparison to the rich elaborate jewellery created by the jeweller. And yet, there was something about the necklace she found peaceful.

Kaper carried the necklace over, fastened it around her neck, and placed the earrings on her ears. He stepped back, bowed, and followed the wig-maker out of the room.

Nothing was said. No laughter. Just uneasy silence.

When the two men left, the matrons burned scented fats, rubbed the fats on her neck, wrists and ankles. The makeup artist used the wooden stick to outline her eyes in black.

Tigris could feel the stick scratch along her eyelids, calling out the tears, which seemed to always be ready to break out these past few months. She willed them away, tried not to think. Her thoughts only caused her pain.

When the matrons finished, they stepped back, bowed. In both of their eyes she could see their pity. No longer was there any bantering or chatter. Instead, awkward silence loomed in the dressing room the past many weeks, obliging the attendants to finish quickly and leave the Pharaoh's presence.

No one knew the cause of the Queen's behaviour. They all assumed it was the demise of Egypt and her enemy's growing power. But, that was not it at all.

Tigris nodded her gratitude. The matrons bowed. One moved to leave the chamber but the youngest chambermaid peered up at Tigris. Her eyes fluttered as she looked into the Queen's face. She dashed forward, took Tigris' hand, kissed it as she dropped to her knees.

"Great Per'a," she said, "you are loved and we pray for your glory." She pulled a charm out from a fold of her skirt and shoved it into the Queen's hand.

Tigris looked into her open palm at the charm. The small silver talisman was shaped like the god Amun—King of Gods. Tigris forced a broken smile. "Thank you, good maiden. You are blessed."

The maiden gave a sorrowful smile. She kissed the Queen's feet, scurried out, leaving Tigris alone in the room.

Tigris examined the small talisman—the god *Amun*—a man with the head of a ram.

An artificial laugh escaped her. *A ram*, she thought holding back her tears. She flipped the charm over in her hand. Amun, meaning, "what is hidden;" the ram—a symbol of fertility; and, Amun himself who was King of the Gods but also a God of War. Tigris began to cry, quiet tears. They poured down her face, stinging her cheeks, forming a painful lump in her throat. To her, the talisman symbolized Euphrates.

The Vizier was buried in parchments and scrolls when Tigris entered his study. Chephren, Commander of the Royal Vessels; Septoy, High Priest of Men-nefer; and, Isetep, Chancellor of the High Courts, were standing near Ibimpetus in quiet conversation.

All of them looked up at her as she entered and immediately fell silent. The Queen could sense her presence was unwelcome—she had interrupted something they didn't want her to hear. They began moving about, changing the topic of their conversation in a fumbled blunder. They all wore gold pendants around their necks, which they one-by-one discreetly tucked into their tunics out of her sight.

Suspiciously, the Queen eyed the men, quietly seething. Normally, she met with the Vizier every evening, but today, she felt to meet early. Indeed, her presence came unexpected.

Why were the four councillors meeting? And, more importantly, why did they try to conceal it from her?

"Euphrates has crossed the border into Lower Egypt," Ibimpetus stated. He stepped away from the other councillors, leaving them to their mutters while he distracted the Queen. "Euphrates has doubled his rebellion. His numbers threaten—"

"Euphrates!" Tigris barked. "Euphrates! Euphrates! I want to stop hearing his name!"

The councillors subtly eyed her, pretending not to listen. Tigris didn't care. She didn't want to hear his name anymore or even think about him. Since the chambermaid gave her the talisman that afternoon, she couldn't get him out of her mind. He brought her pain—thoughts of him brought her so much pain.

"Send twenty thousand more men—fifty thousand, if you must—but make it stop!" Tigris sent a glare past the Vizier to the councillors, giving them a venal look so they dare not open their mouths.

"The inundation of the Nile was low. We cannot possibly afford to pay such an army," the Vizier responded, spitting out the words.

"His army has grown! He is feeding them—"

"*He* has over thrown the storehouses in every town he has been through!"

Tigris' frustration peaked. She threw her arm out, pointing towards the north. "Then why haven't we put more guards on the storehouses?"

"Because *everyone* is turning against you!" Ibimpetus' words lanced the air. No one moved. The room burned with their rage.

Tigris glowered at the Vizier. She turned her attention towards the three councillors hovering around the table. "Everyone?" she accused in a grim tone.

No one answered.

Tigris strode further into the study.

Ibimpetus dropped a linen shroud onto the floor. The ball-like mass rolled towards her unveiling its contents. *Anaten's head.*

"You need to address Upper Egypt," Ibimpetus said, stopping her. "It's chaotic. There's hostility and feuding and already three Waset claims by meagre Lords for the crowns of Egypt. You must put your energy into campaigning this region."

"And, what about *him?*" She couldn't say his name.

"Lower Egypt still remains loyal to you. They do not want a northern heretic on their throne and will fight to keep him out. But, the country is divided. You've already lost half of Egypt. Thus, you must campaign the north; win back these regions and gain their support." The Vizier's voice vibrated through the room in low certitude.

Tigris' temples pulsated under the wrenching pressure gripping her head. She didn't want to go to the north. She wanted to go to Euphrates, and yet, she wouldn't—*couldn't*.

Tigris eyed the Vizier coldly. She deepened her voice. "I said, send twenty thousand men, destroy his army and bring me Euphrates."

Ibimpetus stepped in close to her. He peered into the depths of her eyes with a sinister scowl. His glare made her want to quiver, but she forced her composure, narrowed her eyes and commanded, "See to it." Tigris headed to the door, escaping his questioning look.

"Even if it is his head in a basket?" the Vizier asked, stopping Tigris in her tracks. Her heart sunk into her stomach with the thought. The Vizier's voice echoed with revolt.

Tigris closed her eyes, stole a deep breath, tried to gather herself. Thoughts flooded her mind, wanting to command her response, but she only had the strength to obey one.

Exhaling, the Queen left the room.

LVI

EUPHRATES UNROLLED THE small parchment and read the words, "Please, I beg you to meet me. I must see you. Come alone. Nitiqreti, Tigris of Egypt." Suspiciously, he looked at the messenger. The man was older but still had a strong physique. He was dressed in regal attire holding the messenger flag with a stone cold face. Something about him seemed to lie.

"Where is Allegi?" Euphrates demanded. "Why does he not bring this message?" He flicked the parchment into the air, questioningly.

"Allegi is about to marry."

Euphrates' eyes narrowed. "He *has* been married," Euphrates' said.

A momentary wave of surprise hit the man before his brow furrowed, questioning Euphrates' statement.

Euphrates straightened. "I know many things," he justified. It had been over three months since he was with the Queen. He remembered Allegi saying when he came for him that he left on the eve of his marriage but there was no way Euphrates should have known such information.

Euphrates glimpsed down at the letter. "Wait here," he grunted, turning away.

Somiset was standing next to him. They had set up camp on the southern side of the border, preparing to advance on Lower Egypt. Their numbers now reached nearly ten thousand men and the vast north agreed Euphrates was their King. The self-proclaimed King was no longer self-proclaimed—he was recognized by the people as their Lord.

When he was done securing Upper Egypt, Euphrates intended to settle his throne in Waset. Although in his absence petty warlords were rising up trying to form a government, Euphrates knew they would be no match when he returned.

Stomping away from the messenger, Euphrates made his way across the camp with Somiset in tow. He crushed the letter in his hand. Strange Allegi wasn't sent with the message, and even more strange was the message itself. Tigris was too proud to beg. The words didn't sound like ones that would escape her lips.

"Where are you going?" Somiset demanded, seeing the horse pen in Euphrates' path. He snatched the letter from Euphrates' grip, read it. "You cannot go!" he barked.

Euphrates kept walking.

Somiset glanced back at the messenger. "It wreaks of a trap, great Lord. You cannot go."

Euphrates reached the pen, stopped. He looked around, waved a teenaged boy over. The teenager trotted up to him and bowed.

"Fetch my travel bag," Euphrates ordered. "And, make sure the water pouch is full."

The teenager bowed and scampered off.

"You cannot go," Somiset repeated.

"Nor can I stay." He unlatched the gate, walked into the pen. "What if it is true and she wants to meet with me?"

"What if it is not?"

Euphrates didn't reply. He led his horse out of the pen, shut the gate.

"You are blinded by hope you know would never be delivered in this manner," Somiset persisted.

Euphrates gave him a solemn look. "I'd rather meet death than the treachery of having to face regret."

The teenager was dashing back to them with Euphrates' bag held out. Euphrates climbed onto his horse and looked down at Somiset with a knowing smile. "Besides, I know my loyal comrades will safeguard me."

Somiset grunted, advanced into the pen. He leapt onto a horse, grabbed two more and led them out of the enclosure.

The teenager reached Euphrates and handed him the bag. As Euphrates took off towards the edge of camp where the messenger waited, Somiset went to the teenager. "Find Tuthiken and Storithen. Tell them to meet me at my tent."

The messenger rode his camel across the desert. Euphrates followed. The further they rode from view of the camp, the more Euphrates' instincts tugged at him.

Why wouldn't Tigris send Allegi?

Over three months had passed since he had stole into the palace at Men-nefer and took her in his arms. Three months since his heart felt as if it was ripped from his chest. And each day since, an empty ache grieved in its place.

Euphrates had thrown his agony into the war. He had conquered half of Egypt. He had travelled almost six hundred kilometres, crossing the border into the south. Now, he treaded into Lower Egypt, which would prove a bigger challenge.

For centuries, tension between Upper and Lower Egypt persisted, each vying to house the Great Throne of Geb. Only powerful rulers had ever been able to keep the country united from one Seat of State. Tigris' father Qakare Iby had rejoined Egypt during his reign and Tigris had maintained it until now—until him.

Euphrates spurred the country within less than a year with his quest to win back Egypt, avenge his father's death and return their bloodline to the throne. But now, as he rode across the desert in hopes of seeing the Pharaoh Queen, he no longer cared. If all he had gained was taken from him and he was only left with Tigris, he would be happier.

Euphrates looked around as he followed the messenger into *Kasa* and down a street. He reached into a small leather satchel, pulled out another gold nugget, discreetly dropped it on their path.

LVII

$\mathcal{L}$EAVING THE PALACE confines, Allegi and Deshyre walked hand-in-hand through the city of Men-nefer. The rich aromas of burning incense powerfully drifted through the market strip welcoming the patrons. The variety of smells clashed together, each trying to lure a shopper back to its master's rug where sale goods were sprawled out.

Stopping, Deshyre bent over a jeweller's mat to admire his artistic pieces.

Allegi stepped up behind her and watched from over her shoulder. "Pick one," he said.

She glanced back at him with a smile before she turned to the jeweller who was busy scrutinizing her every move, making sure she didn't rob him.

"I'd like that one," Deshyre pointed.

The jeweller reached for the gold charm. "Ah, *Menat*—fertility," he said as he picked the charm up.

Deshyre sent Allegi a soft smile.

"Fertility?" Allegi grinned. He turned to the jeweller who clenched the piece, unwilling to let it go until he had his payment. "How much?"

"Six," Deshyre whispered in his ear.

"Six!" Allegi exclaimed.

Deshyre giggled. "Yes. Three boys and three girls."

"What do you have?" the jeweller cut in, wanting to make his sale.

"Apparently, a lot of exciting nights," Allegi answered facetiously as he kissed his wife on the cheek and took out a large piece of lapis lazuli from his pouch. He handed it to the jeweller.

The jeweller inspected the stone. "That's not enough."

Allegi wasn't in the mood to barter. He handed him a small gold nugget.

Biting into it, the jeweller grinned. He let go of the charm. "I wish you good health," he said, bowing.

Deshyre took the charm, returned the gesture, "Same to you." She peered down at the amulet and smiled.

Deshyre's smile was stifled. A hand covered her mouth, pulled her back. She began to laugh playfully but then stopped, realizing the hand wasn't Allegi's. Behind her, she could hear her husband's muffled shouts.

Deshyre gasped. She froze in fear. A rope slid down her body, tightened her arms to her sides. She fell back to the ground. *Great gods!* "Allegi!" she cried out. She kicked, trying to look behind her as her body was dragged down the street. Allegi's muffled shouts grew further away.

"*Allegi!*" she frantically screamed.

The people and merchants along the strip stepped back, out of the way, their expressions baffled with fear.

"Do something!" Deshyre begged the onlookers. "Please, help us!"

No one moved, except to cover their mouths.

Deshyre squirmed, tried to escape the rope that held her prisoner. She burst into tears, fearing the worst.

She couldn't make out her captor. She was dragged on her back, only able to glimpse the back of him. All she could see was his long black cape with a hood pulled over his head. But, she was certain she knew exactly who he was.

They rounded a dead-end alley, vacant of any life and stopped. The man let go of the rope. He straddled her body, pushed his foot under her chin, cranked her head backwards and lowered his hood.

Deshyre stopped crying. She panted in anger as she looked up at the cloaked figure.

"This is your last warning, Deshyre. Bring about my request or the next time I take your husband, he won't come home to you."

Deshyre's heart sank. She knew he meant his words. Her body trembled with the thought of not being able to fulfill his demand. Breaking into sobs, she pleaded, "Please Eritum, I can't. The Pharaoh is ill. She refuses to meet or even write to Euphrates."

He pressed his foot harder into her throat.

"It's not possible," she choked.

"Then make it possible!" Eritum growled. "Your husband is *Friend of the King* surely he has influence and you have influence over him."

"No," Deshyre cried. "You ask of me that which is not possible!"

Eritum removed his foot. Bending down, he clasped her neck in his hand and hauled her into the air. He brought her ear to his mouth. She dangled in his grip as he spoke harsh and low, "You've already had a *possible* opportunity," he spat. "He was at the palace during the Great Festival."

Deshyre gasped. "How do you—"

Eritum's powerful hand crushed her throat, cutting her off. "It was the perfect possible moment. You could have invited me to the celebration, said I was your father, and masked by the guests I could have carried out my deed." Eritum squeezed his fist tighter.

Deshyre's eyes watered. She tried to suck in air but he blocked her wind pipe. Her head felt heavy. She tried to gasp but only made a noise. She kicked her feet; her arms still tied tightly to her side.

Two camels stopped at the mouth of the alley. One empty, the other carrying a man dressed in the same attire as Eritum.

Eritum glanced at his counterpart. The camel was crouched to the ground waiting for him. Turning back, he looked into Deshyre's watering eyes and scowled, "Make it happen or your husband dies!"

He threw her against the wall, ran down the alley, jumped on the camel.

The two men were gone.

Deshyre sobbed. Her head throbbed where it had smacked against the wall. She gasped for air, unable to move.

"Deshyre!"

She could hear Allegi's faint voice growing as he repeatedly called out her name. Relief soothed her, knowing he was safe. She tried to catch her breath to answer.

Allegi reached the bottom of the alley and halted. "Deshyre!" he yelled, recognizing her body crumbled against the wall of the building. He raced towards her.

"Oh sweet Deshyre!" he said, taking hold of her. He untied the rope from around her body.

The moment she was free, Deshyre threw her arms around him.

"Did they touch you?"

She shook her head, crying into his shoulder.

"Are you hurt?"

"No," she answered. She sat up to inspect him. "Are you?"

"No. He dragged me away and left." He brushed her hair from her face. "What did they want?"

Deshyre burst into tears. "I don't know," she lied. "I don't know."

Allegi stood. He wanted to find out who the men were. "Wait here, I'll come back."

"No!" Deshyre begged, jumping to her feet. "Don't leave me alone!"

He could see the fear in her eyes. She reached for his arm to hold onto him. Allegi gave in, took hold of her hand, pulled her behind him as he raced down the alley onto the street. He stopped in the middle of the busy roadway where he scanned people's faces to see who looked at them still in shock.

An old man darted his eyes to the ground. Allegi went to him. "Who were they?" he asked the man.

The old man shook his head. "I didn't see."

Allegi could tell the man was lying, but he didn't have time to coerce it out of him. Each moment their attackers got further away. He dragged Deshyre across the street over to a woman who sat outside her door peeling onions. "What did the man look like?" Allegi demanded.

The woman shrugged her shoulders. She didn't look up. Instead, she tilted her head further down as if to hide.

Frustration flooded Allegi's body. He pulled his dagger from his side as he stepped back into the middle of the road. "Someone saw these men!" he yelled, turning around in the street. "You?" Allegi dashed to a man with the same guilt of knowing sprawled over his face. Allegi lifted his blade.

The man raised his arms, eased backwards, shook his head rapidly.

"Tell me!" Allegi ordered. "By order of the Royal Court, tell me!"

The man stepped further back. He didn't speak.

Deshyre hugged Allegi's arm. "Let's just go home."

Allegi looked at her. He noticed the charm he bought her still clenched in her hand.

The jeweller sat on the ground holding a piece of linen over his head to shade himself from the sun. He clambered to his feet when he spotted Allegi marching towards him.

"Who were the men that dragged us away?" Allegi barked as he approached.

The jeweller only shook his head.

"Who were the men!" Allegi clenched his dagger towards the jeweller.

"There... there is no way to know," the man stuttered. "They were cloaked and hooded with only their eyes cut out."

"Seth!" Allegi cursed.

LVIII

TIGRIS HEAVED INTO the large pot placed beside her bed. That was the third time she threw up this morning. Her body felt weak and shaky. She hadn't eaten a proper meal in months for she barely had the will to chew the food or the desire to keep it down.

Tigris clumsily pushed herself back onto the bed. Her heart ached and she cried out of self pity--the kind of cry that shook the core.

Sorrow swelled in her chest. No amount of crying subdued it. She hated herself.

Why couldn't she stop him from leaving that night? Why couldn't she go to him now?

Tears silently burned their trail down her cheeks. She'd been crying since Euphrates left and each day it got worse rather than better. She felt hollow inside. She lost her desire to live.

What was the point? She could never be with Euphrates; she was losing Egypt; everything crumbled around her at a whirling pace and she had no will to fight.

The Vizier sent commanders to campaign Upper Egypt—to win back loyalty in her place. Tigris lay in bed for weeks. She could hardly stand up without becoming dizzy and the nauseous feeling in her belly made her feeble. Her daily meetings with the Vizier ceased and everyone inside the palace whispered, *"The Pharaoh has fallen ill."* The news was beginning to drift past the thick outer walls and onto the streets. A sickly Pharaoh was no good to a country in such turmoil, but Tigris no longer cared. All she wanted to do was sleep in order to escape the reality of this loathsome world. Even worse was the torture that her memory of Euphrates—holding him, touching him, feeling him—had dissipated into delusion, making her fear it had only been just a dream.

Tigris covered her face and cried again. She was alone. She had ordered her chambermaids to leave her bedchamber. They only came in to change her pots, help her to the bath and to bring her food, which they more often than not carried away untouched. Even the palace physician stopped coming to see her by her order. His remedies had failed and most of the time, Tigris refused to take them.

Outside the King's chamber the maidens hung charms across her bedroom door and placed a statue of Bes next to it to ward off evil spirits. When they did enter the room, they said short prayers before they left her bedside, asking the gods to heal her sickness. Even Naat, her childhood maiden, who was granted leave of duty when Tigris moved her throne to Henen-nesut, returned by freewill when she discovered the Pharaoh remained in Men-nefer and had fallen ill. The elderly woman spent most of her time perched outside the main door of the King's quarters, waiting to be called upon, worried and wanting to help more than Tigris would allow. But, Tigris didn't want anyone's help. She knew the cause of her affliction and there was nothing anyone could do.

Rolling over, Tigris hurled her upper body from the bed, over the tall pot. She was sick again.

〜

ALLEGI MARCHED DOWN the hall towards the King's apartments. He had just returned from the city with Deshyre and he was still wound up from their attack. His aggression gave him the will to see Tigris—something he had lately been avoiding.

Seeing him come, Naat leapt from her stool to block the door. "She doesn't want to see you."

"I don't care. Step aside."

The chambermaid shook her head and braced the doorway. "She doesn't want to see you," she repeated, firmly.

"Rarely does the truth spill from her mouth these days." Allegi halted in front of the older woman. Worry cut into her skin deeper than her wrinkles.

Naat helped to raise Tigris. Her love and loyalty brought her back to the palace to nurse the Queen in her condition. She eyed Allegi, knowing he was right and knowing it was his own love and loyalty for the Queen that marched him down the hall.

"Step aside," Allegi said, sternly.

Naat obeyed.

Allegi barged past her into the room. He tramped across the outer chamber, flung open the bedroom door.

Across the room, the Queen hung off her bed over a pot, vomiting. Allegi ran to her side.

"Leave me!" she ordered, but there was no power behind her voice, no strength left within her. She tried to push her body back onto the bed. Struggled. Failed.

In spite of her order, Allegi helped.

Tigris didn't have the strength to fight him. She wiped her eyes to ensure there were no tears for him to see before she propped herself up in the bed.

Allegi poured some water, which she took and drank. He spotted the untouched plate of food on the table beside her bed. He picked it up,

357

set it on her lap. "You have to eat," he said, gently.

Tigris looked at the dish. The sight of it made her sick. "I don't want to eat!" she snapped, flinging the plate across the room. It broke against the wall with a high pitched *crash*.

Allegi eyed his Pharaoh. This was not the Tigris he had known—the sensible Pharaoh, who always managed to remain calm when chaos was at its peak and when most men would have lost their minds. No, this Pharaoh had changed.

Allegi held his head in frustration. "Why?" he asked. "Why don't you send him a letter?"

Tigris looked at him with bitterness. "Because I don't want to."

Allegi dropped his arms, studied her. There was so much pain in her eyes. "Do you ever speak the truth anymore?"

She turned away.

"Why do you do this to yourself?"

"You did this to me," she snarled coldly.

Allegi stepped back; her words stabbed him with their resentment. He shook his head, refusing her blame. "No, Tigris." He continued to slowly shake his head back and forth, denying her words that still stung him. "It's you who prevents it. Do you not want to feel love? Or, have a son to take your throne? Or," he added, raising his voice, "*be with Euphrates?*"

Tigris whipped her head around to glower at him. "Stop it!" she hissed. "How dare you utter his name in my presence. I forbid it!" She struggled out of bed, catching herself from collapsing. She wanted to get away from Allegi; away from all that he reminded her of.

Her head felt light. Her knees buckled. For a moment she saw darkness but she managed to straighten on her feet.

Allegi moved to help. She pushed him away.

"Leave me alone! Just go away!" Tigris turned from him. "I hate you," she whispered.

Allegi stepped back. Her words ripped at him, cutting through his chest like a sharpened blade.

Tigris turned back to him. "You did this to me with your *gift!*" she seethed.

Allegi stepped further back. He sized his Pharaoh with disbelief, her words of hatred filling him with heaviness. "No, Great Per'a," he argued softly, "you did this to yourself, and it is you who chooses to keep your torment."

"Get out!" Tigris shrieked. She grabbed the cup from the table next to the bed and threw it at the wall beside him. "Get out!"

Allegi stared in shock before he was able to stomp from the room.

Tigris stumbled to the door, slammed it shut. *Wailed.* Painful tears bursting from her as she crumbled to the floor with heated sobs.

"I don't care," she whispered. "I don't care."

Allegi stormed across the audience chamber, he could hear the Queen's cry escape the door. The sound of it tore into him.

How could he help her when she refused his help?

Naat dashed into the room. She heard Tigris from outside the main chamber door.

Allegi quickened his pace. He made it to the door before the maiden took four steps into the room and blocked her. He knew Tigris feared anyone seeing her weak, seeing her cry, which was why she shut everyone out—the servants, the doctors, the priests and even him.

"She sleeps," he said, knowing the chambermaid wouldn't believe him. "I will stay with her." Allegi didn't wait for a response. He backed the elderly woman out of the room and closed the door. He dropped his weight against the door, exhaled heavily. He felt swollen with despair—anger, sadness, helplessness.

Helpless—that was the worst of them. What could he do?

Allegi opened his eyes, looked around the audience chamber. He remembered the days in Henen-nesut when he used to stay up all night laughing and chatting with Tigris or playing his music for her. But, the walls of the Great House in Men-nefer seemed only to loom with sorrow.

Allegi went to the seating area. He sat on the floor, leaned back against the pillows. Through the bedroom door, he could still hear Tigris crying.

LIX

$\mathcal{E}$UPHRATES JUMPED FROM his horse. He followed the messenger into the Temple of Sobek. They had cut through the city and emerged in the open desert on the other side of town. Euphrates ran out of gold nuggets before they had left Kasa but the temple was not too far off—within sight.

Like most towns in Egypt, Kasa was built on the bank of the Nile for its water source. The small Temple of Sobek was also built near the river, honouring the crocodile god of the Nile.

Euphrates peered across the river. There was only one royal ship on it and it wasn't the Pharaoh's.

"She travels discreetly to meet you," the messenger said, catching Euphrates' stare.

As they climbed the steps of the temple, Euphrates unsheathed his sword.

The man shot him a questioning look.

Tilting his head, Euphrates responded, "You can never be too careful these days."

The messenger continued through the temple door into its dim lit interior. Euphrates followed, cautiously.

Inside, a single chamber offered sanctuary to the god Sobek. The crocodile god was carved out of limestone and stood opposite the open doorway with offerings placed by its feet. Other than the statue and their presence, the room was empty.

Turning, the messenger answered Euphrates' thoughts. "They are bringing the Pharaoh as we speak."

The two men silently watched the door. Before long, a troop of men grew from the earth as they climbed the temple steps.

Euphrates watched, anxiously—*hoping*.

Silhouetted by the sunlight, the men closed in the doorway blocking out most of the afternoon sun. Two-by-two, they entered the room until there were eight.

Euphrates waited as they filed in, lining up in a row across the door like a barricade. There was no sign of Tigris.

"Where is Nitiqreti?" Euphrates demanded, using her imperial name.

A dark figure rose from the steps behind the row of officers. Moving forward and passing between two men, the figure stopped in front of the line of soldiers. Inside the torch lit chamber, out of the brightness of the sun, Euphrates was able to see his face.

"She sends her wishes," Ibimpetus said coldly. "And, she wishes you dead."

"Lies!" Euphrates shouted, holding out his sword.

"Seize him!" commanded the Vizier.

The eight men surrounded Euphrates. Euphrates swung his weapon. More soldiers entered the temple, climbing the stairs like an army of ants. With only one exit, Euphrates was trapped and severely outnumbered, but he fought until they closed in, disarmed him, and forced him to the ground.

The officers kicked and lashed relentlessly at the self-proclaimed King until the Vizier waved them off. Beaten and bleeding, Euphrates was dragged onto his knees, his arms held out by two officers, his head hung over, defeated.

"Now, why would you think the Pharaoh would not wish to see her *enemy* dead?" the Vizier snarled, stepping closer. Ibimpetus struck him across the face, knocking him over.

The guards held onto him and brought him back up.

Grinning wryly, the Vizier crouched down so he could look Euphrates in the eyes. "Do not fool yourself. Tigris *hates* you." The word hissed out of his mouth like a serpent biting its victim. "She resents the day you ever met and wishes to have your head. But, the rest of you can be picked apart by the scavengers." He ran the tip of his knife across Euphrates' outstretched arm, stopping over his heart, pricking him with the sharp point of the blade.

Blood dripped out of the cut and trickled down Euphrates' chest.

"Of course, it will be hard for you to hold the crown upon your head then." Ibimpetus' chuckle spurned the air. He pulled his knife from Euphrates' skin and stood.

"Consider yourself lucky to have lived this long," he added. "For, had I found you in the Temple of Horu, this story would never have been written." The Vizier looked at the officers of the State Police. "Torture him and kill him." He returned his gaze to Euphrates. "Then bring his head to our devoted Pharaoh." His sinister grin marked his victorious moment.

The Vizier spun on his heels, marched out of the Temple of Sobek and into the sunlight.

LX

*T*IGRIS WALKED INTO the Temple of Horu. She stood for a moment fixing her stare straight ahead. She felt as if she floated along the wide columned Hypostyle Hall towards the Grand Chamber. The massive columns seemed to close in behind her but she did not look back. As she moved forward, she read an inscription on the wall:

> *Glorious, victorious Pharaoh,*
> *Proudly won the battle.*
> *Seizing everything,*
> *Losing nothing,*
> *To gain the Greatest Empire.*

The words left her with a feeling of emptiness; fear of having an Empire instead of her true desire. Her chest tightened. *Painfully tightened.*

Tigris reached the main chamber, floated into the room. She moved towards the four colossal statues, looked up at their faces. The Gods of War—Horu, Mut, Montu, Neith.

Stopping before them she found her gaze locked on the eyes of Horu. Her vision blurred. The longer she stared the more blurry her vision became. When her eyes came back into focus, Horu's face had turned into the face of *Hathor*—Goddess of Love, fertility and the protector of women.

Suddenly, Tigris' head jerked sideways as if possessed by some unknown force. She looked into the face of Mut. Her vision blurred, refocused. She found herself peering again into the eyes of Hathor. Her head uncontrollably jerked again. Montu became Hathor. Another jerk—Neith now Hathor. All four gods had the face of Hathor.

Tigris gasped. Air flooded into her lungs, unleashing her from the grip of the unknown force. Suddenly freed, Tigris fell back to the floor. The Hathors smiled at her in vain.

The Queen crawled backwards away from their mocking smiles. She managed to scramble to her feet. She ran towards the door and into the Grand Hall. The massive columns disappeared in the distance and where they did, a dark figure drifted towards her.

Tigris froze.

The figure moved closer, into the torchlight, where Tigris was gradually able to see it. A long gown draped to the ground, clinging to the body of a woman; in her hands, a reed basket illuminated in the light. The shadowed figure held the basket forward. She floated out of the darkness, her face now in view. Tigris' eyes widened—it was the face of *Hathor!*

The Goddess of Love opened the lid, brought the contents forward, offering it to the Queen. "I bring you the head of the only man you ever loved," Hathor said, drifting closer.

In the basket, Euphrates' severed head peered up at her, his eyes opened, filled with tears.

Tigris shrieked. She turned, ran back into the Great Chamber, away from the goddess. Her heart pounded. *Pounded with self-hatred.*

Tigris halted. Another figure drifted towards her from out of the shadows. She tried to back up but her legs wouldn't move. The figure floated into the light, holding out a covered dish. Tigris looked up into her face.

Great gods, another Hathor!

The goddess lifted the lid, carrying it forward as an offering. "I bring you the heart of the only man you've ever loved."

The heart was lifeless, blood all around it as if ripped out and placed on the plate.

"*No!*" Tigris screamed, allowing the word to ride out of her lungs with all of her breath. She collapsed to the stone cold floor. "No!" she cried, uncontrollably.

Hathor, carrying Euphrates' head, followed her into the room. She drifted in from the darkness, repeating her words, "I bring you the head of the only man you ever loved." She floated out of the light as her twin drifted forward carrying Euphrates' heart, repeating her words, "I bring you the heart of the only man you ever loved."

The two apparitions took turns, moving in and out faster and faster so their words overlapped until all Tigris could hear was, "Head. Heart. Head. Heart...." She couldn't take it anymore. She covered her ears and screamed.

〰

LURCHING UP IN bed, Tigris looked around. Her body was soaked with sweat, she couldn't catch her breath. She was in her bedchamber surrounded by darkness provided by the thick rugs that draped the windows.

Frantically, Tigris threw back the covers and feebly rose to her feet. Although she felt dizzy and weak, she stumbled onto the balcony. The cool air hit her, causing her to shiver under the sweat of her body. She was barely able to walk—but she had to see....

The Queen made her way to the balcony wall. The sunlight stung her eyes but she peered across the land where she set her sight on the Great Temple of Horu. Hardly anything remained of it. She was glad to see it almost destroyed. The temple felt filled with sin and closer to the Underworld than it did to the Heavens.

Tigris was relieved to know the Temple of War would soon cease to exist. Her dream seemed so real. The pain it brought her still clung to her chest. She struggled back to her bed, crawled under the covers.

Tigris lay awake too afraid to sleep. Each time she closed her eyes, her nightmare replayed in her mind, the words of the goddess echoing, *"I bring you the head of the only man you ever loved."*

Tigris burst into tears.

"I bring you the heart of the only man you ever loved," Hathor whispered in her thoughts.

Tigris squeezed her eyes closed under the pressure of her palms, trying to shut out the voice of the goddess but she couldn't. The Hathors kept drifting forward in her mind, offering their gifts, whispering their words.

Hopelessly, Tigris curled into a ball and cried.

LXI

ANOTHER DAY HAD come and gone and still Tigris refused to eat anything more than a few bites of food. Most of the time, she sat up in bed staring at the wall ahead of her or curled on her side with her back to those who came into the room. She rarely spoke and answered most questions with a movement of her head—if she answered them at all.

Allegi stayed with her since their argument but she ignored his presence, not speaking or even looking in his direction. He wanted to help her to get better, but the Queen had given up.

Allegi stepped out of Tigris' bedchamber, closed the door. He had made her drink a full cup of milk with difficulty. She was frail, weak, not composed—everything that went against what the Great Pharaoh, Nitiqreti, Tigris of Egypt once was. Dark circles began to form under her eyes—she didn't sleep much anymore. And, when the door was closed, she cried.

Allegi went to the seating area in the audience chamber of the King's quarters. They were still in Men-nefer and would not return to Henen-nesut until the Pharaoh was better—if she got better. He settled himself on the pillows and laid back.

"You've been in here a week; will you ever return to our bed?"

Allegi twisted backwards to watch Deshyre come into the room. "Come lay here with me," he said, making room for her to lie beside him.

Nestling against his body, Deshyre looked with concern at her husband. His expression was sullen, drained by worry—it made her envy the love he had for the Pharaoh.

"I can't leave her like this," Allegi explained, softly.

"I know. That's why I love you, my faithful Allegi." She kissed his forehead. "Though, you must get them to meet. It is denying herself of him that makes her this way." Deshyre's stomach knotted as she made the suggestion. She knew what she was doing but she cared only to save her husband. His life was threatened for the life of a dying Pharaoh. Why should she feel guilty?

"I can't. Tigris is too stubborn. Her pride rules her. She won't concede."

Deshyre sat up on her knees so she could look at him directly. "You must try—force her, kidnap her—but take her to Euphrates." She glanced at the door of the King's bedchamber. "She is destroying herself." Deshyre took hold of his hands, continued earnestly. "Allegi, other than Tigris, only we know the true cause of her infliction. It is her broken heart that is *killing* her. You must save her from herself."

Her words stabbed into Allegi's chest. He knew Deshyre was right. He looked away, gazed outside, thinking silently to himself.

Darkness took over the sky, forcing the light out of day. Yet, in spite of the darkness, the stars glimmered, reminding that light was omnipresent and more certain than dark.

Suddenly, a thought hit Allegi. He jumped to his feet almost knocking Deshyre over. "Watch over the Pharaoh," he said. Without waiting for a response, Allegi left the King's chambers. He flew to the stairs, descended the steps to the main level of the royal suites in the palace of Men-nefer. He hastened down the hall, headed to the queen's quarters, threw open the door. He stormed through the empty chamber, which was closed off by Tigris' order. All of its furnishings were gone. Tigris wanted nothing around that would spark a memory of her mother—the hated Queen Nefari. She avoided her late mother's rooms, save for the route, which went through them—the route Allegi was now on.

Allegi reached the mirror—the only belonging, which was permitted to remain in the barren room. He grabbed its edge, pulled it open, slid along the dark narrow walkway. The torch, which he stole from the wall outside the queen's apartment, illuminated the tunnel that cut towards Kafate's chamber. When he reached the end of the tunnel, he halted, pounded against the door before he threw it open and entered the room.

Kafate was already making her slow steps towards the mirror. Seeing Allegi, she stopped, looked at him questioningly, but she could sense the answer.

"Tell me, great priestess, what should I do? How can I help her?"

Kafate didn't respond. Concern hazed over her expression. Allegi watched as she shuffled away, grabbing a satchel from a table as she scampered by it. She went to the circular shiny black pond cut into the floor and plumped herself painfully on the cushions.

Allegi followed. He stood over her shoulder, watching.

The priestess dumped her bag of stones out in front of her and scooped them up. For a short while she held them clenched in her fist, praying—hoping not to get the answer she feared.

Allegi looked down on her, forcing his patience to grant the old woman the time she needed to give him an answer. Allegi believed she was the only person who knew.

Finally, Kafate's hand began to move. She cupped her palms together, shook the stones. They clanked like a drum roll as she whispered, *"Through cloud and darkness let me see. May the future's truths come to me."* She let the stones spill into the dark water, their strange etchings falling still in a way that spoke only to her. The white stones seemed to glow on the bottom of pond.

Kafate closed her good eye, leaned forward, peered into the black pond over the stones with her blind eye—the one that let her see all. She stiffened. Her spirit seemed to leave her body vacant as it went out searching for an answer. When she spoke, the voice did not seem to be her own:

> *The ram and fish shall come to meet,*
> *And their souls they will deceive,*
> *For land and throne both hunger for,*
> *Deprives the heart, which makes them poor.*

Kafate fell quiet. Allegi waited. He sidestepped to view her face. He caught her brow twitching. She leaned in closer. Her voice grew more intense, becoming low, resonating deep within her throat:

> *They fight for pride, the sin they bear,*
> *To the detriment of love so rare,*
> *And, if pride does rule then all is done,*
> *Weakness strengthened, all is won,*
>
> *Beware the veil that makes them wait,*
> *Until at last it's much too late,*
> *For in the Nile these rivers part,*

If pride does conquer over heart.

Kafate's eye popped open. Life returned to her body. She looked up at Allegi in shock. "The doors of change are closing. There isn't much time," she whispered, her voice strained with fret. The priestess grabbed Allegi's hand, pressed his palm against her face. The strange voice returned, *"A needless cost! A needless cost! Truth denied—all is lost!"*

"What should I do?" Allegi asked, beginning to feel anxiety form in his gut.

"Great Messenger," the priestess whispered loudly. Her deformed figure hunched further over. She became still.

Allegi crouched down, pushed her up to see her face. "Kafate?"

The priestess was sleeping. The reading drained all of her energy; he would get no more answers from her. But, he knew her answer was in those two words—*Great Messenger.*

Pulling his hand from hers, Allegi charged out of the room.

The messenger's ship quietly rowed out of the barque station of the Great House of Men-nefer and manoeuvred its way up the Nile. The night sky helped to mask its leave. Before daylight would return, the ship would be safely out of sight.

Allegi stood at the bow looking up the river. Although they rowed against the current, their travel would only be five days as Euphrates had entered the south.

Over and over in his mind, Allegi heard Deshyre's voice inform him of what the old chambermaid had whispered to his wife.

She hasn't bled in over four months.

Tigris had lied to the doctors, her illness suddenly making sense as well as her rapid deterioration. She needed to eat for two but she did not eat enough for even one.

Only Naat knew of her condition, until a day ago, when she confided in Deshyre. *She hasn't bled in over four months.*

Allegi couldn't believe it. He pressed his face into his hands as he tried to gather his thoughts. He felt burdened.

Leaving the bow, Allegi found Ramska resting in his cabin. The man was the most pleasant person Allegi knew---true to the core.

"You look like you need to talk," the Captain said, sitting up.

Allegi sat. The stress lightened as he began to divulge everything to the old skipper.

Allegi trusted him.

LXII

DESHYRE RODE OUT of the palace into the city of Mennefer. Allegi had been gone for almost a week. She sat in his place, watching over the Queen in his absence.

The Pharaoh grew worse—single-handedly destroying herself. Deshyre tried to get her to eat but the Queen barely consumed a full meal in a day. She weakened rapidly. As Deshyre watched Tigris killing herself slowly, she wondered whether it was worth risking the life of her husband for a dying Pharaoh.

Slowly, Deshyre rode through the busy streets of the city. She was sent a letter of where to drop her information. Her heart sank deeper with every corner she turned. The streets became less and less populated as she made her way towards the ominous door.

Deshyre could feel her body trembling, not out of fear of where she was headed, but rather out of fear of what she was doing. If the camel didn't carry her forward, Deshyre doubted she would have the courage to take the steps herself.

She looked up into the sky. Although the afternoon sun shone its brightness down on the earth, Deshyre seemed only surrounded by darkness. The gods were frowning upon her, she knew. But, she prayed to Hathor to protect her for it was out of love why she made her way to deliver the information.

Deshyre stopped in front of the black door. She eyed it for a long time. At length, she tapped the camel to sit down so she could climb off its back. She urged herself forward. Knocked.

A small flap opened. There was only darkness inside.

"It will be done," Deshyre whispered. "Arrangements are being set into place. I will inform you again when I know more."

The flap banged closed.

Deshyre stepped back. She had done it. She promised information for the life of her husband. Yet, no matter how relieving it was to know he would safely make it home to her, she grieved nonetheless. Guilt condemned her for her own contempt. How could she? Yet, how could she not?

Crying, Deshyre climbed onto the camel. She whipped at it to run. She wanted to get away from the door as fast as possible. She raced all the way back to the palace, crying, shamefully crying. What had she done?

Looking up at the royal residential building, Deshyre made her way towards it. She eyed the second floor of the King's suites where Tigris lay. She promised Allegi she would look after the Pharaoh. *Oh gods, what had she done?*

Deshyre entered the building. The sunlight shone through the small high windows in the hall, guiding the way to the stairs. As she walked, she felt as if nothing was real; as if she was in a dream.

Was she really in the Egyptian Pharaoh's palace, walking the hallways of the Great House on her way to sit with the Pharaoh? It seemed so surreal.

Deshyre blinked hard. Yes, she was there. She was ascending the stairs towards the King's quarters. She was welcomed, trusted. Oh, what treachery! How could she see out her promise? There was still time to change her mind. But, then what of Allegi? What a wretched dilemma; she was so confused.

Opening the first door of the King's apartment, Deshyre made her way across the audience chamber to the bedroom.

She didn't have to go through with it. She hadn't yet told them anything. Yes, she could change her mind.

Uneasily, Deshyre pushed open the bedroom door. She peered into the bedchamber. The Queen was sitting propped up against pillows, staring across the room. Dark circles held her sadness under her eyes. She barely slept or ate and she refused to take the medicines the doctors gave her.

"Leave me alone," Tigris said, her voice cracking under the pressure of her sorrow as if it took all of her strength to utter the few words.

Deshyre stepped into the room anyway. "I promised to watch over you," she said gently as she headed to the stool and sat down. Her own words rang in her mind with deceit and with them came guilt.

The Queen did not object; she didn't have the strength. Instead, she returned to her distant stare.

Deshyre looked over at the pot beside the bed; it was full. Getting up, she held her breath, picked up the clay pot filled with the Queen's vomit. She carried it out of the room, down the hall to the lavatory where she poured it down the drain. She scooped water from a basin, rinsed out the pot, headed back to the room.

Stepping into the hall, Deshyre stopped momentarily. Ahead of her, the Vizier stormed into the King's chambers. His heavy strides were angry, filling the air with terror. Deshyre doubled her steps.

"Get up!" she heard the Vizier command.

Danger tightened the air. Deshyre dropped the pot, raced into the King's suites and froze.

The Vizier held Tigris by the hair. He pulled her from the bed.

Tigris gripped the Vizier's wrist trying to release the pain he caused her. She whimpered in agony as he tugged her from the bed.

"Get up!" Ibimpetus ordered again. He yanked her roughly.

Tigris fell off the bed out of his grip.

"I said, get up!" The Vizier grabbed Tigris' hair again, pulled her up, threw her face into the bed.

Deshyre watched in horror. Her body unlocked from its shock. She ran to the Queen's side, screaming, "No, Tjat!" She reached out for Tigris. "Please, no!" she begged.

Before Deshyre was able to get her arms around the Queen, the Vizier grabbed her and launched her across the room. Deshyre toppled over a chest and hit the wall.

Enraged, the Vizier pierced the messenger's wife coldly, his eyes narrowing with despise. "I would recommend—*Bedouin commoner*—to stay out of affairs that preside over you."

Fearing him, Deshyre obeyed. She remained quiet, still—watching.

The Vizier spun to face Tigris who knelt by her bed, leaning across the mattress, gasping. Ibimpetus sized the Queen with contempt. "Look at you! You are a disgrace to the country!" He grabbed her hair again and ripped her head back, met his lips by her ear. "Who was in the room with you the night of the festival?"

Tigris didn't answer. No sound escaped her. Tears streamed down her cheeks.

The Vizier pulled harder. "Why would Euphrates think you wouldn't want his head?" He examined her face, watched her silently cry.

Still she said nothing.

He tightened his grip, pulled her in closer so his lips brushed against her ear and whispered, "Your wish is done. His head follows me from Kasa. Believe it is true for I was there." He moved back, witnessed her face crumble with sorrow.

"No!" she gasped. Tigris couldn't hold onto her pain any longer. Her cry erupted. It was the first time the Vizier saw her cry.

Ibimpetus threw her into the bed. He stood straight, eyed her coldly. "Interesting," he mumbled. Fury burned under his skin. "Your father watches from the Fields of Peace ashamed!" he seethed. "Who are you? You were once so virile and now you let your feminine desires destroy you!" He crushed his fingers into her throat, picked her up by the neck. "Get up and act like a Pharaoh!" he roared. "I will not let you take Egypt down with you!"

He threw her back onto the bed and stormed from the room.

The moment he was gone, Deshyre rushed to the Queen's side. She tried to hold her but Tigris pushed her off.

"No," Tigris cried in a desperate gasp. "Oh, Hathor," she wept. "Oh, good mother Eset!"

〰〰

KAFATE OPENED A clay pot, looked down into it and smiled. She reached into the water, pulled out a palm-sized crystal and held it up to watch the light reflect a rainbow.

"There you are my beauty," she said softly. "I knew you would remind me where I put you when you were ready."

The priestess had put the crystal in a bowl of salted water to cleanse its energy. Despite all the times she searched for it, and even in the move from the palace in Henen-nesut to the palace in Men-nefer, the favoured piece went undiscovered until now. But, the special magical crystal always reappeared when it wanted to tell her something.

Kafate gazed into the murky water of the clay pot and closed the lid. She would clean it out later but right now she was interested in the crystal.

She held it up in front of the light again to peer into its core. The weight of the crystal became heavier in her hand. Its depths gloomed with darkness, calling her to look into them.

Lowering her arm, Kafate stood. She stared at the black pond for a moment. The water rippled in the torchlight. She glimpsed at the crystal in her clenched fist and then, as if compelled, she scuffled to the water hole. Before she came to a full stop, she tossed the crystal into the centre of the shallow pond.

The priestess gripped her staff in her bony white hand. She pressed down to help raise her body up far enough to peer across the water at the gem. She stretched out over the black pond and closed her good eye.

"Through cloud and darkness let me see, may the future's truths come to me."

Through the vision of her blind eye, the old priestess saw the crystal break in half, open up. A shooting grey beam rose from its core, out of the water, towards the ceiling.

Kafate watched, entranced by the spell of the magical crystal. She peered harder, leaned in even further. The crystal's power drove through the priestess. Her body began to tremble, shaking the staff she clung to. Kafate tightened her grip to prevent herself from falling.

In the depths of the grey beam, the priestess foresaw the future. Its truths struck her. She gasped, stumbled back. She tried to keep her balance but she continued to stumble further.

Both of her eyes were now open and she stared agape at the foreboding crystal in the middle of the black pond. The water rippled ferociously inside the hole.

"It is done," Kafate whispered, her eyes growing wider. "It is done. It is done."

She fell back against a table, tried to grab onto it but only managed to fumble the tablecloth, yanking it out from under its contents. Everything on top of the table crashed to the floor—rocks, pots, canisters—everything.

A sudden sharp pain pierced her chest, ripping through her heart. The old woman dropped her staff.

In the hidden chamber below the earth, no one would hear her cries for help. She looked at the mirror, which guarded the passage. She pushed herself off the table. The wrenching pain in her chest grew more intense.

The events she had seen replayed in her mind. "No. No," she gasped. Kafate tried to walk but she couldn't stay on her feet. She reached out, grabbed the tall stand—keeper of the *Am Duat*. It teetered under her weight as her body clumsily banged against it, knocking the stand to the floor, taking the priestess with it.

The old woman crashed to the cold stone floor and toppled into the shallow water of the black pond. She cried out in agony. The pain in her chest was crippling. She gargled on the saliva that began to foam up in her mouth. She glared at the ceiling, unable to speak or scream or utter a sound. Her body was paralysed.

LXIII

SOMISET RODE THROUGH the streets of Kasa with Tuthiken and Storithen. He spotted the gold nuggets Euphrates had dropped on his path but now they ceased to show the route. The three men rode along, trying to find something sparkling on the ground. They stopped. Looked hard. One was due to be set on the path.

"Perhaps he is in one of these buildings," Tuthiken pointed.

Somiset looked up at the mud-brick complex. On either side of them, two-story buildings built side-by-side in rows, lined the roadway. Without hesitation, he jumped from his horse, drew his sword and stormed into the first doorway.

Tuthiken and Storithen glanced at each other as they made their decision. Following suit, they leapt from their horses and unsheathed their weapons.

The three men split up. They charged through the rooms, startling the occupants on their quest to find Euphrates. All of them came up empty handed and before long they were back on the sunlit street, looking at each other in contemplation.

"Maybe he was dragged off at this point," Storithen suggested.

"Great!" Tuthiken exclaimed, whacking the blade of his sword against the mud-brick wall of a building with frustration. "Dragged to where? How are we ever going to find him!" He glared down the street, rage burning his cheeks. Spinning, he pointed at Somiset. "Why would you let him leave?"

Somiset ignored him. He climbed onto his horse and observed their surroundings.

"We now have an army with no leader and without him we have no cause!" Tuthiken blared.

"The temple." Somiset eyed it in the distance. He could see its high roof towering over the short buildings of the town.

"What?" Tuthiken asked not seeing how the temple had anything to do with what he said.

"The temple." Somiset drove his horse forward.

The temple appeared to be the perfect place. Next to the river, away from the city, it offered unobserved admittance and solitude.

Somiset sped through the streets towards the sanctuary. Behind him, Tuthiken and Storithen tried to catch up.

The men rode up to the small, yet, grand Temple of Sobek set in the desert away from the city. Somiset halted to examine the sand around it. Many footprints led both into and back out of the building. The prints were of sandals, which few commoners wore and which meant they were made by officials.

Tuthiken followed Somiset's glare to the dirt. He finally understood. "The temple," he said, resolutely.

"I have a feeling it's empty," stated Storithen as he raised his stare from the ground, up the steps to the doorway. From their level, they couldn't see inside.

"There's only one way to know." Somiset hurled himself from his horse. He darted up the stairs, weapon held out. His two comrades jumped from their steeds and charged close behind him.

As Storithen predicted, the temple was empty.

"How long ago could they have left?" asked Storithen.

"Maybe he did meet the Queen and they have run off together," Tuthiken offered.

Somiset bent down. He wiped blood off the floor—it was still fresh. "He didn't run off with anyone." Somiset followed its trail with his eyes until he found their answer. Standing, he rushed across the room, lifted a trap door on the floor and descended the steps.

A tunnel led straight along to an open doorway at the end of the corridor. There were no turns, just one path. A glowing light flickered in the cellar.

Somiset slowed his stride, looked back at Tuthiken and Storithen. "One of you go back. Remain on the steps in case anyone gets past us."

A thud came from the room followed by a groan of pain. The groan was definitely Euphrates.

Rage burned in Tuthiken's eyes. He tried to squeeze past Somiset down the hall towards Euphrates. But, the walkway was too narrow and Somiset held him back.

"At least we know he is still alive," Somiset whispered. "Patience," he urged. "We don't know how many there are." He looked forward to the light.

Another yelp of pain soared through the hall. Somiset tightened his grip on Tuthiken. He gestured to Storithen who went to the steps.

Cautiously, Somiset led the way along the passage. When he got to its end, he pressed himself against the wall, peeked into the temple's storage cellar.

Inside, there were only three officers of the State Police.

Good, thought Somiset, their numbers were even.

The small room was lit by torch and save for a few pottery jars and a stuffed crocodile, the cellar was empty. Two of the officers faced the door holding Euphrates up between them by the arms while the third beat him with a club.

"Mark this moment as the trampling of the *nine bows!*" declared the Lieutenant as he cracked his club over Euphrates' arm.

Euphrates grimaced in pain. The force of the blow pushed his arm out of the officer's grip, sending him to the floor. The second officer dropped Euphrates' other arm allowing him to fall the rest of the way.

"The Pharaoh wants you dead," the Lieutenant jeered.

"I don't... believe you," Euphrates managed through his pain.

The Lieutenant's brow furrowed as his eyes pinned Euphrates. "You know, I thought the Vizier's accusations were insane but I see now for myself." He squatted down and cranked Euphrates' head back. "Tsk. Tsk. In love with the enemy? How beautiful. Too bad the feeling only goes one way..." he smirked, "to a *dead* end." His last two words were delivered low. They smacked the air with a sense of serenity as they entered Euphrates' faltering consciousness. *Dead end*, he thought before his eyes rolled closed.

Somiset eased his throwing stick from his belt. He only had one chance to throw it before their presence would be known. He would first target one of the officers facing him; his last target would be the Lieutenant whose back was to them, thus, still had to turn around. With the walkway being so narrow, Tuthiken was useless until they were in the room.

Somiset made slow movements until his arm was in position. Locking his eyes on his target, he whipped the stick towards the man's forehead. It struck, knocking him over. Quickly, Somiset reached back, grabbed the stick out of Tuthiken's belt and whipped it at the second officer before the man had the chance to register what was happening.

The Lieutenant spun on his heels, drew his weapon. Somiset lunged towards him but the Lieutenant was too slow. Somiset jabbed his dagger into the man's gut, twisted. He stepped back, pulled his knife from the Lieutenant's body. Blood splattered. The Lieutenant dropped.

Somiset hurtled forward to the officers knocked out on the ground. He slit the first man's throat, moved over and did the same to the second. All three were dead.

Straightening, he glanced back at Tuthiken who stepped into the chamber, holding his weapon forward.

"You didn't even give me a chance," Tuthiken complained.

Somiset smirked. He went to Euphrates, scooped him up, slung his unconscious body over his shoulder.

Tuthiken led the way down the hall. They reached Storithen who guided them out of the depths of the cellar.

Arriving in the single chamber of the temple, the three men halted. Footsteps sounded on the steps outside, bringing forward shadows of the men of whom they belonged. There was only one way out of the temple and it was blocked. Waiting, the three men watched five officers of the State Police follow their shadows into the temple.

Storithen glimpsed at Tuthiken; Tuthiken in turn, looked at Somiset.

"Here's your chance to kill someone," Somiset quipped. He placed Euphrates on the ground, drew his sword.

"Did you think to grab those throwing sticks?" Tuthiken grumbled as he unsheathed his weapon.

"Seize them!" commanded an officer of the State Police.

The three men stood ready as the five officers advanced with strong, steady steps.

"Well, I'm not waiting," Tuthiken growled, holding out his sword as he charged forward.

Storithen shrugged and followed.

Somiset guarded Euphrates' body.

Weapons clashed, sounding the air with their ring. Tuthiken fought against two men as did Storithen. The fifth man ran towards Euphrates. "Just kill their King!" he bellowed out. "Kill their King and it will be done!"

Somiset blocked his path, slashed his sword.

A cry shrieked the room—one officer dead. Tuthiken pulled his axe from the man's chest.

Another royal officer raced towards Euphrates. Somiset saw him coming. Now, he had two men on him. He tried to push them back but his movement was limited—he would not step away from Euphrates' body. Somiset jerked his axe out of his belt and whipped it at one of the officers. The man deflected it.

Storithen glimpsed over his shoulder. He backed away from the officer whom he fought, gave himself the distance he needed so he could turn to Somiset's aid. He held his sword, snatched his throwing stick from his side and chucked it forward. The stick sailed through the air meeting its mark. It whacked an officer by Somiset on the back of his head, sending him to the floor.

A sharp pain pierced Storithen's back as a weight pushed him to the ground. He smacked the hard stone floor, unable to move. His back stung. He felt as if he was suffocating. Then, the weight disappeared.

"Get up. You're only scratched."

Storithen rolled over to see Tuthiken bearing down on him with a proud smile. Beside him, the body of the officer that fell on top of him bled.

Tuthiken held out his hand, helped his friend to stand. They looked over at Somiset. Two soldiers lay at his feet. All five officers were slain.

Tuthiken smirked at Somiset. "That's three for me and two for you."

Raising his eyebrows, Somiset returned, "That's five for me. I have three downstairs." He picked up Euphrates and carried him out of the dim temple into the sunlight.

LXIV

"A MESSENGER OF the Queen rides towards the camp!" the sentry yelled out. He squinted in the bright afternoon sunlight to make out the intruder's flag. Satisfied he was right, the young man raced through the campsite towards Euphrates' tent.

Euphrates had stayed in bed the past three days. His rib cage was cracked from his lashing; he was still sore and bruised. More so, his spirit was broken and he lost his will to fight. But, despite his depression, the warrior King would not allow it to bring him down. He decided to allow himself a few days rest before he would rise and storm the deserts again.

"A royal messenger of the Pharaoh rides in!"

Euphrates could hear the watchman's call making its way towards him. He watched the tent door, waiting for the man to arrive.

The flap opened and the thin man, no more than twenty, stuck his head inside. "The—"

"Send him away," Euphrates ordered. "I am not accepting messages from the Pharaoh anymore."

The sentry nodded, disappeared.

〰

BY THE TIME the young man scampered back towards his post, Somiset stood watching the rider draw in.

Somiset looked down at the frail young watchman as he came up beside him.

The watchman repeated Euphrates' order, "He's not accepting

messages from the Pharaoh anymore."

Somiset looked away—towards the rider.

At length, the messenger trotted up to them, jumped from his horse. "Where's Euphrates?" Allegi asked in a demanding tone.

"He is not accepting messages from the Pharaoh anymore," the sentry echoed.

"Good," Allegi nodded. "This message comes from me and not the Pharaoh." He directed his attention to Somiset, knowing the burly man was the one he needed to get past. "Where is he?"

Somiset inhaled a deep breath and shook his head in disbelief of his own decision. Against his better judgement, he commanded, "Follow me."

The large, muscular soldier led the way through the campground, abruptly halting near Euphrates' tent. "Wait here," he insisted before he treaded onward, continuing the short distance to the tent door.

He went in.

〜

EUPHRATES LOOKED UP, surprised to see Somiset.

"There's a message for you—"

"I told the sentry—"

"It's Allegi."

Euphrates sat up. His stomach rose and fell with desire, but he forced it away, shook his head. "I don't care. I don't want his message."

Somiset turned. He went to the door. "I'm sending him in anyway."

He was gone. A moment later Allegi stood in his place.

Euphrates rose to his feet, grimaced in pain, tried to conceal it. He glanced around the tent, spotted a figurine on top of a chest, went to it. For some reason he couldn't face Allegi. He put his back to him, picked up the sculpture, turned it over in his hand. The small hand-carved sphinx with Euphrates' face was given to him as a gift by one of his men. The resemblance to himself was astounding.

"You must see her."

"No hello?" Euphrates retorted.

"You *must* see her."

Euphrates ignored him. He rolled the statuette over again.

"For your good and hers, you *must* see her." Allegi insisted, delivering the words as if they were an order.

Euphrates whipped around. "We already tried that—it didn't work."

"She loves you."

"She denies it!" Euphrates stomped across the tent to a trunk. He wanted to storm out, but he wouldn't—wouldn't for the shame. He opened the trunk, reached in, pulled out his dagger and a sharpening stone. He fixed his attention on sharpening the blade.

This time Allegi spoke slowly, begging instead of commanding. "You must see her again."

"I don't ever want to see her again."

"Liar."

Euphrates scratched his blade harder.

Allegi studied him for a moment. "You love her and she loves you and you both know it."

"Love?" The word fell from Euphrates' lips with disgust. "It's a curse."

Allegi moved in closer. "It's not your love that is your curse," he argued. "It is your *pride*."

Euphrates' blade froze.

"You must see her, Great Lord."

"No," Euphrates decided, drawing away from his thought. "I won't put myself through that again."

"Please."

"I won't."

"You must."

"*No!*" The knife hit the stone harder. It scraped along the rock cutting the air with its noise.

Allegi calmed his tone, pleaded. "I beg you to see her—for your sake and hers—I beg you!"

"*I will not!*"

Allegi stepped closer. His expression flooded the tent in its desperation. "You *must!*"

"Why *must* I?" Euphrates scowled.

Allegi met his eyes. He swallowed hard, contemplated whether he should tell. Slowly, he responded, "Because she carries your child."

Euphrates froze.

Allegi held his stare. "She is dying," he whispered. "Destroying herself because she's too afraid to love you and too afraid to let you know."

Euphrates set the dagger and stone down on top of the trunk. He turned to face Allegi. Worry showed its cruelty on his face.

"She won't eat or sleep and the once virile Pharaoh cries every night since you left her."

"I did not leave her!" Euphrates stormed away, halted. His head fell with a sense of defeat. "What use is it? She's more stubborn than me."

"She's too weak to be stubborn now. Her heart grieves too deep. Her pride crumbles."

Euphrates didn't move. Allegi watched him.

A long moment of silence lent thought its serenity before Allegi ended the muted moment. "Agree to meet her."

Euphrates didn't move. He kept his back to the Royal Messenger.

Tension swelled; the silence grew unbearable; and then, just when Allegi lost all hope, the rebellious King of Northern Egypt turned to face him.

LXV

ALLEGI RACED INTO the palace at Men-nefer. He was gone for almost a week but he returned with great news. Euphrates would meet Tigris.

He sped through the halls, went to the forbidden queen's apartments and dashed through the empty rooms to the mirror. He barely stopped to open its secretive door. He was elated with the thought of bringing them together but he needed Kafate's help to convince Tigris. Indeed, if the Queen would listen to anyone it would be the old priestess.

Sliding down the tunnel, Allegi charged into Kafate's chamber and stopped.

The old woman lay awkwardly in the black pond with tables and sacred objects capsized around her. "Kafate!" he called as he ran over to her and stepped into the forbidden water. The pond was only a

382

couple inches deep. The priestess lay on her back, her long grey hair floating around her. "Kafate!" Allegi desperately cried out again. He tried to lift her head. The priestess was stiff and if possible, more white than ever. Allegi jumped back. He backed out of the room in shock, unable to think.

Kafate was dead.

The Pharaoh's Royal Messenger walked sombrely along the grand hallway of the royal residential building and out onto the courtyard. Looking up into the speckled night sky, he found some refuge in its quietude as he pondered, *Kafate is dead.* What was he to do now? He couldn't tell the Queen—at least not until she was better. He was left to convince Tigris to meet Euphrates on his own.

Allegi sat on the stoop of the inner building. He felt as if all he ever did was race against time. The Queen would have to leave tomorrow in order to meet Euphrates at the Temple of Sobek by the city of Kasa on the decided day. Worry pounded his head. He rubbed his temples. How could he get Tigris to agree without the help of the priestess? She didn't even look at him anymore.

Allegi covered his face in his hands. When will this end? *How* does this end? he questioned as he raised his head to peer across the court at the administrative building. The Vizier's torches shone brightly in his room. Allegi stood. Did the man ever sleep? he wondered.

Allegi climbed the steps of the royal apartment building. He took his time travelling down the grand hallway. He did not look forward to confronting the Queen. He felt drained, heavy, tired. If only she wasn't so stubborn.

He entered the King's bedchamber. Deshyre looked up. She sprang from her stool, raced into his arms. "She won't eat or sleep. I can barely get her to drink water. She hasn't moved or spoken in days except to say, 'I don't care.'"

Allegi looked at the Queen. She was sitting up in bed staring at the wall ahead of her.

Deshyre let go of her husband and slipped out of the room.

Allegi went to the stool, picked it up and moved it to Tigris' bedside. He sat quietly for a moment.

"I've come from seeing Euphrates," he finally said.

Tigris whipped her head around to look at him. "He's alive?" she asked, her voice almost inaudible.

Allegi's brow furrowed. Why would she ask such a question? But, he didn't inquire; what he had to say was more important. "He wants to see you."

Tigris turned her head to face the wall in front of her again.

"Why won't you see him?"

Tigris didn't reply. She turned her head further to the right, completely away from her messenger as if to end the conversation.

Allegi slid off the stool, knelt beside her bed. He took her hand and cupped it in his. "Why won't you see him?" he repeated, his tone strained and desperate.

Slowly, Tigris moved to face him. Her eyes became glassy. "Because he makes me weak." She pulled her hand from his.

"Is that what you call love?"

Tigris looked away. She gazed at the wall, finding her escape in the dark shadows. Tears ran down her cheeks. She couldn't control them nor did she have the will to hide them anymore.

Allegi pressed his hands over his face and breathed. "Love is a wonderful thing," he whispered. He lifted her hand again and kissed it. "I promise you, Tigris, if you lay aside your fears its path will be easier than the one you take now."

Tigris glowered at him. She yanked back her hand. "I have no fears!" she said in a deep tone, which had found some power inside her weakened body. She shifted on the bed.

"Then if you have no fears, let yourself be with him. You *love* him."

The truth made Tigris cringe, but only for an instant. Her face hardened. "I'm no messenger who can marry some poor, desolate, uneducated Bedouin commoner. It's not that easy for me."

Her words cut into Allegi. He stood, shaking his head, incensed. Hurt and angered, he headed to the door, reached for the handle. But, then he stopped. He wouldn't let her win.

"How many nobles in my position wouldn't have married?" Spinning, Allegi eyed Tigris ruefully. His glare burned his anger into her eyes compelling her to look away.

"You see, when they quietly scorn me, it doesn't matter because I've already won." He side stepped so he stood in her view. "I am with the one I love and their frowns pale by comparison to the pains my heart would cause me had I made the other choice."

Tigris was looking through him but Allegi knew she had heard every word. Tears poured faster down her cheeks. Seeing her sorrow pained his heart. His own tears began to well up in his eyes.

Allegi sat on the bed. "Oh, Tigris, I care too much to watch you destroy yourself." He lay across her lap. "I beg you to go see him. He loves you and you him, what is so horrible about that?"

Tigris covered her face. She was trembling. "I can't," she whispered through her tears.

"You can. I will take you."

"I can't."

"Egypt will still love you."

"I can't," she cried, shaking her head no.

"You will lose *everything* if you don't!" Allegi grabbed her hands and pulled them from her face, forcing her to look at him. "Love is worth so much more than pride."

Tigris broke down, crying deeply. Her body trembled even harder.

Allegi held her but he said no more.

≈

DESHYRE WAS WAITING up for Allegi when he finally made it to bed. It was late, dawn still many hours away.

He looked into her worried face and smiled. She was his happiness. Allegi removed his kilt, slipped into bed and held her.

"They will meet," he grinned.

Deshyre beamed. "You got them to meet? Oh, what a romantic hero!" She rolled onto her back and laughed. "It should be written for all time: Allegi, the Great Messenger of Love." Laughing again, Deshyre looked at her husband. "Do you think they will run into each other's arms and win back Egypt together?"

"I think I love you," Allegi smiled. "I truly love you, Deshyre. I want you to know that."

"I know—Messenger of Love," she teased.

He laughed. "I even love your hairy arms." Allegi tackled her.

"What? They're not hairy!"

He tickled her. Deshyre let out a scream as she squirmed out from under him.

"It's only because you Egyptians tweeze and shave everything." She sat on top of him, pinned him down. "Say they're not hairy." Deshyre grabbed a pillow and pushed it over his head. "Say it!"

"Okay!" Allegi's muffled voice begged from under the pillow.

The door flung open. A servant darted into the room.

Deshyre gasped, scrambled under the sheets to hide her nudity. She pulled the pillow off of Allegi and clutched it in her arms.

"You must come! You must come quickly!" the servant panicked.

Allegi didn't ask questions. He jumped out of the bed, wrapped his kilt around his waist, followed the middle aged man out of his chamber and down the hall. They exited the royal residential building, ran across the courtyard to the administrative building. The servant led Allegi through the hall, around a corner and down the stairs to a corridor scarcely lit. They went deeper down the incline, passing small chambers and other hallways. As they came to the last turn, the servant slowed down. He cautiously peeked around the corner before he stepped out.

Down the hall, a chamber shone brightly. Along with the light that spilled out into the hallway were voices of men. The servant motioned to Allegi. They tiptoed down the hall, its excessive width concealing them from the view of the centred doorway.

Allegi listened.

"We need someone to lead Egypt, someone strong!" It was the voice of the Vizier, his low curt tone distinguishable by its constant harshness. "Tigris is weak and useless with no hope for the better. We must rid ourselves of the Pharaoh's infirmity and save Egypt!"

Allegi gasped. *Treason!* They were planning to kill the Pharaoh. He spun.

Not seeing the table, Allegi bumped into it, knocking a decorative urn to the floor. It smashed into pieces, echoing throughout the hall.

The servant's mouth fell open. "Go!" he urged.

Allegi ran down the corridor and around the corner.

The servant slowly turned, fearful of what was to come. He watched the councillors rush to the door and into the hall.

Chephren studied the servant. "Who was with you?" he demanded.

"No one," the servant mumbled, frozen with fear.

"There was someone with you. Who was it?"

The servant looked nervously at the eight men crowded before him. "I swear, it was only me—I'm sorry. I was passing to check the lights."

"Then why were you looking down the hall?"

Fear and desperation showed their presence on the servant's face. "I swear," he begged.

The Vizier came forward. "He lies. Kill him." He marched past the servant.

"No!" cried the servant, stepping back as Isetep, Chancellor of the High Court, stepped up to him, his dagger held out. Swiftly, the Chancellor slit the servant's throat.

The servant fell to his knees, gargling in his blood.

"Check the palace!" Ibimpetus ordered. "Find Allegi."

〰〰

ALLEGI RAN INTO his room and grabbed his sword. "Get up!" he shouted at Deshyre. "We must get Tigris and get out of here!"

Deshyre jumped out of the bed and dressed. She didn't question him; his expression told more than enough.

Allegi grabbed his sack, swung it over his shoulder. He took hold of Deshyre's hand, pulled her from the room, down the hall and to the stairs. He dragged her behind him as he bolted up to the second level, along the hallway to the King's quarters. He violently threw open the door and hurried across to the bedchamber.

For the first time in a long while, Tigris was sleeping in a deep sleep. She didn't hear the door hit the wall or Allegi call her name.

Allegi raced to her bedside, pulled the covers off of her, took hold of her body and pulled her up. Startled out of sleep, the Queen looked at Allegi in surprise.

"We must go *now*," Allegi answered. "Ibimpetus plans your assassination."

Tigris' eyes grew wide. She could barely muster strength. Deshyre helped the Pharaoh onto her feet.

Outside the room, the sound of a door banging open against the wall gave its warning.

"We're trapped!" Deshyre cried, looking around the room.

"There's a route behind the chests," Tigris managed feebly.

Allegi left his wife to hold up Tigris on her own. He pushed a tower of stacked chests out of the way, pressed on the wall. Hidden behind the wall was the King's escape route.

Deshyre guided Tigris into the passage. Allegi pulled the chests back behind them and closed them in.

〰〰

THE VIZIER ENTERED the room. Tigris was gone. Rage flushed his cheeks. He grabbed the sheets from the bed and whipped them across the room in fury. He headed to the door.

Seven officers were searching the palace—they would be found.

From the corner of his eye, the Vizier noticed something that made him stop. He looked at the stack of chests not set flush against the wall.

Of course, he thought.

Yanking the chests forward, Ibimpetus slipped into the darkness.

〰〰

ALLEGI AND DESHYRE slid against the walls, holding Tigris between them. The Queen's head hung forward. She tried to keep her eyes from rolling back from exhaustion. Her body was so weak—she had deprived it of nutrients for much too long. Her knees buckled. Allegi forced her back onto her feet.

Deshyre glanced at Allegi, fearfully. Behind them, they could hear someone following.

They reached an intersection of tunnels, stopped. Deshyre shot Allegi another look.

Considering his choices and where he thought they were under the palace complex, Allegi chose a corridor. They continued to race down the hall, around a bend.

Behind them, the footsteps closed in, sounding like the beat of a warrior's drum.

"Oser—a dead end!" Deshyre gasped, seeing the wall at the end of the route.

"No," Tigris whispered, almost inaudibly.

Allegi nudged them forward. As they got closer to the wall, a door revealed itself. He pushed it open and they stepped into the wide hall, which led to the chamber Allegi had just spied on.

Deshyre shrieked. Beside her feet, the servant who had warned them lay in a pool of his own blood.

"Don't look," Allegi said calmly, breaking Deshyre out of shock. He guided them away from the chamber.

A sudden strength came from Tigris. She tugged them to stop. "No," she huffed. She managed to lift her head. "The chamber."

Allegi looked back at the room, which ended the hall. They would be trapped if they went inside. He was unsure whether to obey. The Queen was groggy, not completely conscious and probably didn't realize their bearings.

"The chamber," Tigris repeated.

Something compelled him to listen. Allegi turned, dashed forward, dragging both Tigris and Deshyre with him. He rushed into the chamber and froze.

A large round stone table dominated most of the room. Chairs lined the table but at the far end, a throne was raised up on a platform and looked down on everything. Allegi glanced around. The circular room was enclosed by stone walls. Torches burned on them but there was no way out aside from the door they had entered.

"We're trapped," he uttered with a sense of defeat. Allegi let go of Tigris, gripped his sword tighter, and turned to the door. It would only be a matter of moments before their pursuer reached them.

"Open the throne," Tigris said weakly. She pointed across the table to the Throne of Geb.

Deshyre looked at Allegi hoping he would understand, but his expression was just as puzzled. She looked back at the throne—it was their only hope.

Pushing the Queen into Allegi's arms, Deshyre ran around the table and up the steps to the throne. She examined it—seeing if it hid an exit.

The throne was made of large slabs of limestone. The bottom was a solid box that grew up out of the stone floor. The thick arms were also made of stone as well as its high back. It was solid.

Deshyre looked up at them, helplessly.

"The seat," Tigris managed. "Lift the seat."

Deshyre leaned over, gripped the thick slab, tried to move it. The stone top cracked open—only a bit, but that slight crack promised their lives. Deshyre tugged it again. The seat was too heavy for her to manage.

"Take her," Allegi commanded.

Deshyre took hold of Tigris as Allegi darted to the royal chair.

The wide seat of the throne allowed space for the slab to be lifted. Allegi gripped the stone, raised one side of it and leaned the heavy seat against the chair arm. Inside the base of the throne, a ladder descended into the earth.

"Quick!" Allegi exclaimed, excited to see an escape.

Deshyre helped Tigris up the steps to Allegi.

"You go down first," he told his wife. He looked at Tigris. "Can you climb down?"

Tigris nodded. She forced her strength and disappeared into the escape behind Deshyre.

"You only help to destroy Egypt," Ibimpetus' voice thundered.

Straightening, Allegi held out his sword and turned.

The Vizier entered the Chamber of Council. He edged his way around the table. "There is still time to seize control," he breathed. "In the name of Kemet, let me do it!"

Allegi moved down a step and stood between the Vizier and the throne, sword raised, flesh burning with rage.

How dare he—how dare he ask him to step aside to allow him to do away with the Pharaoh. Repulsion laced Allegi's tone, "You lost your chance the moment you plotted instead of preserved. You had the power to unite Egypt. All it took was your blessing with two simple words, *marry Euphrates*." Allegi raised his voice in anger. "It was *you* she feared!"

He watched as Ibimpetus gradually came towards him, clasping a sword at his side.

"Tell me," Allegi asked, condemning the Vizier, "what ill would have come of it?"

Ibimpetus reached the bottom of the steps and lifted his blade. "Let me pass. I can still restore Egypt."

Allegi descended another step. He shook his head. "With sedition and murder? No, Tjat, you have caused enough ruin."

The Vizier drew his sword, swung it forward. Their weapons clanked with hatred propelling their blades. Allegi pushed the Vizier backwards.

Yet, as old as Ibimpetus was, he still had strength.

Allegi was faster. With each strike the messenger forced the Vizier back until he was trapped against the stone table.

Allegi wielded his sword in the air. He brought it down full force. Ibimpetus rolled along the edge of the circular table out of the way. The blade hit the stone with a piercing ring, causing sparks to fly from its bronze edge.

The Vizier stumbled to his feet, lifted his sword, pointed it towards the *Friend of the King*. But, Allegi didn't stop. In a continuous movement, he elevated his blade and twirled. He hit the Vizier's weapon, knocking it from his grip.

Ibimpetus scrambled backwards. He watched his sword fly across the room. He was weaponless.

Allegi moved towards him. The Vizier pressed up against the wall in horror as Allegi pinned him with the tip of his sword.

"Please," the Vizier begged in desperation. "I only ever sought to protect our beloved land."

Allegi shook his head with despise. "No, Tjat," he responded. "You only sought to protect yourself. *You* destroyed Egypt. Bear that burden in death." Allegi pushed his blade into the Vizier's chest. "Ammut comes for you. At last, Oser calls." He pushed harder.

〰

THE VIZIER GAPED in agony. He looked at his chest as Allegi removed his sword. He slid down the wall, fell to the floor and stopped in a sitting position, back against the wall. He raised his head, watched his fellow councillor, *Friend of the King*, race up the steps and into the throne. Allegi pulled the stone seat down, concealing the escape.

The Vizier gasped. His arm felt incredibly heavy. He struggled to lift it, to force it up so he could pull out the gold amulet hanging around his neck under his tunic.

The large pendant was covered in blood. He wiped the blood away with his thumb, revealing its carved symbol—a pyramid overlapped by the Eye of Horu. The pyramid symbolized the greatest structure built by man—superior architect of design. And, the Eye of Horu, *udjat*, represented strength, protection, perfection and the act of "making whole." It was a perfect symbol that meant the superior architect would perfect the world, make it whole, give it strength.

Ibimpetus gazed at the amulet with hope. Powerful men could make that ambition real—he was their leader but his time had come to an end. He clung to the symbol of the sacred order praying his followers would carry on the spirit he had created.

Prayed.

Isetep raced into the circular Chamber of Council. He froze in shock. "No—Tjat!" he cried as he rushed over and crouched down beside the Vizier.

The Vizier opened his eyes: *Isetep. Hope.* He tried to speak, desperately tried to fight his death. He gasped continuously but he could barely utter a sound. How could he tell him? So much to tell in these last minutes.

The Chancellor of the High Courts watched in despair, not knowing what to do. He looked at the Vizier for answers.

The Vizier attempted to lift his hand, he wanted to point towards the throne but his arm was too heavy. His arm dropped. The amulet fell from his grip. His eyes fluttered.

"No!" Isetep cried out. He glared at Ibimpetus, trying to think. His eyes fell to the pendant, the symbol of the sacred order of power and greatness—only privileged members knew of its values or even its existence.

Isetep ripped the pendant from around the Vizier's neck. No one could see the amulet, no one but its members. Protectively, he cupped the pendant in his fist and stared at the Vizier in shock. The Chancellor of the High Courts suddenly felt lost. Their leader, Ibimpetus was dead.

〰

ALLEGI DUCKED THROUGH the low dark tunnel. He sped along the straight pathway, which was carved into the earth. The tunnel squeezed so tightly around him he choked on the scent of dirt. In its confined space, the escape threatened all travellers with claustrophobia. Allegi could feel his lungs tighten, his breaths become difficult. Yet, before the pressure became too much, he reached the end. A ladder led out of the tunnel.

Allegi climbed the ladder. He made it to the outer world, outside the thick protective wall of the palace. He crawled away from the wall, looked back. A stone was pushed out revealing the escape. He looked around for Deshyre and Tigris but there were no signs of them.

Allegi went back to the wall, lifted the stone slab, and placed it back into the hole, covering any trace of their path. As he fixed the stone in place, a hand gripped his shoulder.

Allegi froze, slowly moved for his dagger, drew it, aimed to plunge his weapon.

"This way."

He turned to see Deshyre standing over him. He dropped the dagger and exhaled with relief—he had almost slain his wife.

Deshyre led Allegi along the wall and down the hillside. The palace was built on an incline to make it difficult for enemy attacks. The darkness helped to mask them as they raced down to where rocks jutted out of the ground. They slipped around them away from the view of the palace.

Tigris lay half unconscious against the rock.

"Per'a?" Allegi whispered as he raised her head to make sure she was breathing.

The Queen opened her eyes. "All is lost," she huffed. "All is lost." Her eyes rolled closed. Her head fell forward.

Allegi picked her head up again, shaking her to bring her back to consciousness. "No, Per'a," he insisted with a promising undertone. "We will meet with Euphrates and together you will win back Egypt." Allegi looked up at Deshyre. She stood over top of them, grieved with worry. "Stay here," he told her. "I am going back in to get horses—"

"No!" Deshyre exclaimed in a loud whisper. She fell to her knees beside him, took hold of his arm. "No, Allegi, it's too dangerous!"

"I have to."

"No, you can't!" She shook her head rapidly, holding onto him tighter. "You can't! Let's just go away from here!"

"On foot?"

Deshyre began crying. She hugged his arm with all her strength.

"Deshyre." Allegi gently tried to peel her off of him but her clasp was too strong. "Deshyre!" he yelled in a low voice, using more force to pry her loose. He held her away from him by her shoulders.

She sobbed, fervently shaking her head. "No, no," she continually whispered.

"Deshyre," Allegi repeated. He shook her hard to snap her out of it. "Listen to me."

Deshyre looked at him, her big brown eyes soaked with tears.

"I will return but if I don't, go down to the shipyard and find Ramska. He will know what to do." Allegi let her go and took off down the hill before she was able to take hold of him again.

The Pharaoh's escape led out to the Nile side of the palace. At the bottom of the hill was the shipyard—the escape route well planned.

A small village housed the crews of the Royal Vessels next to the barque station. The men lived in the village with their families, ready to be called upon at a moment's notice. Allegi dashed along the street of the low homes to Ramska's door and pounded on it.

His wife, half asleep, opened the door.

Allegi stood panting from his sprint. The Captain's wife said nothing. Instead, she rushed off to fetch her husband.

By the time Ramska got to the door, Allegi caught most of his breath. "We must leave now," he managed.

For the first time, Ramska didn't smile. He nodded earnestly before he turned to go dress and prepare.

Allegi looked up at the Great House on the hill. Now, for the horses, he thought.

〰〰

RAMSKA BANGED ON his first mate's door. The man opened it, rubbing his eyes, disturbed from his sleep.

"Wake the men," Ramska ordered. "We leave tonight without anyone knowing."

The order whispered though the village, waking each member of the crew. *"Silent sail,"* was all he was told. Having been rehearsed, everything was prepared hastily. The men carried out their tasks of loading the vessel--some responsible for food, some for gear. But, everyone knew his exact duty and he fulfilled it quickly and quietly.

Before long, the ship was ready. Once everyone was aboard, Ramska waved them to attention. The men pushed in so they could hear their Captain's low voice.

"I have one more task for you to do. But, when you see the flame of my torch, whereever you are, you must return immediately to the ship."

〜

ALLEGI SCURRIED AGAINST the outer palace wall. The massive complex caused the distance to the other side to be long. Other than the escape he discovered tonight, there was one other way into the palace, which he knew of that was not through the front gate.

The Queen had mentioned it in one of their many long discussions. They were talking about the priestess; Allegi asked if the old woman ever left her chamber.

"Her chambers are constructed exactly like the ones in Men-nefer," Tigris answered. "She only ever goes outside at night to get herbs and ingredients for her potions. A secret tunnel leads from her room outside the palace wall. There is a black mark on the stone so she can find her way back to it."

"Isn't that dangerous?" Allegi questioned. "What if someone was to follow her back?"

Tigris laughed. "I'd feel sorry for their life. The priestess has put a curse on the passageway. Any enemy who walks through it shall not live out the day."

Allegi frowned. The safeguard did not sound too safe.

〜

RETURNING FROM HIS memory, Allegi stepped back. He reached the southern side of the outer wall and stood opposite the royal residential building, which was tucked safely inside the middle of the palace complex. He knew approximately where the queen's quarters were and Kafate's chambers were beneath the earth beside them. If the tunnel was dug straight, then the marking had to be close.

Scanning the wall outside the palace at Men-nefer, Allegi looked for the black mark, wondering how the half blind old woman could see it at night. But then, as if illuminated by the moon, he saw the blot—a black scarab—symbol of protective powers, which warded off evil.

Allegi went to the stone. The mark was indefinable for anyone who wasn't looking for it, but for the selective eye, it was definite. Allegi pulled out the stone, disappeared into the tunnel, shutting the moonlight out behind him as he closed the hidden door.

The tunnel was low and narrow. Unlike him, the hunched old woman wouldn't have had to duck. Allegi gulped in air. The walls closed in on him, making it hard to breathe. *Don't think about it,* he coached himself as he crawled along.

He remembered the priestess' curse. An eerie feeling added its misery to his chest. Allegi clutched the pin on his skirt—the Golden Scorpion—symbol for *Friend of the King,* and prayed if the curse was real it would not view him as an enemy.

Allegi crawled through the darkness, unable to see the tunnel's end. He felt the air grow thick, crushing his lungs. He hated tight spaces. His head began to feel dizzy; his breaths became short and quick. Panic gripped him. Was he dying? Was it the priestess' curse? But, just when he thought he wouldn't make it, he arrived at the end of the passage.

Allegi pushed on the wall and fell into Kafate's bedchamber. Gasping for air, he looked around the room. The room was sparse. Only a bed sat in the middle; nothing touched the walls.

Allegi clambered to his feet, raced from the bedroom, down the short hall to the main chamber. The stench stopped him in his tracks. Kafate's rotting corpse made him suddenly feel ill. He gagged, covering his nose as he stumbled through the chamber to the mirror. He couldn't look; the thought of her body lying there dead made him uneasy along with the guilt of having forgotten.

Allegi ripped open the mirror and ran from the room. He charged through the empty suites of the late Queen Nefari and stopped at the main door to listen. Drawing his sword, Allegi cautiously stepped out into the grand hallway of the royal residential building. He moved down the hall, observing the shadows. Every several strides, he spun to look behind, walked backwards a few steps then turned forward again. He scanned the hallway and saw a shadow move behind a column.

Allegi darted to the pillar, slid around it with his sword pointing out, ready. As he came face-to-face with the person, he stopped. The old chambermaid of the Queen pressed against the column. She was shaking, her eyes tightly closed.

"Naat," Allegi whispered, lowering his weapon.

She opened her eyes. "Allegi?" The elderly woman looked around apprehensively. "What's happening? They're looking for Tigris."

"I know. I need to get some horses and get out of here."

"Horses? They will see you."

"I have no other way."

Naat looked fearful but the disparity in his eyes made her find courage. She glanced around the empty hall, linked arms with Allegi's and rushed him down the hallway towards the back entrance. They went from column to column, using the large structures to help mask them. At the end of the last column, a corridor led out of the grand hall to the King's private garden. On the other side of the garden were the stables.

"How do you plan to get horses out of here?" she asked firmly.

"I will have to charge the front gate," Allegi answered, quickening their pace through the corridor.

"Then you'll never get out alive."

They stopped at the back doorway, cautiously peered out. Ahead of them was the private garden. Allegi searched for any signs of guards. Naat just stared with fret.

Suddenly, a memory hit the old chambermaid. "The garden!" she exclaimed.

Allegi held out his sword ready to pounce at their attacker.

"No," Naat said, holding his arm. "You can get out through the garden."

He looked at her confused.

"At the back behind the obelisk there is a thick bronze metal door hidden in the thicket." She looked up at him. "The horses can fit through."

Allegi kissed her on the cheek and ran off towards the stables.

Naat went into the garden, found her way along the paths to the obelisk.

Good, she thought, as she stopped in front of the tall structure. The path was safe.

Soon Allegi arrived, guiding three horses, on foot. Behind him, the horses brushed through the narrow walkways in a row. Allegi held the reigns of Nefer; Qare followed the tail of the chain. The trees and shrubs of the King's garden helped to hide the creatures.

Allegi reached the back of the garden where it opened up into a small patio. He stopped in front of the obelisk. The magnificent structure pointed up to the heavens, representing a ray of light from Ra. Allegi moved towards the pillar, jumped back, startled by a movement.

Naat stepped out from behind the obelisk. "The door is open," she said softly. Tears began to fill the chambermaid's eyes and the sternness she had always managed dissipated. "You truly walk on the path of the gods, Allegi. May they protect you." She kissed his hand, stepped aside allowing him to pass.

Allegi rode Nefer along the outer wall of the palace, his one hand wrapped in the reins of the second horse, Qare following. He went down the incline, headed to the rocks where Deshyre and Tigris waited.

Deshyre jumped up the moment she saw Allegi. She raced to him and hugged him when he got off his horse.

Allegi hugged her before he pushed her back so he could look steadily in her eyes. "I have a house in Khem. Go to it. The people in the village will help direct you. Wait for me there."

"No," she began to cry. "No, I won't go. I want to go with you, Allegi."

"You will be safer there."

"I don't care," Deshyre sobbed uncontrollably. "I want to go with you."

"I care." His expression softened. "I will come to you as soon as I can."

She cried harder. "No. Please, Allegi."

He signalled Qare. The horse pranced forward. Qare was the easiest horse to ride and Allegi felt some security that his faithful steed would help watch over his wife.

Allegi kissed Deshyre's quivering lips. "Please, if you love me you will go to where I know you will be safe so I can have hope."

Deshyre stood trembling, crying. She wanted to be with her husband but he was sending her away. Reluctantly, Deshyre obeyed, his words guilting her to grant his wish. She cried harder, her body shook. Allegi helped her onto the horse.

"I love you," he said.

Deshyre's lips quivered. She tried to respond but her cry wouldn't let her; her sobs broke her voice.

Allegi kissed her hand. "I know you do."

He smacked Qare, sending the horse running. A stabbing pain lanced his chest as he watched her ride away, hoping this wasn't the last moment he had with his wife.

Allegi lifted the Queen to her feet and helped her on Nefer's back. He jumped on the last horse and took the reins of both. Through the darkness, he trotted down the hillside to Ramska's ship—*Vessel of the Royal Messenger*. He glanced up the hill and looked at the *Great House* one last time. The gate was still closed.

LXVI

DESHYRE RODE THROUGH the city feeling lost and alone. The stillness of sleep brought a death-like silence over the streets of Men-nefer and even the stragglers and homeless lay silent in the deep hours of night.

Wiping the tears from her eyes, she opened the pouch Allegi left tied to her horse. Her hand trembled as she reached in and pulled out the contents one at a time: gold pieces to buy her way, the Golden Scorpion and their marriage contract so she could prove her tie to Allegi when she reached his home in Khem. Seeing the marriage contract made her tear again. They were married and she didn't yet have the chance to be his wife.

Deshyre slowly unrolled the contract and peered at it through blurred vision. Although she couldn't read, she noticed Allegi added something to the bottom. Deshyre stared at the script wishing she could decipher it. She ran her fingers over the ink feeling connected to Allegi. At her first opportunity, she would have someone read it to her. She rolled up the scroll and slipped it back into the pouch.

Deshyre opened her hand and glared at the Gold Scorpion. It had helped get her into the palace to be with Allegi but it also symbolized the reason why he was never with her. *Friend of the King*, Deshyre thought with despise. She almost felt to toss the golden pin; to break it out of resentment but she held back. What she hated the most was also what she loved the most in her husband—his loyalty and allegiance.

Deshyre put the scorpion back inside the pouch and glanced around. She didn't know where she was; she had steered Qare aimlessly through the streets. She didn't even know which direction led to Khem. Regardless, Deshyre decided to spend the night in Men-nefer and inquire about her route in the morning. She was Bedouin, a traveller of the desert and sea. If any woman could make it on her own, Deshyre knew she could.

She glimpsed at the pouch hanging from the horse, grateful her husband was wise to place it there.

"Allegi," she whispered up into the heavens, "return to me safely." Deshyre remembered the amulet of *djed* hanging by a braided string around her neck. She hadn't taken it off since Allegi put it on her the night of their marriage.

Stability, she thought as she ripped it off. She hadn't had one day of stability since they were married.

Glaring down at the cursed symbol, Deshyre didn't notice the two horses pull up beside her until it was too late. She frantically glanced at the two Sumerian men caped in black, their long curly hair and dark beards distinguishing them as foreigners. She tried to flick Qare's reins to make the horse go faster but Eritum grabbed them before she had the chance.

"No, Eritum," she begged. But, her plea barely left her lips. A sack dropped over her, draping her in darkness. "No!" Deshyre screamed. "Please!"

She was pulled from her horse, draped onto another. "No!" she screamed as they sped away.

Their ride was short. They reached the black door. Eritum went into the dim lit room. Behind him, his ally yanked Deshyre from his horse and carried her in. He pulled the sack from her body, dropped her to the floor.

"Where is your husband taking the Pharaoh?" Eritum demanded in Summerian.

Deshyre didn't answer. She lay on her stomach, clasping the amulet *djed* in her fist.

Eritum kicked her in the ribs. Deshyre grunted with pain. She rolled onto her side, curled into a ball.

"Where is Allegi taking the Pharaoh?" he asked again, articulating each word.

She didn't answer.

He grabbed her by the hair, pulled her to her feet. "Tell me where!"

Deshyre closed her eyes, shaking, crying but not answering.

Eritum burned with rage. He belted her across the face with his free hand. "You protect the chosen enemy of your country."

"It is *not* my country."

"Travelling with the Bedouins doesn't make you one of them. Your roots are Summerian."

"I was referring to Egypt. I am married. I'm Egyptian now."

Eritum grabbed her throat, slammed her into the wall. "Then you are a traitor!" He spat on her face.

Deshyre winced.

"Before your death, you will speak!" Eritum spun to look at his comrade. "Tie her to that chair."

A sinister grin curled his ally's lips as he stomped across the room and grabbed Deshyre's arm. He dragged her along the floor, threw her into the wooden seat.

Struggling and screaming, Deshyre fought helplessly against the tall strong man. He held her down, tied her wrists to the chair arms. As he pulled tighter on the rope, the amulet she had clung to fell to the floor. The man stepped aside, allowing Eritum to stand before her.

"Where is he taking the Pharaoh?" Eritum demanded, giving her a final chance to tell.

Sobbing, Deshyre shook her head.

Eritum's powerful hand struck her again. "Where?"

"I don't know."

Another hit. "Where!" he bellowed with fury.

"Please—I don't know."

His blows came fast, becoming increasingly harder each time. Deshyre's face bled, bruised and swelled but she didn't answer him.

Spurning her with anger, Eritum growled, "This all ends once you tell me where." He drew out his knife, placed the blade under her breast. "One tit or two?" He cut into her flesh.

Deshyre screamed.

"Will your husband still love you mutilated, ugly and no longer a woman?" He cut deeper.

Deshyre screamed in pain and horror. Her eyes and lips were already swollen. Her nose bled. Her head throbbed. Now, he added a burning feeling of torture as he cut at her breast. She was weak—drained of all her strength. She couldn't take it anymore. "Stop!" she begged. "Please!"

"Then, where?" Eritum demanded in an evil snarl.

"The temple..." The answer fell from Deshyre's mouth, she couldn't hold onto it any longer. Her agony robbed her of her loyalty. "The Temple of Sobek."

Eritum stepped back and smiled. He went to the door.

His ally pulled out his dagger. He moved in to slay Deshyre.

"No," Eritum ordered, stopping him. He halted in the doorway, stood with that evil sneer, scorning Deshyre. "Cut her loose. Let her live."

The man eyed Eritum questioningly.

"She had her chance to die but she chose betrayal. Let her live to suffer with the knowledge she betrayed the man she loved and with it took his life."

Cutting the rope, the man freed Deshyre then walked away.

"Live long," Eritum said before he disappeared.

Deshyre slid off the chair onto the floor, wailing loudly with debilitating sorrow. She wailed until she had no more strength, no more air to scream any more. She opened her eyes as much as the swelling would allow. Beside her face on the floor was the amulet *djed*—symbol of stability. She observed its shape and what it represented—a pillar with three cross bars symbolizing the backbone of Oser, *God of the Dead*.

Deshyre's heart sunk. "What have I done?" she cried.

ON THE THRONE of Sumer in the city of Kish, Yarlaganda watched his faithful nobleman approach. Caped in black, the man walked up the length of the room with his head bent over but his eyes and his smile graced his King.

Yarlaganda knew his time had come. Egypt was crumbling.

His father, Puzur-Sin, had attempted to overtake the Egyptian Empire but was defeated by Wadjkare when the Pharaoh had conquered their land between the two great rivers of Tigris and Euphrates. Puzar-Sin attempted once more as the country began to fall under the once glorious Egyptian King's rule. Again, he was thwarted-- cast out of the country by Qakare Iby, the King's General who had suddenly become Pharaoh upon Wadjkare's death. But now, the country perished in the hands of their heirs and the heir of Puzur-Sin would see to his father's dream of conquering the exalted Empire of Egypt.

Bowing, the man bent over and whispered in the King of Sumer's ear. Yarlaganda smiled.

LXVII

*T*HE SUN BEAT directly down on the earth, burning the air but the moving ship created a light breeze, which offered some comfort. Already it was three days since they left Men-nefer.

Allegi tramped along the length of the boat to the stern. He peered down the Nile. The sharp cut rocks of the water way blocked his view.

"What do you keep looking for?" Ramska asked, stopping behind him.

"Chephren should have dispatched his fleet already." Allegi looked at Ramska. "He should have dispatched them that night."

Placing a hand on Allegi's shoulder, the Captain laughed. "Come," he said, walking away. He led Allegi to the centre of the boat where a trap door opened up into the bowels of the ship.

Allegi stared down in shock. He looked at Ramska.

The Captain chuckled. "It will be days before Chephren will be able to get even one ship anywhere."

Looking down again, Allegi gazed into the hole amazed. Beneath the deck floor several hundred—maybe more—oars piled high.

Ramska forced a heavy sigh. "Though, the weight of them is slowing us down. We will have to dump them on the shore if we're going to make it in time."

Allegi stared at the Captain dumbfounded, making Ramska laugh again.

"I couldn't bring myself to destroy a good oar."

"How?" Allegi asked—it was all he was able to utter.

"My men work fast." Ramska patted Allegi on the back with a huge grin covering his face. He allowed the trap door to drop close.

"You're a good man," Allegi complimented still in shock.

Ramska chuckled.

They turned. Stopped abruptly. The Pharaoh was headed towards them. She was up and walking on her own, her beauty glowing. They bowed.

Tigris stopped before them. "Good day," she said, gesturing for them to rise.

"Per'a, you should be resting," insisted Allegi.

"I wanted fresh air, sunlight on my face." Her face was still pale but the dark circles had disappeared. She slept and ate every day since they left the palace in Men-nefer. Her broken heart seemed to be rejuvenated by hope. Tigris glimpsed into their eyes. "More so, I wanted to say I am grateful for you both."

"Prosper and live long," Ramska bowed.

"Friend of the King," Allegi winked.

Tigris smiled back at them. She turned to leave, buckled.

Allegi caught her. "You should lie down again. You need your rest for when we arrive."

Tigris didn't argue—she felt light-headed and still somewhat weak.

Allegi guided her back to the cabin. He helped her to lie down onto the long cushion, piled with pillows on the floor. He handed her the cup of water near the bed.

Sipping it, she looked up at him. "You are a loyal friend Allegi." She glanced away for a moment before she was able to look back at him again. "I am so sorry."

"Don't be—"

"I must be—for all I've said and for how I've treated you, I must be and I am."

Taking the empty cup, Allegi kissed her forehead. "Everything will be made right."

"A new beginning?" Her tone was doubtful.

He nodded.

Tigris pulled the charm of *Menat* out from under her pillow.

Allegi eyed the beaded necklace that curved over and held a golden crescent shaped piece at one end and a counterpoise at the other—the symbol of fertility as well as joy, life, birth and rebirth. He recognized it as the one he bought his wife in the market.

"Deshyre—" Tigris whispered, looking up from the charm. "You know?"

Allegi nodded.

Tears swelled up in Tigris' eyes. "I am afraid I might lose it." She held her stomach.

"No," Allegi refused. He took the charm out of the Queen's hand and laid it over her abdomen. "He comes from strong parents. He is a fighter."

Tigris cried softly. "I don't want to lose it," she whispered through her tears. "What have I done?" Her tears streamed faster, burning her cheeks. For the first time in her life, Tigris submitted herself. She curled into a ball, held Allegi's hand and cried.

LXVIII

*C*HEY STOPPED BETWEEN *Smed-Hor* and *Dep-Ehet* where Ramska was able to bring the ship near the shore. The crew emptied the oars out of the boat and laid them up on the land. With all thirty men working, it took less than an hour before they were ready to sail again.

Two days later, the Vessel of the Royal Messenger reached their destination just as night began to descend upon the earth. They arrived less than a day early. Tomorrow when the sun reached its highest point in the sky, Euphrates and Tigris would meet.

≈

TIGRIS LAY ON the bed running the charm Deshyre had given her across her palms. She couldn't sleep—her nerves shook with anticipation and fear. She felt so exposed. All her internal walls were broken down leaving her open and weak.

Yes, she thought, *weak*.

Tigris cried quietly. At first, she didn't know what her tears were for but the longer she cried, the more she understood them. She was scared. For the first time in her life she let go and she feared not having control. The loss of control made her feel helpless, exposed, vulnerable. To Tigris those were the most frightening feelings in the world.

A soft tap on the door ended her thoughts. She wiped away her tears, shoved the charm under her pillow, sat up. "Come in."

The door opened and Ramska brought his radiant smile into the room.

Tigris returned the smile.

"My wife packed this sack for you," he said, reaching in and pulling out a wrist cuff. "It's not as fine as the garments you're accustomed to but it's her finest."

Tigris looked at him confused.

He dropped the cuff back into the sack and handed her the bag. "She can't fit into the dress anymore," he chuckled as he patted his round belly, "she's trying to keep up with me."

Digging into the bag, Tigris pulled up a piece of the dress. It was made from fine white linen and it was scented with a soft perfume. Tigris sniffed it.

"It's *metopian*," Ramska said. "She sprinkled it over the dress before she put it in the bag."

"It smells lovely," Tigris replied.

He nodded at the dress. "She only wore it once, on the day of our marriage."

"It's lovely. It's all very lovely," Tigris repeated, lost for words.

Ramska's smile brightened. "She wants you to keep it as an offering—a gift to know you will always be loved by your people."

For a moment, Tigris couldn't speak. She felt touched by his wife's gesture, honoured to know some of her people still loved her. When she found her voice, she said, "Tell your wife I am eternally grateful and the first day I return to Men-nefer I will thank her in person and shower her with gifts."

Ramska bowed. "She would be satisfied just to kiss your hand, Great Per'a." He backed out of the door, closing it behind him.

Tigris sat silently, taken aback by the warm feeling that came over her; and yet, she felt guilty—she didn't even know the woman's name. "Bless her, Eset," she whispered as she pulled the items out of the bag and laid them on the bed next to her: a white linen dress, two gold cuffs embedded with lapis lazuli, a matching gold collar and a braided wig cut in a short bob with bangs.

Tigris ran her fingers over the wig. It was well made and looked new. She felt the bottom of the bag and lifted out a small makeup box. Inside was *msdmt* for the eyes and crushed powder for the cheeks.

Tigris took the items from her bed and sprawled them out over a trunk. Her head spun, suddenly dizzy. She staggered uneasily back to the bed and eased herself down.

"Please be better by tomorrow," she whispered into the air as she lay back against the cushions.

Tomorrow, Tigris thought. Something to hope for; something to fear.

Reaching under a pillow, Tigris pulled out the *Menat* charm. She placed it over her abdomen, closed her eyes, and prayed for strength.

LXIX

EARLY THE NEXT morning, fear and worry woke Tigris from her sleep. She lay still on the bed realizing today she would face Euphrates. The thought made her stomach fill with nervousness and her mind fill with doubts.

How could she confront him after all she said, after the way she behaved? Marching into battle was easier than this moment.

Tigris eased herself out of bed. She found a pouch with writing equipment and rolls of papyrus in it. She carried them over to the table, sat down. She flattened the edges of a parchment, picked up the brush. Her hand shook over the paper but she wouldn't let her fears reign. Instead, she forced the brush down onto the page and wrote, for once, the truth.

When she finished, Tigris set down her writing utensil and breathed. In spite of how frightening it felt to write the letter, it did indeed feel right.

The cabin door swung open after a short rap, startling Tigris. Two men carried in a tub of water from the river. They placed it down in the middle of the small room. A third man followed with a towel and a wooden box filled with oils and scented fat. He set them down on a chair next to the tub and then trailed the first two men out. Before the door was closed the last man entered with a tray of fruit and cheese.

Tigris rolled up the parchment and laid it on her lap. The man set the tray on the table and left.

Tigris looked at the food. Her stomach was too nervous to eat but she decided to force herself anyway—she needed her strength. She picked up a grape, popped it into her mouth. The breakfast actually helped to settle her stomach and for the first time in months, Tigris managed to eat the entire dish. By the time she was done, she felt full, satisfied.

The Queen leaned back in her seat, glanced out the cabin window to judge the position of the sun. She still had several hours before she would depart the vessel and head to the Temple of Sobek.

Tigris went over to the basin of water, removed her long tunic and stepped in. The water was moderately warm but felt refreshing. Crouching down into the cramped basin, Tigris submerged her body. She leaned back against the tub and held her stomach. Inside grew a child, she thought. *Euphrates' child.* And, soon Euphrates would know—what then? Could everything be made right after having been made so wrong?

Tigris opened her eyes to escape her thoughts. She eyed the makeup box on the trunk next to her dress. Never before had she applied her own makeup or even dressed herself. Everything felt surreal and for a moment she wondered if she was dreaming.

What if it was all just a dream? What if she awoke and none of this had happened? She thought about it for a moment and realized she would be afraid of what she would wake up to find. War? Her mundane life before this chaos? Not ever knowing Euphrates? She couldn't bear the thought. Tigris splashed her face with water.

If only she could wake up to the beginning, knowing what she knew now—how she would have done things differently.

Tigris drew in a heavy, deep breath of air. Why didn't the priestess foresee all of this?

Sinking deeper into the tub, Tigris closed her eyes.

A memory rose into view: the first reading Kafate gave her when she was a child—the look on the old woman's face after she threw the stones.

The priestess' voice echoed in her head: *There is to be war; unlike any you know.*

Tigris' memory fast forwarded to the palace at Henen-nesut after she returned from her first meeting with Euphrates. She was standing before Kafate saying, "I have to go to war." The priestess was mixing a potion. Her words hit Tigris with more understanding now than when she first delivered them. *"You have to follow your heart,"* Kafate had replied.

Tigris' memory flashed: Kafate was lying down. This time she was saying, *"Only when you've opened yourself to the possibilities of change can guidance be given, unless you've travelled so far down a road that you've sealed the passages to change it."*

Tigris bolted up. Water spilled out over the tub, slapping the floor. She grabbed the towel off of the chair, pressed it into her face.

A wrenching pain twisted in her chest.

Oh gods, she agonized. What if the passages are sealed? It wasn't my heart I had listened to.

Tigris stood. The water rushed off of her body. She wrapped herself in the towel, stepped out of the basin and sunk onto the chair next to it. Worry trembled through her belly and sat like a lump in her chest. Why hadn't Kafate warned me?

You have to follow your heart, the priestess' voice echoed.

Tigris' heart pounded. She had never listened to it. Her ego had drowned it out convincing her it was Egypt she wanted—*such lies!* Why? she tortured herself. *Why didn't I listen?*

Tigris' memories resurfaced with brutal force. Kafate's words hit her with the meanings she couldn't see before.

Deprives the heart! You both to marry...unite like the rivers. Listen to your heart. The old priestess' statements haunted her with sudden impact. They continued to surface, faster and faster.

One choice will put an end to all your troubles. This choice you're unwilling to make. Marry Euphrates, she heard Kafate whisper. *Marry Euphrates.*

Tigris' head began to spin. Kafate had known. She had tried to tell her but Tigris had only understood what she wanted to, and in so doing she denied the truth. And, for what? Her father's sin? Why didn't he tell her *he* had saved Euphrates. *He* had seen to it that Euphrates was raised a warrior. *He* had put the battle axe in Euphrates' hand. Why did he not say to her, if I should die and he should come, unite with him?

Tigris remembered her last moment with her father. *Do not let anyone take Egypt from you*, he had said. But, what if she was to *give* it?

Tigris felt betrayed. Why didn't Kafate tell her—force her?

You are not willing to change. You are not ready for anyone's advice, the priestess taunted in her mind. *Only when you've opened yourself to the possibilities of change can guidance be given, unless you've travelled so far down a road that you've sealed the passages to change it.* Kafate's words burned her soul.

"Oh, Great Anqet," Tigris whispered, sliding off the chair and onto her knees. She clasped her hands together and looked up towards the heavens through the small cabin window. "Good Goddess Anqet, grant me redemption."

LXX

ALLEGI WAS SITTING on a crate reading when she found him. He looked up at her, his mouth fell open. The Queen appeared radiant, beautiful and alive. He hadn't seen her so alive in what seemed a very long time.

Smiling softly, Tigris sat beside him. "What are you reading?" she asked to make conversation rather than to be nosy.

Allegi shrugged. "Something I wrote the first time I sailed the river to take your message to the self-proclaimed King."

Tigris looked at him confused. "The letter I had you deliver?" she asked.

"No," Allegi answered, "a poem I wrote."

Tigris leaned back against the wall of the vessel. "Read it to me." She noticed him hesitate as he glimpsed over the parchment. "Please, Allegi."

Taking a deep breath, Allegi gave in:

> *Beneath your murky currents,*
> *I hear you call my name,*
> *Cleanse me from my conscience,*
> *My spirit empty,*
> *Lets me go.*
> *Your undertow so strong,*
> *Whispers...*
> *So I come to you,*
> *Falling towards your depths,*
> *I collapse slowly.*
> *You hold up your mirror,*
> *And, I see the way you ridicule my frown—*
> *I am crying,*
> *Painful tears racing to you,*
> *Leading the way.*
> *My last memory is yours,*
> *Thus, you will not let me forget,*
> *So, you deliver me to my conscience,*
> *And, reflect upon your glistening surface,*
> *As I fall closer,*
> *My wisdom;*
> *   Closer*
> *My ignorance;*
> *   Closer*
> *My happiness;*
> *   Closer*

My sorrow;
Until, at last, I am submerged,
And, you rush over me,
Cleansing me,
Everything now so perfectly clear
From washing away the sins
That I had clung to with a mortal price,
'Til finally, so surely I see
My errors.
I smile.
My last labour bears only regret.

Tigris tensed her eyebrows. "That's so morbid, Allegi. What did you name it?"

"River of Redemption."

"Redemption?" she thought out loud. How odd to hear the word after she just prayed for it.

The Queen twisted around to look at the reflective surface of the river over the short wall. After a moment, she turned back to Allegi, took his hand. "I believe you've finally found purpose for your life," she said softly. She looked into his eyes. "Love." The word rolled off her tongue cradled with desire. "When this day is over, I relieve you of your services to me."

Allegi went to speak but Tigris cut him off. "Go to your wife, make many children. You will be well looked after by the state." Kissing his hand, Tigris looked at him solemnly. "You are a noble dignitary, a loyal friend, your name will be written in my tomb for all time." Tigris looked up towards the sun.

Allegi followed her gaze. "It's time," he said.

She glanced at him. "It's time," she repeated. She met his eyes. "I need your service one last time for in this matter called love, I am weak." For the first time in her life, Nitiqreti, Tigris of Egypt admitted weakness.

Allegi leaned over, kissed her forehead. Still holding her hand, he stood, pulled her to her feet. They walked along the ship.

Ramska brought their horses forward. He bowed as the Pharaoh approached. "Your loveliness outshines the sun," he beamed.

Smiling, Tigris took the reins of Nefer and climbed onto the horse's back. Allegi climbed onto the second horse.

"To the end of sorrow and the beginning of a new life," Ramska wished as he hit Allegi's horse on the rump, sending them off.

Tigris followed her messenger into the water and up onto the sandy shore of the desert. They raced across the dry sands towards the Temple of Sobek, which was set a little ways in from the Nile. The old temple was no longer in daily use since the main temple of Sobek was built in the Faiyum. Only twice a year did the priest of Kasa attend the temple to honour the crocodile god in order not to anger Sobek. Today, there would be no one there, save for the Queen, the King and the Messenger.

Tigris and Allegi reached the temple around the time when the sun loomed mid-day. Euphrates hadn't arrived.

Dismounting their horses, they sat on the temple steps looking across the Eastern desert. It was barren as far as the eye could see.

They waited in silence, baking in the sun, hoping to see Euphrates appear on the horizon, but time dragged on.

After a long while, Tigris sadly whispered, "He's not coming."

"He will come," Allegi assured.

An hour slowly moved the sun across the sky.

"He's not coming," Tigris whispered again.

Allegi looked at her. The radiance she had earlier began to lose its glow. "Have faith. He will come."

They returned to the silence, watching the sun sink towards the horizon. Time continued to pass, hope dwindled. Tigris began to lose belief but then something caught her eye. Squinting, she bolted upright. Allegi followed her gaze. On the horizon a figure finally appeared, riding towards the Temple of Sobek.

Tigris grabbed Allegi's hand and squeezed it. The realness of the moment made her skin burn more than the Egyptian sun. She was trembling. "What am I doing? I can't do this."

"Yes you can," Allegi urged.

Euphrates closed the distance, racing towards them. Anxiety swelled inside Tigris until she couldn't hold herself back. She rose to her feet, moved out towards him. Allegi came up beside where she stopped. Together they stood waiting for Euphrates.

Tigris' attention was suddenly drawn towards the south. Her eyes widened. A second horseman rode in—clearly not travelling with Euphrates.

"Allegi?" she asked, tugging his arm. "Who is that?"

Allegi squinted against the sunlight. The rider was on a dark horse, caped in black.

"Who else would know we are here?" Tigris watched with worry as the unknown rider moved in behind Euphrates. "Who else would ride a horse?"

Allegi was speechless. No one could have possibly known save for Euphrates' comrades, but then why wouldn't the man ride *with* him?

〰

EUPHRATES HADN'T SEEN the man. The rider had come from behind, out of his view and now the unknown horseman was gaining on him. By the time Euphrates became aware of his presence, the cloaked man was at his side.

Euphrates looked into the bearded face of the stranger. Evil glowed in his eyes. Euphrates sensed his danger, drew his sword.

The man fell back a few paces out of Euphrates' reach. Euphrates glanced over his shoulder, watched as the caped rider lifted his hand to his lips. The man held a short hollow wooden tube. He took a breath and blew into it.

A second later, something stung Euphrates' back. Euphrates reached around, pulled a thick copper needle from his body and looked at its tip.

Poison!

Euphrates went white. He looked in horror at the rider who raced past him towards the Queen.

〰

ALLEGI WATCHED.

The strange rider sped by Euphrates and was heading towards Tigris. Danger shot through the air hitting Allegi like a club. Instinctively, he spun, ran back towards the temple steps to grab his sword and horse. As he charged the distance, he glanced back at the rider. A man caped in black—the feeling was familiar.

〰

STILL NO WORDS could escape Tigris. She was dazed by the moment, watching everything in confusion. Her eyes locked on Euphrates. He still rode towards her but his horse had slowed down and he looked as if he was wavering on top of it.

Something wasn't right. Tigris' legs unlocked from beneath her. She began to stride forward, watching him in fear. *Unbelievable fear.* Her steps became a run.

Tigris reached for the letter—the last letter she had written to Euphrates—and pulled it out from where she had tucked it into her dress. She didn't want to lose it. More than ever she wanted him to read her words, words she should have written long ago.

Tigris raced into the desert towards Euphrates, clenching the parchment in her fist, hoping. She wanted what she saw to not be real. She wanted to be in Euphrates' arms. She wanted everything to be good, happy....

Euphrates fell from his horse.

Great gods, what had the rider done? But, she knew the answer. A pain soared through her. "*Nooo!*" Tigris screamed in terror as she watched Euphrates hit the earth. Her knees weakened. They gave out beneath her. She crashed down on them. Her voice carried across the desert, screaming *No!*

This couldn't be happening. Great Oser, why? No, this can't be happening! Tears poured down her cheeks. Her body trembled more than it ever had in her life.

The rider rode up to the Pharaoh. Stopped. She looked at him with hatred.

He raised the tube to his mouth, blew a copper needle into the Pharaoh's chest. Tigris glared down at it, fell backwards to the earth. The letter she clung to escaped from her grip. She gazed up into the clear Egyptian sky. Everything was blurred by her tears. She watched the letter swirl above her before it blew away. She could hear Allegi's voice filling the air with fury. "*No!*" he was yelling.

What was happening? She felt so weak. Maybe I am dreaming, Tigris thought as she closed her eyes.

〰

THE HORSEMAN TURNED away. He raced off in the direction he had come. Allegi chased after him on horseback, weapon raised, rage pumping his blood. He was in shock. Could it be? He had seen the man's face though he didn't believe it and yet, he was sure he had seen him.

Eritum? Allegi questioned.

At high speed, Allegi pursued. He wouldn't stop until the man was dead.

〰

EUPHRATES FORCED HIMSELF to his feet. His horse stood over him. He used its reins to help pull himself up. His body was tingling, becoming numb but he wanted to see Tigris.

Mustering his strength, he heaved himself onto his horse. The horse walked forward with casual steps. He feared he wouldn't have the strength to hold onto the animal if it moved any faster. The poison slowly overtook him, making his body feel incredibly hot. He lifted his head, forced its weight up to look into the distance at Tigris' figure lying in the sand. She was so still.

Please, he prayed, not daring to think the worst.

Gradually, Euphrates made his way towards Tigris. He slid off his horse, crashed to the ground. He feebly pushed himself onto his knees and crawled.

The warrior King dragged his limp body with difficulty to the Pharaoh's side. He looked down on her. Her eyes were closed. She was still. Her face was so pale.

"No," Euphrates whispered, stroking her head. He spotted the needle protruding from her chest, pulled it out.

Tigris' eyes opened. She looked up into Euphrates' eyes where she had always found happiness but had always denied it. Tears streaked down her face. "I'm sorry," she wept. "I'm so sorry." She couldn't stop apologizing. In some way she felt as if this had been all her fault— if she had only followed her heart; if she had been willing to change— where would they be now?

Euphrates wiped away her tears. "Don't apologize, Per'a." He was crying. His tears fell onto her and their warmth broke her heart even more.

Euphrates laid a gentle hand on her belly.

Tigris studied him, realizing he knew. She cried harder. "I don't want to die like this," she sobbed. "Take me to Kafate; she can cure us." Tigris tried to lift her arm. It was so hard, so heavy but she managed. She grasped his hand. "Please don't let me die like this. I want to give birth to our child."

"You're not going to die." He steadied himself, mustered his strength. "We will live and rule both Egypts together."

He picked her up, rose to his feet. Unsteadily, he carried her to his horse and helped her to sit on top.

Tigris slumped forward against the horse's neck. Euphrates climbed up behind her. He held her on the horse with the weight of his body as he steered the animal towards the Nile—to where the Pharaoh's ship waited.

Tigris tried to fight against the poison running through her blood. She forced herself to stay conscious. "I feel so weak," she muttered. "I can barely feel my limbs."

"I know," Euphrates whispered, his eyes rolling back into his head. He forced them to stay open. Being bigger, stronger, he knew he could withstand the venom longer. "Do not close your eyes," he told her. "Fight it."

At length, they reached the Nile, left the sandy shore, trampled into the shallow water.

Euphrates looked up. The Queen's vessel was in the distance, downstream. He didn't have the strength to yell. In front of him, Tigris' body slipped from the horse. He tried to hold onto her but his arms and legs were almost paralyzed. His body felt incredibly heavy. All his strength was gone.

His eyes rolled back.

〰

TIGRIS FORCED HER eyes open. She was sliding from the horse, she couldn't prevent it. Below her, she could see her reflection in the river. In her thoughts, she could hear Allegi's voice reciting his poem, *River of Redemption*.

Beneath your murky currents,

417

I hear you call my name,
Cleanse me from my conscience,
My spirit empty,
Lets me go.
Your undertow so strong,
Whispers...
So I come to you,
Falling towards your depths,
I collapse slowly.
You hold up your mirror,
And, I see the way you ridicule my frown—
I am crying,
Painful tears racing to you,
Leading the way.
My last memory is yours,
Thus, you will not let me forget,
So, you deliver me to my conscience,
And, reflect upon your glistening surface,
As I fall closer,
My wisdom;
    Closer
My ignorance;
    Closer
My happiness;
    Closer
My sorrow;
Until, at last, I am submerged,
And, you rush over me,
Cleansing me,
Everything now so perfectly clear
From washing away the sins
That I had clung to with a mortal price,
'Til finally, so surely I see
My errors.
I smile.
My last labour bears only regret.

I come to you, thought Tigris as she relaxed, letting go, allowing herself to fall from the horse. She slid down, dragging Euphrates' limp body with her.

The Queen fell into the shallow waters of the river landing on her stomach, her head smacking a rock. Beside her, Euphrates splashed down on his back.

Blood trickled from Tigris' temple over the stone and into the Nile. She opened her eyes, looked at Euphrates through her tears. The sun shone down on him and even in his weakened state, he looked like a god.

With everything left in her, Tigris lifted her arm and stretched it out towards him.

"Euphrates," she whispered, straining, trying to reach him. More than anything, she wanted to touch him, feel his skin under her fingers one last time, hold him. God, how she wished to hold him! Why didn't she hold him when she had the chance? Why didn't she leave with him? Where would they be now? Surely, in each other's arms *together*. Oh, what tragic choices she had made! And, for what?

Her arm felt incredibly heavy, she could barely lift it up. She couldn't bear its weight any longer. Against her will, her arm collapsed, splashing down into the water. She stretched out her fingers. He was so close but she couldn't reach him. Sadness engulfed her.

Oser! Eset! Hathor! Tigris called out within. *Please great deities, grant me one last touch! One last moment!*

The river ran between them, glistening in the sunlight.

Euphrates turned his head towards her. His eyes fluttered open. They were filled with tears.

Tigris' heart screamed with self hatred. *Why? Why did you do this!* It felt as if her heart was tearing apart, ripping inside her chest. But, then she realized it was speaking—making one last request. *One last solemn request.* This time, Tigris obeyed. She laid aside her pride, allowed her heart to break from the prison she had confined it. And, at long last, Tigris let go.

"My King," she whispered.

Euphrates' eyes focused on her. She looked into their depths and finally saw the truth.

"I love you," Tigris admitted.

Euphrates' eyes closed. Tigris' eyes rolled back and the river washed over them.

...and, all things must end.

To read the last letter Tigris wrote, which escaped from her grip and blew away, go to the "Lost Letter" page at

www.jjmakins.com

And enter the password:

Iloveyou2

I would love to know what you thought about
The King of Egypt
Review the book at:
www.amazon.com (search j.j. makins)
or at www.jjmakins.com and enter the password:
Tragedy9809

Any questions? Want to share your thoughts
with the author?
Contact J.J. Makins at www.jjmakins.com

Keep watch for the next novel by J.J. Makins
www.jjmakins.com

About the Author

J.J. Makins lives in Toronto, Ontario, Canada. Her love for writing first shone in grade three when her book, *Boy, I Wish It Was Another Day*, received so much attention from her teacher and principal that it was elevated all the way up to the district school board. Again in college, her English professor encouraged her writing with a note on a short story, which read, "You should think about turning this into a novel." From that story *The King of Egypt* was born.

J.J. Makins has worked in interior design and TV production. She has been educated in advertising/ marketing. She loves social settings, dancing and traveling along with anything adventurous.

Find out more about the author and the book at:

www.jjmakins.com

CPSIA information can be obtained at www.ICGtesting.com
Printed in the USA
LVOW11s1525220215

427897LV00001B/44/P